CALL
Environments

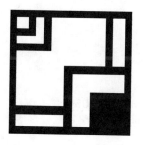 Research, Practice, and Critical Issues

Joy Egbert and
Elizabeth Hanson-Smith,
Editors

TESOL   Teachers of English to Speakers of Other Languages, Inc.

Founded 1966

Typeset in VAG Rounded and Novarese
by Capitol Communication Systems, Inc., Crofton, Maryland USA
and printed by Pantagraph Printing, Bloomington, Illinois USA

Teachers of English to Speakers of Other Languages, Inc.
1600 Cameron Street, Suite 300
Alexandria, Virginia 22314 USA
Tel 703-836-0774 • Fax 703-836-7864 • E-mail tesol@tesol.edu •
http://www.tesol.edu/

Director of Communications and Marketing: Helen Kornblum
Managing Editor: Marilyn Kupetz
Copy Editor: Ellen F. Garshick
Cover Design: Ann Kammerer

ISBN 0-939-791-79-2
Library of Congress Catalogue No. 98-061417

Dedication

We dedicate this work to our friends and families and to the memory of Brooke Brummitt, colleague, friend, and inspiration.

Table of Contents

Part VII: Atmosphere

Part VIII: Control

References

Appendixes

Contributors

Preface

Computer-assisted language learning (CALL) is changing so quickly and significantly that the only constant is change itself. As access to hardware, software, and telecommunications spreads throughout the world, the need for an underlying pedagogical framework to support the use of these new technologies in the language classroom becomes ever more critical. Although most CALL texts are themselves technology driven, that is, organized around the types of activities computers are able to do, few have spoken to the need for a specific framework based on the best of second language acquisition (SLA) research. This volume fills that need.

In addressing CALL issues, we conceive of technology as support for a total environment for learning rather than as a single tool or a source of information only. Our premise is that using technology can change not only *how* teachers teach but *what* they can teach—in the most positive sense—and whom they can teach: Technology reaches out to the most distant learners in the most isolated places and offers a hitherto undreamed-of richness of experience.

Purposes

Our purposes are several:

- to provide a sound theoretical framework based on ESL and SLA research

- to describe theory-based practice for high-technology and low-technology environments and a variety of learners

- to tackle critical issues within the CALL environment

- to communicate our own excitement about the potential of technology-enhanced education

Thus, the book is organized around the major themes of SLA research: input and negotiation of meaning, communicative activities, content-based learning, and so on. It offers practical suggestions for contexts ranging from the one-computer classroom to the fully wired, turbo-charged, Internet-based learning center. It also offers advice for individuals who choose software, train other teachers, and organize labs.

Our primary audience is teachers-in-training, both graduate and undergraduate students in TESOL methods courses—particularly those focusing on CALL. We expect, however, that classroom teachers will find the book a rich source of ideas and inspiration.

Organization

In keeping with our focus, chapter 1 introduces the scaffold for the entire volume: eight linking and overlapping conditions for language learning that have informed the best known practices in the field. Each of Parts I–VIII then treats current research on one of the eight areas of SLA, its application in classroom activities, and related issues that affect the success of the CALL environment.

As an emerging field, CALL desperately needs more research. Thus, chapter 1 also discusses the need for research and guidelines for its conduct in the CALL environment. Additionally, each part contains ideas for further exploration of classroom-based, hands-on observation for the working teacher as well as questions for academic research.

The final chapter looks cautiously and pragmatically at the future of CALL, although we feel the injection of technology is a singular cultural event that will dramatically change the way teachers live and work in the next century. To paraphrase Claire Bradin, technology will not replace teachers; teachers who use technology will replace those who don't (C. Bradin, personal communication, March 1996, cited in Hanson-Smith, 1997b, p. 14).

Acknowledgments

This book is the result of a lot of hard work by many dedicated people. We thank all of the contributors for their outstanding effort in making this text a seminal work in the field. We also thank Gary Rhoades and Gavriel Salomon, who helped get the whole ball rolling; Larry Mikulecky for advice; Cindy Chan and Stephanie Essington for invaluable editorial work; and Chin-chi Chao for her willingness to "road test" the text in her graduate CALL distance course.

We are also grateful to Marilyn Kupetz, TESOL's managing editor, who provided encouragement and the answers to myriad questions; to David Nunan, president of TESOL, and Helen Kornblum, TESOL's director of communications and marketing, who saw the potential of this text and brought it to the TESOL publications list; to Ellen Garshick, copy editor, who had the patience to make it work; and to Ann Kammerer, for her invaluable technical assistance in preparing the many images that appear in the text. We also thank all of the software publishers and World Wide Web site developers who gave us permission to use images from their products in this volume.

Finally, and most important, we would like to thank our families for their support of this 2-year project. Jack Thompson's encouragement was essential—and sustaining. Thanks are also due Len Jessup—for listening, suggesting, supporting, and babysitting—and to Jamie Erin Jessup, whose arrival did not make the job easier but definitely made it worthwhile.

Chapter 1 ▣

Computer-Enhanced Language Learning Environments: An Overview

Joy Egbert, Chin-chi Chao, and
Elizabeth Hanson-Smith

World Wide Web, Internet, multimedia, CD-ROM, *technology coordinator, chat room,* MOO, *e-mail, virus, newbie*—educational technologies involve a lot of scary-sounding jargon. In fact, technology presents a whole new language, but the language of technology, although important, is not the most crucial information that educators need in order to use technology effectively in their language classrooms. More important is an understanding of good pedagogy and the relationship among teaching, learning, and technology.

Levy (1990) and other second language educators have pointed out the need for a theory of computer-assisted language learning (CALL) that would provide educators with a framework for teaching and learning with technology. He notes that "our language teaching philosophy, method, or approach needs to be broadened to encompass new technologies, and the inter-relationship between language teaching and computing needs to be carefully explored" (p. 5). Supporting the need for a theory of CALL is the increase in the number of computers available to language educators and learners and the desire of educators to apply theories of second language acquisition (SLA) to the computer-using classroom. Hypothetically, a theory of CALL could assist teachers in making decisions about ways to prepare language learners for the high-technology future that they face; in describing the kinds of theoretically sound, vital changes in curricula that can and should be made; and in assessing the types of technology needed to assist in the effective and efficient learning and teaching of additional languages. A theory of CALL could help educators evaluate how and which students learn with different kinds of technology, identify factors that must be addressed in the application of the technology, and serve as a guide for research on language learning.

If *technology* is replaced with *textbook* in the preceding paragraph, the hypothetical theory of CALL sounds not much different from an integrated theory of language acquisition; in fact, it is the same. A theory of CALL is a

1

theory of language acquisition; the fact that the technology changes does not mean that the principles of language development do. Therefore, before talking about the use of technology in language classrooms, we must talk about how additional languages are learned.

Language Learning Theory and the Learning Environment

The number of theories of language acquisition and knowledge of the processes underlying these theories increase slowly but surely. Researchers and teachers generally accept that language acquisition is the result of an interplay between some kind of cognitive mechanism and environmental factors. They also acknowledge that not all language learners learn in the same way, at the same rate, or for the same purposes. Spolsky's (1989) general theory of conditions for language acquisition encompasses these variables in the form of the equation in Figure 1-1. According to this theory, *abilities* include physiological, biological, intellectual, and cognitive skills. *Opportunity* implies the learning environment, or time multiplied by exposure to the language. In the classroom, how or when a learner acquires language depends on the optimal strength of each of these variables for each learner.

Although it is not yet known for certain whether nature (cognition) or nurture (the classroom environment) is more important in the acquisition of additional languages, researchers have shown that the learning environment (*opportunity*, the term used by Spolsky, 1989) is a critical component. In addition to being a valid predictor of learning outcomes (see, e.g., Fraser, 1986), the classroom environment can mediate between the learner and macroenvironmental variables such as socioeconomic status, family circumstances, and language status. Most important, the classroom language learning environment is also the component of language acquisition that teachers, researchers, learners, and technology can directly influence.

Figure 1-1. Spolsky's (1989) Theory of Conditions for Language Acquisition

	The learner's:	
	Kp	Knowledge in the present
	A	Abilities
	M	Motivation/affect
+	O	Opportunity
	Kf	Knowledge and skills in the future

Understanding and creating optimal language learning environments is the essential business of the language teacher. Understanding this, educators and their language learners can observe circumstances under which learners acquire language and make adjustments to the classroom environment, thereby playing an instrumental role in students' learning. Because computers are becoming an increasingly significant element in the teaching and learning environment, a clear theory of language learning that takes into account the significance of that environment in turn has critical implications for CALL. In other words, educators do not need a discrete theory of CALL to understand the role of technology in the classroom; a clear theory of SLA and its implications for the learning environment serves this goal.

A variety of classroom environmental variables may affect learners' acquisition. These variables form the theoretical framework for this volume's discussion of CALL.

Conditions for Optimal Language Learning Environments

In the SLA, ESL, and learning theory literatures, research repeatedly points to eight conditions (see the box) that, when present in the language learning environment in some form and in some amount, seem to support optimal classroom language learning. Although other factors may come into play, these eight are the most widely researched and supported in the literature and make up a general model of optimal environmental conditions. Below is a brief overview of these conditions, each of which is described in more detail in later chapters. This model forms the book's theoretical framework, one that you as a teacher can use to guide your deployment of technology in the language classroom.

Condition 1: Learners Have Opportunities to Interact and Negotiate Meaning

Many researchers have noted that learning is essentially the result of interaction between learners and others (see, e.g., Ahmad, Corbett, Rogers, & Sussex, 1985; Kelman, 1990; Levin & Boruta, 1983; Vygotsky, 1978). If learning is a social process, then interaction with other people is necessary. This concept, addressed in Part I, is not new to second language instruction, as many researchers have called attention to the importance of the negotiation of meaning and modification of interaction in second language development (Long, 1985; Long & Porter, 1985; Pica, Holliday, Lewis, & Morgenthaler, 1989; Porter, 1986).

Conditions for Optimal Language Learning Environments

1. Learners have opportunities to interact and negotiate meaning.
2. Learners interact in the target language with an authentic audience.
3. Learners are involved in authentic tasks.
4. Learners are exposed to and encouraged to produce varied and creative language.
5. Learners have enough time and feedback.
6. Learners are guided to attend mindfully to the learning process.
7. Learners work in an atmosphere with an ideal stress/anxiety level.
8. Learner autonomy is supported.

Condition 2: Learners Interact in the Target Language With an Authentic Audience

Other researchers (see, e.g., Ernst, 1994; Pica, 1987; Pica, Young, & Doughty, 1987; Webb, 1982, 1985) have found that language learners must be involved not only in social interaction but in *purposeful* interaction, which includes a real audience that is actively involved with the learners. The implication, then, is that involving learners in authentic social interaction in the target language with a knowledgeable source (e.g., the teacher, another learner, a family doctor, or another person who can negotiate in the target language) facilitates language acquisition. The question of audience is taken up in Part II.

Condition 3: Learners Are Involved in Authentic Tasks

Many researchers (e.g., Chun, 1994; Kelm, 1992; Meagher, 1995) have reported that learners tend to be inspired by having not only a real audience but also an authentic goal for their work, and in this context the language used tends to be candid and heartfelt. Authentic tasks are those having the same types of cognitive challenges as complicated real-world tasks do. The cognitive demands, that is, the thinking required, should be consistent with the cognitive demands in the environment for which the learner is being prepared. In the context of language learning, this means, for example, that language teachers want students not simply to learn *about* English or French but rather to be engaged in the use of English or French in ways that native speakers normally are. It is important to design tasks so that students can use their current proficiency level to function in authentic communications. Even less proficient students should have the ability to handle the task well and gain confidence from it. As Vygotsky (1978) believed and research has shown, learners grow into an activity that has meaning for them in its own right and at the same time grow out of the need for external support in the activity. The notion of task is addressed in Part III.

Condition 4: Learners Are Exposed to and Encouraged to Produce Varied and Creative Language

Spolsky (1989) claims that "whatever the language learner brings to the task, whether innate ability, a language acquisition device, attitudes, previous knowledge, and experience of languages and language learning, the outcome of language learning depends in large measure on the amount and kind of exposure to the target language" (p. 166). An authentic task alone, therefore, may not be sufficient for language acquisition; the phrase *varied and creative language* implies that learners are involved in a diversity of tasks with a variety of sources of language input (Krashen & Terrell, 1983). Output is thus also a means to language development (see chapter 12). The use of varied and creative language also means that learners tap both receptive and productive language skills and that the tasks take into account the multiple learning styles and preferences among learners. Research on and examples of exposure and production are discussed in Part IV.

Condition 5: Learners Have Enough Time and Feedback

Learners need adequate time and feedback, both of which facilitate the formulation of ideas. Within the classroom, individual differences in ability, motivation, and other factors determine how much time each learner requires to complete a task successfully. This fact implies that some flexibility must be built into the time line for the task. In this way, all learners have the opportunity to reflect on and communicate their ideas.

In addition, explicit, appropriate, individualized feedback is critical in helping learners reach the goals of a task. *Explicit* feedback addresses the learner's task-related questions; an example is help with the ordering of subtasks, with a relevant grammar point, or with general task instructions. *Appropriate* signifies as much assistance as the learner needs but neither less nor more. Learners also vary in the amount and kind of task feedback that they require. This condition does not indicate, however, that teachers must act as private tutors; it suggests that tasks, the grouping of learners, and learners' opportunities to receive help should be planned carefully. Part V addresses this topic.

Condition 6: Learners Are Guided to Attend Mindfully to the Learning Process

An authentic task and audience, exposure to and opportunities to produce language, and sufficient time and feedback do not imply that learners will take these opportunities or make the best of them. During the learning process, learners must be *mindful* (Salomon, 1990); that is, they must be motivated to take the opportunities presented to them and to be cognitively engaged as they perform them. A certain degree of metacognitive guidance (instructions and examples about how to learn), whether from peers, teachers, or others, may facilitate learning and promote cognitive engagement (Vygotsky, 1978; Zellermayer, Salomon, Globerson, & Givon, 1991). Research has repeatedly shown that the conscious or deliberate use of learning strategies is related to language achievement and proficiency (Oxford, 1994). By consciously understanding and applying metacognitive strategies, learners are prompted to be aware of their language use and learning and thus become more efficient in both. Learning styles and strategies and related issues are discussed in Part VI.

Condition 7: Learners Work in an Atmosphere With an Ideal Stress/Anxiety Level

Before becoming mindfully engaged and willing to communicate their ideas, learners must experience an optimal level of anxiety in the language learning environment; any feelings of worry or apprehension must be facilitative rather than debilitative (Brown, 1987; Krashen & Terrell, 1983; Lozanov, 1978). Educators can assist in the development of an environment with an optimal stress level by creating a learner-centered classroom, which implies that learners have some control over their learning (see, e.g., Bereiter & Scardamalia, 1987; Kremers, 1990; Robinson, 1991). A learner-centered environment also suggests that the teacher's expectations are reasonable and that goals are attainable. Peyton (1990b) suggests that giving more control to the learner removes the confounds of teacher, learner, school personalities, styles, and goals. These issues and their applications in the language classroom are discussed in Part VII.

Condition 8: Learner Autonomy Is Supported

Thein (1994) describes a learner-centered classroom as one that develops learners' confidence and skills to learn autonomously and to design and coordinate tasks in a variety of contexts. In a learner-centered classroom, learners are given ownership of the process of developing solutions to their learning task and may, in fact, with the teacher's guidance or mentorship, devise their own learning agenda. This does not mean that learners have complete autonomy in the classroom; the instructor should determine boundaries so that learners can develop meaningful problems or tasks in that domain. Savery and Duffy (1995) believe that a teacher's role is to challenge learners' thinking, not to dictate or attempt to regulate their thinking for them. In this context, the learner decides on learning goals, but the modeling, mediation, and scaffolding provided by the instructor are indispensable. Consultation with and feedback from the instructor are crucial, as students require varying degrees of control. Issues of autonomy and their relationship to the CALL environment are discussed in Part VIII.

These eight conditions affect and overlap each other; thus, so do the chapters in this volume. The literature does not suggest the nature or impact of interactions among the conditions or their necessary or relative optimal strengths. What is known, however, is that the eight conditions act and interact in different ways in different classrooms depending on variables such as student population, content area, and learning context. Therefore, teachers must attempt to tailor these conditions in ways that are best for the learners in their specific classrooms. Classroom-situated research, discussed in the next section, is one way to determine if and how the conditions are being met.

Exploring the CALL Environment Through Research

Throughout this text we propose questions that should be asked about CALL; however, even if all these questions are answered to our satisfaction, there will still be much to learn. The brief discussion below presents general guidelines for developing inquiries in the area of CALL. The purpose of classroom research is to find out what works for you as a teacher and to add to the growing body of knowledge concerning the CALL environment. The framework provided below for the exploration and presentation of research on CALL should have the very practical effect of leading you to uncover ways to meet the eight conditions for learning in your own setting.

Purcell (1996) notes that research generally has six levels—observation, recording, investigation, use of a model, experimentation, and enlightenment; he adds that the conduct of research involves six steps of analysis, synthesis, and evaluation:

1. Describe a question significant enough to merit research.

2. Review in the relevant literature the knowledge to date about the research question.

3. State a tentative answer to the research question, or declare the further knowledge required to answer the question.

4. Determine how to test the research question or gather the required information, and state it as an *if-then* sentence.

5. Test the hypothesis or gather the data carefully.

6. Refine the tentative answer to the research question, or present the clarification derived from the data; generalize the result of the particular research performed, and suggest further study about the research question.

Although most CALL research follows Purcell's (1996) guidelines in some form, these generic steps do not speak to specific research methods or measurement tools; researchers should use whatever is appropriate to the study. These steps pertain to the presentation of any research project, but they require further consideration when the CALL environment is the focus. Even though conducting research following these guidelines seems simple enough, unfortunately it is not. The most critical step in conducting research is formulating a research question of significance, Purcell's Step 1.

Step 1: Ask the Right Questions

A common complaint is that current CALL research does not tell teachers anything. Teachers who make this claim often mean that research results do not speak specifically to the best methods of using computers in the language learning classroom. However, just as there seems to be no one right way to teach or learn language (see Stevick, 1976, for numerous examples underscoring why this is so), there is most likely no one best way to use computers for language learning. Researchers and other educators looking for the CALL research study that can answer specific questions about the best way to teach must instead look to the large body of research in SLA and language learning; in fact, most of the outstanding research cited in this volume comes from these and other academic fields or areas of study, as has the framework of environmental conditions that serves as the structure for this book. As we suggest above, perhaps the best way, if there is one, to teach in a CALL classroom is to create an optimal language learning environment for each learner.

Clearly, much remains to be learned about how to create optimal CALL environments. Most research has failed to shed light on this area, perhaps because of the questions asked and the methods used. One common type of research study compares a classroom with computers to one without and measures productivity gains or language achievement on standardized tests to show whether computers are effective. As Ehrmann (1995) notes, such questions imply that if technology performs better than traditional methods, everyone should use it—a neat picture, but one that poses three problems. First, the concept of *traditional methods* is unclearly defined at best, and research does not support the idea that one single set of methods is typical across classrooms. In addition, in most cases, an invalid assumption underlies this type of research: that nothing else changes when computers are introduced into the classroom. On the contrary, as Salomon (1990) and Ehrmann (1995) point out, computers (or the introduction of any new factor) can radically change the environment. New skills are needed to perform the task; motivation to do the task may increase; and the task itself may be defined in new and different ways. Because the technology introduces many new variables and myriad other, even more subtle changes, the comparison of a CALL with a non-CALL environment is misleading and can rarely describe accurately the effectiveness of computers for language learning.

Finally, a third problem in comparing CALL to non-CALL environments is that such comparisons ask whether the teacher or the computer is better for a specific task when, in fact, each may be better at performing very different kinds of tasks. Especially when the results of the research are unfavorable for learning with computers, such comparisons may ignore other things that might be learned—effects of the technology that cannot be measured with simple linguistic measures, with standardized tests, or even by looking at discrete environmental variables (Salomon, 1990). Questions should focus on whether the *system* of teacher, student, and technology is working for the learners (see Egbert, 1993, for an example of a systemic approach to CALL research).

The Explorations sections at the end of each part of this volume demonstrate what we consider to be some of the *right* questions to ask about the CALL environment. Questions that focus on conditions in language learning environments go far toward educating teachers about the effectiveness of technology in language learning. For example, the questions that Pica (1994) asks of language learning research are just as critical in the computer-assisted classroom:

- How effective is group work as an aid to second language learning?

- Should students drill and practice new structures?

- What can be done to encourage participation among students who seldom ask questions or initiate interaction?

- To what extent does the correction of errors assist second language learning?

In addition, as Ehrmann (1995) notes, some technologies support some teaching methods better than others do, leading to the question:

- Which technologies are best for supporting the best methods of teaching and learning?

Studies of the CALL environment must consider other important factors in SLA research. Ehrmann (1995) points out that one teacher using technology can influence a student's learning but that the cumulative effects of many teachers supporting good learning across the curriculum are far more significant. Therefore, what is needed are questions that address the study of CALL within and across courses and programs. Along the same lines, Chapelle (1995b) notes that the many layers of the language learning environment can affect what happens in the classroom. Questions that investigate the political and social milieus in which CALL takes place are no less important than those that investigate CALL activities within one classroom; one may ask, for example, What are some of the assumptions that come with technology? What are the goals of technology use?

Step 2: Review the Literature

In CALL research, Purcell's (1996) Step 2 may involve more careful selection and analysis of research literature than is the case with typical SLA research. Much that has been written about using computers in language education has been descriptive rather than analytical: Technology-using teachers explain their program and curriculum and the way they have integrated CALL. Although these anecdotes are useful, they do not constitute rigorous research and should be used as guidelines for practice and as a starting point for scientific inquiry rather than as support for specific theories. A large body of research regarding educational technology does exist; this might be one place to start in conducting a research review for answers to theoretical CALL questions.

Another pitfall to watch out for in the literature (and in any SLA research) is the *Hawthorne effect*: Any group that is being studied while doing a new or different activity usually performs better. As noted above, this is only one way that the language learning environment changes upon the introduction of technology.

Step 3: State a Hypothesis

Your search of the literature, beginning perhaps with some of the articles cited in the chapters in this volume that are pertinent to your inquiry, should give you a fairly comprehensive overview of what has already been accomplished in CALL research. Your study might lead you to replicate prior research, making appropriate corrections in procedures, or you may wish to strike out in a new direction. A tentative research question reflects only what you hope to find.

Step 4: Determine How to Test the Research Question

Purcell's (1996) Step 4 is fraught with hazards. One truism of quantitative research in the past was the attempt to reduce or eliminate all variables except the one to be researched. However, testing pedagogical theory and application is one of the most difficult undertakings in the social sciences, because so many variables are at work at the same time. A quantitative focus cannot deal adequately with this "anarchic" environment. Happily for both researchers and classroom educators, many paradigm shifts have taken place since the days when only quantitative methodologies constituted "real" research. Structured qualitative studies, complementary analytic and systemic views, and many other designs have successfully shed new light on what occurs in language classrooms (see Johnson, 1991, for an overview). Rather than forcing the design to fit into expected or traditional paradigms, you as a classroom CALL researcher should consider a design that takes into consideration what your questions are really asking.

Step 5: Gather Data

Purcell's Step 5 cautions researchers to gather data accurately in order to test the hypothesis carefully. The swing away from quantitative research toward qualitative research in the past 10 years is noted in chapter 8. As we point out above, however, the CALL environment does not fit neatly into either of these two compartments and should be viewed through a lens that either combines these two paradigms or considers the classroom as the interacting system that it is.

The computer itself allows the generation of considerable data for many kinds of analyses. For instance, the usefulness of saving students' e-mail files to study as examples of interaction strategies is demonstrated in chapter 12. You might also have students save all drafts of an essay and might later use them for an analysis of composing and editing styles. Some software programs, for example, NewReader (McVicker, 1995a, 1997), also assist in data collection because a built-in record keeper notes the parts of the software that were accessed, the time spent on task, and the results of tests or exercises. Collecting the same information about students working in a traditional classroom or studying the same material at home would be very difficult. At the University of Puerto Rico, Cayey's self-access lab, the coordinator has created a similar but far simpler record keeper with HyperStudio (1997): Students write up a record of their work with any questions they have after each session in the lab. A brief video clip on the first card explains how to use the software.

The computer combined with video and audio recording also presents interesting opportunities to collect data about students' behavior with technology. Pujol (1995/1996) provides an excellent model for CALL research in which learners were video- and audiotaped as they used software. Although video and audio recording may be used successfully in a traditional classroom for data collection, professionally developed software may allow sound files to be kept as records and later reviewed by the teacher, researcher, and student with regard to such variables as pronunciation and accent. A record of all keystrokes as students work at a terminal would allow close observation of how they use a tutorial, compose and revise an essay, or conduct an Internet search.

Many research models can be used to collect data for the study of a CALL environment, among them a discourse model with a hierarchical analysis of the interaction (Chapelle, 1990), a systemic model of the language learning environment like the one proposed in this book (see also Egbert, 1993; Egbert & Jessup, 1996), and a set of indicators like those proposed by Jones, Valdez, Nowakowski, and Rasmussen (1995) and by others. Regardless of the model, technology clearly does not dictate methods or questions; however, the model chosen must be appropriate to the setting and the technology under study. Questions of media are not of prime importance—questions about what is being taught and what is being learned must be the focus.

Step 6: Refine Your Answer

In both CALL and non-CALL research, Purcell's (1996) final step is sometimes treated with the perfunctory phrase "more research is needed in this area." A considerably more useful approach is to determine exactly where your research design may have gone astray or how data unaccounted for by your initial hypothesis might be incorporated into a different design or analytical framework. A number of the studies cited throughout this volume follow the latter approach and thus present useful starting points for your own research project.

Conclusion

The eight learning conditions presented above can be put into effect in the language classroom by means of many general strategies, including using group work, providing concrete opportunities to interact in English, focusing on survival skills and functions or on content-based tasks, using problem solving, employing a multitude of media, and recycling lesson content in various ways while providing open-ended opportunities for meaningful language use. In addition, you can provide adequate time for tasks, adequate feedback, appropriate prompting and other assistance, and adequate information or research resources while giving learners opportunities to choose goals and participate consciously in the learning process. The environmental conditions, however, do not dictate specific methods, techniques, content, or tools. Language educators are now using technology effectively to support these learning conditions in a wide variety of settings.

Chapters 2-27 explore in more depth the research that provides the empirical basis for each learning condition. Each part of the book contains a chapter detailing research and describing the present state of theoretical knowledge about classroom language learning, especially as it relates to CALL (Theory and Research). Subsequent chapters discuss current teaching practices that apply the theory to computer-enhanced instruction, including activities, software, and hardware that support an optimal learning environment (Classroom Practice). Also included are chapters on matters related to the environment in which technology is used—including access, policy, and fear of technology (CALL Issues). Each part closes with suggestions for projects and questions for reflection that will help you understand more about CALL practices and conduct research with your own students in a computer-enhanced learning environment (Explorations). The text concludes with a look at what the future of CALL may hold (chapter 28). The Appendixes provide names and uniform resource locators (URLs) for key World Wide Web sites, names and contact information for software publishers and professional organizations, and other resources to help you explore the CALL environment.

PART I

Interaction

Chapter 2

Theory and Research:
Interaction via Computers

Joy Kreeft Peyton

Computer networks as a medium for communication have created opportunities for writing and learning that were never before possible. These opportunities include synchronous (real-time) and asynchronous (time-delayed) interaction, one-on-one interaction between students and teachers or among students within classrooms, and wider communication with individuals and groups around the world. Text and talk are available within the classroom and in a rapidly expanding universe of resources not bound by physical space.

In this chapter, I describe the importance of interaction and negotiation in learning in general and the promises and challenges that interaction over a computer network presents to teachers and students. Although the focus of this chapter is network interaction, the principles hold true for interactions in a variety of computer-supported contexts. I argue that, as new contexts and opportunities for learning and interaction are created, teachers need to continually examine the types and quality of those interactions and find ways to shape them so that they are consistent with the needs and learning goals of teachers and students.

The Central Role of Interaction

As Vygotsky (1934/1962, 1978) has argued so effectively, all human learning is mediated through interaction with others. In interactions with parents, peers or colleagues, and teachers, all learners move, in their speaking and thinking, toward stages at which they can function alone. A number of scholars, particularly in the 1970s and 1980s, demonstrated that oral interaction for authentic social purposes and with a knowledgeable partner is essential to first language development (e.g., Cazden, 1988; McNamee, 1979; Snow & Goldfield, 1982; Wells, 1981) and to second language acquisition

(SLA; e.g., Hatch, 1978a; Long, 1983a; Pica, 1991b; see Pica, 1996, for a comprehensive review of the literature).

More proficient language users or more knowledgeable conversation partners facilitate the participation of less proficient participants by modifying their own language in a number of ways, including asking questions so the learner has something to talk about; repeating, rephrasing, and extending the learner's utterances to provide a language and thinking model; and simplifying their language so the learner can understand it, thereby supporting negotiation. Thus, learners receive *comprehensible input* (Krashen, 1981, 1982), language that they understand but that is slightly beyond their expressive ability, and are encouraged to produce *comprehensible output* (Swain, 1985), when they are "pushed toward the delivery of a message that is not only conveyed, but that is conveyed precisely, coherently, and appropriately" (p. 249). The use of language in interaction with others "provides opportunities for contextualized, meaningful use, to test out hypotheses about the target language, and to move the learner from a purely semantic analysis of the language to a syntactic analysis of it" (p. 252).

Moving beyond language acquisition to the development of thought and the gaining of new knowledge in a content area, Lemke (1990) argues that interaction (or *communication*) is crucial to the learning of science. Scientists and science teachers belong to a community of people who know how to speak the language of science, but students do not, and they need to learn to speak that language. "We have to learn to see science teaching as a social process and to bring students, at least partially, into this community of people who *talk* science" (p. x). This is accomplished at least in part by classroom interaction, through which a learning community is created.

Most work on the dynamics of interaction and their effect on learning has focused on oral interaction. However, research on written interaction in dialogue journals with teachers (notebooks in which students and teachers write regularly with each other; Peyton & Staton, 1993; Staton, Shuy, Peyton, & Reed, 1988) and in letters exchanged with older students (Heath & Branscombe, 1985) has shown that these interactions can also develop language, thought, and reading and writing abilities. As Staton (1984) points out in describing the dynamics of dialogue journal writing,

> To be able to think in new situations—which is the real goal of all education—[learners] need a lot of experience in thinking with someone who is good at it. Just as we learn language by talking with someone who is good at it in specific situations concerning tangible, shared experiences, so we learn to think by thinking with someone to solve a joint task or problem. (p. 145)

In teacher-student and student-student interactions written in dialogue journals and letters, teachers and more knowledgeable students can "engage individual students in active mental processing of their current experience and knowledge in such a way that both new concepts and general strategies for thinking and writing are introduced" (Staton, 1984, p. 147).

In summary, both the interactionist perspective of those studying "language learning through interaction" (Pica, 1996, p. 1) and the sociocultural perspective of Vygotsky (1934/1962) and the many scholars who have studied the development of cognitive abilities and independent judgment show clearly that interaction and negotiation are crucial for learning and language development. Within this general claim, it is also clear that certain types of interactions promote learning and language development more than others do (for a discussion, see Lemke, 1990; Pica, 1996).

Patterns for Computer-Mediated Interaction

Computer networks expand opportunities for written interaction beyond the one-to-one interactions possible in dialogue journals and pen-and-pencil letters, allowing *many-to-many* (Warschauer, 1996) communication with a wide variety of partners. Trent Batson and I first realized the power of computer-mediated communication for promoting language use and development in the mid-1980s at Gallaudet University and Kendall Demonstration Elementary School, both in Washington, DC. Batson and his colleagues in the English department had developed a local-area computer network and software that allowed students and teachers to communicate with each other in writing in real time within the classroom, as a whole class or in pairs and small groups (on separate channels). These network interactions allowed the deaf students in the classes to use English in ways that had not been possible before—in authentic social interactions with others that developed in real time, comparably to oral and signed interactions. The software design, which was at the time revolutionary, allowed messages typed by individuals on a private screen to be sent to and scrolled up a public screen so that the whole class or the conversation partner(s) could read them. Transcripts of these interactions were saved, stored, and printed for analysis and reflection and as the basis for further writing.

Because we were using the local area network (LAN) with deaf students learning English, we initially focused our attention on the ways that these interactions could promote English language acquisition. It was clear to us that as the college and elementary school students interacted with each other and their teachers via computers, the more competent English language users' language provided an interactional *scaffold* (Bruner, 1983; Cazden, 1988), or an expansion of the students' language on which the students could build. For example, in a university literature class, a student and the professor had the following network exchange (excerpted from a much longer conversation that involved the whole class) about a text they had read:

Sharon: the little girl is struggled between her parents
Teacher: She's struggling between life and death, I think.
Sharon: she is struggling between her parents and the love for them . . . .

In another interaction at the elementary school, in which older and more English-proficient students were paired with younger, less proficient students, the following exchange (excerpted from a much longer conversation) took place between Robin (a more proficient English user) and Pam (a beginning English user who was working far below grade level and having difficulty writing independently on the network):

Robin: . . . oh i am fine too do you have any pets?
Pam: yes i have my pet is fish.
Robin: oh i see i have a pet too i have a dog.
Pam: oh you have baby dog?
Robin: no before that dog was baby baby dogs are called puppies. My dog is girl. She is 4 years old.
Pam: oh
Robin: Do you want to know what's her name?
Pam: yes i want your name.
Robin: Okay, Her name is Tina. Do you like cats?
Pam: who is's cats.
Robin: No I dont have cats I want to know if you like cats?
Pam: oh i like cats yes

In both interactions, more proficient and knowledgeable language users were helping their partners communicate by asking them questions, answering their questions, and repeating and expanding on what they were writing. As these interactions continued throughout the school year, we watched the students become more independent and develop more complex and sophisticated English (see, e.g., Peyton & Mackinson, 1989).

As news about network use spread to schools and universities for hearing students and a number of researchers began to explore networking as a potential means to develop the writing skills of hearing and deaf students, it became clear that computer-mediated interaction revolutionizes notions about writing, radically challenging traditional distinctions between speech and writing—for example, that speech is social and interactive and that writing is solitary and monologic (Peyton, 1991; Warschauer, 1996).

Kemp (1993), an early network enthusiast and developer of Daedalus® InterChange®, a part of Daedalus Integrated Writing Environment (1997), contrasts *network theory* with what he considers to be its antecedents in writing theory—formalist theory, process theory, and collaborative theory—and argues that network writing revolutionizes writing instruction because it textualizes it:

Almost all of the interaction among students takes place on screen and in written text. Critiques are written using split screens and mailed electronically to the writer, in text. Negotiations concerning the markers of effective and ineffective writing are written and distributed to a student or a group of students on screen and in text. And all of this text is saved and retrievable by any student practically at any time to read and review and reread. . . . What networked computers allow us to do in the writing classroom is emphasize reactions in text to text. (pp. 171–172)

With a computer network, a lively class discussion about a topic can begin in writing. The text of that discussion can be stored and printed, or the electronic version can be used to spark thought as students write individual pieces, which they can then post on the network for class members to read and critique, again in writing, after which the student can revise. The process then continues, all in writing.

This process not only takes place continuously in writing but is also continuously collaborative, a notion that is very different from previous visions of a writer working alone to produce a text that others (possibly) comment on later. Instead of one author, there may be many authors, each expressing ideas and building on (or completely ignoring) the ideas of the others. Langston and Batson (1990) go so far as to argue that network writing abolishes the notion of the original thinker and the solitary author and gives rise to the image of "a precipitating solid in a supersaturated solution . . . the speck of dust around which crystals form" (p. 153). The individual in this new image is suspended in ideas and concepts that crystallize in a community. In a similar vein, Sirc and Reynolds (1993) describe network interaction as "sampling" (p. 154), a construction of meaning built from a blend of one's own ideas, others' ideas, and material one has read or heard in discussion. This shift carries many benefits, particularly for students who have difficulties making the transition from oral to written expression.

Studies of participation patterns in computer-mediated discussions also show their benefits for students' learning. Studies in business settings among professionals (e.g., Kiesler, Siegel, & McGuire, 1984; Sproull & Kiesler, 1991; see Warschauer, 1996, for a review of several such studies) have shown that participation in computer-mediated discussions is more equally distributed than in face-to-face discussions, with women and groups of people with low social status, for example, participating more than they normally do. This difference seems to be attributable to the reduction of social context cues that indicate race, gender, and social status. According to Warschauer's review of studies of computer-mediated communication in second language composition and foreign language classrooms, researchers found that the amount of student participation and student-to-student interaction in the computer-mediated discussions was dramatically higher than in face-to-face discussions among the same individuals. In addition, students took greater control of discourse management, and their language was lexically and syntactically more complex. These findings indicate that computer networks provide a positive environment for learning.

Challenges in Computer-Mediated Interaction

Although network interaction can provide a powerful context for language and writing development, it can also present considerable challenges to both teachers and students. In the late 1980s, a group of college and university professors and researchers formed the Electronic Networks for Interaction Consortium to use and study real-time network interaction within college and university writing classrooms. In a number of publications, the members of this group described the following challenges, which are also relevant to K–12 settings (as described in Peyton & French, 1996).

One challenge probably results from the newness of the medium. Initially, students seem to feel a certain sense of anonymity; they often have the urge to play with language and display their wit and verbal audacity. Even if students use their real names, which they don't always do, they are sitting in front of a computer screen and are not necessarily seeing others or being seen by them. The result can be confrontational and insulting dialogues. The following example (excerpted from a longer discussion) comes from a small-group discussion among students in two developmental writing classes in two community colleges in Virginia, communicating at a distance. The two groups identified themselves as "Group3" and "Chris."

Group3:	Hello, my name is Charles and this is Karen
	HEY, WHAT'S UP! THIS TOMSON AND THIS IS SUSAN
Chris:	Hello our names are Alice, Helen, Bill, Ernie and dora.
	Yes were the Fatboys! to bad you guys don't drink! . . .
Chris:	Of course we drink beer and etc. . . .
Group3:	Are you guys single.
Chris:	some of us are and some of us aren't
Group3:	What is the etc.
Chris:	Bill has been divorced 3 times and he's only 18.
	Etc. . . . is other types of alcohol!
	Ernie does crack!!
	Dora does Dallas!!!
	Bill smokes candy!! (Thompson, 1993, p. 222)

One writing professor using the network at his university for the first time found that his students, also new to the network, began to "curse obsessively" in "a tidal wave of obscenity and puerility" (DiMatteo, 1990, pp. 79–80), similar to the *flaming* that Sproull and Kiesler (1991) found in network communications among more experienced users. A female writing instructor at the same institution described her students' initial network behavior as a "combination of unbridled bigotry and heady power," producing exchanges that were "less interactive than interinsultive" (George, 1990, p. 49). The conversation in the example above, which began with a game of mutual insults, degenerated over time into increasingly more hostile exchanges (not shown here).

Another challenge probably results from the immediacy of the medium. Some teachers and researchers have argued that students have more time to think and compose their thoughts in written than in oral interactions. However, other scholars have found that, rather than write complex thoughts or extended, logical, thoughtful prose, students trying to keep up with the constant flow of language scrolling up their screens and the sudden linguistic competition with their classmates may fire off humorous zingers and "graffiti-like messages" (Kremers, 1990, p. 40) or "cheap shots" and "easy insults" (Miller, 1993, p. 131). These might be regularly interspersed with more serious writing and can take it over completely. For example, the following conversation took place in a network small-group discussion among first-year basic writers in college who were giving feedback on Nick's paper. The critique rapidly degenerates:

Kevin:	it was a pretty good paper. Just spelling mistakes kinda crippled it.
Jim:	yeah
Nick:	jerald what about your shoes?
Kevin:	Avia
Nick:	I was rushed
Jerald:	That's the problem you wait till the late minute
Nick:	Jerald get a Life, a real life
Kevin:	get rid of them did'nt you say you had them ever since jr high.
Jerald:	I have seen some of your writing before you are a good writer
Kevin:	your shoes.
Jerald:	It just takes nick longer to put his thought together.
Kevin:	Avia are one of the finest most comfortable shoes you can buy
Nick:	Jerald you do smell like you want to be alone, and so does your shoes (Sirc & Reynolds, 1993, p. 55)

A third challenge for teachers comes from the very sense of community fostered by the medium. Even when students are trying to collaborate, network discussions can seem fragmented, diffuse, and off the topic until students and teachers find ways to establish and follow topic threads. These patterns were reported by professors using LANs for synchronous written interaction within classes, but Black, Levin, and Mehan (1983) found that discourse in asynchronous interaction with distant audiences was also structured with multiple, interwoven topic threads. In addition, teachers accustomed to having a considerable amount of authority in the classroom initially find it difficult to maintain control and establish order when students are free to write whatever they want, to whomever they want, whenever they want. Kremers (1993), for example, describes his first experience with leading a classroom discussion on a LAN as follows:

> Expecting that my students would follow me in discussion, I found instead that they much preferred to converse with each other, forcing me to the sidelines. I could not imagine that happening in my conventional classroom. No student had ever tried to take over the discussion in all my 20 years of teaching, even during my progressive period, when I arranged the desks in a circle. I had always set the direction, and the students had always done more or less what I wanted. But interaction in real time on the LAN was totally different because it seemed to give all the power to the students, who outnumbered me 20 to 1. (p. 113)

Finally, how do teachers monitor writing development and account for individual students' progress when it is difficult to separate the individual from the group and written exchanges are often so free and casual? DiMatteo (1990) points out that

> the product of such writing is a text that reaches no conclusion . . . . Not only does no one have the final say, but even the notion of a final say is brought into doubt. The text, traditionally understood as a stable piece of organized and fixed language, disappears. (p. 76)

Electronic writing is like communal free writing or like an unmonitored discussion in an oral, face-to-face setting. Making students fully aware that the electronic text is monitored, saved, and printed—and therefore has a more formal nature than out-of-class conversation—seems difficult.

The Explosion in Electronic Interaction

Very early in the current revolution in the use of computer-mediated interaction in classrooms, Langer (1986) predicted its promise:

> Such possibilities for literacy activities may greatly enhance first language learning, second language learning, and literacy development in contexts where words like "natural" and "functional" are no longer used to stimulate "pretend" activities, but to carry on purposeful and sensible communication about the content the students are learning in a social context where students can learn from and help each other (and receive the teacher's help when needed) as they work toward a joint goal. (p. 119)

Cummins and Sayers (1995), writing nearly 10 years later, provide an illuminating glimpse at the explosion of such possibilities for interaction and the creation of learning communities within classrooms and around the world—through the World Wide Web, electronic journals and newsletters, electronic discussion groups, newsgroups, and bulletin boards—taking students and teachers far beyond the one-on-one interactions of Gallaudet's early days. The simultaneous explosion of computer software and hypertext environments provides a multitude of texts to interact with and about.

Kemp (1997) recently argued that computer networks create "the intensely interactive classroom, whose controlling instructional principle is student interactivity managed by the computer, the software, and the instructor" (n.p.). In this environment, traditional notions of what writing and learning involve and traditional patterns of teacher-dominated talk are not appropriate, possible, or even desirable. The challenge now is to think carefully about new ways to write and learn and about how to structure the computer network's intensely interactive environment and use of texts so that they meet students' and teachers' needs and goals. Kremers (1990), who was shocked and affronted when he first began using a LAN in his writing class and struggled long and hard with the interactional dynamics it created, provides some insight into how to start:

> I am in favor of taking this risk because after three years of experimenting with real-time network writing, I am convinced that students working in the heady atmosphere of written interaction can, with careful guidance, learn to handle it. The teaching model I am trying to develop is a networked writing class in which authority is shared, decentralized, distributed, even communal; a class in which teachers sometimes participate directly in the discussion and at other times stay out of things, letting their students take control of their own dialogues; a class in which students compete among themselves for influence in the group through the force of their language and the clarity of their arguments. (p. 33)

In Kremers' vision of a "reconceived and redesigned classroom that supports the theory and pedagogy of collaboration" (p. 33), the teacher does not leave students alone to develop their own ways of working and interacting, or even to work through topics of their own choosing, but rather stays involved. At times the teacher might prompt and lead a discussion, contributing questions and comments to help students focus on and explore a topic. Kremers calls this arrangement an *intervention model*. At other times, the teacher structures the discussion and work ahead of time by creating scenarios and problems for students to work through together. Kremers calls this arrangement a *nonintervention model* because, once the scenario is created, the teacher stays out of the discussion. For example, when students in Kremers' basic reading and writing class in college read a series of articles about the plague of fires in the Amazon rain forest, he wrote a script, involving a Japanese timber merchant (Sako), an American environmentalist (Pat), and a Brazilian cattle rancher (Landis), for them to act out on the network. (The creation of scenarios to guide students' interactions and writing is also discussed in Miller, 1993.) The discussion, excerpted below, lasted for about an hour:

Sako: We are not going to chop down all the trees. There are a lot of trees in this rain forest. And you, Landis, could use the cleared land for a new and bigger ranch to hold your cattle.

Pat: I've been down to look at the land and it looks bad. it will only be fertile for one year. then become nothing. IT WILL NEVER REJUVENATE ITSELF BECAUSE ONCE ITS CUT DOWN THATS IT.

Sako: If we could just draw up a little agreement saying Landis will not cut more than 2% of his trees, and he will build some kind of ranch or something to utilize the land—would everyone agree?

Landis: You do not understand local politics. Local politics are settled in blood and the law is carried in pistols. (Kremers, 1990, p. 40)

In the following class session, Kremers posed a number of provocative questions addressing issues that arose in the discussion, and the students wrote essays individually to address them. To his surprise, Kremers found that

after a few such scenario-writing sessions, some of the students started appearing at the door of my office just before class to help create that day's scenario by looking over my shoulder at my composing screen and offering suggestions. So not only did they collaborate with each other to create the types of writing they found meaningful, they collaborated with me on how to teach the course. (p. 40)

Conclusion

Two crucial points emerge from this discussion. First, no matter what new opportunities are created for interaction and learning, the quality of the interactions is critical and needs to be taken seriously and examined. Second, teachers are central to the process of creating opportunities for students to interact with individuals and need to continually shape and examine those opportunities and their outcomes. Computers are not replacing teachers but rather are changing the nature of their work.

Perrone, Repenning, Spencer, and Ambach (1996) have argued that if teachers expand their thinking about computers as simply tools and use them as a medium to facilitate communication and sharing, they can fundamentally change their ways of thinking and learning. As they expand their thinking to consider new opportunities and contexts, teachers need to look continually at the patterns of interaction that emerge so that they meet the ideals of equity, productive exploration, and educational excellence.

Chapter 3

Classroom Practice: Creating Interactive CALL Activities

Joy Egbert

Clearly, social interaction is a critical component of the language learning environment. Authentic social interaction is that which occurs for a good reason—for example, to solve a problem or address an issue important to learners—with an authentic audience (see chapter 5). Social interaction may take place among participants in many configurations: one to one, one to many, and many to many.

The fact that learners are put into work groups or given a task, however, does not mean that they will interact, that they will interact in the target language, or that the interaction will facilitate language learning. As noted in chapter 2, the quality of interaction is important and often takes careful planning on the part of the teacher. One guideline that may help teachers ensure that learners engage in high-quality social interaction, including the negotiation of meaning, is to build in specific roles or assignments for individuals during tasks so that each student's contribution is necessary to achieve the group's or team's goal.

Having established goals and created roles, the teacher can integrate computer technology into the task, if needed. In some cases technology will play a peripheral role; in others it will help create an environment that is unique in the way it supports interaction. This chapter focuses on the *who* and *how* of computer-assisted classroom social interaction. The chapter is organized around the participant configurations most likely to be used in the language learning classroom: learners interacting with classmates, with the teacher, with other students in their school or in other schools, and with community members and experts. These divisions can be considered arbitrary, however, as most of the activities can be adapted for use with more than one grouping.

Interaction With Classmates

Language learners probably interact more often with their classmates than with other people, although such interaction is not always productive from a language learning perspective. Many of the variety of ways to make this interaction more productive can be enhanced with computers.

When Is a Drill Not a Drill?

As many of the contributors to this volume suggest, computers are very useful as drillmasters. However, unlike texts with drill-and-practice exercises, the computer can provide instant feedback to learners, and unlike teachers, the computer can easily repeat questions endlessly and in exactly the same manner. Although drill-and-practice software is useful for some individuals and for remediation, it does not provide opportunities for learners to engage in authentic social interaction.

When is a drill not a drill? The answer is, when it's an interactive activity. Not all teachers have the latest multimedia software or integrated learning systems available to them, and the majority of computer-using language teachers worldwide do not have access to the Internet. What can these teachers do to add interaction among students to the grammar drill software, the vocabulary-based, fill-in-the-blanks computer exercise, or the electronic text without hyperlinks that might be the extent of their software library?

External documents such as handouts and graphic organizers can enhance drill software, and assigning different roles to students and varying the group configurations can also increase the chances that students will interact while using such software. Suppose, for example, that in using a traditional grammar drill package (many of which are available free or very cheaply through Internet software archives; see chapter 14 and Appendix D), Student 1 is manipulating the computer to complete a basic exercise in which sentences with no semantic relationship to one another are to be completed with the correct preposition. Student 2, who cannot see the computer screen, has a handout prepared by the teacher that (a) asks the students to join the computer-generated sentences in the exercise in a logical way, changing them as little as possible (and without changing the prepositions), and (b) supplies vocabulary words and a topic to use in this endeavor. Together, the students must correctly complete the software exercise (which only Student 1 can see), share information about the sentences on the screen, and develop a way to form the sentences into a story using the vocabulary and topic from the worksheet (which only Student 2 has). The task has changed from an isolating, closed-ended drill to an interactive, creative exchange in the target language during which learners are still performing the original drill.

Another example of an interactive drill uses MacTrivia (Killion, 1985), available free from software archives through the Internet (see chapter 14 and Appendix D). In this software, the students see a question at the top of the screen and four answers from which to choose the correct one (see Figure 3-1). The instructor can easily change the content of the questions and answers (see chapter 25 on authorable software), but this capability does not change the individualized, drill-and-practice nature of the software.

One way to use the software more creatively and to provide opportunities for learners to interact is to add a reference text in which students must find the answers to the questions. For ESL learners in the United States, a good choice is *Living in the* USA (Lanier, 1988), which covers a wide range of important cultural and living issues in relatively simple prose. The teacher can use important information from the text as the basis for questions and answers written in the MacTrivia (Killion, 1995) framework. With one student doing the screen work and another looking up information in the book, the chance of interaction goes up at least slightly. Adding a paper worksheet on which students have to supply short answers extrapolated from the answers to the screen questions raises that chance even more. The question and the choices of answer might be arranged on the screen as in Figure 3-2. The book's explanation, once the learner locates it, reads,

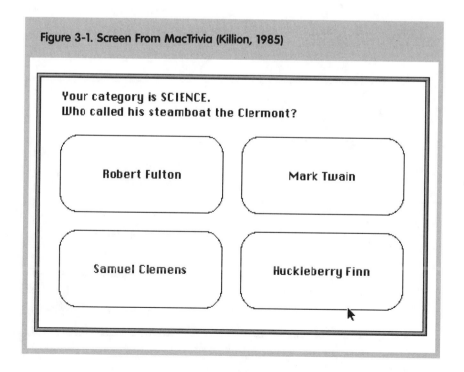

Figure 3-1. Screen From MacTrivia (Killion, 1985)

Your category is SCIENCE.
Who called his steamboat the Clermont?

Robert Fulton

Mark Twain

Samuel Clemens

Huckleberry Finn

> Nearly all large offices and factories have mid-morning and mid-afternoon coffee breaks. Although 15 minutes are allotted twice a day for relaxation and chatter, many office employees take coffee to their desks and keep on working . . . . (Lanier, 1988, p. 62)

The question on the worksheet might read, "During a coffee break, employees _____." Completing this work correctly within an allotted time period takes coordination, communication, negotiation of meaning, and the use of a variety of language skills and modes. The task is not just a drill any more. Creative teachers can find many other ways to use their computers as a basis for offering learners opportunities to interact.

Decision Making in the Classroom

Problem-solving and decision-making tasks can support classroom interaction if they are well planned. Again, each student must have a role or a task that contributes to the group's goal. The huge databases of organized material available to students in computer software packages and on the Internet can save teachers preparation time and effort. Most of the software published by Tom Snyder Productions (TSP; see chapters 10 and 13) is excellent for this type of activity.

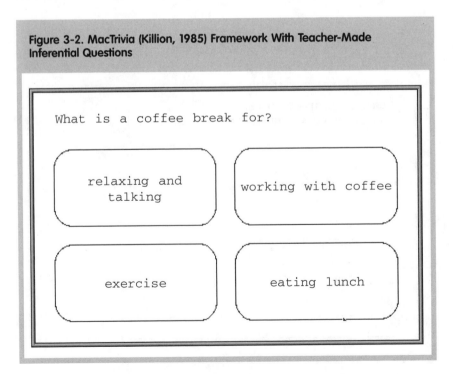

Figure 3-2. MacTrivia (Killion, 1985) Framework With Teacher-Made Inferential Questions

What is a coffee break for?

| relaxing and talking | working with coffee |
| exercise | eating lunch |

The software from TSP's Inspirer series is one way to help learners ask questions, request and use information, and share information clearly. For ESL learners, National Inspirer (1996) and International Inspirer (1996) are appropriate, and for EFL, TSP offers Europe Inspirer (1997) and Africa Inspirer (1997) as well. Within the classroom the whole class, teams, or individuals can use these packages.

Here is a scenario for a class using National Inspirer (1996). In teams of up to six learners, each team member receives a map of the United States (hard copies are included with the software). Each map is different and shows, in graphics and text, important information on one or two topics about the United States (e.g., population density, gross national product, ethnic makeup, major products). The software presents an assignment in which each team must start in a specific state and move to contiguous states to achieve a certain goal within 10 moves (see Figure 3-3). The goal could be to land in the states with the highest population density or with the

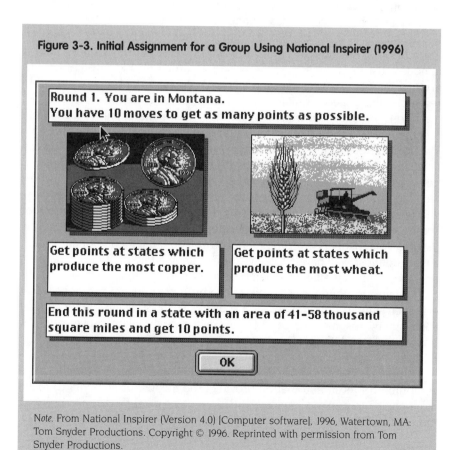

Figure 3-3. Initial Assignment for a Group Using National Inspirer (1996)

> Round 1. You are in Montana.
> You have 10 moves to get as many points as possible.
>
> Get points at states which produce the most copper.
>
> Get points at states which produce the most wheat.
>
> End this round in a state with an area of 41–58 thousand square miles and get 10 points.
>
> OK

Note. From National Inspirer (Version 4.0) [Computer software], 1996, Watertown, MA: Tom Snyder Productions. Copyright © 1996. Reprinted with permission from Tom Snyder Productions.

greatest export of dairy products. The team may earn a bonus for landing in a state with the highest elevation. After the team discusses and makes its moves on the computer, the software calculates the team's score before giving another assignment.

Because the students each have a map (containing information that is essential to meeting the team's goal) and may say anything they like to their teammates without sharing their maps, teammates must negotiate among themselves as they decide where they should go in each move. This activity can lead to collaborative research projects and a host of other activities in which interaction is a vital part of the learning environment.

TSP's TimeLiner (1994) is also valuable in helping students visualize content, summarize, compare and contrast, and use graphic organizers to arrange information in the target language. Because the software is content free, it can be used for almost any area of study—for example, to trace the biography of a famous person, help students define life plans, compare the gestation periods of various animals, or graphically display the history of English. Like the Inspirer series, TimeLiner allows students to take on roles. For example, a team of two to four learners could conduct research individually on a musical figure, a political figure, an entertainer, and a famous artist from the same time period and then decide together how to arrange the comparisons on a time line. Or each student on a team could research one aspect of a famous person or time period—for example, inventions or social movements—and the team members could decide together which information is important enough to include on the time line. TimeLiner affords many opportunities for interaction while focusing on the language and content that are important to the teacher and learners. To help students with public speaking, speech making, and similar activities, teachers could have teams present the results of their time lines to the class and answer questions from the class. Students could create other types of presentations using graphics or presentation software, such as Kid Pix (1997) or Microsoft® PowerPoint® 97 (1996). The critical component is that each student should have a role—visual designer, audio mixer, text preparer, and so on—so that all group members must participate in each step.

Numerous other in-class projects can promote interaction among learners. Even simple computer-assisted activities such as having learners create each others' résumés instead of their own can stimulate conversation. It takes a great deal of interaction to obtain a satisfactory result from this type of task.

Students could probably do all the activities described here without the computer; however, automation provides the means for students to focus more completely on the language and ideas being presented and to proceed more efficiently in their team efforts.

Teacher-Student Interaction

For teachers, learning about their students—their strengths and weaknesses, their concerns, and other characteristics that might affect them in the language learning classroom—is crucial. The importance of teacher-student interaction cannot be overstated, and a variety of ways exist for teachers to individualize interaction in the target language.

In addition to the feedback and discussion resulting from other kinds of CALL activities, computers can help by enabling electronic journals (discussed further in chapter 6). Electronic journals not only give teachers valuable insight into learners' progress and problems but are also a wonderful way to integrate e-mail into the classroom. In addition to saving paper, electronic journals avoid the problems of messy handwriting and of the journals being lost or damaged, and they can help ensure privacy, as only learners have access to their individual e-mail accounts.

Interaction Among Classes in the Same School

School is often an isolating environment in which one classroom rarely communicates with others. Electronic media can make communication quicker and easier, overcome space and scheduling problems that make physical contact difficult to arrange, and organize large amounts of data in useful ways. At Palomar Community College in San Marcos, California, starting a simulated business was D. Hanley's way to get her learners to interact among themselves and with others in other classes. The general steps for the project were

1.   Choose a business venture.
2.   Vote on positions and roles (for everyone).
3.   Make business cards.
4.   Develop the product or service.
5.   Advertise in other classes.
6.   Distribute the product.

At Palomar, the students decided to develop a matchmaking enterprise that would help all students in the ESL program meet other learners for "friendship or love." After deciding on jobs, the students created business cards with word-processing software. They then developed a survey that they used to interview students throughout the program who wanted to participate. This information was then put into a database, in which matching was to take place. The final goal was a party at which the matched students would meet. Interaction took place among class members, who each had a job to do, and during the interviews. The computer played a support role in this multiweek project; without the database capabilities, making the matches would have been a very time-consuming process.

At the elementary level, many projects have involved students at different grade levels. Language learners in higher grades might interview younger students about their interests or problems and, in teams, design target-language electronic books for the younger students to read and discuss with them. As noted in chapter 6, e-mail exchanges between classes can involve discussions of course content or critical issues, or the sharing or presentation of research projects across the school. The possibilities are almost limitless.

Interaction Among Classes in Different Schools

Technology as a tool for communication becomes even more important in the design of interactive tasks between language learners at physically separated schools. Numerous ways exist to assist language learning between two classes or among several. The exciting results of these projects can be found all over the World Wide Web and in journals and magazines dealing with educational technology (see chapters 6, 7, and 26; see Appendix H for a list of organized curricular exchanges).

Literature Circles

One idea for promoting interaction between schools is the use of literature circles. Classes of students in different schools read the same article or articles about the same topic and use an e-mail or Web-based discussion list to exchange views and opinions and explore the topic more deeply. Teachers can create their own lists or use one of the many resources available on-line. For example, the Orillas Project (Sayers, 1989; see http://orillas.upr.clu.edu/) has been assisting K–12 class-to-class EFL and native speaker exchanges for over 15 years, and the SL-*Lists* (Holliday & Robb, n.d.; see chapter 6 and Appendix B) also provide an excellent forum for learner interaction. The HUT Internet Writing Project (Vilmi, 1998b; see chapter 26) promotes exchanges among college- and university-level students. Controversial issues seem to work very well as topics for this type of exchange, as they promote many clarification requests and the negotiation of meaning, as discussed in chapters 2 and 12.

Other kinds of information exchanges to use as a basis for a research project or other task involve geographic or cultural information and topics. The Oregon Trail project, for example, involved classes or groups within schools along the original Oregon Trail. Students used the software Oregon Trail (1991), in which students take on the roles of pioneers as they trek across the country following the trail (see Figure 3-4). As the students

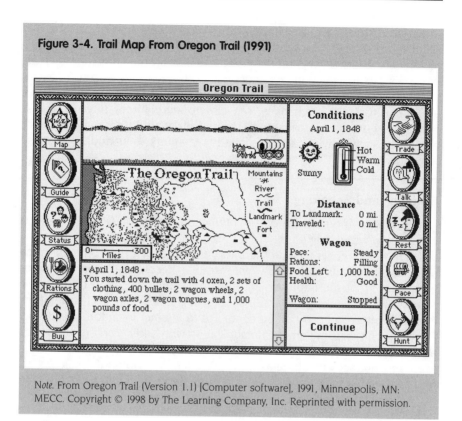

Figure 3-4. Trail Map From Oregon Trail (1991)

Note. From Oregon Trail (Version 1.1) [Computer software], 1991, Minneapolis, MN: MECC. Copyright © 1998 by The Learning Company, Inc. Reprinted with permission.

approached each town or important landmark in the course of taking their journey across the U.S. Wild West, they contacted other students in that place for additional information about its history, its present-day conditions, and any other information they needed to perform tasks related to learning about the trail.

The Amazon Trail (1994) and The Yukon Trail (1994) are appropriate for learners who live in or are studying about these regions. Many Web sites put students in touch with others working in the field on ocean research, culture, rain forest ecology, and other content areas (see chapters 7 and 10). The World Wide Web site for the King's Road 2001 Project (see Vilmi, 1997b) contains links to several such projects in Canada and Europe.

Language classes in different countries have collaborated on many occasions. In a private language school in California, a class of Japanese students wanted to write a Mexican cookbook. They contacted local informants and counterparts in Mexico for recipes and help with the actual cooking of the food; the collaborators then received a copy of the cookbook.

Some classes have used HyperCard® (1997), an authoring program (described in more detail in chapter 25), to produce electronic postcards and other types of short applications to share with other classes, which then reciprocate. Learners separated by distance have worked together to create pages for the World Wide Web, help each other learn how to use specific technologies, and publish joint texts. The Internet and file transfer programs are useful to these exchanges, but classrooms without Internet access successfully use the postal service to send disks and other materials back and forth. Such activities are described in chapters 9, 10, and 26 (see also Appendix H).

Listening and Speaking

At this writing, the majority of the interaction in school-to-school projects occurs asynchronously (at different times) and in writing. For teachers and learners whose goals include the improvement of written communication skills, these projects are an excellent resource. Recent preliminary research even shows that the improvement in written communication translates in some ways to speaking skills (see chapter 12). This is especially true of the informal written speech that students use to interact in chat rooms, a tool for synchronous (same-time) communication with other learners and teachers. Multiuser object-oriented domains (MOOs) are also a great place to meet and interact with students from other schools. Both MOOs and chats for language learning are discussed in more depth in chapter 22.

Learners with the goal of improving speaking skills or teachers with the desire to give learners practice in integrated skills might find tasks such as those mentioned above to be unsuited to their needs. There is hope, however, for incorporating listening and speaking into reading and writing projects over distance. One innovation in sharing information among language classrooms that is not far off is videoconferencing. With the advent of inexpensive computer-based video cameras, free software such as CU-SeeMe (1997) and Microsoft NetMeeting™ (1997), and easier access to the Internet and other transmission media, the prospect for oral communication in the target language over distance is improving quickly. The software mentioned allows users to see each other via video; use audio to communicate; and at the same time use drawing, typing, and other software tools. Figure 3-5 shows a screen from a videoconferencing session using Microsoft NetMeeting conferencing software. The small window at the top right displays the local user, and a similar window below it displays the distant user. Microsoft NetMeeting also has a whiteboard that allows distant users to design graphics together as a chat window displays messages.

Figure 3-5. Interface in Microsoft® NetMeeting™ (1997)

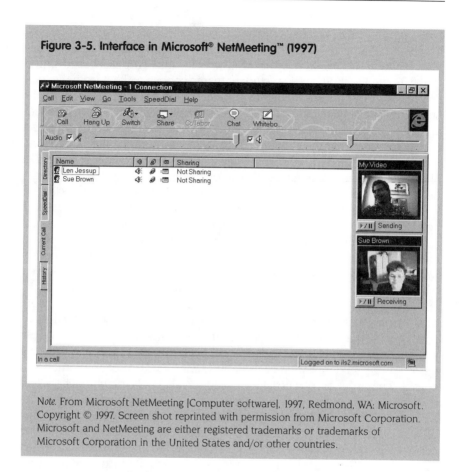

Note. From Microsoft NetMeeting [Computer software], 1997, Redmond, WA: Microsoft. Copyright © 1997. Screen shot reprinted with permission from Microsoft Corporation. Microsoft and NetMeeting are either registered trademarks or trademarks of Microsoft Corporation in the United States and/or other countries.

Interaction With Local Community Members

Until videoconferencing technologies are commonplace, learners can take advantage of opportunities to interact in the target language with members of the local community. Getting students into the community to interact with native speakers is critical, even in EFL situations. Teachers can use e-mail for this purpose (see chapter 6), but this medium, like most of the school-to-school projects described, involves a limited set of primarily written language skills. Other kinds of computer-supported activities can help accomplish the goal of authentic interaction between students and community members.

A good example of a project demanding oral, written, and organization skills is the small-scale systems analysis and design (SAD) project for the World Wide Web done by a group of future business students (Egbert & Jessup, in press; see Egbert, 1996a, for sample forms and handouts). The purpose of the SAD business process is generally to help organizations use computer information systems successfully. The process requires consulting, analysis, design, and other oral, written, and graphics-based procedures. In the ESL/EFL setting, student teams choose a client from the local community (e.g., a nonprofit organization, a branch or department of the school, a small business, or even the leading local employer) who has agreed to participate. The students interview the client about the organization; determine what the client needs to include on a Web page; and obtain any graphics, photos, or other materials that the client would like to include. The students then summarize this information and make a preliminary design for the page(s), which is approved after discussion with the class or instructor. Students then create the pages and, when finished, print out the needs summary and Web pages and return the entire package to the client for review. The final steps are to make changes requested by the client and undergo a final review by the client. This project is not just an exercise in Web page building. Often the clients choose to keep the pages as their official home pages on the Web, making the experience highly authentic.

Arranging for students to visit other schools or organizations and work with participants there is another way to give students opportunities to interact with the local community. Having international or immigrant ESL students work with children in local schools (or, in an EFL context, having the language students work with native speakers at a local international school, embassy, or business) can lead to all kinds of interaction and learning. For example, international students at Indiana University met with a Grade 2–3 class for 7 weeks (see Egbert, in press). Each team, consisting of a university language learner dyad and four native-English-speaking children, used Kid Pix (1997) to create an electronic presentation called "All About Us." The international students were thrilled to interact with native-speaking children (a low-pressure situation for them), learn a great deal of slang and idioms, and teach about their home countries.

Newspaper production also provides learners with opportunities to interact with the local native speaker community. Conducting interviews and research, soliciting advertising, learning about the news, and performing other tasks involved in developing a newspaper require many contact hours with community members from local organizations, newsworthy institutions, businesses, and so on. Sharing the newspaper with other members of the community makes the task authentic as well.

Cultural Reporter (1995) is a curriculum kit that can promote interaction with the local community. The purpose of the activities is to help students look at the community around them and think about why it looks and acts the way it does. In addition to a video, a student workbook, and teacher-guided activities, the kit includes computer templates for students to use in constructing their projects. Using this curriculum as a basis, teams of students in the Intensive English Program at Indiana University have looked at the differences in the social choices of U.S. and foreign students and have researched the relationship between a university and the local community surrounding it (see Figure 3-6). In conducting interviews and gathering information, students used tape recorders and cameras. Students employed computers to type and display their results in a variety of ways, from making Web pages to developing display boards to be hung in the local library.

Any of the activities described here could be adapted for varying grade levels within a school, for a one-computer setting, for different groups within the class, or for connecting with world community members, as discussed below.

Interaction With World Community Members/Experts

The "Born on the Fourth of July" project (described in Mejia, 1995) is an excellent example of how second language students can interact with experts or other people in different parts of the world outside of the purely

Figure 3-6. Cultural Reporter (1995) Project Published on the World Wide Web

THEIR VIEWS

on the relationship between
Bloomington & *I.U.*

For WHAT? HOW? WHEN? WHY?

This project belongs to the curriculum of I.E.P of IU. The class is "Cultural Reporter" and our instructor was **Joy Egbert**.
We want to understand why citizens and students are proud of being here or complain of the surroundings made by IU. So, during two weeks, we met several people in Bloomington. Though a camera and a cassette tape recorder were all our equipment, we tried to do our best. and we could reach the result as follows. It began on January 15th.

Our members were...
Lyu-Kyung Jang, Yongji Zhao, Sung-Su Hong and Kyo-Beom Lee
● Click here to see us

Note. Produced by students L.-K. Jang, Y. Zhao, S.-S. Hong, and K.-B. Lee, 1996, Indiana University, Bloomington, Intensive English Program.

academic domain. During a thematic unit on the Vietnam War, Mejia's students read the book *Born on the Fourth of July* (Kovic, 1976), viewed the film of the same name, and discussed various aspects of the war. To provide authentic information and interaction for her students, Mejia asked members of a Vietnam War veterans' electronic discussion list if they would be willing to participate. Mejia's students interviewed the veterans via e-mail and composed essays centering on themes that emerged from the class materials and the students' conversations with the veterans. They then sent the essays to the veterans for comments.

Experts on almost any topic are relatively easy to find through an Internet search. They can provide valuable, content-based interaction in the target language with language learners at all levels and abilities.

Summary

This chapter has suggested many ways to build interaction into language learning activities and has described how computers can enhance interaction in language learning tasks. Among the ways to build interaction into activities are supplementing software with external documents, using software with built-in interactivity, and teaming learners with others inside and outside the classroom. Two principles for building interaction can serve as guidelines for creating additional activities and groupings: (a) each student's role should be clear, and (b) each student should possess information that is crucial to the learner's or team's goal.

Chapter 4

CALL Issues: Building a Computer-Enhanced Language Classroom*

Shayla Sivert and Joy Egbert

Traditionally, getting a class to use computers has meant going to the computer lab. There, each learner walks into a cold, sterile environment of 20–30 computers, each set on a desk designed to hold nothing more than the central processing unit (CPU), monitor, and keyboard and placed in rows, all facing the front of the room. As class begins, learners sit in their seats, stash their books next to their chairs, crouch in front of their computer screens, and work individually through drill-and-practice grammar software. As they finish, they print out a copy of their score and take it to the instructor as proof of their success in completing the assigned task.

Fortunately, times are changing. Although the traditional lab is still commonplace in many academic institutions, a new scenario is emerging: that of the computer-assisted classroom. The word *classroom* implies a place where different kinds of learning can take place and where technology use is subordinate to discovery and understanding. In this setting, learners enter a classroom designed for comfort and collaborative learning. They ideally find a cushioned seat equipped with casters in front of a large desk with a recessed monitor; each desk is part of a group of four desks facing one another. Books, papers, and pens are spread over the quad of desks. As learners begin their work, they move easily among other members of their quad and even among other members of the class and the instructor. Instead of concentrated silence, one hears the lively discussion of learners working together on task-oriented and project-based assignments. The software available assists in driving the assignments, and several other media are used in developing and completing the tasks.

---

*This chapter draws on S. Sivert and J. Egbert, 1995, "Applying the Principles: Using a Language Learning Environment Framework to Build a Computer-Assisted Classroom," *College ESL*, 7(3), pp. 53–66.

41

This situation sounds idyllic, especially when compared with the isolating audio language labs that many programs still have, but creating such a learning environment requires the resolution of a variety of issues dealing with the physical environment of the computer-assisted classroom. Palomar College in San Marcos, California, has developed what Hanson-Smith (1991) calls the "ideal lab" (p. 15). With federal grant money aimed at providing computer access to learners in basic skills classes, we began building a computer-assisted classroom. A description of this process serves as the basis for our discussion of the impact of the physical environment on the learning environment.

Getting Started

Building a computer-based lab, classroom, or learning center usually involves at a minimum making educated decisions about hardware, software, furniture, and the configuration of all this equipment in the physical space available (or, for a few lucky programs and institutions, designing a new facility from the ground up). Within each of these categories, issues such as cost, relevance, usefulness, and longevity must be taken into consideration. In the year preceding the actual purchase of hardware, software, and furniture at Palomar College, we had these and other decisions to make. A committee of ESL instructors, several of whom use the classroom today, was formed to assist in this process.

Our first task was to decide on the rationale and objectives for the room. Hanson-Smith (1991) describes three main types of technology-based environments, each of which has its own goals and uses: the self-access lab, the computerized instructional classroom, and the language development center. At Palomar, we chose to make decisions based on the framework of environmental conditions that also serve as a basis for this book (see chapter 1); this would, we felt, help us establish an optimal technology-enhanced language learning environment. (Other programs following the same framework might choose radically different solutions if they fulfilled the needs of the context and the student population.) Our rationale for the classroom was based on our students' needs to become familiar with technology and to gain the language, content, and social skills that would help them succeed in both employment and academics. In keeping with the framework and our rationale, our goal was to create a language development center where students could choose and use materials themselves, where groups of students could work comfortably inside or outside class, and where both student-centered and teacher-led lessons could take place.

Because classroom space has always been at a premium on campus, finding an adequate facility was a challenge. Political wrangling over classroom space was the least of our critical concerns; room size and shape determined not only the number of workstations we could plan for but also their layout. We also had to consider that, given the age of the buildings on campus and the lack of electronic infrastructure, renovations would include special wiring and the installation of dry-erase boards, windows in the laboratory technicians' and director's offices to comply with federal regulations, and a security system. In addition, we needed to obtain nongrant funding for the renovations and for ongoing costs such as lab technicians, supplies, and professional development; sources included the department, division, and college. Some of the costs, such as those involving staffing, training, repairs, upgrades, and software purchases, would require an ongoing financial commitment from the college's administration. Because of problems with space, several times during the process of development it looked as though we would need to relinquish our goal of trying to construct an optimal CALL classroom; however, a lot of hard work and rethinking helped us find different ways to achieve the same ends.

Hardware

Sachs (1996) states, "Before considering hardware, I'd suggest hunting for software to use within your program and then determining the hardware needed to run it . . . . My recommendation to anyone is to first identify what you want to do in the lab space . . . and then and only then seek the hardware . . . . My experience has been that a lot of time and money is spent on hardware with little thought given to the software that will sit on it and how it is to be integrated into the program" (n.p.). Bishop (see chapter 17) agrees that software choices should come before hardware choices. However, there are still major differences between hardware platforms, and for our committee and teachers, hardware was a more vital initial issue than software was. We needed to make a choice that would allow our teachers and adult beginning learners (many of whom have not had much previous schooling) the greatest flexibility and the most chances for exposure and production without creating an overly stressful environment. The 29 networked Macintosh® computers that we chose have a consistent user interface with pull-down menus and icons that learners with limited English can learn to operate quickly. More recently, MS-DOS®-based platforms (e.g., those running the Microsoft® Windows® operating system) have begun to offer this type of interface, but it is neither as intuitive nor as transparent as the graphical user interface on the Macintosh computer. Learners, we reasoned, may be less apprehensive about using a variety of software on Macintosh computers because the screens in programs for those machines look similar and function similarly across different software packages and because the ability to use a mouse to point and click avoids the need for language input or memorization of commands.

Other decisions about the hardware had to be made. Among the concerns to deal with were connections among the workstations, features such as CD-ROM drives and sound cards, and projection equipment. In the completed classroom, a network allows learners to work together in certain applications, thus promoting interaction as well as establishing a potential authentic audience for each learner. Furthermore, an Internet connection in the classroom provides access to authentic audiences around the world and allows learners to work with a rich variety of sources; two-way communication between learners and other resource people would otherwise be unavailable or impractical.

Microphones and built-in sound equipment on each computer provide the means for listening and speaking, and CD-ROM drives allow access to graphics and video. With this hardware configuration, teachers can reach learners in different ways and appeal to individual learning styles and preferences. In addition, a presentation station with a 35-inch direct-view monitor connected to a networked CPU permits the teachers or learners to demonstrate, present, or teach whole-class lessons. With a direct-view monitor, there is no need to dim the lights, as there might be with a liquid crystal display or another projection system; therefore, learners can manipulate paper documents while participating in an activity involving the monitor.

Clearly, hardware selection should be driven by goals that extend beyond a preference for one kind of computer over another, for these decisions can greatly affect the types of input and output learners have access to and can promote a positive learning environment. In addition, because the technology changes so rapidly, the specific models and makes of computer hardware purchased will depend on the desired features, the time frame, and the funds available. Programs should buy the best and most appropriate equipment that they can with the money available.

Furniture and Room Layout

In implementing technology, lab developers should not only concentrate on hardware and software decisions but also emphasize the importance of room configuration and furniture selection in creating an optimal language learning environment. State-of-the-art labs in which the computers are arranged in rows of desks may actually obstruct teamwork and other useful activities by creating barriers of computers or seating students in positions from which it is difficult to maneuver into others.

The layout of Palomar's computer classroom is a critical factor in maximizing interaction and meeting the conditions for an atmosphere in which learners are comfortable and are encouraged to participate. To facilitate group work and other kinds of interaction in the ESL classroom, we purchased 20 desks with recessed monitors (see Figure 4-1), two of which

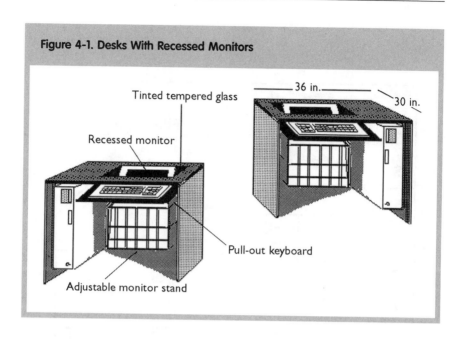

Figure 4-1. Desks With Recessed Monitors

Tinted tempered glass

Recessed monitor

36 in.

30 in.

Pull-out keyboard

Adjustable monitor stand

are wheelchair accessible as required by the Americans With Disabilities Act of 1992. These desks, in addition to helping students assume a position that is more comfortable for the neck, allow an unobstructed line of sight from learner to learner, learner to teacher, and learner to presentation station, supporting interaction and encouraging learners to help each other.

We arranged the desks in five pods of four desks each (see Figure 4-2); this arrangement creates a conference effect and a very large work space, avoiding the artificial barriers found in many labs. In addition to the recessed desks, comfortable swivel chairs (with casters) allow for an unimpeded line of sight and access to other areas of the classroom. Instead of isolating pairs of learners behind computers as many lab settings do, we encourage all learners to consult, to feel that the whole classroom is theirs, and to view technology as something under their control rather than as something that controls them. Ten traditional desks along the outside walls provide alternatives to the recessed framework. All the desks in the classroom are large enough to support pair work, but the arrangement also supports teamwork and work in large groups.

White dry-erase boards span the entire front wall behind the presentation station, making a variety of written and graphics-based teaching tools available within the same area. Finally, at the back of the classroom is a glassed-in file server room with a Dutch door. This room, which contains the computer that runs the network, disk copies of software, and the documentation for the software, is typically staffed by one of three bilingual technicians. Because information and technical personnel are located

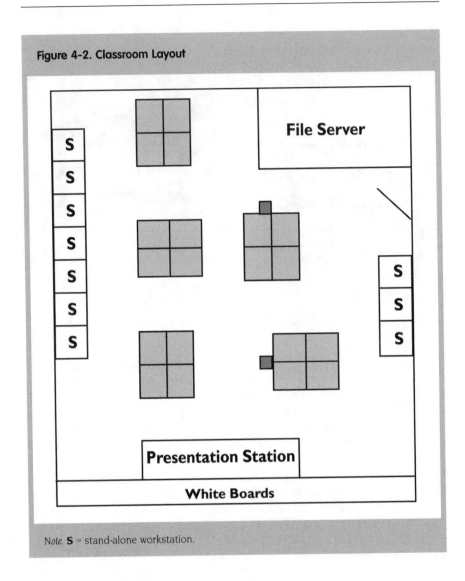

Figure 4-2. Classroom Layout

Note. **S** = stand-alone workstation.

within the classroom, learners and teachers have easy access to assistance and guidance.

Software

During the development of the computer-based classroom, we emphasized course content, not the computer, as the focus of instruction. Several members of the technology committee and other faculty members reviewed each piece of software borrowed for previewing purposes; sent to us by commercial software companies; or suggested by faculty, staff, or learners. Because we had to support curricular goals and the conditions of our environmental framework as well as possible, much of the ESL software currently available (particularly of the drill-and-practice and textbook-on-disk types) did not meet our needs. We did find, however, a variety of applications intended for ESL and non-ESL audiences that, with some adaptation, have assisted us in meeting our goals.

In following the guidelines for technology use, we looked for applications that teachers could change to suit their needs (i.e., that were authorable) and that were adaptable to a variety of purposes and learner populations. To this end, we chose content-free applications such as Microsoft Works (1994), which has a simplified database, spreadsheet, and word processor, and the collaborative writer GROUPwriter for the AppleTalk® Network (1991), which allows learners to create group documents or hold electronic conferences for brainstorming and prewriting activities. We have found these programs to be simple and powerful, to have a variety of uses, and to be the most familiar to faculty members and students. Students have used these applications in conjunction with regular classroom activities, for example, to simulate the creation of a business by designing résumés and business cards (described in chapter 3). Other content-free or authorable applications include Paint, simple painting and graphics software that at the time came preloaded on computers made by Apple Computer, Spell-It-Plus (1991; a spelling tutorial), and shareware such as Phraze Craze Plus (Pettit, 1986), a *Wheel of Fortune* takeoff.

Faculty also use authoring software such as HyperCard® (1997) and Authorware Star (1994) to create new applications; learners use such programs to create presentations and interactive reports (see also chapter 25). Because these programs are open ended, they promote the development of a great variety of applications. Texts such as *HyperCard Projects for Teachers* (Ventura & Grover, 1992) and many others available from associations such as the International Society for Technology in Education (see Appendix A) provide step-by-step instructions for creating HyperCard-based games, presentations, and other educational applications. Several faculty-developed applications, including scrambled-sentence activities and grammar- and paragraph-writing tutorials, are currently in use in the ESL program.

Software chosen for our lab that provides authentic content and promotes interaction and critical thinking includes the Decisions, Decisions series (1996), Wagon Train 1848 (1997), National Inspirer (1996), and International Inspirer (1996). These programs feature information-gap activities, which encourage learners to rely on each other for information; learners must successfully complete the activities to achieve their goal. In Decisions, Decisions, learners make a series of decisions in order to solve problems based on such real-life issues as prejudice and the environment; the goal is to make those decisions in accordance with a list of priorities set by the group(s) at the beginning of the program. In Wagon Train 1848, the goal is to complete a cross-country journey in the manner of pioneers. External documents and activities incorporate reading, writing, and other skills. The goal of both Inspirers is to travel to a number of locations to collect the geographic, geological, and economic data requested in the activities. These programs can be used with small groups, individuals, or a whole class and with one computer or with several. (See chapter 3 on using these programs and incorporating teams of learners.) All of these programs come with external documents, such as booklets for reading critical information and worksheets for decision making, resulting in multisource tasks. In addition, the software packages include lesson plans and handouts for reading, writing, and speaking activities and for integrated-skills tasks. Faculty can easily incorporate these applications into the existing curriculum to assist in meeting students' needs.

The Palomar faculty constantly review other computer programs and applications, adding the most valuable to the software library. Most commercial publishers are willing to lend software for previewing purposes; Tom Snyder Productions (TSP; see Appendix E) distributes demonstration versions of many of its titles and the accompanying documentation. Shareware, for which users pay a nominal fee, and freeware applications, which are freely distributed, are available through TESOL's Computer-Assisted Language Learning Interest Section, through state-based computer-using organizations such as Computer-Using Educators, and from the World Wide Web and other Internet sites (see chapter 14; see also Appendixes A and D). Several of these types of programs, which teachers can adapt to their learners' needs, are also available in our computer classroom.

The One-Computer Classroom

The Palomar College ESL program was lucky to have the funds to build its computer-assisted classroom, but many language programs around the world have neither the funds nor the space to develop a complete electronic classroom. The good news is that many pedagogically sound language-based activities and projects can be completed successfully in the one- or two-computer classroom. Most of the software by TSP (see also chapters 9, 10, and 13) and much of the other software described here is useful in a variety of physical settings. In fact, some educators advocate the use of one computer over a lab, resource center, or other multicomputer setting (see Dockterman, 1991, for a convincing argument).

Summary

No hard-and-fast rules exist for building technology-enhanced learning environments; however, experienced computer-using language educators offer some advice for labs and the one-computer classroom (summarized by Lunn, 1996):

> Labs will be pretty much wasted if teachers are not encouraged to integrate it into their instruction.
>
> It is essential to take advantage of CALL's ability to provide self-paced learning.
>
> One piece of software is never enough.
>
> Using computer [sic] to accomplish real tasks has more value for students than being plugged into language software.
>
> School must provide faculty and staff training and a place and time for faculty to use the computers.
>
> Danger of setting up lab without proper preparation: may sour the faculty on computers and wreck any chance of establishing a proper facility in the future. (n.p.)

In developing the computer-assisted classroom at Palomar, we chose hardware, furniture, the room's layout, and software according to theory-based conditions for an optimal language learning environment. We are therefore confident that we have created an atmosphere in which effective language learning can take place. Although the federal funding for the classroom has long since ended, the classroom is still developing. We continue to update and expand our software resources, and our computer lab staff (director and technicians) continues to provide orientation and training to faculty and students in software-specific workshops and one-on-one sessions. Our faculty continue to design computer-related activities and supplemental materials. As our teachers and learners have become more familiar with the technology, they have also become increasingly comfortable with the idea of the computer as a tool rather than as a teacher. We are confident that, in partnership with the teachers, learners, and other members of the Palomar College community, our ESL computer classroom supports the kind of language learning environment that encourages successful language acquisition.

Explorations

Projects

1. Briefly describe any two noncomputerized tasks you have been involved in as either a teacher or a student in the language learning classroom. Explain the kinds and purposes of the interaction included in the task, if any. Explain how technology use might change the interaction patterns of these activities for better or for worse.

2. You have been given a modest but adequate budget to design a computer-enhanced classroom that would be appropriate for your learners. What questions would you need to ask? What other considerations would there be?

3. Visit at least two differing language learning centers or instructional computer labs on your campus or in your region. Describe in detail how the layout of each lab or learning center reflects assumptions about (a) computer-student interaction and (b) student-student interaction. Give some examples of each type of activity as observed in the centers or labs.

Guided Research

1. Test the hypotheses you formulated in Projects, No. 1. First, choose one of the two activities that you described. Next, prepare a lesson plan to use with actual software and students in pairs or small groups in a CALL learning center or lab. Take careful notes on two to four students as they use the software. What kinds of verbal interactions take place? Which interactions are focused on computer use, and which on language learning? (For greater accuracy in reporting, you may wish to make an audio or video recording of your subjects—with their permission.)

If possible, interview the students afterward to determine what their attitudes toward the experience are and how they feel about the task's interaction.

2. Compare and contrast computer use by one student and computer use by groups or pairs. What instructions and organizational tips does the teacher need to provide to make group or pair interaction successful? Test your instructions by preparing a lesson, executing it, and taking notes as in No. 1 above, or observe another computer-using teacher over a number of class sessions.

3. Formulate a research question related to interaction and technology and do a literature search. Go to AskERIC's Web site (http://ericir.syr.edu/) for help. What descriptors are most effective? What are the criteria for a search? How can you make your search more efficient? (Use the ERIC *on Silver Platter* CD-ROM index for your search if neither you nor your school has Internet access.)

Questions for Further Investigation

1. What can teachers do to encourage participation by students who do not commonly interact in class? How can technology assist in supporting such interaction?

2. How effective is group work around the computer? How can teachers determine students' achievements in language and gains in other areas?

3. Do certain students learn better with less interaction? Why might this be the case?

 PART II

Authentic Audience

Chapter 5

Theory and Research: Audience, Language Use, and Language Learning

Bill Johnston

Theoretical and applied linguists and language teaching professionals have long recognized the importance of audience in the study of language. A consideration of audience has been central in at least two areas: language use and language learning.

Audience and Language Use

In linguistics, it has long been known that the nature of the audience and, specifically, the nature of the speaker's relation to that audience has a crucial effect on the forms of language chosen to encode the message. A simple and widespread example is the choice of second-person pronoun. Many languages have a T/V distinction (Brown & Gilman, 1960); that is, they have formal and informal (or intimate and nonintimate) forms of the second-person pronoun, such as *tu* versus *vous* in French. These are sometimes called *referent honorifics* (Levinson, 1983, p. 90). In other languages, address forms are more complex: Japanese and Korean, for instance, have intricate addressee honorific systems whereby the identity of the person spoken to affects not only the choice of pronoun used to refer to the addressee but also other lexical and morphological choices. In other languages, like Dyirbal, *bystander honorifics* are used when certain parties (e.g., taboo relatives) are witnesses to a conversation (Levinson, 1983, p. 90). In each of these cases, the nature of the audience has a direct and structured impact on the language produced.

In fact, linguistic messages are influenced by addressees in a wide range of subtle and not-so-subtle ways. Within sociolinguistics, it is known that variation in audience accounts for a great deal of social and stylistic variation, and a number of theoretical approaches take some notion of audience as a central construct.

Bell (1984), for example, offers the concept of *audience design*, a notion clearly related to that of *recipient design* proposed by Sacks and Schegloff (1979) for conversational analysis. Bell takes as his axiomatic starting point the idea that persons respond mainly to other persons; that is, speakers take most account of hearers in designing their talk. He argues that variation in linguistic style can best be explained by variation in audience; he proposes a nested model of players in speech situations in which *audience* constitutes a scale from addressee through auditor and overhearer to eavesdropper.

Another theory in which the role of audience is central is Giles' speech accommodation theory (Giles & Smith, 1979; Thakerar, Giles, & Cheshire, 1982). Giles' basic claim is similar to Bell's: that speakers adjust their language according to who their interlocutor is. Giles' theory differs in that he argues that this adjustment involves either convergence (moving toward the addressee's style) or divergence (deliberately sounding different from the addressee). In Giles' theory, convergence and divergence can be explained largely by reference to social identity and membership in a class or another social group.

Finally, notions of audience have featured prominently in many post-modern approaches to language and communication. Bakhtin (1986, p. 95), for example, points to the *addressivity* of language, meaning that any language addresses a particular listener and by the same token contains the anticipation of its own response. He also states that "every word is directed toward an answer and cannot escape the profound influence of the answering word that it anticipates" (p. 280). For Bakhtin, the dialogical character of language in use means that audience is a fundamental part of the very structure of language.

This notion is reflected in other postmodern work that emphasizes the *situated* nature of texts (e.g., Green & Meyer, 1991), that is, the fact that the writing and reading of texts do not take place in a vacuum but are located in a very specific social and cultural context. Every reading of a text, for example, is conducted by a particular reader in a particular place in space and time. Thus, there is no such thing as an objective, decontextualized meaning of a text; each reading is unique, so each new reader constructs the meaning of a text afresh. In this way, the audience is crucial in the process of creating meaning.

To sum up, language scholars working in a variety of fields (socio-linguistics, pragmatics, literary studies) are in accord that the nature of audience and, specifically, the speaker's relation to the addressee are a central concern in describing and understanding features of language use.

Audience and Language Learning

Just as they generally acknowledge that audience is a fundamental part of the way language is used, so a wide range of specialists working in disparate areas connected with the acquisition and teaching of second and foreign languages agree on the importance of audience in the learning of languages. These specialists include both researchers in the field of second language acquisition (SLA) and scholars and practitioners focusing on second language education.

In first language acquisition, even hard-line nativists (those who follow Noam Chomsky in believing that the ability to learn language is innate, forming part of the human biological endowment) acknowledge that babies need proper interlocutors to provide the necessary input for the innate *language acquisition device* (Pinker, 1994) to go to work. Studies have suggested, moreover, that passive input, such as that provided by television, is not sufficient for language acquisition to take place; acquisition requires person-to-person interaction, for example, between parent and child.

In first language acquisition, however, some scholars have argued that such interaction plays a secondary role and that, even when input is severely limited, children still have a natural drive to learn language, just as they have a natural tendency to learn to walk (Pinker, 1994). In SLA, on the other hand, there seems to be more of an argument for saying that interaction—that is, the availability of authentic audience—is a necessary (though perhaps not sufficient) condition for learning (Spolsky, 1989). A well-established line of research in SLA, often labeled *interactionism* in surveys of the field (Ellis, 1994; Lightbown & Spada, 1994), claims that interaction is a crucial prerequisite to acquisition (e.g., Long, 1983b; Long & Porter, 1985; Pica, 1987; Pica, Young, & Doughty, 1987). To simplify, the basic argument is that interaction provides opportunities for the negotiation of meaning; for enriched, suitably modified, and negotiated input; and for enhanced output. (See chapters 2 and 12 for further discussion; for a recent pedagogical application of this work, see Ernst, 1994.)

This research is rooted in a belief that audience is a crucial factor in the acquisition of the second language—specifically, that the availability of an authentic audience affects the rate and extent of language learning. In other words, audience is not merely an important element in language use; it is also a vital part of language learning.

Audience in Language Teaching

The Emergence of Audience

In what might loosely be called *traditional* language teaching—approaches such as grammar-translation, audiolingualism, and the like—little or no real audience exists for the linguistic productions of the learners. When they write, it is for "an audience of one" (Murray, 1982, p. 40). When they speak, it is generally only in the presence of classmates and the teacher; the substance of the message is either completely immaterial (e.g., in the case of drills and rote exercises) or secondary to the grammatical form, as with real-life questions that are intended to see whether the learner has mastered a particular morphological or syntactic structure. Schmidt (Schmidt & Frota, 1986), for example, tells of his sense of frustration in his own learning of Portuguese in Brazil when his teacher insisted that he answer the question, "Are you married?" with the factually incorrect "yes," for the reason that "we are practicing affirmative answers" (p. 243).

The recognition of the importance of audience in language and language learning eventually led to a reevaluation of the question of audience in language teaching. Although in different ways, a broad range of methodological approaches and techniques of language teaching have incorporated issues of audience into their underlying philosophy and pedagogical practices. For the purposes of brevity, I focus on three such approaches: whole language, process writing, and English for specific purposes (ESP).

In whole language approaches to language teaching, the question of audience has been central. Part of whole language's insistence on *real* language use (Rigg, 1991) has resulted from a reappraisal of the audience for students' writing and oral production (for a parallel in reading, see, e.g., Edelsky's 1991 distinction between "reading" and "not-reading," p. 77). In the whole language class, instead of writing for the eyes of the teacher alone, students write compositions for classmates, students in other classes, parents, and members of the community. Furthermore, an important part of the writing process is the writer's awareness of the audience; consideration of the actual or potential audience and its possible reactions forms an important part of feedback on and revisions of successive drafts of compositions.

In the domain of writing pedagogy, in ESL as well as in mainstream education, a prominent movement in recent years has been the process approach, whereby the focus of writing instruction is not simply the finished product but the process of brainstorming, writing drafts, revising, gathering feedback, and organizing all the procedures that real writers in the real world use all the time (Emig, 1977; Raimes, 1983, 1991). A major part of the process writing approach is an emphasis on treating one's writing as something to be read by a real audience (Beach & Liebman-Kleine, 1986). Considerations of audience, then, play a significant role in the development of the text.

Finally, a narrower understanding of audience emerges from the approach to writing taken within the tradition of ESP. A concern of certain scholars in ESP was that process writing focused too much on writing as expression and thus failed to address adequately the particular expectations of specialist disciplines (Horowitz, 1986; Johns, 1986). ESP, then, evidences what Raimes (1991) calls a *focus on the reader* in a different way. Here the idea of audience is associated with that of the discourse community within which particular texts are generated. This approach has tended toward a more prescriptive, norm-focused pedagogy and a view of second language writers as outsiders needing to follow preestablished rules in order to be accepted by the academic community.

Thus, as mentioned above, by different paths the concept of audience has found its way into many approaches and areas of language pedagogy, in particular into the teaching of writing.

What Does *Audience* Mean in Language Learning?

The differences referred to above may be more significant than they seem at first, as they indicate alternative understandings of what exactly *audience* is in language teaching. I address this problem here.

Kirsch and Roen (1990) point out that even within composition studies there are at least two divergent understandings of what *audience* refers to. They cite Park (1982):

> The meanings of "audience" . . . tend to diverge in two general directions: one toward actual people external to a text, the audience whom the writer must accommodate; the other toward the text itself and the audience implied there, a set of suggested or evoked attitudes, interests, reactions, conditions of knowledge which may or may not fit with actual readers or listeners. (p. 249, cited in Kirsch & Roen, 1990, p. 14)

The former understanding is clearly that of the ESP camp; the latter, that associated with the process writing approaches outlined above.

The more one analyzes the nature of audience, the more complex the picture becomes. Kroll (1984), for example, draws a three-way distinction among audience as "target receiver" (the intended audience of the writer), "needy reader" (one who wants to extract specific information from the text), and "constructive participant" (for whom reading is a social act) (p. 183). The contributors to McGregor and White (1990) point out that the way audiences of various kinds receive and interpret messages is never entirely predictable, yet it is a crucial part of linguistic interaction.

In the area of language teaching and learning, further complications arise. Second language learners are often at best marginal members of relevant discourse communities; furthermore, they may have differing notions of *audience* either in the sense of actual readership (what Ede & Lunsford, 1984, have called the *addressed audience*) or the audience they create through their own texts (Ede & Lunsford's *invoked audience*). Limitations in their command of linguistic style in the target language may make Bell's (1984) notion of *audience design* difficult for them to implement. Finally, as

Widdowson (1990) points out, second and especially foreign language classrooms tend to be somewhat artificial places by nature; this fact may mean that notions of audience in a classroom context need to be considered and evaluated in their own right.

The truth, of course, is even more complex than any of these analyses. *Audience* in reality is both imagined and real; it is interested in both information and attitude; it is both social and individual. Language learners are sometimes like native speakers and sometimes not. Rather than conclude in any definitive way, I end this section with a set of questions to guide a consideration of audience in relation to language teaching and learning in particular situations:

- To what extent can speakers or writers control or predict who the audience for their linguistic productions will be? To what extent can the speaker or writer be said to know this audience? How immediate is the audience in time and space?

- How much shared knowledge can speakers or writers assume? To what extent can speakers or writers count on the cooperation of the audience?

Authentic Audience

The notion of *authenticity* is commonly invoked in language learning (Breen, 1985), yet the field's understanding of its meaning is to a large extent purely intuitive. What authenticity might mean in terms of audience and what an authentic audience might be merit some discussion.

Most language teaching professionals agree that it is desirable to aim for authenticity in the classroom: to use authentic texts and materials, encourage real conversations, and find genuine purposes for language use. Yet, as Widdowson (1990) points out, authenticity is a slippery concept in pedagogical terms, above all because, as Widdowson argues, "meanings are achieved by human agency and are negotiable: they are not contained in text" (p. 45). Thus, in the case of audience, authenticity really dwells not in the audience itself but in what the audience chooses to do with the text. In light of this, I offer a single criterion to determine whether an audience is authentic:

> An authentic audience is an audience that is concerned exclusively with the meaning of the speaker's message.

This criterion discounts the teacher as audience insofar as the teacher is really interested in what forms the learner can produce in nativelike ways. When teachers are indeed interested in the meaning of what their students write and say, then they may be seen as an authentic audience. This criterion also automatically excludes all evaluators of tests, examinations, and so on.

Of course, other criteria might be proposed. For example, an authentic audience might be said to be the audience that a native speaker would have when speaking or writing in the same context. Yet the audience for many native-speaker texts may itself not be authentic (native speakers also take exams); in other cases, the audience may not be well defined. For example, if I as an adult pick up and read a magazine intended for 4- to 6-year-old children, do I constitute an authentic audience? I suggest that the definition given above, which takes into account the intentions of the audience as much as it does those of the speaker or writer, de facto includes as a subset those cases legitimately incorporated in native-speaker audiences.

For the purposes of this chapter, then, I argue that the only necessary criterion for the authenticity of an audience is whether or not the message is being read or listened to for its meaning. This definition will prove instrumental in analyzing the usefulness of computer-mediated communication for language learning.

Authentic Audience and Computer-Mediated Communication in ESL

The emergence of computer-based technologies and new forms of communication quite clearly has radically altered the state of affairs in language teaching in terms of authentic audience. In this section I explore the various ways in which computer technology is affecting the conception of audience in language teaching and learning and the significance this has for the field. I touch on issues that are explored in more detail in the other chapters in this book.

The Size of the Audience Available to Learners Has Increased Dramatically

A common complaint of ESL and especially EFL learners is that it is hard for them to find native speakers to interact with. The development of computer-mediated forms of interaction, such as e-mail, electronic discussion groups, and multiuser domains (MUDs) or object-oriented MUDS (MOOs; see chapter 22), has vastly increased the potential audience. Learners are no longer restricted to their physical geographical location. Along with this change is an increase in the range of potential interlocutors, who may be of any age, background, and so on.

The Nature of the New Audiences Is Hard to Judge

In spoken and written interaction previously, the audience was either unknown and remote (in the case of writing) or immediate and visible (in the case of speaking). Now audiences can be invisible but immediate (Anderson, 1994). Interactants in MOOs and MUDs, for example, respond in real time to each other's contributions, as in face-to-face interaction, yet the additional paralinguistic information available in the latter—eye contact, accent, tone of voice, proxemics—is totally absent. Participants have no knowledge of their interlocutors other than what the latter say (or, more accurately, write). Such a situation creates the need for radically new conceptualizations of audience.

Electronic Audiences Are Authentic Audiences

Whatever else may be said about audiences in computer-mediated interaction, clearly these audiences are by and large focused on the meaning of messages rather than on their form. Thus, by the definition offered above, they constitute authentic audiences for the linguistic production of learners.

Computer-Mediated Interaction Is Intensely Language Based

Some observers have claimed that society is shifting from logocentrism (a reliance on language-based communication) to iconocentrism (communication primarily by images). Ironically, much computer-mediated interaction, whether in a MOO or by e-mail, is intensely grounded in language and language alone. As mentioned in the preceding section, without visual cues to provide additional information, participants must judge their interlocutors based entirely on what they write; likewise, a participant's own presentation of self is completely reliant on what that participant writes. Thus, communication is language based to an even greater extent than before. This change offers new and exciting possibilities for language learners; it also presents a tough challenge to them, as they cannot use many of the compensatory communicative strategies (Tarone, 1977) learners customarily draw on.

Written and Spoken Forms of Language Are Converging

Studies of e-mail and other forms of electronic communication (e.g., Naumann, 1995; Uhlirov, 1994) have found that the forms of language used in this medium occupy a middle ground between conventional written and spoken forms. The language of e-mail, for instance, is less formal than other written language because it is written with greater speed and less attention to detail (e.g., spelling mistakes are tolerated) and because it is generally private rather than intended for large audiences; yet, because it is written rather than spoken and because of the distance between sender and receiver, e-mail retains some qualities of written language (e.g., the absence of fillers and of repetition, less use of indeterminate reference, and the use of more complex forms of subordination and relativization). This *intermediate* language also presents new challenges to language learners already struggling with variations in genre and style in the target language.

The Distinction Between Hearers and Eavesdroppers Is Less Clear

A problem with much language learning, especially in the receptive skills and especially in listening, is that the learner is often obliged to take on the role of eavesdropper rather than that of hearer. Prerecorded tapes in listening tasks, for example, relatively rarely address the learners themselves; more often the content of the tape is something like a conversation that they hear only because it is on the tape. Although it would be more tenuous, a similar argument could be made about reading.

In many computer-based forms of communication, the distinction Bell (1984) draws among addressees, auditors, overhearers, and eavesdroppers is significantly eroded. On electronic discussion lists, for example, anyone may read the messages that are posted. Although some lists (e.g., managed lists) involve gatekeepers who determine which messages are sent in the first place, the gatekeepers do not attempt to control who the recipients are. Likewise, access to the World Wide Web is spectacularly uncontrolled. Thus, it is easier for learners to become an authentic audience themselves and, in this domain at least, to transcend the status of eavesdropper.

New Conventions Are Emerging

Partly in response to some of the problems identified above, electronic communication has begun to produce its own set of conventions for interaction (Cathcart & Gumpert, 1994; Naumann, 1995). Examples include the emoticons used in e-mail and the often elaborate stage directions found in contributions to MOOs. These new conventions again present a challenge to second language learners trying to interact effectively with the unseen electronic audience, and they suggest a useful role for instruction.

Summary

The issue of audience in language learning and teaching is highly complex. In a variety of ways, audience has been seen as crucial in both language use and language learning. At the same time, language learners are potentially disadvantaged both in their understanding of audience-related issues and in their productive capacity for audience design in target language contexts.

Computer-mediated communication offers new opportunities and new challenges to learners. Although the size and range of potential audiences have increased dramatically, and although learners also have a greater chance of becoming an authentic audience themselves, language learners must become familiar with new conventions and new conditions if they are to participate effectively in these new forms of communication.

Chapter 6

Classroom Practice: An Introduction to E-Mail and World Wide Web Projects

Susan Gaer

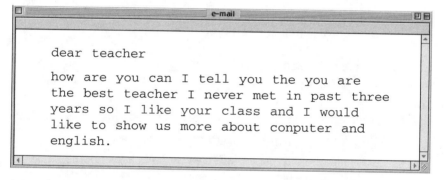

dear teacher

how are you can I tell you the you are
the best teacher I never met in past three
years so I like your class and I would
like to show us more about conputer and
english.

(E-mail message by Israel Carmargo, ESL student)

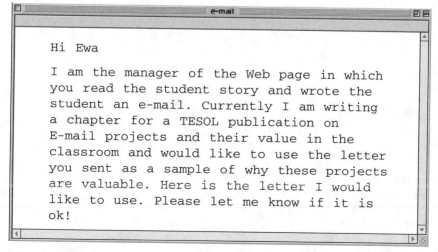

Hi Ewa

I am the manager of the Web page in which
you read the student story and wrote the
student an e-mail. Currently I am writing
a chapter for a TESOL publication on
E-mail projects and their value in the
classroom and would like to use the letter
you sent as a sample of why these projects
are valuable. Here is the letter I would
like to use. Please let me know if it is
ok!

(E-mail message from the author to a student)

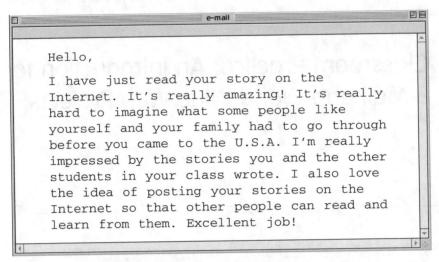

(E-mail response to a student's story on the Internet)

Each of the messages above represents an authentic voice speaking to an authentic audience in order to accomplish real purposes. Electronic mail (e-mail) projects

- give learners opportunities to interact and negotiate meaning
- give learners authentic tasks to perform
- expose learners to varied and creative language and encourage learners to produce it
- give learners enough time and feedback
- guide learners to attend mindfully to the learning process
- help learners work in an atmosphere with an ideal level of stress and anxiety
- support learner autonomy

The most profound effect of e-mail projects, however, is to provide an authentic audience for the language learner. As defined in chapter 5, whether an audience is authentic or not depends on "whether or not the message is being read or listened to for its meaning" (p. 61).

This chapter first explains what the Internet is and describes e-mail as a process. Following that explanation is a discussion of basic e-mail literacy and its uses in the classroom.

The Internet and the World Wide Web

The Internet is a vast system involving a multitude of computers, and it is rather hard to navigate without tools. Some Internet tools include software with which to send e-mail and use the World Wide Web (the multimedia version of the Internet).

E-mail involves transmitting data, either over a telephone via a modem or through a cable line, over a network of computers and satellite relays called the *Internet*. If you have access to a computer terminal, modem, and telephone line, you can, with the appropriate software, connect to the Internet. Many school settings (and most big businesses) use a cable connection, which is faster than telephone and modem links and is becoming more common among home users as well. It is also possible to connect to the Internet through *Web* TV, a cable system that allows you to view graphics and text, hear sounds, and send e-mail through a television receiver, although the system does not have the functionality of a computer.

You can connect to the Internet by contracting with a commercial carrier (an Internet service provider [ISP]), through a university, or through a school district or other community system. Many public libraries are now getting Internet access as well, but access is not free. The educational institution, the local community, or the individual picks up the cost. Most Internet providers offer an e-mail account and World Wide Web access using software called a *Web browser*, which allows the user to see graphics and video and hear sounds. (Web access is not necessary to send and receive e-mail, however.) Providers usually charge a fixed rate for these services; usually users pay a monthly fee for unlimited time on the Internet.

E-mail addresses are made up of a name plus information about the account (Figure 6-1). For example, my e-mail address is *sgaer@earthlink.net*. My account name is *sgaer*, my account is with Earthlink (my ISP), and it is an Internet account. The last three letters tell what kind of service the account

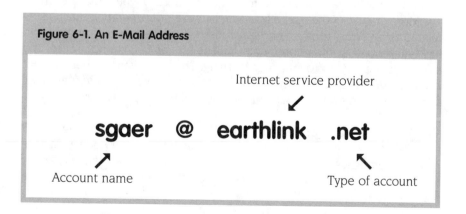

Figure 6-1. An E-Mail Address

Internet service provider

sgaer   @   earthlink   .net

Account name   Type of account holder is affiliated with: the government (*.gov*), an educational institution (*.edu*), or, in my address, a commercial provider (*.com* or *.net*).

With an Internet account you can send e-mail to anyone who is also connected to the Internet. You can send and receive letters, photographs, video clips, and sounds. You can send e-mail down the hall or around the world in less than a microsecond. If the receiver of the message is not on-line, the message stays in the recipient's "mailbox" until it is opened. Because e-mail messages are usually text-only files, any computer and any word processor can read the document, regardless of what kind of computer and platform created it. After you open an e-mail message, you can read it, save it to your computer's hard drive, print it to share with others, or forward it to someone else via your ISP.

Electronic Discussion Lists

Imagine asking a question and being able to receive hundreds of responses to that question in a few seconds. Discussion lists, often referred to by the type of software that manages them (e.g., Listserv, Listproc, Majordomo), make this possible. Lists are valuable for discussing issues, asking questions, and giving and receiving information. Basically, a discussion list is similar to a mass mailing. A message is posted to a certain address via e-mail, and everyone on the list is then sent the message to read and respond to at leisure.

Discussion lists connect groups of people with similar interests. To participate in a list, you must first subscribe to it, usually free of charge. Messages posted to a list are sent automatically to every member of the list. You receive the messages from a server along with your regular e-mail. Some electronic discussion lists are very small, and some are huge; the larger the list, the more messages generated. To stop messages from coming into a mailbox, you must *unsubscribe* from the list. Each discussion list has its own rules for subscribing and unsubscribing and its own etiquette, and messages describing them are usually sent to you automatically when you subscribe.

More than 50,000 e-mail discussion lists are now operating. Each list is related to a certain topic of particular interest to the group of people who have subscribed, such as community college ESL or ESL literacy issues, and many lists are related to language learning. The ways lists can benefit your students are described below, but as a teaching professional you also will probably want to sign on to one or more lists in order to stay current in your field.

One of the major ESOL lists for teachers is TESL-L. Founded in 1991, it is supported by a grant from the United States Information Agency. TESL-L has many branches, reflecting the wide variety of teachers' interests. To join any of the branches, you must first become a member of TESL-L. The branches are

- TESLCA-L: TESL and technology
- TESLFF-L: fluency first and whole language pedagogy
- TESLIE-L: intensive English programs, teaching, and administration
- TESLIT-L: adult education and literacy
- TESLJB-L: jobs, employment, and working conditions in the TESL/TEFL field
- TESLMW-L: material writers
- TESP-L: teachers of English for specific purposes

A sister list, TESLK-12, is for teachers of English to children.

Several options available to subscribers, described briefly here, determine how and if you receive messages from the list. The functions and instructions on setting and using them are described in the information you receive when you sign up with any list. The volume of mail you will receive is enormous, so you may want to set the main list to the *index* or, at times, the *nomail* function. Under the *index* option, you receive only the titles of messages; you may then automatically receive only those you select. Under the *nomail* function, you remain a list member, but you don't receive messages from the list. You can begin to receive messages again by activating the *mail* function. Warschauer (1995a) provides further information about the organization and goals of TESL-L; see Appendix B for instructions on joining TESL-L and its sublists and for information on other lists for teachers.

Why Should Students Use the Internet?

E-mail and electronic discussion lists benefit learners by serving as learning networks among nonnative speakers of different ages and cultural backgrounds. Internet communication can help teachers and learners create many of the conditions for optimal learning environments. It

- increases self-esteem by empowering both the teacher and the student (As one Laubach Literacy tutor said, "You do it because once you've seen what happens to your students, you can never go back," Turner, 1992, p. 3.)

- accommodates different learning styles and empowers learners regardless of physical challenges or social and cultural differences (Berge & Collins, 1995)

- encourages and motivates students to become involved in authentic projects and to write for a real audience of their peers instead of merely composing for the teacher (Berge & Collins, 1995)

- promotes critical thinking because students move from being passive learners to participants and collaborators in the creation of knowledge and meaning (Berge & Collins, 1995)
- makes learning relevant by teaching students the skills they need when they are most ready to learn them
- allows learners to participate cooperatively in the educational process, as in the following e-mail, written to an instructor while she was absent due to jury duty:

---

e-mail

Hello teacher. How are you? I think that you are very busy with the Jury Dury. But I hope and you have a few minutes to read and answer my letter.

You know that is very difficult for me write a letter if you don't help me. I know that you won't be with me always thats why I have to practice.

The substitute is so pretty. She teaches very well. But you are our teacher and we miss you so much. We are studying very hard so don't worry about us.

Today we are going to have a test so "haga changitos"

Before that I finish my letter. I want to know about the e-mail project. What happen with them?

I hope and see you soon!

Sincerity: LUCY GARCIA SANDOVAL.

Although at a modest level of accomplishment thus far in the learning process, Lucy is using conscious processes to analyze her progress and her needs. Even though part of the purpose of the e-mail message is to practice letter writing, as expressed in the second paragraph, the message is also filled with authentic chat ("We are studying very hard so don't worry about us.") and contains a real request for information ("What happen with them?"). Throughout, an authentic voice speaks to a real person and expects an authentic reply.

How Can Students Learn to Use the Internet?

Although more and more schools are getting access to the Internet, many teachers still operate in unconnected classrooms. The ideas and projects in this section consider both environments.

Using E-Mail

The following is an outline of a process I have used for teaching e-mail to adult immigrant students at Rancho Santiago College in Santa Ana, California.

- *acquiring basic computer literacy* (1 week): Students learn how to use the mouse, keyboard, and word processor by typing in exercises from their textbooks.

- *learning about e-mail* (1 week): Students learn what e-mail is and how it works. The class sets up an e-mail account and sends a letter to a collaborating teacher.

- *getting an e-mail account* (2 weeks): Students learn to use the local e-mail system and are taught the steps involved in signing up for individual e-mail accounts. In classes with only one computer linked to the Internet, the students are grouped, and the groups rotate until all the students have accounts. Student assistants (peer tutors—students who seem to learn computer skills quickly or have some knowledge of computers) help the groups.

- *using e-mail* (until the end of the semester and beyond): Students start off by e-mailing the teacher and each other. As they become accustomed to using e-mail, students are assigned various tasks to help them write to a keypal. (See the next section for ways to find keypals.) Students need to learn how to write a letter to a person they don't know, how to ask questions, and how to use information in a letter when replying to it. For this reason, students are asked to save all their letters so that the teacher can help them continue with the communication if a problem arises.

Keypals

Finding Keypals
   One way for students to find keypals from around the world is to join an electronic discussion list. Just as teachers have their own discussion lists,

the SL-*Lists* specialize in cross-cultural discussion and writing practice for college, university, and adult students in English language programs around the world. There are currently 10 lists (listed below with their topics), but more may be added as demand for them becomes evident.

- INTRO-SL: new members
- CHAT-SL: general (low level)
- DISCUSS-SL: general (high level)
- BUSINESS-SL: business and economics
- ENGL-SL: learning English
- EVENT-SL: current events
- MOVIE-SL: cinema
- MUSIC-SL: music
- SCITECH-SL: science, technology and computers
- SPORT-SL: sports

To use the lists, students must have individual e-mail accounts. For a description of the SL-*Lists* and instructions for signing on, see Holliday and Robb, n.d., http://chiron.latrobe.edu.au/www/education/sl/sl.html, and Appendix B.

Another way to use e-mail is by connecting to another classroom or school site and finding keypals. If your language learning classroom has only one Internet account (yours), students can still post messages to a particular individual. If your students have their own e-mail accounts, they can write private messages back and forth, creating a truly authentic audience for their work.

Keypalling allows for authentic communication between and within different cultural groups. One benefit of a cross-cultural pen pal exchange on the Internet is that students from nonnative-English-speaking backgrounds can communicate with native speakers of English without the communicative pitfalls of pronunciation or accent. Intergenerational communication can form bonds between the young and the old, as e-mail is independent of sound and age.

Keypalling for Language Learning

Keypalling is a rather free-form activity. This section explains how to maximize the pedagogical value of e-mail correspondence.

The following process gets students started in keypalling.

1. Prekeypalling activities
   - Find another class or several other classes that are willing to be keypals.

- With the other teacher(s), decide on a topic that is relevant to each class's curriculum, and formulate questions for students to answer in their letters.

2. Keypalling

   - Have the students write individual letters in a text file, making sure to include their partner's and their own first and last names.

   - Develop a grid of partners.

   - Have the students send letters to the participating class.

   - As the students receive letters from the participating class, have the students respond.

3. Postkeypalling activities: Begin the cycle again.

If students have their own e-mail accounts, management is much simpler, but focusing the students is a little more difficult. Students who have their own e-mail accounts must learn how to send and receive messages independently. To ensure that the students stay on task in the messages, you can assign a summary or report based on their conversation topics.

Once students are familiar with computers and the technical aspects of e-mail as a process, the teachers of two or more classes can collaborate on assignments and arrange for students with keypals at different schools—perhaps in different countries—to collaborate on a cyberproject. Some examples of keypal assignments used in an academic setting are

- *reading journals:* Instead of keeping a reading journal for you, students can write their journal to other students. They might write to each other about the same book or about two different books. Two students reading the same book can collaborate on a review to submit to an on-line magazine or Web site (see On-Line Projects below).

- *authentic information search:* Students find a Web site that interests them and ask the developer of the site questions in an e-mail. For example, during a discussion of voting, students read about the Los Angeles voter registration rate. A student from Mexico wanted to know what the voter registration rate was in Mexico. He found the Web site of a Mexican newspaper, e-mailed a journalist, and got the information.

On-Line Projects

Writing to an authentic audience also involves creating authentic tasks that will spark meaningful exchanges. Assigning projects for students to complete through on-line collaboration can provide the necessary spark.

The Basics

In on-line projects, either individual or collaborative, students use e-mail to obtain information from other participants or use the on-line environment as a means of publishing class work for others to read. Projects help students develop language skills because they involve the creation of a product, and completed projects can be placed on the World Wide Web for display and as an authentic form of publication.

The Email Projects Home Page (Gaer, 1997, http://www.otan.dni.us/webfarm/ emailproject/email.htm; see Figure 6-2), supported by the Outreach and Technical Assistance Network (OTAN), lists current and completed projects that are offered worldwide. At this site, prospective teachers and students can see what types of projects are currently in progress and get ideas for their own. Among the many projects accessible from the Email Projects Home Page are the following:

- Intergenerational Project: Parents share traditional cultural practices with their children.

- Health Chats: Developed by the Quincy Adult Learning Center in Boston, Massachusetts, the site sponsors student chats focused on certain health topics, such as stress and nutrition.

- Annotated Booklist: Students summarize books they have read for pleasure or books they read with their children (see Figure 6-3 below).

- International Home Remedies: Students write descriptions of home remedies for various ailments.

- Cookbook: In this project, started in 1995, students prepare a recipe, write it up, and post it.

Several other World Wide Web sites offer examples of projects (see chapters 7 and 14). The following sampling was collected by Thalman (1997b, http://www.wfi.fr/volterre/inetpro.html; see also Appendix H):

- International Tandem Network (http://www.slf.ruhr-uni-bochum.de/)

- HUT Internet Writing Project (Vilmi, 1998b, http://www.hut.fi/~rvilmi/ Project/)

- Write AWAY! A Showcase of Writing by Australian and Adult Migrants (Oriti, 1998, http://137.111.169.8/writeaway/projects.htm)

Figure 6-2. *Email Projects Home Page* (Gaer, 1997)

Email Projects Home Page

For project information, contact <u>Susan Gaer</u>.

This is a picture of my village in Laos. I do this picture.

Click on a project to visit it

How to Buy a House in the USA	Intergenerational Project	Health Chats	Pizza Project	Annotated Booklist
Cookbook 1997	Cost of Living Data Project	Price Comparision Project	Writing Projects	Home Remedies
Student Stories	Workshop Handouts	Resource Library	Completed Projects	New Project goes here

- *Blue Web'n: A Library of Blue Ribbon Learning Sites on the Web* (1998, http://www.kn.pacbell.com/wired/bluewebn/; a compendium of projects for all content areas)

- *The Global Schoolhouse* (http://www.gsn.org/; projects hosted by teachers in schools throughout the world)

- *Intercultural E-Mail Classroom Connections* (http://www.iecc.org/; exchanges facilitated by Craig Rice, Bruce Roberts, and Howard Thorsheim at St. Olaf College)

Participating in an On-Line Project

To complete an on-line project,

1. Choose a project that fits your curriculum guidelines. Write to the teacher coordinating the project; indicate your interests in detail so that a match can be found.

2. Have your students find and examine some projects on the Web.

3. Depending on your students' level, develop a model for them to follow, or guide them in developing a model that will help them conceptualize the steps involved in completing the project.

4. Allow plenty of time for communication with your collaborating teacher and classroom to finalize the project design and curricular area.

5. As students are completing their sections of the project, make sure the correspondence between the collaborating teachers and classes highlights the progress made.

6. Send the completed project to the coordinating teacher, or post it on the appropriate Web site.

Figure 6-3 shows a sample from the *Annotated Booklist* project on the *Email Projects Home Page* (Gaer, 1997, http://www.otan.dni.us/webfarm /emailproject/email.htm). To join this project,

1. E-mail the instructor and indicate an interest in participating.

2. Print out a model entry by choosing one of the completed annotated book titles and clicking the mouse on the "Print" button.

3. Use the model to explain to the students how they will annotate their books.

4. Have the students each choose and read a book.

5. Have the students write a draft of a summary of the book either on paper or by using a word processor.

6. Using peer correction techniques, have the students revise their writing. Optionally, correct some of their work yourself.

7. Have the students return to the project and click on "Add a Book Here."

8. Have the students copy the information they have written onto the form in the appropriate places.

9. Have the students submit the work by clicking on "Submit Query."

Figure 6-3. Entry From the Annotated Booklist Project on the Email Projects Home Page (Gaer, 1997)

INTERNET LIBRARY PROJECT

TITLE: House on Mango Street

AUTHOR: Sandra Cisneros

This story is about a Mexican family living is some place in U.S. on Mango St. It tells mexican traditions, and describes each personage of the neighborhood very well.
I recommend this book because you will really enjoy it. It send you back to your ancestors and customs.
Level: Adult

Submitted by Cutberto Molina

School: JobLink at BISC, Santa Ana, CA

[Main Page] [Booklist Project Main Page] [Add a book here] [Learner Stories]
[Current Projects] [Completed Projects] [Resource Library]

Note. From "The House on Mango Street," in *Email Projects Home Page: Annotated Booklist,* by S. Gaer, 1997, Staff Development Institute/Outreach Technical Assistance Network, http://www.otan.dni.us/webfarm/emailproject/mango.htm. Copyright © 1997 by S. Gaer. Reprinted with permission.

On-line projects are enjoyable for the students, they foster language learning as students collaborate on the development of the project, and they are driven by the necessity of writing to an authentic audience of peers on the Internet. As a result of students' writing and posting on the World Wide Web, cultural and cross-generational understanding has improved, and tolerance for others has increased. In addition, students' work has been published in real magazines. These benefits are evidenced by two responses that students have received about their writing:

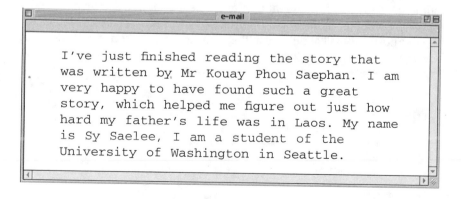

I've just finished reading the story that was written by Mr Kouay Phou Saephan. I am very happy to have found such a great story, which helped me figure out just how hard my father's life was in Laos. My name is Sy Saelee, I am a student of the University of Washington in Seattle.

```
┌────────────────────────── e-mail ──────────────────────────┐
│                                                             │
│   Dear Vladimir,                                            │
│                                                             │
│    I got interested in your story because                   │
│   you and I have some things in common. For                 │
│   one, we both have Russian first names; my                 │
│   name is Ivan. I also come from Latin                      │
│   America (born in Ecuador) and am an                       │
│   immigrant to the U.S. I've lived here most                │
│   of my life and, two years ago, became an                  │
│   American citizen, something I am                          │
│   particularly proud of.                                    │
│                                                             │
│    I would like to congratulate you on your                 │
│   progress in English and your determination                │
│   not to let personal hardships deter you                   │
│   from persevering in your education. I am                  │
│   glad you are a resident of my country and                 │
│   encourage you to someday contribute to the                │
│   betterment of others who find themselves in               │
│   the circumstances you have found yourself                 │
│   in during your stay in this country. God                  │
│   bless you.                                                │
│                                                             │
└─────────────────────────────────────────────────────────────┘
```

Summary

Electronic discussion lists, e-mail keypals, and projects on the World Wide Web promote reading and writing skills in English by providing an authentic audience for students' writing. These projects also help students develop computer literacy and Internet skills as they use the computer for real purposes. E-mail and the resulting projects can be used with students at any grade level and any English proficiency level.

Chapter 7

Classroom Practice: Authentic Audience on the Internet

Leslie Opp-Beckman

The rapid-paced, transitory nature of technology is both thrilling and daunting. In fact, by the time this text reaches its intended audience, the computer technology that this chapter refers to may have changed dramatically and, in some cases, will even have become obsolete. However, the human need to communicate and the desire to do so in languages other than one's native language will remain constant, and you as an educator can build on what is written here and what is in the world around you. This chapter examines the notion of *audience* as it pertains to TESOL and CALL and offers current examples of communicative, language-based activities that incorporate technology.

Definitions and Roles

Authenticity, Audience, and the Internet

The ever-swinging pendulum of education has, in recent times, endorsed and incorporated the use of *real* or *authentic* language and, by extension, developed the notion of *authentic readers, writers,* and *interlocutors*. Computers are but one of many means by which language students can be exposed to authentic materials, discourse, and culture. Through the Internet, for example, students can reach others outside their physical setting, expanding their opportunities to interact with the target language. In short, computers have the capacity to enhance language learning in ways that complement other methods and activities.

Chapter 5 outlines some of the pedagogical issues surrounding the concepts of *audience* and *authenticity* and defines *authentic audience* as "an audience that is concerned exclusively with the meaning of the speaker's message" (p. 60). In a computer-assisted context, the word *speaker* is understood to encompass both oral and written communication. For example, one can chat in real time using a keyboard and text or talk in near-real time with video or voice software such as CU-SeeMe (1997). The notion of *audience* on the Internet can also be defined in many ways, including but not limited to native speakers, peer groups, and specific discourse communities. Technology further allows students to place themselves in the role of being an audience, reaching out to an audience, or engaging in two-way communication or interaction between audiences.

Authenticity across discourse communities and communicative style in CALL, particularly in the uncontrolled universe of the Internet, can be wildly variable and requires careful matching of the relative goals and needs to any particular set of students. For example, you might give a group of students whose knowledge of technology is at a low level and whose English is at the intermediate level the task of visiting five or six teacher-selected World Wide Web sites to gather information on a given topic rather than turning the students loose on the Internet and its search engines, which yield millions of Web sites to sort through (see Boswood, 1997, esp. Pt. III).

The Learner's Role

Given the wide array of media available (e.g., the Internet, CD-ROMs, software, multimedia devices), in what concrete ways can language learners benefit from CALL? Rather than review the more than 30-year history of computer-assisted instruction, I frame the answer to this question in the context of *audience* from the language learner's perspective. The terms *passive*, *active*, *receptive*, and *interactive*, which have been used in many ways in the field of language acquisition and teaching methodology, are defined as follows for the purposes of the hands-on CALL activities described in this chapter:

- *passive*: Language learners are not engaged; they are not involved in any language-based, cultural, or technological communication (e.g., sleeping).

- *receptive*: Language learners function as an authentic audience, that is, as receivers (e.g., reading a newsgroup posting) or by *lurking*, that is, reading messages but not actively posting on an electronic list.

- *active*: Language learners address an authentic audience (e.g., writing a poem for publication in an electronic magazine [e-zine]).

- *interactive*: Language learners communicate both as and to an audience, in whole or in part by means of technology (e.g., exchanging e-mail with a keypal or taking part in a real-time electronic discussion).

I purposely omit passive activities from consideration, as I know of no CALL activities that fit that category (see below).

The Teacher's Role

What about the role of the educator? More than ever, technology has the capacity to free you as a teacher from the role of lecturer or dispenser of knowledge and to move you toward the role of facilitator or mentor, putting the learner at the center of learning and communication. In any setting, you need to

- *assess the students' level and needs*: Set expectations relative to students' language, cultural, and technological experience.

- *assess the students' access to technology*: Be realistic but creative, and find support.

- *determine language and course goals*: Plan how technology will enhance or improve what can already be done; integrate CALL purposefully and meaningfully.

Hands-On Activities

The activities described in this section are classified by three of the types of audience defined above—receptive, active, and interactive—and further by the type of technology employed. Note that Web sites change rapidly; if you find that a uniform resource locator (URL) is incorrect, try searching for the site by its name or by the author's or Webmaster's name.

Receptive Activities: Language Learners as Authentic Audience

In receptive activities (see the box on p. 82), the language learner primarily receives information—in the form of text, sound, images, and even goods (e.g., electronically transmitted software)—through technology. In CALL as used in English language learning, this received discourse or communication should be processed and contextualized within the overall language learning environment. Nonnative speakers need practice in functioning as the audience in the target language. How they decode incoming information or communication is the prime question. At the simplest level, students may read documents at a site such as *Folktales From Around the World* (Scott, Gaer, & Hopper, 1998, http://www.otan.dni.us/webfarm/emailproject/folk.htm; see Figure 7-1).

Imagine, for instance, a class of 15–20 adult students who are all at an intermediate level of English but who have varying degrees of experience and comfort with technology. In a reading-writing unit with a theme such as "leisure time across cultures," students could gather information from a range of resources: face-to-face surveys, assorted readings, collaborative vocabulary-building exercises, introspective journal entries, community observations, video, and electronic sources. The final project might be to work

Receptive Activities

- Reading electronic documents
- Listening on-line
- Using search engines and downloading files
- Receiving simulcasts
- Lurking on a list or a MOO

toward a definition of *leisure* according to cultural values represented in the class, produce a piece of process writing, give oral reports in small groups, or all of these. A supportive menu of technology-enhanced language learning activities is discussed below. You can do most of these activities with even a modest degree of technology as long as access to the Internet is available.

Figure 7-1. *Folktales From Around the World* (Scott, Gaer, & Hopper, 1998)

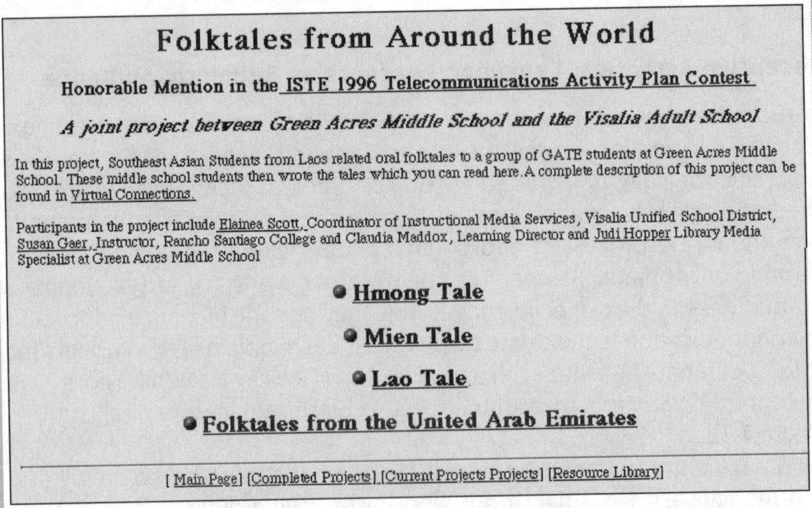

Folktales from Around the World

Honorable Mention in the ISTE 1996 Telecommunications Activity Plan Contest

A joint project between Green Acres Middle School and the Visalia Adult School

In this project, Southeast Asian Students from Laos related oral folktales to a group of GATE students at Green Acres Middle School. These middle school students then wrote the tales which you can read here. A complete description of this project can be found in Virtual Connections.

Participants in the project include Elainea Scott, Coordinator of Instructional Media Services, Visalia Unified School District, Susan Gaer, Instructor, Rancho Santiago College and Claudia Maddox, Learning Director and Judi Hopper Library Media Specialist at Green Acres Middle School

- **Hmong Tale**
- **Mien Tale**
- **Lao Tale**
- **Folktales from the United Arab Emirates**

[Main Page] [Completed Projects] [Current Projects Projects] [Resource Library]

Note. From *Folktales From Around the World,* by E. Scott, S. Gaer, and J. Hopper, 1998, Staff Development Institute/Outreach Technical Assistance Network, http://www.otan.dni.us/webfarm/emailproject/folk.htm. Copyright © 1998 by S. Gaer. Reprinted with permission.

Electronic Books and CD-ROMs

Encyclopedias and interactive texts available as software (on floppy disks or CD-ROMs) and increasingly as downloadable files on the World Wide Web (in the form of freeware, shareware, and commercial software) can enhance paper-based classroom resources. You can preview the software, create a set of four or five tasks per application, and have students work in small groups to complete tasks, discover information, or win the game, for example. If resources are limited and only single copies of software are available, they can be loaded onto separate stations; students can rotate through the stations individually or in groups. CELIA *at La Trobe University: Computer Enhanced Language Instruction Archive* (Holliday, 1997a, http://chiron.latrobe.edu.au/www/education/celia/celia.html) is a good place to start looking for language software to download (see also Appendix D).

Reading Software

Reading skills software that allows the importation of text or personalized vocabulary (for example, NewReader, McVicker, 1995a) can be adapted to particular themes and topics. A free corpus of reading matter is found at *Project Gutenberg* (Michael Hart, http://www.gutenberg.net/). Select materials that are relevant to the topic and allow students to work at their own pace. Students can also use their own compositions and texts they have read in class as reading matter for skills enhancement.

Internet E-Zines, Web Site Sound and Video Clips

With sufficient resources, a class or department can maintain an intranet or bulletin board system on which all members can read about, view, or listen to relevant information, events, and materials. You (or your students) can create Web pages with links to topic-related texts and to sound and video clips in order to make tasks and activities more concrete. Web-based news sources, such as CNN *Interactive* (http://www.cnn.com/), PBS *Online* (http://www.pbs.org/), and USA *Today* (http://www.usatoday.com/), provide adaptable educational materials in support of current news events. A sample task would be to have students answer three questions based on a speech by Hillary Rodham Clinton. (See Appendix F for a variety of resources.)

Real-Time Sound

Streaming sound transmissions through applications such as RealPlayer™ (1998), which plays audio files without tedious downloading, open up endless possibilities for tapping into ready-to-go audio programming on a variety of topics. Software to play audio files and audio content is widely available free of charge through the World Wide Web. Students can use audio clips for receptive activities, such as listening dictations using whole or partial cloze, or for note-taking practice (see Appendix F).

IPTV Real-Time TV or Video

A wide array of streaming video and satellite transmissions (in Internet Protocol for Television [IPTV]) can bring topic-related current movies, news broadcasts, and popular programming into the classroom. Check on-site or local technology services to see if the wiring and infrastructure exist for this type of service. Comprehension and listening activities can be structured in much the same way as they would be for a regularly broadcast TV or video program. Many of the sites listed in Appendix F also have short videos.

Newsgroups

Lurking on select newsgroups (e.g., the news source *ClariNews*, 1997, http://www.clari.net/newstree.html) is a good way to gather information on specific topics. Web browsers such as Netscape Navigator® Gold (1997) offer direct access to the newsgroups themselves and the archives that store past files. Students can decide on topics ahead of time and do focused research and reading. These articles also copy and paste handily into word-processing applications so that you can create reading packets, cloze exercises, and other activities.

Electronic Discussion Lists

As noted in chapter 6, in an electronic discussion (or mailing) list, server software automatically posts e-mail messages to a list of the mailboxes of all subscribed members. As a means of getting to know how to navigate an electronic mailing list, students can lurk on a list until they feel ready to contribute. (See Appendix B for information on lists for teachers and students.)

The SL-Lists (Holliday & Robb, n.d., http://chiron.latrobe.edu.au/www /education/sl/sl.html; see chapter 6 and Appendix B) consist of 10 lists differentiated by level (beginner, intermediate, and advanced) and by topic (e.g., sports, movies) and are for English language learners only (the list runs a teacher-only support strand as well). A number of electronic lists archive important strands or topics on the World Wide Web, and these can be downloaded as a resource for class activities and student reading.

Push Technology

Push technology can send information to your computer over the Internet whenever you go on-line. With the free *My Yahoo!* service (http:// my.yahoo.com/), for example, you can ask to receive local or global news, computer news, sports scores, information on movie releases, weather reports, stock market updates, your daily horoscope, and so on—all rich teaching resources. Students can follow an unfolding news story or create a hypothetical stock portfolio, which is updated automatically through their Web browser each time they enter *My Yahoo!* Individual accounts are private and must be accessed by password. Students may need some help in setting up the parameters they wish to have reported, and your lab must be able to allow *cookies* (packets of identifying information) to be sent to and stored on the hard drive.

Search Engine or Gopher Research

Browsers can link users to one or more Internet search engines (e.g., *Dogpile: A Multisearch Engine,* http://www.dogpile.com/; *Infoseek,* http://www.infoseek.com/; *Lycos,* http://www.lycos.com/; *Yahoo!,* http://www.yahoo.com/; see Appendix C), in which the organization and operators differ slightly. Advanced students can be directed to on-line search engines and appropriate databases, archives, and other sites for individualized research projects. Prior training in search methodology, as well as site evaluation and verification, are critical for this level of research.

File Transfer Protocol

File transfer protocol (FTP) is a means of rapidly downloading files, including software, to individual computers. Web sites that provide access to FTP archives of downloadable software include *The U-M Software Archives* (1995, http://www.umich.edu/~archive/), CNET (http://www.cnet.com/), and *Jumbo!* (http://www.jumbo.com/); see Appendix D for others. Students can survey types of software that people use in their leisure time or for work and can download software to try out for themselves.

MOOs and MUDs

Multiuser virtual spaces—multiuser object-oriented domains (MOOs)—centered around a number of topics and themes, abound on the Internet (see chapter 22 and Appendix B). By signing on as a guest, students can visit the ESL MOO called *schMOOze University* (Falsetti, n.d., http://schmooze.hunter.cuny.edu:8888/) in an all-class adventure and practice navigating the space without posting. In this way they can experience a potential new hobby and learning experience and can evaluate it without getting entangled in the technical aspects of writing and responding live. *schMOOze University's* Web site provides information about how to navigate this virtual space; direct access requires free, downloadable Telnet software that is compatible with the user's local computer system (most new computers come with a version of Telnet installed). Several other Web sites (e.g., Frizler, 1997, http://thecity.sfsu.edu/~funweb/schmooze.htm) provide helpful downloadable software and instructions for using MOOs.

Active Activities: Language Learners Address an Authentic Audience

In active tasks, the student continues to function as an audience by receiving information, goods, or experiences as outlined in the previous section, but with the added dimension of actively reaching out to submit or contribute information in some way (see the box). These activities are less

---

Active Activities

- Producing formulaic, short writings
- Producing short answers on electronic quizzes
- Commenting on other students' writing
- Playing simulation games on-line
- Telephoning in to satellite broadcasts
- Creating a World Wide Web page

---

taxing than those in the interactive category, which involve give-and-take on both sides. In an active task, the student neither receives any kind of conversational reply nor is part of a real-time, bidirectional interaction or communication.

In a technology-enhanced setting, the students' audience (i.e., the entity to whom they are sending a communication of some kind) may not be human. Formulaic responses, answers to on-line quizzes, and courtesy confirmation messages are all examples of communication with and limited, fairly predictable responses from an electronic audience. Many teacher-made Web sites offer such opportunities, such as *Talking About Daily Routines* (Trickel, 1997, http://grove.ufl.edu/~ktrickel/teslmini/activity.html; see Figure 7-2); see Appendix G for other sites. Successful completion of active tasks with a nonhuman audience is a valid language learning activity and provides students with an element of control that is missing in spontaneous, interactive communications. It is fairly easy to predict what will happen when the audience is receptive, not interactive.

Consider, then, the same intermediate-level ESOL reading-writing class of 15–20 adult students, who now have a growing degree of experience and comfort with technology. They need to reach out to authentic audiences but in a sheltered way. A class theme such as "styles in communication" can tap into a wide range of resources through traditional readings and media (e.g., newspapers, magazines, pen pals) and can be enhanced through resources such as those described below.

Activities at World Wide Web Sites

The number of Web sites explicitly for ESOL audiences and of general sites that are useful in and adaptable to ESOL is growing day by day (see Appendix G). Many ask for responses to questionnaires and surveys, promising to send results. Some offer English tests for students to take and have scored on-line. Several Web-site-based activities offering opportunities for limited and safe interactions are described below.

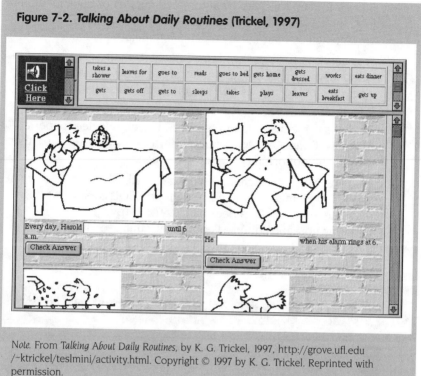

Figure 7-2. Talking About Daily Routines (Trickel, 1997)

Note. From Talking About Daily Routines, by K. G. Trickel, 1997, http://grove.ufl.edu/~ktrickel/teslmini/activity.html. Copyright © 1997 by K. G. Trickel. Reprinted with permission.

- Letter-writing and guest registries, especially those that offer spaces in which to type in comments, are an easy avenue of communication for nonnative speakers. Students often enjoy a visit to the U.S. White House on-line (http://www.whitehouse.gov/), where they may leave a message for the president. A special section of the site, The White House for Kids, uses the presidential cat, Socks, as a guide to help youngsters learn about citizenship, and it has its own message box.

- Formulaic responses to topics or tasks on Web sites can provide enjoyable, finite tasks. For example, students can put a message in a bottle at Smithsonian's Ocean Planet (n.d., http://seawifs.gsfc.nasa.gov/ocean_planet.html), the on-line version of the traveling exhibit (as of autumn 1998).

- Voting and opinion polls, in which other individuals post and read results, provide chances for nonnative speakers to comment in a controlled way. The Feedback page on CNN Interactive (1998, http://www.cnn.com/feedback/) is one such Web page.

- Stories to read followed by automated quizzes or questionnaires (e.g., the fables at *The Comenius English Language Center*, http://www.comenius.com/) give students immediate feedback.

- Free services such as *The Electric Postcard* (Donath, 1996, http://persona.www.media.mit.edu/postcards/) allow students to send electronic postcards, as well as bouquets and songs, to each other.

- Students can construct a personalized electronic newspaper at CRAYON: *Create Your Own Newspaper* (http://www.crayon.net/), thus creating an opportunity to read on a regular basis.

- Students can submit creative writing for publishing or contests at various sites, many of them listed in the ESOL creative writing resource, PIZZAZ! (Opp-Beckman, 1997b, http://darkwing.uoregon.edu/~leslieob/pizzaz.html; see Figure 7-3).

Figure 7-3. Creative Writing Resources at *PIZZAZ!* (Opp-Beckman, 1997b)

PIZZAZ!... People Interested in Zippy and ZAny Zcribbling

An Online Resource since 1995 for
Scribblers and Teachers of English as a Second Language
by Leslie Opp-Beckman

URL: http://darkwing.uoregon.edu/~leslieob/pizzaz.html

Poetry ||| Fiction ||| Bag of Tricks ||| More Publishing Opportunities ||| Other Teacher Resources

Description: PIZZAZ! is dedicated to providing creative writing activities and copyable (yes, copyable!) handouts for use with students of all ages. Permission is given to use these resources for in-class, non-profit use only.

Prerequisite: An interest in using English in fun, dynamic ways!

ESL Student Level: High Beginner +

Poetry

- Cinquaine Poems Five-line poems that are very easy to write.
- Diamante Poems Diamond-shaped poems - real gems! Seven lines in all.
- Haiku Poems A short, three-line poem (originally from Japanese) with the form: 5,7,5 syllables. Resources, examples, publishing opportunities.
- Headline Poems, courtesy of my colleague Iris Moye.
- Limericks Resources, teaching ideas and contests.
- Persona-Poems A structured 8-line poem, biographical in nature.
- Renga and Renku Poems from Japan.

Note. From PIZZAZ!, by L. Opp-Beckman, 1997, University of Oregon, American English Institute, http://darkwing.uoregon.edu/~leslieob/pizzaz.html. Copyright © 1997 by L. Opp-Beckman. Reprinted with permission.

Software

Many educational Web sites and software now come with games related to their materials and topics. Highly commercialized Web sites, such as Disney.com (http://www.disney.com/), often put out free, downloadable games in English in conjunction with current films. The table of contents on the dust jacket of an old encyclopedia on CD-ROM may also reveal that it contains useful activities or games that students would enjoy (and learn from).

Local Network Simulations and On-Line Games

Collaborative simulations, either in a lab setting on a local area network (LAN) or on the Internet, offer opportunities for students to interact with classmates and outsiders in a controlled way. CD-ROMs from educational publishers are now beginning to include direct Web links so that students can jump from the disc to a Web-based game almost without realizing it. Collaborative, team simulations and games such as Oregon Trail II (1997) or Tom Snyder Productions' software (see http://www.teachtsp.com/) are effective in ESOL settings. Because such games come and go very quickly, check for current listings in archives of search engines (e.g., Lycos, http://www.lycos.com/) in the "Games" category, and screen game sites especially carefully for content, appropriateness, and stability.

Synchronous Communication

Real-time communication, an integral part of many satellite broadcasts, requires telephone lines, microphones, and video hardware and software. Watching real-time televised presentations and shows requires minimal, if any, communication when an individual telephones in to ask a question, so it presents a relatively safe, modest level of interaction. This type of opportunity may be offered in conjunction with Web-based distance education courses appropriate to a content or adjunct course. Check local technology and telecommunications resources, for example, your local school district office, for current satellite broadcast offerings.

Web Page Creation (Electronic Publishing)

Web-based publishing can be an empowering tool in the ESOL classroom, as students can incorporate original text, sound, image, and video files into Web pages. As any Web site producer does, students need to carefully assess their intended audience and design the format and content of the Web page(s) accordingly. Beware of copyright infringement, especially with images. You will probably need the school's or district's approval for content if you work in a public school system. Most browser software has Web page templates built in to get you started. (See chapter 25 for more information on authoring Web pages.)

Interactive Activities

- Holding asynchronous text-based conversations
- Holding synchronous text-based conversations
- Participating in audio exchanges
- Videoconferencing
- Taking distance-learning courses

Interactive Activities: Language Learners Involved in Authentic, Two-Way Communication

In interactive exchanges, students act both as receivers and senders of information (see the box). Communication takes place between two or more participants. In most cases, nonnative speakers will benefit from a guided tour of the technology coupled with an overview of the corresponding tasks that they are to complete.

Imagine now that the intermediate-level ESOL reading-writing class of 15–20 adult students has completed several on-line tasks and has acquired a modest degree of experience and comfort with technology. In a reading-writing unit with a theme such as "changing work habits in the information age," students could once again gather information from a range of resources: face-to-face surveys, assorted readings, collaborative vocabulary building, dialogue or double-entry journals, community observations, video, and electronic sources. The final project might be to build a community model showing demographics and traffic flow patterns, produce a piece of process writing, give oral reports in small groups (perhaps with the help of presentation software; see chapter 25), or do all of the preceding tasks. Many aspects of these projects will involve interactions with native speakers in relatively unstructured situations. Supportive CALL activities are noted below.

Asynchronous Communication: Text

Asynchronous (time-delayed) exchanges can be a great way to share information and socialize with native speakers or other ESOL students. Asynchronous communication requires either e-mail accounts or software such as Web-B-Mail (Pfaff-Harris, 1996). You can either structure exchanges or turn the students loose on a safe discussion list, such as the SL-Lists, mentioned above (Holliday & Robb, n.d.; see chapter 6 and Appendix B). Once students have visited and lurked on a list, they can begin to participate in threaded discussions and debates by reading messages and posting replies to newsgroups, discussion forums, bulletin boards, and Web-based conferencing on virtually any topic. Consider whether private or open discussions will best serve the students' needs. To break students out of the habit of lurking, you can require them to ask a question and post a specific number of responses within a given time frame.

A structured cross-classroom exchange works best when the teachers are in explicit agreement on grading criteria, number of exchanges, topics, and course goals. *Intercultural E- Mail Classroom Connections* (http://www.iecc .org/), facilitated by Craig Rice, Bruce Roberts, and Howard Thorsheim at St. Olaf College, is a high-quality, free service assisting cross-classroom exchanges with teacher support at a Web site; a form to use to request keypals is also available on the Web page (see Figure 7-4; see chapters 6 and 26 for additional exchange ideas).

A number of Web sites, such as bulletin boards, joint authoring sites, and publishers' sites related to elementary and high school curricula, provide the opportunity for asynchronous written exchanges of the following types:

Figure 7-4. E-Mail Exchanges at *Intercultural E-Mail Classroom Connections* (http://www.iecc.org/)

Intercultural E-Mail Classroom Connections

http://www.iecc.org

The **IECC** (Intercultural E-Mail Classroom Connections) mailing lists are provided by St. Olaf College as a free service to help teachers and classes link with partners in other countries and cultures for e-mail classroom pen-pal and project exchanges. Since its creation in 1992, IECC has distributed over 19,000 requests for e-mail partnerships. At last count, there were more than 7300 teachers in approximately 73 countries participating in at least one of the IECC lists: how many teachers are participating today?

- **General information about IECC**
- **About using this page**

- **Books of Interest** [New]

- How to Subscribe to IECC

- **Submit a request to IECC**
- **Search all IECC Archives**

- Related Resources

- Browse IECC-HE
- Browse IECC
- Browse IECC-PROJECTS
- Browse IECC-SURVEYS

The graphic above is used with permission of Hecklermedia, Inc.

Note. From *Intercultural E-Mail Classroom Connections*, by C. Rice, B. Roberts, and H. Thorsheim, 1998, St. Olaf College, http://www.iecc.org/. Reprinted with permission of the authors.

- Questions to and answers from on-line advice columns are entertaining and make for authentic exchanges.

- Opportunities to write fiction and poetry with other authors are available through the ESOL creative writing resource at PIZZAZ! (Opp-Beckman, 1997b, http://darkwing.uoregon.edu/~leslieob /pizzaz.html).

- On-line writing labs (OWLs), such as Purdue University's *Online Writing Lab* (http://owl.english.purdue.edu/), provide personalized writing assistance.

In-house intranets can provide opportunities for two-way communications. Several pages at the University of Oregon's American English Institute offer examples of projects that began as intranet writing. For example, *Sanno College Summer 1998* (Opp-Beckman, 1998a, http://darkwing.uoregon.edu /~aei/sanno98memories.html) displays photos, poetry, and stories (Figure 7-5). PIZZAZ! *Magazine Marvels* (Opp-Beckman, 1997c, http://darkwing.uoregon .edu/~leslieob/magmarvel.html) contains instructions for teachers on motivating students to write.

Synchronous Communication: Text

Once students have visited a MOO and have seen how it operates, synchronous (real-time) Internet Relay Chat (IRC) and MOO/MUD conversa-

---

Figure 7-5. Sanno College Student Projects (Opp-Beckman, 1998a)

Sanno College Summer 1998

Student Project "I Saw, I Heard, I Learned, I Am..."

The poem and pictures below reflect the experiences of Sanno students at the University of Oregon in Eugene.

Visitors to this site can see, hear, read and share these students' memories from the Summer of '98!

Click on any of the following pictures to see larger ones:

Note. From *Sanno College Summer 1998*, by L. Opp-Beckman, 1998, University of Oregon, American English Institute, http://darkwing.uoregon.edu/~aei/sanno98memories.html. Copyright © 1998 by L. Opp-Beckman. Reprinted with permission.

tions using keyboarding offer 24-hour practice with real people. They require Telnet software, which is often built into Web browsers and may be obtained free on-line. Additional software to filter real-time input and output, so that messages are not interlaced on the screen (which can be confusing even for native speakers), is downloadable from most MOO sites. You can also set up synchronous chatting or debating off-line on a LAN with chat software, such as CommonSpace (1997) or the InterChange® module of Daedalus® Integrated Writing Environment (1997). Students who are otherwise quiet in class may open up when they can express their thoughts in writing. Two reputable ESOL Internet MOOs can be accessed through their Web sites: *schMOOze University* (Falsetti, n.d., http://schmooze.hunter.cuny.edu:8888/) and ESL *Chat Room Central* (Sperling, 1997, http://www.eslcafe.com/chat/chatpro.cgi). (See chapter 22 for details on MOOs and MUDs.)

With special software (downloadable on-line), students can access Virtual Reality Modeling Language (VRML) three-dimensional chat rooms with avatars (fictional characters created by the users). However, these rooms may be frequented by avid players of complex on-line games who may not welcome *newbies* (newcomers to the on-line world). Check sites thoroughly in advance, and make sure the students have considerable confidence in their technological and linguistic skills before attempting to visit VRML chat rooms.

Audio Exchanges

Real-time, voice-to-voice conversations (e.g., with the software CU-SeeMe, 1997) can take place through the Internet. Students should prepare for synchronous voice exchanges as they would for any oral presentation. Practice with social exchanges, such as turn-taking strategies and polite requests and interruptions, can make the experience more harmonious.

Sound and image *packets* (files) can also be sent as e-mail attachments. Students can create their own sound files in response to those they receive. Most presentation software, such as HyperStudio (1997), now allows users to upload files to the Web and to display or play them on the Internet (see chapter 25).

Videoconferencing

Real-time, face-to-face videoconferencing is also improving in quality and becoming more accessible though the Internet. A videoconference requires a video camera (about $200 in 1998) and a modem allowing a Web connection speed of at least 28.8 kilobytes per second. In the future, Web browsers and telecommunications software will support this function globally. As with audioconferencing, a smooth exchange via synchronous video communication requires good preparation.

Distance Learning

Taking on-line courses that incorporate various facets of the Internet (e.g., the Web, e-mail, conferencing, newsgroups) allows nonnative speakers and educators access to information, educational experiences, and audiences far removed from their local physical environment and expands opportunities for homebound people. Distance-learning courses can be easily located through Internet search engines, such as *Infoseek* (http://www.infoseek.com/), and metasearch engines such as *Dogpile: A Multisearch Engine* (http://www.dogpile.com/). *The Homeschool Zone* (http://www.homeschoolzone.com/) provides excellent links for the independent language learner or ESL/EFL classroom as well as for individuals schooling their children at home. (See chapters 14 and 26 and Appendix H for more information on distance learning.)

Conclusion

Given enough time, the mechanics of technology should become so transparent that it is seamlessly woven into a variety of daily experiences, educational and noneducational. The increasing ease of access to the Internet can bring people together in ways that were formerly impossible.

Authentic language opportunities abound via the Internet and World Wide Web. Students can converse with keypals in Asia, chat with peers from around the world in a virtual university or MOO, receive assistance from educators in an OWL, do research in databases and archives across Europe and North America, and check up-to-the-minute news at their convenience. Educators should consider the following guidelines and questions when students take the role of a receptive, active, or interactive audience vis-à-vis the World Wide Web:

- Build students' awareness of stylistic variations across discourse communities. For example, what is appropriate discourse in an OWL versus in a MOO? What are the general rules of *netiquette* (Internet etiquette)? How does on-line discourse differ from face-to-face discourse in pacing and approach?

- Facilitate the building of a language and cultural framework from which students can approach tasks. For example, what does it mean to hold up one's end of a conversation? What constitutes a personal question in a given culture, and how is such a question best handled?

- Discuss security issues. For example, what are the pluses and minuses of assuming a cloak of anonymity in a chat room or in a discussion group? How much personal information should students divulge to a keypal?

- Provide technology-based opportunities that are relevant to students' interests and needs. For example, what activities will best prepare them for their life goals? Are there ways in which technology can help them learn faster or more efficiently? If so, is there a trade-off (i.e., is something lost in exchange for the speed and efficiency of technology)?

With talk of the development of Internet II (a national network for higher education that will offer high speeds and reliable service), the exponential doubling of hardware speed approximately every 18 months, and the emergence of futuristic gadgets, such as cochlear implants, virtual retinal displays, and digital pets that live in your computer and come when you call them, it's easy to become overwhelmed and give up before you start. But the adage still applies: It's not how much technology you have that counts; it's what you do with it.

Explorations

Products

1. Design a keypal project for your students so that they can interact with an authentic audience. With whom would your students be connected, and why? What would the requirements of the assignment be? How would you assess the results?

2. Search the World Wide Web for sites that meet your students' learning objectives and also provide ways for them to interact with an authentic audience (several starting points are listed in chapters 6 and 7 and in Appendixes B and H.) Make an annotated list of your favorite sites.

3. Develop and describe an interclass project using the Web. How will students interact with this audience? What kinds of help will they need from the teacher or technical personnel? How will the project attain closure?

Guided Research

1. How do the content, style, and tone of e-mail messages change in writing to different audiences? Collect sample data by having students copy e-mail messages to you or by checking students' bulletin board, electronic discussion list, or electronic chat room on a regular basis. Using existing discourse research, develop a content-coding scheme that accurately captures the changes that you anticipate.

2. How do content, style, and tone change over time in writing to the same audience? Collect samples for analysis over an extended period of time. A write-up of results might also include interviews with student participants: How did they approach the writing task? Did they feel their language was more formal or less

formal on the Internet? Did they find themselves making adjustments or corrections for their intended audience(s)?

3. Implement the interclass project you developed for Projects, No. 3. Keep a record of student processes. How do students go about designing the project? How do they formulate their roles in the project? At what point is teacher intervention most effective? Include an exit interview in your data collection: What changes do students feel occurred in their language growth? How did students feel about their participation in the project?

Questions for Further Investigation

1. At what level of language ability are students able to meet the needs of their audience? Are there other factors that determine how language students understand and meet the needs of their audience?

2. How can technology best assist in the growth of an awareness of audience?

3. Which audiences in what contexts do second language learners consider authentic? How do these considerations differ from teachers' considerations of authenticity?

PART III

Authentic Task

Chapter 8

Theory and Research: Investigation of "Authentic" Language Learning Tasks

Carol A. Chapelle

Many researchers believe that learners best acquire the target language by engaging in activities resembling those they will encounter outside the classroom. Such classroom activities are often referred to as *tasks* even though researchers differ on exactly what qualifies as a task. Despite differences in the precise definition of a task, researchers generally agree that tasks must have goals and that they are carried out through participants' engagement in goal-oriented behavior.

Tasks for language learners, therefore, require learners to use the target language to accomplish something, but differences of opinion exist on just what they must accomplish. Some researchers see tasks as any goal-directed behavior in the language classroom (Breen, 1987), whereas others consider the most useful and interesting tasks to be those whose goals require communication in the target language (Pica, Kanagy, & Falodun, 1993), in other words, authentic tasks. A communicative task requires learners to accomplish something through the construction and interpretation of linguistic meanings. Communicative goals might include coming to a compromise on an issue or finding out the prices of plane tickets to various points in Mexico, for example.

This chapter details two approaches to investigating learning tasks that may strengthen teachers' understanding of computer-assisted tasks. Because the two methods provide complementary information, they should not be seen as mutually exclusive or as two different routes to the same information. The first method, which is based on teachers' judgments of the relationship between the second language task and the tasks that learners might encounter outside the classroom, can be thought of as a way of evaluating the authenticity of the task relative to learners' language use in other settings. The second method relies on detailed observation of the language that learners produce during the second language task.

Method 1: Judging Authenticity

The title of this chapter places the term *authentic* in quotation marks, for it is obviously difficult to have a fully authentic language task in a classroom where teachers have a role in deciding what is to be learned and grades are assigned. Evaluating the authenticity of second language tasks relies on an analysis of the correspondence between a second language learning task and tasks that the learner is likely to encounter outside the classroom. Such an analysis requires the definition of a set of features relevant for describing the second language tasks both in and out of the classroom. A complete set of features would come from a fully elaborated theory of context, which articulates interdependencies between contextual features and context-embedded language (see Halliday, 1977; Halliday & Hasan, 1989). However, to illustrate this type of analysis, I examine one part of context theory, *field*, here renamed *frame*, to adapt to the study of CALL tasks (see also Chapelle, in press). The frame of a second language learning task consists of five features: (a) goal, (b) process, (c) topic, (d) location(s), and (e) duration (see Table 8-1).

The task's *goal* refers to what the learner is trying to accomplish in the task. The concern here is tasks with communicative goals, those which focus on accomplishing something through the use of language. Research on

Table 8-1. Features and Questions for Analyzing the Frame of a Second Language Task

Feature of task	Questions for analysis
1. Goal	Is the task communicative? Is there one or more than one possible outcome? Is the conveyance of information necessary for reaching the goal?
2. Process	What are the learners engaged in—in everyday terms (e.g., listening to a lecture)? How can the process be characterized as a genre (e.g., a service encounter)?
3. Topic	What is the content? Is it personal or nonpersonal? Is it field specific or general? How precisely is the topic defined? How cognitively complex is the topic?
4. Location	Where are the participants located as they work on the task?
5. Duration	What is the duration of the task? Under what time constraints is the task performed?

second language tasks (Pica et al., 1993) indicates that tasks with communicative goals should be further defined according to whether they have one or more than one possible outcome and whether or not conveyance of information is necessary for reaching the goal, because these features affect the language associated with communicative tasks. Communicative goals might include self-expression or self-definition and establishing social bonds as well as giving and receiving information.

The task's *process* refers to what the learners are engaged in while completing the task. Task processes can be described in everyday terms, such as listening to a lecture or making an airline reservation. The task process might also be characterized as a genre (Halliday & Hasan, 1989; Martin, 1985), such as a service encounter (e.g., buying a plane ticket) or a descriptive essay (e.g., describing Bloomington, Indiana).

The *topic* of a communicative task is some content other than the linguistic forms of the target language, because communicative goals require learners to use language to do something other than learn language. Topics are further categorized as field specific versus general (see, e.g., Alderson & Urquhart, 1985; Clapham, 1996; Douglas, in press). Field-specific, classroom-focused topics might include the language of an academic area (e.g., math) or of a profession (e.g., airline attendant). General topics might include the description of a house to another person in a jigsaw task. Other aspects of topic believed to be important are how complex it is, how personal it is, and how precisely it has been defined. Skehan (1996) suggests that both the specificity and the cognitive complexity of the topic are other significant factors. Duff's (1993) study of second language tasks suggests that whether topics are personal or nonpersonal is also relevant for second language performance, and Pica, Holliday, Lewis, and Morgenthaler (1989) suggest that how precisely the topic is defined is also important.

The fourth and fifth variables, the *location* and *duration* of the task, refer to where each participant works on the task and within what time period. Most task-based second language research has been conducted on oral, face-to-face communication in the classroom. In such studies the location and duration have not been considered variables because communication takes place in a single location and within the time period of a class. Computer-mediated second language tasks expand the duration and location options, and these variables should therefore be important in defining the frame of a second language task. For example, a multiuser object-oriented (MOO) setting (see chapter 22) can allow on-line checking of grammar and spelling during a real-time (synchronous) conversation, something not ordinarily possible in face-to-face exchanges.

Note that the research does not clearly define how much of each characteristic or which specific features make a task authentic. The definition, therefore, is that authentic classroom tasks are those which are most like natural communication outside class. A comparison of an out-of-class discussion with an in-class task illustrates how these task features can be used to analyze the authenticity of classroom tasks. The out-of-class model is a hypothetical discussion between two friends about the homes of mutual acquaintances. Each of the two participants knows about a set of friends' houses, and therefore each has unique information to contribute to the discussion. Table 8-2 shows an analysis of the resulting speech event using the frame features.

An in-class communication task that is comparable to this conversation is a jigsaw task, which is thought of as useful for second language acquisition (SLA). In a jigsaw task, a pair of learners exchange information to reach a goal. Each participant holds unique pieces of information; in other words, pieces of the communication puzzle. Table 8-3 shows an analysis of a jigsaw task in which native speaker–learner dyads were to "reproduce an unseen sequence of pictures of houses by exchanging verbal descriptions of their own uniquely held portions of the sequence" (Pica, Lincoln-Porter, Paninos, & Linnell, 1996, p. 69; see Table 8-4 below for some of the actual dialogue).

By comparing the analyses in Tables 8-2 and 8-3, one can determine how authentic the task is. The goals of both the in-class task and the out-of-class conversation are communicative because they require the use of language to construct the meanings required for conveying information, yet the two speech events differ in important ways. For example, the out-of-class task has the additional interpersonal goal of maintaining the friendship of

Table 8-2. Analysis of "House Description" Speech Event

Feature	Values for speech event
Goals	Communicate; maintain friendship Achieve multiple possible outcomes Convey information about mutual friends' houses to fill in gaps in each other's knowledge
Process	Interactive dialogue
Topics	Houses: physical characteristics and locations Other information about people who live in the houses Opinions about the houses Topic not field specific, not cognitively complex, not precisely defined Some personal involvement (e.g., opinions, personal stories)
Location	Cafeteria
Duration	Moderate rate of speech No time pressure; flexible 45-minute duration

Table 8-3. Analysis of "House Description" Jigsaw Task

Feature	Values for jigsaw task
Goals	Communicate Achieve the one correct outcome Convey information about houses to complete picture
Process	Interactive dialogue
Topic	Houses: physical characteristics and locations Topic not field specific, not cognitively complex, not personal, precisely defined
Location	Classroom
Duration	Moderate rate of speech Some time pressure to finish during class

the two participants and is less precisely defined than the goal of the classroom task. The process of the two speech events, in general terms, may appear the same even though a detailed empirical investigation of the language of the two would no doubt reveal some differences. The topics of the two tasks overlap in their inclusion of house vocabulary, physical characteristics, and locations, but the out-of-class discussion contains topics in addition to houses, such as information about the people who live in the houses and opinions on the characteristics of the houses (i.e., more personal topics). In both tasks the participants sit face-to-face in one location, but, of course, the out-of-class task takes place in a different location from the in-class task—in this case in a cafeteria, a more informal setting. In neither task is time pressure imposed; however, the classroom task has a more fixed duration because it must be completed during the class period. On the basis of this analysis, the second language task can be considered authentic to some degree. The primary difference between the two is that the classroom task is more narrowly focused; this characteristic shows up in the goal, topics, and duration of the exchange.

Method 2: Empirical Investigation of Oral Texts

A second means of evaluating tasks is empirical examination of the actual language produced in classroom speech events during communicative tasks. Table 8-4 shows a part of the conversation produced in the jigsaw task described above (Pica et al., 1996).

Researchers usually investigate learners' language in a second language

Table 8-4. Conversation From "House Description" Jigsaw Task

Exchange	Move	Participant	Text
1	1	Taro	the house has maybe two stone steps
	2	Ichi	two stone steps?
	3	Taro	yeah steps its a entrance
2	1	Taro	its wall is completely white
	2	Ichi	completely white?
	3	Taro	yeah completely white
	4	Ichi	it looks not wood it looks ah concrete

Note. From Pica, Lincoln-Porter, Paninos, and Linnell (1996, p. 76).

learning task with some assumptions about what language use is beneficial for second language development. For example, in Exchange 1 in Table 8-4, Ichi's first move (1.2) acts as a signal to indicate uncertainty: "two stone steps?" This utterance focuses Taro's attention on the linguistic form of what he has just said and produces a response in the third move (1.3) that expands on his previous language: "yeah steps its a entrance." Exchange 2 illustrates a signal—again focusing attention on language—in Ichi's move (2.2), which again elicits a repetition from Taro (2.3) and an expansion on previous language: "yeah completely white." These types of moves, which focus attention on language and repeat and expand what was previously said, are believed to be beneficial for SLA, and identifying such sequences has therefore been a means of investigating second language tasks. The assumption is that tasks that produce these beneficial moves may be ideal for second language learning. Examining the language of these task-related exchanges has therefore been an important method of investigating second language tasks, and that method might profitably be used to investigate CALL tasks as well.

Empirical research methods for evaluating second language tasks have evolved from the second language classroom research methods of the 1980s, which to a large extent abandoned the evaluation of language instruction by measuring learning outcomes in favor of the investigation of classroom processes (Allwright, 1988; Allwright & Bailey, 1991; Chaudron, 1988; Day, 1986; Gass & Madden, 1985; Long, 1980; van Lier, 1988). Second language classroom researchers found that the most revealing way to document the processes occurring in a language classroom appeared to be to describe the language of the classroom participants. Second language task research follows in this tradition of investigating oral texts. In this section I outline two ways of looking at textual data from second language tasks. The first provides general categories for a description of task-based texts, and the second adds some precision to the analysis by identifying particular aspects of a text, using the conversation from the jigsaw task in Table 8-4.

Description of Task-Based Second Language Texts

Second language researchers' descriptions of task-based language center on three aspects of the second language text: the input provided to the learner, the learner's output, and the interaction between the learner and the interlocutor. Each of these aspects of the language can be analyzed in greater detail through five descriptive categories: (a) pragmatic function, (b) linguistic characteristics, (c) quantity, (d) nonlinguistic moves and forms, and (e) medium. Tables 8-5 and 8-6 show just a few of the many ways to describe the linguistic characteristics of the data.

The *pragmatic functions* in the jigsaw task exchanges detailed in Table 8-6 include describing and signaling; other functions in a task might include giving instructions or transmitting information. The *linguistic characteristics* of the oral text can be examined descriptively in terms of its semantic and grammatical systems—the vocabulary, grammatical features, and forms of the text structure. The description in Table 8-6 is purposely very simple, noting sentence structure, verb tense, and some vocabulary. The *quantity* of the language input and output—that is, how much target language input is received and how much output is produced—can be described very precisely in terms of time or number of words; however, I have described them more holistically as *short turns*. The form and function of *nonlinguistic moves* refer to such features as body language or icons and mouse clicks that are used to communicate during the task. Despite the role that they might have played in the jigsaw task, no information is given with the text to indicate how nonlinguistic moves were used. Finally, the *medium* of language refers to the manner in which the language is transmitted: orally through face-to-face conversation, as in the jigsaw task, or through electronic mail or hypermedia text on a computer screen, for example.

These descriptive categories can guide the researcher to include a great deal of detail in the analysis of second language texts and therefore help illuminate the nature of the second language practice the learner engages in during a particular task. This information is useful, and it is different from what is provided by analyzing a task's authenticity. On the other hand, a neutral description might be viewed as limited because it does not reveal what language experiences might be beneficial for learners. Attempting to move beyond the neutral description of second language texts, researchers have hypothesized some of the characteristics of "good" task-based

Table 8-5. Categories for Analyzing Features of Second Language Text

Feature of task	Questions for analysis
Input to learner	1. What functions does the target language input perform in the task (e.g., give instructions; provide comprehensible input)? 2. What are the linguistic characteristics of the input to the learner (i.e., the lexicogrammatical features, such as syntactic and morphological forms)? 3. How much target language input does the learner receive? 4. What nonlinguistic moves and forms are used as input, and what functions do they perform (e.g., give instructions, offer options)? 5. Through what medium is the input transmitted (e.g., oral-aural/face-to-face, written on a computer screen)?
Output from learner	1. What functions does the target language output perform in the task (e.g., ask questions, display knowledge)? 2. What are the linguistic characteristics of the output from the learner (i.e., the lexicogrammatical features, such as syntactic and morphological forms)? 3. How much target language output does the learner produce? 4. What nonlinguistic moves and forms are used as output, and what functions do they perform? 5. Through what medium is the output transmitted (e.g., oral over the phone, written on paper)?
Interaction	1. What functions does the target language interaction perform in the task (e.g., negotiation of meaning, response to questions, signaling)? 2. What are the linguistic characteristics of the interaction, of the coherence and cohesion of the text, and of the structure of the text (e.g., openings, adjacency pairs; are functional sequences adapted or modified, such as with additional turns)? 3. How much interaction does the learner engage in? 4. What nonlinguistic moves and forms are used to accomplish interaction, and what functions do they perform (e.g., negotiate meaning, respond to questions, focus on form)? 5. Through what medium does interaction take place (e.g., oral over the phone; written via e-mail)?

Table 8-6. Analysis of Oral Text From Jigsaw Task

| Oral text | Descriptive category | | | | |
	Pragmatic role	Linguistic characteristics[a]	Quantity	Nonlinguistic characteristics[b]	Medium
1. its wall is completely white	Description	Simple declarative present tense	Short turn	–	Spoken face-to-face
2. completely white?	Signal	Noun phrase	Short turn	–	Spoken face-to-face
3. yeah completely white	Repetition	Noun phrase	Short turn	–	Spoken face-to-face
4. it looks not wood it looks ah concrete	Expansion (more information)	Simple declaratives More complex syntax: "looks" (i.e., "looks like") More complex vocabulary	Short turn	–	Spoken face-to-face

[a]Entries represent examples of the many ways one might choose to describe the linguistic characteristics of the data.
[b]The nonverbal communication accompanying the language might be described; however, the transcriptions I worked from do not note them in any of the data given.

exchanges on the basis of SLA theory. These hypotheses offer a starting point for a more focused description of second language texts.

Focused Investigation of Second Language Task-Based Texts

One way to evaluate the success of task language is by applying the criteria of accuracy, complexity, and fluency. Skehan (1996) suggests that the goal of task-based instruction should be for learners to develop an effective balance between fluency and accuracy and to become able to increase the complexity of their language use. An instructor could set pedagogical goals in terms of fluency, accuracy, and complexity and assess the extent to which learners have achieved them by examining the learners' language. A more precise way to investigate task language, however, comes from the interactionist tradition.

Generally, SLA theory and research in the interactionist tradition assume that learners acquire the second language through interaction in the target language because interaction gives learners opportunities to (a) comprehend message meaning, which is believed to be necessary for acquisition of second language forms; (b) produce modified output, which drives development of the specifics of morphology and syntax; and (c) attend to second language form, which helps develop the learners' linguistic systems (Krashen, 1982; Larsen-Freeman & Long, 1991; Nobuyoshi & Ellis, 1993; Pica et al., 1989; Swain, 1985; Swain & Lapkin, 1995). These hypotheses provide a basis for identifying the ideal qualities of second language input, output, and interaction.

Target Language Input

Speculation about target language input once suggested that quantity was all-important, and most researchers would still agree that a large quantity of target language input is good for second language development. However, theory suggests that not just any input is likely to prove beneficial; the quality of input is also important, and the quality of the input in turn depends on its pragmatic function and linguistic characteristics. With respect to pragmatic function, good input should require the learner to comprehend its semantic and pragmatic function in order to complete the task. In addition, the linguistic characteristics of the input should provide new data for the learner's developing system. Input that meets these conditions is called *comprehensible input* (Krashen, 1982).

In the analysis of task-based texts, the researcher would want to ask whether the learner received input conveying a message that was essential for completing a communicative task goal and that contained linguistic forms the learner was ready to acquire. The problem with this definition is that examining the input alone is insufficient to determine whether it can be considered comprehensible for a given learner. The input's comprehensibility depends not only on the nature of the input but also on the language ability of the individual student.

Despite the slipperiness inherent in a definition of comprehensible input, some input characteristics can be identified as potentially comprehension enhancing—and these may help focus the description of task-based texts. First, the researcher might note whether or not the input has been modified through simplification, elaboration, added redundancy, or sequencing to make it comprehensible (Chaudron, 1988; Larsen-Freeman & Long, 1991). A second key question is whether or not the input is marked to help learners notice particular linguistic features (Doughty, 1991; Schmidt & Frota, 1986). Marking might take the form of additional stress, a higher pitch, or a pause before or after a vocabulary word or grammatical form.

Potentially Valuable Output

Potentially valuable output is described in terms of the pragmatic role and linguistic characteristics of learners' language (Swain, 1985). Comprehensible output is believed to be valuable when it plays a role in helping learners convey meaning by stretching their linguistic resources, as Swain and Lapkin (1995) explain:

> In producing the L2, a learner will on occasion become aware of (i.e., notice) a linguistic problem brought to his/her attention either by external feedback (e.g., clarification requests) or internal feedback. Noticing a problem "pushes" the learner to modify his/her output. In doing so, the learner may sometimes be forced into a more syntactic processing mode than might occur in comprehension. (p. 373)

The hypothesis is that the syntactic mode of processing helps learners internalize new forms (Pica et al., 1989) and improve the accuracy of their existing grammatical knowledge (Nobuyoshi & Ellis, 1993). The "syntactic processing mode," of course, is not itself directly observable but can be inferred from observation of comprehensible output in learners' texts.

Comprehensible output, as it is defined in second language research, occurs when learners produce language to achieve communicative task goals. Comprehensible output is observed in a sequence of text consisting of the learner's unsuccessful attempt at expression followed by a linguistic modification of the form perceived as problematic. The trigger that causes the learner to notice the problem in the original output may or may not appear in the text. If another participant in the task draws the learner's attention to the problematic form, the text may reflect the interlocutor's clarification request, as the questions in Moves 1.2 and 2.2 in Table 8-4 illustrate. However, under Swain and Lapkin's (1995) definition of *beneficial output*, learners may recognize a problem in their own output without external prompting. In such cases, the text would display only the learners' original form, the process of correction (e.g., restatement or editing), and the learner's second attempt. Something like this process may be seen in Table 8-4, Move 2.4, in which Ichi corrects himself from "not wood" to the more specific "concrete." (See chapter 12 for a more detailed discussion of input and output.)

Interaction

Hypotheses about the value of interaction for second language development refer to its pragmatic role in negotiating the meaning of input (Long, 1985). Such negotiations result when the learner has requested, for example, a repetition, clarification, or restatement of the original input. Larsen-Freeman and Long (1991) summarize this view of *interactional modifications* as follows:

> Modification of the interactional structure of conversation or of written discourse during reading is a [good] candidate for a necessary (not sufficient) condition for acquisition. The role it plays in negotiation for meaning helps to make input comprehensible while still containing unknown linguistic elements, and, hence, potential intake for acquisition. (p. 144)

Ideal second language texts, then, would display learners' moves that request modifications of the input they receive. One type of modification would be learners' requests for clarifications, restatements, definitions, and explanations—all of which are intended to help them understand the meaning of the input they receive. A second type of interactional modification believed to facilitate SLA is an interruption in the normal interactional structure of an exchange to focus on linguistic form; that is, overt correction or self-correction of linguistic errors to clarify meaning. Chapter 2 of this volume contains several examples of self-correction in e-mail exchanges between deaf students of varying language ability.

Questions that may help researchers focus their investigation of second language tasks using SLA hypotheses are shown in Table 8-7. Although these questions delineate a starting point for a focused description of CALL tasks, they have limitations. First, the questions are based on research on classroom tasks in which oral face-to-face language was the medium of communication. Research is needed to seek a systematic understanding of these textual features in a variety of contexts, such as contexts in which the computer plays a role or in which written language is used. (See chapter 12 for references to studies that have begun to expand the research into the electronic realm.) Second, the characteristics of speech events outlined above are only hypothesized to be positive; they do not constitute direct evidence of learning. Thus CALL tasks must be investigated in combination with learning outcomes. Finally, for a particular CALL task, it may be useful to specify particular beneficial features that the task planner hopes will result rather than to look for all the positive qualities at one time.

Table 8-7. Focus Questions for Examining CALL Task Language

Aspect	Questions
Input	Is the input modified to make it comprehensible (e.g., through simplification, elaboration, added redundancy, or sequencing)?
	Is it flagged to focus learner's attention (i.e., on form or on meaning)?
Output	How much output does the learner produce?
	Does it contain interlanguage forms that appear to be competence stretching?
	Does it contain linguistic modifications of previous output?
Interaction	Is negotiation of meaning achieved through interaction?
	Is the interaction adapted or modified to focus on form through signaling? Corrections? Reference to previous discourse? Requests for target language reference materials?

The Dual Goals of Authentic Second Language Tasks

If the benefits of language practice during a second language task are the reason that the task is used in the classroom, then classroom second language tasks clearly have a goal besides the communicative one. In other words, communicative second language tasks have two simultaneous goals: one communicative, one pedagogical. In a larger framework for analysis of CALL tasks (Chapelle, 1995b, 1997), each of these goals can be thought of in connection with one of two levels of task analysis: the second language activity and the second language task. These two levels correspond to the two perspectives on tasks that Breen (1987) takes when he distinguishes between *task-as-work-plan* (i.e., second language activity) and *task-in-process* (i.e., second language task) to underscore the fact that what is planned and what actually happens in the classroom may differ. Breen notes, for example, that the learner plays a significant role in defining the character of the actual task-in-process observed in the classroom. This distinction between task and activity is also useful for anchoring the two task goals required for the two types of research described earlier in this chapter.

Task as Work Plan: Second Language Activity Goals

The second language *activity*, or work plan, is a general description of what learners are expected to do in a task, how they are to go about doing it, and what they are expected to learn (the pedagogical goal, or what learners are expected to do from the perspective of the planner, who intends the task to be beneficial for second language development). For example, the instructor assigning the jigsaw task is not really concerned about the learners' producing correct pictures of houses. The task is assigned to engender language learning through the negotiation of meaning as identified in specific textual features, such as signals, repetitions, and modification of previous language. Further, the activity is intended to "engage learners in describing attributes, states, and conditions in their pictures" (Pica et al., 1996, p. 69). This goal names some of the functional and, very generally, the grammatical features of the language that learners should work with in the task. Such pedagogical goals would be considered part of the instructor's plan for the learning activity—a plan that is crucial in guiding the empirical analysis of the language associated with the second language task.

Task in Process: Second Language Task Goals

The second language *task* refers to the specific conditions and processes that actually occur as the learner works. At the process level, the goal of the jigsaw task is communicative because, as learners work, they are exchanging information by using language to construct meanings. It is unlikely that they are attempting to produce repetitions and signals indicating lack of comprehension simply for the sake of language learning. During the task, the learner uses language for the sake of communication. Table 8-8 summarizes how the activity and task goals can (or cannot) be used to investigate second language learning tasks through the two methods of research treated in this chapter.

Table 8-8. Using Activity- and Task-Level Goals in the Investigation of Second Language Tasks

	Type of investigation	
Level	Analysis of authenticity	Empirical analysis of language
Task as work plan (activity goal)	Cannot be used because activity goal is pedagogical	Is required to guide discourse analysis by specifying intended benefits of the task
Task in process (task goal)	Is required for authenticity analysis because of focus on successful communication	Provides inadequate guidance for empirical language analysis because goal can be communicative

Conclusion

The two approaches to the investigation of second language tasks—
authenticity analysis and empirical language analysis—can lead to a better
understanding of the authenticity of CALL tasks and the quality of the
language they produce for second language development. Studies that have
used empirical analysis to probe the quality of various types of classroom
tasks have led researchers to draw some generalizations about task characteristics (Pica et al., 1993). However, applying these generalizations, which
are based on face-to-face oral tasks, requires the investigation of a range of
other tasks, including CALL tasks. In such research, empirical discourse
analysis can consist of a neutral description of the learner's input, output,
and interaction during the task; however, a more efficient and revealing
analysis would involve setting a pedagogical activity goal beforehand to
guide the analysis of the language.

CALL tasks should also be analyzed from the perspective of authenticity. Because second language tasks are designed to provide practice with
language similar to that found outside the classroom, authenticity analysis
can reveal important information about the quality of the classroom task.
The task goal is the most salient feature for defining a task as communicative; however, the degree of task authenticity depends on more than the
goal. A classroom task should be compared with an out-of-class speech
event through an analysis of multiple relevant task features. I have illustrated
how the features of the task frame would be used for this purpose; a
complete set of context features and other examples of analysis are laid out
elsewhere (Chapelle, 1997, in press). Through authenticity analysis and
empirical text analysis, future research should lead to a better understanding of the value of CALL tasks for second language development.

Chapter 9

Classroom Practice: Communicative Skill-Building Tasks in CALL Environments

Deborah Healey

Current language teaching methodology focuses on getting learners to communicate in the target language and, as discussed in chapter 8, emphasizes the importance of authentic language tasks. However, communication does not occur in a vocabulary and grammar vacuum, and communication generally improves with some practice in listening, speaking, reading, and writing on the part of the learner.

This chapter offers teachers ways to incorporate technology in communicative skill-building activities. The examples of authentic tasks addressed with specific types of software show some of the many possibilities for employing technology effectively in the classroom. The point is neither to use technology for its own sake nor to practice skills for their own sake, but to keep the focus on the communicative goal—and to achieve it in a variety of ways.

A typical language program offers work in reading, writing, listening, speaking, grammar, and vocabulary. Even when the curriculum is not skills based, teachers often cover specific points related to writing academic essays, taking notes from lectures, improving reading speed and comprehension, and performing similar tasks. Certainly, no communication can occur if learners have no vocabulary to work with. Underlying the discussion in this chapter is the assumption that teachers want to employ a variety of methods to introduce language skills and offer learners a choice in how they practice. Wherever possible, teachers should set frameworks for learning so that learners who work well by starting with language rules or guidelines and trying to apply them can do so while those who prefer to start with language data and generate their own rules have that option.

The information in this chapter overlaps to a certain extent with that in chapter 10, which explains where to find electronic support for authentic tasks in content areas. The difference in perspective, however, will be quite valuable for teachers.

Teaching Reading Skills With Technology

Reading skills fall into two basic categories: skills that help learners find information from a reading and those that help learners enjoy reading. These categories are not mutually exclusive, as learners who enjoy reading often have skills that help them find information more easily, and vice versa. As a result, some of the subskills below are assigned rather arbitrarily to one category or the other.

The skill of finding information includes the following subskills:

- skimming
- scanning
- recognizing topic sentences and supporting details
- predicting what will come next
- recognizing transition markers
- reading quickly
- evaluating the validity of a source

Computers can help in all these areas, though some types of software lend themselves better to authentic and communicative tasks than others do.

Simulations

Students can use a simulation to work on a number of these subskills. SimCity (1995) is one software package that can provide learners with opportunities to build their reading skills. Students working as a class or in a small group each take a role within the simulation, such as police chief, city planner, or mayor. The software asks players to make the decisions necessary to run a city and gives them information in a variety of categories. The task is to create a city that survives and prospers. Students need to skim the on-screen information quickly to find facts relevant to their role. Because the simulation imposes time limits, quick, accurate reading is essential.

A simulation that uses longer readings helps students work on scanning to decide whether a specific reading covers a topic they need to know about—and gives practice with prediction. Learners need to recognize topic sentences and supporting details if part of their task is to justify, either orally or in writing, the decisions they make. If students work in small groups, the groups can compare their results when the time is up, explaining their basic decisions and their results to the whole class. Extensive material to read, a time limit, and some element of competition can motivate students to read faster and more efficiently, and the right technology can help.

Speed-Reading Software

Learners who believe that the practice they are doing meets a need they have are also engaged in an authentic task. The real-world task that it emulates may be somewhat different, but the learners' motivation will be high. One example of such practice is speed reading. University-bound students are often highly engaged when using speed-reading software, as they see an immediate or imminent need for that skill. The software makes the logistics easier, computing reading speed and turning pages at a pace set by the student much more smoothly than the combination of a stopwatch and a book can.

Students should help set their own goals for speed reading based on what they feel they need to and can accomplish. By the same token, students who do not feel a need to read much will likely see speed reading assignments as arbitrary and unnecessary; simulations may motivate such learners more effectively.

The World Wide Web

Another approach to reading skills is to use the World Wide Web. Teachers can give a group of students a list of Web sites related to a specific topic and the task of gathering information about that topic. Each person can quickly scan a different site and report the main idea and a few significant details back to the group, as in a communicative information-gap activity. If the learners themselves generate the topics and the questions they are researching, the task becomes both appealing and authentic.

Having students use a Web search engine offers additional possibilities (see chapter 7 and Appendix C). In that case, students can look at the brief summary of each site generated by the search engine and predict whether or not the site is likely to be useful. Search engines are notorious for returning results that often have only the most marginal relationship to what learners really want to find out from the Web. For learners who are engaged in workplace-related or academic Web work, finding reliable information on the Internet is a real-life task.

Hypermedia

To enjoy reading, learners need to know about

- invoking background knowledge
- asking themselves questions while reading
- finding similarities and differences in their own experience
- applying information to a wider context

These subskills lend themselves to the use of software built around specific, preferably learner-selected, readings. Hypermedia—text, graphics, sound, video, or a combination, with links among them that let learners jump from one medium to another and from one topic to a related one—allows the teacher to bring out learners' background knowledge of a topic. An element that is unfamiliar as text may be recognizable to the learner as a graphic or in music. Clicking the mouse on the audio symbol in a Microsoft® Book-shelf® 95 (1995) entry pronounces the name of the entry, and users can view an explanatory animation. In other entries, a video or sound file may be played. A click on a related hyperlinked term within the text, such as comet, links to other articles in the CD-ROM's seven resource books.

In hypertext, links to related topics can help learners see how reading material applies to a wider context. Questions that pop up in the midst of a reading, such as those provided in HyperStory (May, 1993), help weak readers focus on ideas that are important to the progression of the text and model good reading behavior. Pop-up questions also remind readers to think about similarities or differences in their own experience in order to personalize what they are reading, and the questions prompt learners to generalize from the specific reading to a wider context.

Software for Extensive Reading

Nothing improves reading and reading enjoyment like extensive reading. Software that encourages learners to reread a text helps them achieve the goal of spending more time reading, even if what they are doing does not appear to be directed toward a specific reading-related skill. For example, in whole-text deletion software like Storyboard (Jones, 1990; see Figure 9-1) and Eclipse (Higgins, 1995), every letter in the text is replaced by a dot, and students guess words to fill in the text. Learners can turn these exercises into games for pairs or groups by adding a competitive element.

The learning comes not so much from guessing as from repeatedly reading the text in order to fill in the gaps left after the learners have inserted the obvious words. In group tasks such as simulations, members of the group push each other to be sure they understand what they are explaining, generally encouraging repeated reading.

Teaching Writing Skills With Technology

Just as reading is improved by reading, writing is best improved by writing. Teachers are constantly looking for ways to motivate writers to reach inside themselves, connect to what they are writing, and touch their audience; in other words, to make writing a communicative and authentic task. Teachers are also always trying to improve writers' ability to communicate with their

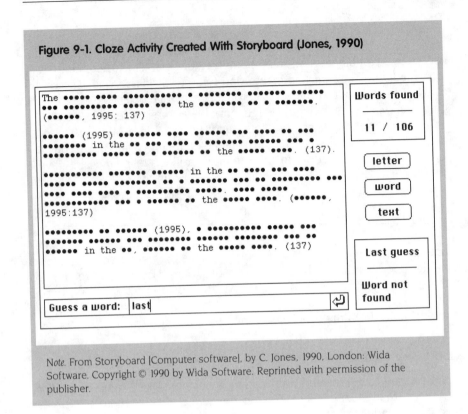

Figure 9-1. Cloze Activity Created With Storyboard (Jones, 1990)

Note. From Storyboard [Computer software], by C. Jones, 1990, London: Wida Software. Copyright © 1990 by Wida Software. Reprinted with permission of the publisher.

readers, including having a sense of audience and writing to the expectations of that audience, using peer review effectively, and revising and editing as needed rather than assuming that the first draft is all they need to worry about. Technology can help in many ways to achieve these goals.

Increasing Motivation

Learners who are struggling to find a voice in a second language (and perhaps don't see the point in going through the process anyway) find writing even more difficult. Teachers have attempted to motivate writers by creating authentic tasks that give learners a reason to endure the struggle of writing. Teachers can motivate learners to write by

- creating a reason for writing in the target language
- broadening the audience base

One of the great benefits of having students write e-mail to a partner (keypal) is that even students in EFL settings can see the point in writing in the target language if it is the only language they can use to communicate with the keypal. Doing an interesting group project with someone in another town or halfway around the world is a reason both to write and to use the target language.

Similarly, broadening the audience base can enhance students' motivation to take the time to write and rewrite. Class projects can be put in a public space, such as a newsletter distributed in the library or published on the World Wide Web. Also on the Internet, students can participate in mailing lists or newsgroups, many of which have an audience of thousands. Even posting a message to a class newsgroup gives the sense of an audience larger than one consisting only of the teacher. Most people are quite motivated at the thought of their work being read publicly.

Improving Communication

Writing isn't solely a matter of feeling motivated. Communication requires at least a second person who understands what the writer is trying to say. Better communication can be achieved in several ways:

- prewriting
- establishing and visualizing the audience
- writing to expectations, particularly academic and business expectations
- using peer review
- revising
- editing

Most prewriting programs explicitly encourage the user to describe the anticipated audience. With a sense of audience, the learner can work on writing to the expectations of that audience to enhance communication. Software such as Writer's Assistant (1996) helps learners practice academic and business writing. Also, teachers can have students look up information about specific writing skills at interactive Internet sites such as Purdue University's *Online Writing Lab* (http://owl.english.purdue.edu/; see Figure 9-2). Some on-line labs, in fact, offer e-mail interaction; learners write in with their questions about grammar and rhetoric, and someone at the other end responds. Human interaction via writing makes this exchange an authentic task.

Simulations can help teachers create writing tasks that are similar to real-world ones. Students in a business simulation might create charts and graphs, then explain the information in the chart in writing as they would for an actual business report. They might use presentation software, such as Microsoft PowerPoint® 97 (1996), to create an on-computer presentation with a related handout from the outline. Students who are giving a talk to a large group, especially as part of a business simulation, may pay a bit more

Figure 9-2. *Resources for Writers* in Purdue University's *Online Writing Lab* (1997)

Resources for Writers

OWL Handouts:
An Outline of all the Documents

This site lists over 120 handouts available on the following major categories, many of which are subdivided. So be sure to browse around. We also have a summary of these categories.

General Writing Concerns

Writing Research Papers & Citing Sources

Writing in the Job Search

Provessional Writing

English as a Second Language

Parts of Speech

Sentence Construction

Punctuation

Spelling

Purdue Writing Lab Information

Note. From *Online Writing Lab: Resources for Writers,* 1997, Purdue University, http://owl.english.purdue.edu/writers/introduction.html. Copyright © 1997 by Online Writing Lab. Reprinted with permission.

attention to form on their overhead projector transparencies than they would if they were writing only for the teacher. (See chapter 25 for more information on student presentations.)

Teachers using the process approach to writing often make extensive use of peer reviewing. One problem with peer review is that it can be very intense and personal and, therefore, difficult to get students to do well. When both the writer and the reviewer are anonymous, as is possible with some collaborative writing software, such as LiveWriter (1990), Dialectical Notebook (1996), and Daedalus® Integrated Writing Environment (1997), the reviewer can feel freer to ask questions and give a critical response. Internet Relay Chat (IRC, or Chat), although it can seem like a free-for-all in writing (as discussed in chapter 2), also provides a space for anonymous comments and real-time written communication between writers and readers.

Writing comments in the margin is a perennial activity of writing teachers. Unfortunately, margins are rarely big enough for comments of any depth. When writing comes to the teacher electronically, however, having a more extensive dialogue with the learner is easier. Exchanging writing on diskette can also have considerable advantages, as some word-processing programs have the electronic equivalent of stick-on notes—with the benefit that the note can expand in size to fit the length of the comment or even be an audio recording (see Figure 9-3). One advantage of using this type of software is that electronic commenting is increasingly a feature of corporate communication, in which more than one person goes through a report or other document before it is submitted. Thus students are learning a useful skill as they participate in the writing process.

Other real-world tools for writing are on-line dictionaries, thesauruses, and style and grammar checkers. These widely available tools wait in the background for the writer to invoke them as needed—not just in the language classroom. The ability to use such tools is a real-world skill.

Figure 9-3. Voice Annotation in a Text Document

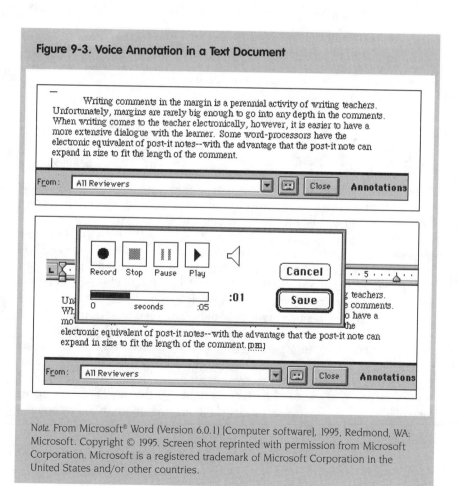

Note. From Microsoft® Word (Version 6.0.1) [Computer software], 1995, Redmond, WA: Microsoft. Copyright © 1995. Screen shot reprinted with permission from Microsoft Corporation. Microsoft is a registered trademark of Microsoft Corporation in the United States and/or other countries.

Teaching Listening Skills With Technology

CALL software has incorporated listening and speaking practice relatively recently but with great enthusiasm. New multimedia products on CD-ROM incorporate extensive graphics, audio, and sometimes digitized video (digitized audio and video files are generally very large). Because a great deal of face-to-face communication is nonverbal, seeing while listening can be very helpful in preparing learners for encounters with real (i.e., actual, not virtual) native speakers.

The skills learners need in listening include many of those needed in reading:

- invoking background knowledge
- asking themselves questions while listening
- finding similarities and differences in their own experience
- applying information to a wider context

and

- asking clarifying questions of a speaker
- interpreting phrasing, intonation, and body language
- recognizing important ideas
- noting transitions
- understanding the speaker's attitude toward what is being said

There are two basic styles of computer-generated speech. In *synthesized speech*, which is the easiest way for programmers to incorporate many different spoken words, phrases, and dialogues, the computer scans typed text and interprets it according to a set of fixed rules. Unfortunately, computers don't imitate a human voice very well, much less figure out how to pronounce words in English according to their spelling. If the teacher puts in phonetic rather than actual English spelling, the machine does better. Still, it's hard to mistake synthesized speech for human—and nearly impossible to interpret phrasing and intonation in synthesized speech.

Digitized speech is of the same quality as recorded speech; in a way, that's exactly what it is. As in a tape recording, if the software does not have a specific word or phrase in digitized form somewhere on disk, it can't produce that word or phrase. As a result, programs that use digitized speech are more comprehensible but less flexible. All the major producers of language teaching software have opted for the more natural-sounding digitized speech.

The Internet

One of the most authentic computer-aided tasks for listening comes from the Internet. Voice of America (http://www.voa.gov/) allows users to hear its broadcasts on the Internet using RealPlayer™ (1998), add-on software to Web browsers like Netscape Navigator® (1997) and Microsoft Internet Explorer (1998). Other sites on the Internet also offer RealPlayer files containing information in spoken form. Teachers can ask students to listen to the news, tell their classmates what they heard, and perhaps discuss some of the stories. Learners can look for background information electronically as well. The advantage of digitized news over radio or television news is that listeners can save it (and find it again) easily for later playback. A variation on this theme is in LiveChat (1997) with audio, in which learners and speakers are on-line simultaneously. With this software users can ask clarifying questions, although these are usually typed rather than spoken.

Listening can have a visual element with digitized video. Unfortunately, the quality is not as good as that on a videotape, and the image size is far smaller. Movie sites on the Internet offer an interesting way to use digitized video, as some producers put digitized video clips of previews of their current movies on those sites (see *Internet Movie Database*, http://us.imdb.com/). Because the files are large, a fast connection is essential to use digitized video successfully on the Internet. Teachers can ask students to watch a preview, tell the class what they saw, transcribe the dialogue, and watch the full-length movie, looking for the preview they saw. Because the clips are from current movies, the real-world connection is very strong.

Software for Listening Practice

CDictation (Herren, 1995) is a program that helps teachers create dictations with audio CDs. Learners who like music and whose listening skills need improvement often get quite excited about using class time for such an enjoyable activity. The teacher sets up one or more tracks on an audio CD by marking logical breaks and typing in the lyrics that go along with those tracks. Students can bring in CDs and lyrics for songs they want to practice with and can either set up an exercise themselves or ask the teacher to do it for them. A great deal of focused listening goes on when learners are motivated to understand.

Songs are not the only incentive for focused listening. Unlike many listening practice programs, HyperACE Advanced (1996) demands some thought on the part of the learner. Students are expected not only to recall information given orally but also to manipulate that information in some way in order to select the correct answer. The situations and questions are similar to those students encounter in academic classes. When learners recognize them as such, this type of practice becomes an authentic activity.

For example, students may be asked to select which of three diagrams best represents a specific statement, such as "Which of these three figures has dots on the top and right side?" (see Figure 9-4). To choose the correct answer, students need to understand the whole statement, not just pick out a few words in an otherwise unintelligible stream of speech.

A different approach to using technology to enhance listening and note-taking skills has been developed by Project Connect. This grant-funded project uses Aspects (1994), a collaborative writing software program, to help learners see how to take notes from a lecture. Students with weak listening and note-taking skills are paired with skilled note-takers in a lecture. During the lecture, the weaker students can see the note-taker's computer screen on their own and watch as that person takes notes. They can begin to take their own notes, ask a question in the question window, or show the note-taker their own notes as the lecture continues. This software helps learners understand the thought process that goes on while skilled note-takers listen to a lecture. At the same time, by watching what learners do as they take lecture notes, teachers learn about students' weaknesses in listening comprehension and can plan accordingly. Unlike most of the other approaches and software mentioned above, this software creates a truly interactive listening environment.

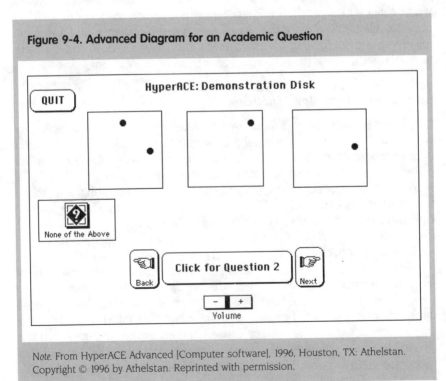

Figure 9-4. Advanced Diagram for an Academic Question

Note. From HyperACE Advanced [Computer software], 1996, Houston, TX: Athelstan. Copyright © 1996 by Athelstan. Reprinted with permission.

Teaching Speaking Skills With Technology

Speech Recognition

One of the newest enhancements in commercial software for language teaching is *speech recognition*, the ability of a machine to process spoken input and respond. This technology does not approach the level of human-computer oral interaction seen in science fiction movies and television shows—computers are a long way from being able to understand natural, rapid speech on an unexpected topic. However, the technology has reached the point at which the computer can judge a student's oral response to a multiple-choice question, as in programs such as Triple Play Plus! English (1995), Dynamic English (1997), and See It! Hear It! Say It! (1996). Taking another tack, Practice Makes Perfect French (1994) has a meter (similar to a speedometer in appearance) that indicates to learners where their speech falls on a continuum from "tourist" to "native."

Increasingly, teachers will see educational applications for software that can transcribe oral input. Such programs are reasonably good within restricted domains, such as business news reports. When this technology filters down to education, teachers can expect to see open-ended dialogues and more realistic simulations, although computer responses will probably include much recourse to such phrases as "Excuse me, I don't understand" or noncommittal comments.

Features likely to be available in the future, however, do not help today's teachers address most of the basic subskills in effective speaking:

- invoking background knowledge
- choosing an appropriate register
- signaling a turn
- using body language appropriately
- responding to the listener or audience
- selecting the most effective grammar and vocabulary for the communication task
- adjusting the pace and register
- self-correcting and focusing on form as needed

As computers become still more powerful and fully video capable, students will be able to practice some of these subskills with technological assistance.

Simulations

What software can do well at present is set up an environment that encourages learners to speak. Simulations such as Where in the World Is

Carmen Sandiego? (1996) and Decisions, Decisions (1996) help teachers create a microworld in which students can operate in the target language. The simulated world can take on a life of its own, making communication within that context feel authentic. Simulations often require reading, note-taking, writing, and group discussion, making simulations a versatile tool in the language classroom. (See Crookall & Oxford, 1990, on using simulations for oral proficiency practice, both on and off the computer.)

Another angle to take is to have students create their own simulations and role plays. In such tasks, students communicate with each other as they decide what the simulations should look like as well as during the simulation itself. One application that focuses on dialogue writing is Hollywood High (1996; see Figure 9-5). In this software, students receive raw material in the form of sets and stock characters to choose from and decide what the characters will say and do, typing in the dialogue. The program then animates the characters and synthesizes their speech based on the dialogue. The synthesized speech is robotic-sounding and not good as a model for speaking, so the process of creating the script is the most useful aspect

Figure 9-5. Script and Scene From Hollywood High (1996)

MATT: Hi. Can I come in?
(Matt points) Do you play drums? *(Matt with his arms crossed)*
JENNY: *(Jenny points)* Are you talking to me? *(Jenny with her hands on her hips) (Jenny faces left)* or to her? *(Jenny points)*
LILLY: Me?

Note. From Hollywood High [Computer software], 1996, Emeryville, CA: Theatrix Interactive. Copyright © 1996 by Theatrix Interactive. Reprinted with permission of Theatrix (SWMC).

of the program. Learners can certainly also use a word-processing program or even pen and paper to write scripts, but the animation in Hollywood High is quite engaging.

Pair or Small-Group Tasks

Students can also be given tasks to accomplish in pairs or small groups while working on any kind of computer software. Teachers should make sure that the tasks require more than just giving affirmative or negative responses and pointing at the screen. Collaborative writing, gap filling, whole-text reconstruction, and some competitive word games lend themselves to group interaction. Arcade-style games generally do not work well in group mode.

Video

In the noncomputer realm of educational technology, video is an important tool in speaking improvement. When students can see themselves on videotape, spotting their own weaknesses is much easier. Watching video-tapes recorded at different points during a semester or term gives learners a sense of progress, which is very helpful in language learning. Students who will make presentations in the scientific, business, or academic realm need to know how to look as well as sound good in a presentation, and video offers them a full picture of what they do well and what they need to improve.

Digitized (computer-based) video is still too raw for effective use in more than a very short clip. The picture is quite small, often only 2 in. by 2 in. or 4 in. by 4 in., and may be jerky and unclear, especially if blown up to a larger size. Still, digitized video holds promise for the future: Because presentation software allows the insertion of video clips, a teacher could view and annotate a digitized video clip, and students could record portions of a presentation (see chapter 25).

Pronunciation Software

Although fluency is the first goal of most learners, accuracy also plays an important role in speaking competence. Pronunciation is one of the few areas in language learning in which sheer repetition can be helpful, and it is one area in which the ability of the computer to repeat as often as the learner desires is a great asset. I have taught pronunciation to learners with fossilized errors and learned a language (Chinese) whose phonemic distinctions I had a hard time hearing and reproducing. As a teacher, I was unable to repeat a phoneme, word, or phrase as often as my students wanted and maintain my sanity. As a learner, I wanted far more repetition than the teacher was able to provide and maintain his sanity, along with the sanity of other students who could hear and repeat the sounds better than I. I would have happily worked with a computer program that repeated endlessly and identically to meet my needs. The authenticity of the task, in this case, is in the ear of the learner.

Besides infinite patience, a computer can bring multiple modes of displaying information to the learner. Most pronunciation software, such as Accent Lab (1995), TEAM: Technology-Enhanced Accent Management Program (Schwartz, 1995), and VideoVoice (1995), incorporates some types of waveforms (see Figure 9-6), and some also offers formant diagrams to translate sound into graphic representations. In addition, some software, such as ELLIS Master Pronunciation (1994), includes video clips of a speaker's mouth in motion during pronunciation of words or sounds (Figure 9-7). The video allows the learner to stare far longer and more directly than is comfortable with a human interlocutor. A few programs, such as VideoVoice and SpeechViewer III (1996), let learners practice in a wide variety of ways. Teachers should keep in mind that, in general, the more features the software offers, the more expensive it is.

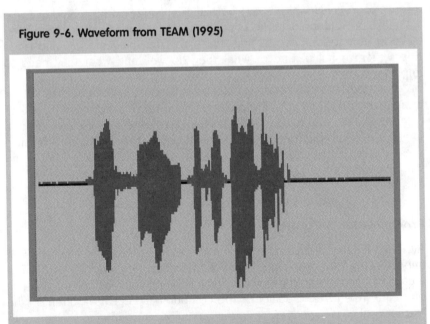

Figure 9-6. Waveform from TEAM (1995)

Note. From TEAM: Technology-Enhanced Accent Management Program (Version KMA.CSU) [Computer software], by A. H. Schwartz, 1995, Cleveland, OH: Cleveland State University. Copyright © 1995 by A. H. Schwartz. Reprinted with permission of the author.

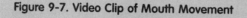

Figure 9-7. Video Clip of Mouth Movement

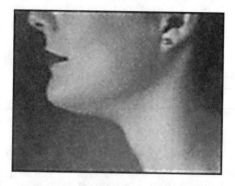

Note. From ELLIS Master Pronunciation [Computer software], 1994, American Fork, UT: CALI. Copyright © 1994 by CALI. Reprinted with permission.

Teaching Grammar With Technology

Grammar and vocabulary practice are the two areas many people think of first when CALL is mentioned. Discrete-point drill and practice have their place, particularly with learners who prefer to go from rules to data rather than vice versa. If nothing else, drill and practice give some learners a sense of security about getting answers right (much as some learners enjoy doing workbook drills). Still, far more than just workbook-style drill is possible on the computer, and far more is required to learn some of the grammar subskills needed for effective communication. These grammar subskills include

- attention to form as well as fluency
- grammar consciousness
- attention to form as used by others
- attention to salient features in grammar that affect meaning
- self-correction

On-Line Writing

In terms of authentic tasks, the best approach to learning grammar may be on-line writing with e-mail, multiuser object-oriented domains (MOOs), and IRC. If learners are trying to do a joint project and the grammar of one or more of the partners causes a miscommunication, the other partner(s) will encourage attention to grammatical detail, usually by requesting clarification. A MOO like *schMOOze University* (Falsetti, n.d., http://schmooze.hunter.cuny.edu:8888/; see chapter 22) and chat rooms function in real time, which means that readers can ask for clarification and negotiate meaning immediately. Just because this is possible does not mean that it happens, however; students are more likely to negotiate if teachers encourage them to do so. When a task requires a clear sense of the facts—who, what, where, when, and why, as in writing a city guide that includes historical details—then grammar will follow.

Software With a Narrow Scope

The very rigidity of the computer can be another incentive to pay attention to form. In a conversation simulation like Eliza (Bender, 1989), the computer "reads" what the learner has typed in and responds according to specific key words and structures. If the student's grammar is inaccurate, the computer's response will likely be unsatisfactory or nonsensical. The human in this case must conform to the machine's expectations about grammar in order to make a conversation work.

Grammar or style checkers (available in many languages besides English) are similarly unable to make sense of what has been written. Rather, they operate by applying relatively rigid rules of grammar and rhetoric (such as a frequent use of the verb *be*) and bringing inconsistencies to the attention of the writer. Although not notably accurate in flagging typical ESL grammatical problems, such software does a good job of raising learners' consciousness.

Hypertext

A different way of approaching grammar on the computer is through hypertext. Learners can read an electronic text until the point at which they do not understand, then request grammar help. In a program such as Language Now! (1996; see Figure 9-8), learners open a window to see a gloss of a certain element in the reading—a sentence, phrase, or word—in terms of the grammatical structures used. This technique might be thought of as "just-in-time" grammar; students learn what they need to know only when they request it. Such software tends not to include elaborate grammar explanations, however, so teachers may want to direct students who want more information to other sources.

Concordancing Software

Another learner-centered approach is data-driven learning, in which learners who have a question about how language works receive data to look at

Figure 9-8. Grammar Window in Language Now! (1996)

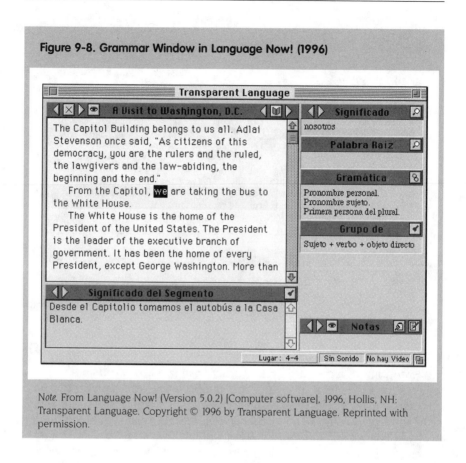

Note. From Language Now! (Version 5.0.2) [Computer software], 1996, Hollis, NH: Transparent Language. Copyright © 1996 by Transparent Language. Reprinted with permission.

and draw their own conclusions from. For example, the difference between *by* and *for*—a question that often arises among Spanish speakers—can be difficult to turn into a rule. Instead, a concordancer searches its large text database, finds all the occurrences of *by* and *for*, and presents them to the learner (see Figure 9-9). Learners can scan the examples, clicking the mouse on a specific sentence as needed to see the paragraph in which it occurred. As the learners look through the examples, they start to draw their own conclusions about the use of a specific word or structure. The process works better if the teacher has made specific suggestions on formulating rules about typical contexts. Concordancers, such as MicroConcord (Scott, 1994), MonoConc (Barlow, 1996), and Conc (Thomson, 1991), allow users to select the text file to search, which lets learners see how words are used in different ways in different styles of writing or (with speech transcripts) speaking. Using a concordancer works best with advanced learners who can understand the sentences presented to them well enough to see the differences in meaning.

Figure 9-9. Concordance of the Word *for* in Conc (Thomson, 1991)

```
non-technical knowledge. This  follows a line of thought proposed by Ellul
for this curious child was very  fond of pretending to be two people. 'But it's
    you might have to adjust the  fonts a bit. Version 1.70 has only minor bug
      they have access to a teacher  for advice, but where the teacher does not
         students become teachers  for each other by sharing their separate
  :omplete shift of responsibility  for learning to the learner. Teachers and
    arise. The concept of authority,  for example, is culturally defined. This holds
     the workforce and responsible  for themselves may resist a completely
   and setting their own standards  for evaluation. Field dependent people, like
      risks with language; looking  for and remembering patterns in language
    work in a self-directed setting  for adult language learners. These are the ne
```

Note. From Conc: Concordance Generating Program (Version 1.70) [Computer software], by J. Thomson, 1991, Dallas, TX: Summer Institute of Linguistics. Copyright © 1991 by Summer Institute of Linguistics. Reprinted with permission of the author and publisher.

Even without a concordancer, learners can see how words are used by taking advantage of the "find" function in most word processors and in Web browsers, such as Netscape Navigator (1997). Using this procedure is not nearly as tidy as using a concordancer. Still, learners can see the difference in usage by selecting different types of writing in which to search for target structures. Searching for a structure in a long article in an encyclopedia, for example, gives different results than searching in a long, rambling, colloquial narrative on a Web page does. Concordancing is also a way for learners to see how they have used a target structure in their own writing and compare their usage with what they have found elsewhere.

Vocabulary Teaching With Technology

In sheer number, vocabulary practice programs are probably the largest category of language learning software. Learning vocabulary takes much practice, and students generally have to progress from recognition to use in a structured context to active, creative use. Some of the subskills for vocabulary learning are

- attention to form rather than just fluency
- self-correction
- awareness of usage when reading and listening

- knowledge of grammatical aspects
- awareness of register
- focus on recognizing and trying to use new vocabulary

At the recognition level, well-designed software can help learners fit a word into a semantic category. Programs that incorporate graphics and sound can be especially helpful in creating multiple connections to the new word. As with grammar software, having students work in pairs and small groups encourages more time on task and more communication.

Vocabulary work can also be done on a need-to-know basis. With an electronic dictionary, such as the Longman Multimedia Dictionary (1996), that can run in the background and be consulted as needed, or with an on-line dictionary, like *The Newbury House Online Dictionary* (http://nhd .heinle.com/), learners have access to definitions and often graphics, sound, video, and sample sentences for unfamiliar words they come across while perusing a CD-ROM-based encyclopedia or a Web page. Having a dictionary a keystroke away means that readers do not have to completely break their train of thought by going to get a paper dictionary and thumbing through to find the word in question—a process that may take so long that readers forget what they were looking for. An on-line thesaurus helps build vocabulary while learners are writing, especially if the thesaurus also gives some definitions for the words. Like an on-line dictionary, an on-line thesaurus is easier to use than its paper counterpart and is therefore more likely to be used.

Hypertext programs also generally have vocabulary help that users can link to while going through the text. Depending on the author, learners may get far more than just a definition: graphics, sound, and video clips may also be available to elucidate a concept, as in CD-ROM-based encyclopedias. Software like VersaText (Woodbury & Smith, 1990) and NewReader (McVicker, 1997) allows teachers to add their own glosses, customizing the definitions to their students. The readings included in Language Now! (1996), described in the grammar section, have extensive vocabulary glosses as well as direct translations into selected languages. All these types of software give the learner control over vocabulary study—the learner chooses which words to look up, when to do it, and how long to spend on it.

Conclusion

Computers are often thought of as automated taskmasters, offering practice in specific skill areas via drills. This type of practice is possible for skill-area work and is useful at some stages of language learning. Drills are authentic tasks when learners find them useful and look for that type of practice, as in learning vocabulary, improving pronunciation, or coming up with an irregular past form without having to think about it. Beginning learners are well aware of how utterly unable to communicate they are without vocabulary, for example, and will seek a variety of ways to build their repertoire. Once learners have passed the stage of actively seeking drills because they feel they need them, teachers should be ready to move on to different types of activities.

Collaboration between learners, whether they are sitting next to each other in chairs or linked electronically, sets a communicative stage for learning. Computers can make it easier for learners to interact with language and with each other, but the teacher as task setter has a critical role. The colors, bells, and whistles of multimedia software can draw in both adults and children, but teachers cannot take for granted that learners will benefit linguistically from one-on-one interaction with software. Tasks that require creative language use and have a connection to learners' real-world needs and desires are essential. Adult learners should take part in the task-setting process, helping the teacher find activities that are appropriate for them as individuals and as language learners.

Technology alone does not create language learning any more than dropping a learner into the middle of a large library does. Teachers who know how to exploit computer resources can use them to create authentic tasks that vary in level and learning style and that demand attention to form as well as to content. With better resources available, the learner's demanding job of internalizing the language becomes easier.

Chapter 10

Classroom Practice: Content-Area Tasks in CALL Environments

Elizabeth Hanson-Smith

One of the most significant contributions that technology can make to the teaching and learning of language resides in its power to store, organize, and search vast quantities of data. Data management capability lies behind the power of video arcade games, adventure simulations, and the flow of information around the globe on the Internet.

Unfortunately, what the computer is least able to do is respond to and interact with humans in natural language. However, as computer-using teachers have become more savvy and more numerous, the pedagogy of instructional technology has moved away from simple drill-and-respond tasks to more authentic tasks that use the computer's data management power and that are motivating enough to fully engage learners and so enhance their opportunity to master the language structures and content they need. Brinton, Snow, and Wesche (1989), Chamot and O'Malley (1989), and Nunan (1989a), among many others, have emphasized that a curriculum constructed around tasks rather than just around drills and exercises can provide significant, motivating practice. Once teachers have decided on the kinds of tasks appropriate to a content area (perhaps using one of the models suggested in chapter 8 to determine authenticity), they may well find content-based software that creates or shapes relevant tasks to allow learners to practice language skills in an environment safe from misunderstandings or social ridicule.

This chapter describes types of software that support authentic tasks and activities for the language learner at a wide variety of levels in all content areas. The simulations, adventure games, and content-based Internet searches facilitated by computers can promote in students an intensity of purpose that well deserves the term *virtual reality*.

Authentic tasks are well suited to content-based teaching and learning rather than to the study of language itself. Cantoni-Harvey (1987), Snow, Met, and Genessee (1989), and more recently Short (1991, 1994) have described fairly completely how students can acquire collocations and related vocabulary items by studying them not in isolation but with the purpose of mastering an area of learning that the students are already interested in or have some expertise with in their own language, such as business, geography, history, technology, literature, and art. For the younger student, sheltered English or specially designed academic instruction in English (SDAIE, as it is known in California) is an outgrowth of the belief that students learn best when the content of instruction is subject matter rather than the language itself, particularly when the student may be too young to have developed a strong sense of or interest in the fine points of grammar. At the most local level, students may perform authentic tasks related to the "content" of their own community: bus routes, movie schedules, supermarket ads in the newspaper, maps, demographics, and historical background. At the global level, the Internet provides the means to authentic, but still very safe, communicative tasks, both learner to learner and learner to native speakers from many different countries, both asynchronously (through e-mail and lists or bulletin boards) and synchronously, and either in real-time videoconferencing or at live chat sites (see chapters 3, 7, and 22). The content of such communications is often cultural differences and similarities or the sharing of a social science or science curriculum.

In a computer-assisted environment, complex tasks can be broken into small, safe, manageable stages while still providing a high level of interest and motivation; with the best software, the technology becomes a virtually invisible servant to the students' own goals. This chapter describes both the highest levels of activities and some of the more limited but still productive tasks that computer enhancement can provide.

Games for Language and Strategy

Drill-and-practice activities in a content area might be termed *authentic tasks*, as they are often the type of activity students are expected to perform in school subjects without reference to language teaching or learning functions. However, the concept of authentic task as a learning strategy is transforming the sciences and social sciences for native speakers, and mathematics and science teachers have become increasingly cognizant of the role of language in learning or understanding fully the higher level concepts of these subject areas. (See Kaufman & Brooks, 1996, for a fuller discussion of language and content area collaborations by professional organizations, such as the National Council of Mathematics.) Games that improve estimating abilities, deductive and inductive reasoning, and prediction strategies, such as those in the Thinkin' Things collections published by Edmark, meet many of the criteria for authentic tasks because they can become absorbing in and of themselves while imparting the language appropriate to certain kinds of reasoning. In the simulation from Thinkin' Things: Collection 3 (1995) shown in Figure 10-1, the student must trade items in the lower box to get those in the goal box. Conversations with animal characters around the world include a few common social expressions in each language, such as *ní hǎo* from Ping in China. Trades become increasingly complex as students succeed in the trading process.

In the area of language arts, teachers have long found that word games, such as Hangman (Winograd, 1985, for Macintosh® computers; versions are available for all platforms) or Hangman Plus (Winograd, 1991; this version can involve phrases rather than just words), and crossword puzzle software can help students practice vocabulary. A wide sampling of free or inexpensive computer language games used by language teachers is to be found on the CD-ROM TESOL/CELIA '96 (1996) and in CELIA *at La Trobe University: Computer Enhanced Language Instruction Archive* (Holliday, 1997a, http://chiron .latrobe.edu.au/www/education/celia/celia.html); see also the archives listed in Appendix D. Even more effective is to have small teams of students use the authoring or editing programs built into such games to generate puzzles

Figure 10-1. "Stocktopus" From Thinkin' Things Collection 3 (1995)

Note. From Thinkin' Things Collection 3 [Computer software], 1995, Redmond, WA: Edmark. Used by permission of Edmark © 1997.

for their peers (see chapter 25 for other ideas on authoring). If learning a vocabulary word requires six or seven exposures to it in context, then a task such as developing the clues for a crossword puzzle virtually guarantees sufficient contact with the words to learn them. The computer does all the detailed, nonlanguage work of figuring out where the boxes should go and which words will intersect. Language games can be used in content courses to help students practice definitions, collocations, part-to-whole relations, and so on—in the context of a particular discipline or field of study.

In using games as tasks for language practice, the teacher must be especially careful to give accurate directions for team use of the software and hardware. Although winning a game becomes a goal in itself, to learn as much language as possible from a game session, students should follow a set of lesson plans that includes time to share with other students what has been learned. Teachers should also indicate, as appropriate to the level of the students, the instructional value of the activity; adult students coming from a traditional educational background in another country might be puzzled by the use of games to learn language.

Simulations for the Social Sciences

Simulations can be a significant educational use of the computer's power to do calculations if teachers provide tasks that build language skills in the process. In simulations, the computer stores data and applies them when students make decisions about what to do next—for example, grow more rice or build more houses. Although simulations can be done with paper and pencil, technology-enhanced simulations include realistic color and sound, respond instantly to students' decisions in multiple ways, can suggest alternate strategies, and can be deeply absorbing.

For example, in SimCity (1995; discussed in chapter 9), the goal is to build an entire urban environment from scratch. A version for elementary schoolchildren, SimTown (1995), is perhaps more effective for low-level ESL learners, both youngsters and adults. In SimTown, the town can be constructed much faster, and the program features people (or animal characters) to dress up, a panel of experts (such as a town planner and an ecologist) to consult, and a newspaper to report on how the town is doing. In an adaptation conceived by Egbert (Hanson-Smith & Egbert, 1996), students can be put in groups and take on the roles of members of a town council (e.g., the editor of a newspaper, a geologist from an oil company, the leader of the Sierra Club), which will produce discussion about urban design and ecology. The data management features of the computer handle the results of the council's decisions, but it is up to the teacher to design careful lesson plans so that students will try out the various aspects of the software and learn appropriate language in the process. The task should be organized into small steps that the team of students can complete in a reasonably short time. Then, away from the computer, the teams can write up what they have done, develop maps for other students, and plan their next steps. Most simulations have a "save" or "pause" feature that allows the students to stop work and regroup. For the ambitious teacher, Maxis has developed a whole series of "Sim" CD-ROMs involving tasks ranging from building an ant farm to creating new species on a virtual planet; a CD-ROM containing demo versions is available from Maxis's Web site (http://www.maxis.com/).

For advanced students in the area of business and economics, simulations can extend the concept of the case study by providing enormous amounts of data with which to experiment as well as offering changes based on students' input in various areas. Capitalist Pig (1994) is one such simulation that is fairly easy for lower level adult students to run: Changes in the sales force, the number of workers in the mail room, and the number of managers, for example, each produce changes in profits and losses. The simulated business also responds to news flashes that appear regularly on screen (watch out for the stock market crash!). For much more advanced, older students, the more sophisticated Capitalism Plus (1995) provides futuristic or historical scenarios. Students plan production by using maps to locate raw materials and react to events such as riots, plagues, and technological breakthroughs. Also for the more advanced learner, quite a number of on-line services, such as America Online (see http://www.aol.com/), and search engines, such as Yahoo! (see http://www.yahoo.com/), have created portfolio trackers that allow users to follow a set of designated stocks. Each time the user goes on-line, the stock information is updated from the tickertape, thus creating the opportunity for students to learn about the workings of Wall Street and the news stories, economic factors, reports, and political scenarios that influence stock prices. Although the teacher must plan how best to use the data, students can simulate all the variables of the stock market without risking a penny.

The social sciences are particularly fruitful territory for curriculum-related simulations. For example, in a version of the classic simulation Oregon Trail (1991), called Wagon Train 1848 (1997), groups of students can each organize a covered wagon as part of a 19th-century wagon train to the West. They must decide how much to spend on oxen, provisions, and bullets to hunt game and then determine the best route to follow to the Pacific Ocean. An unusual feature of this software is that each computer station becomes a wagon in the train, and groups can communicate from wagon to wagon by e-mail over a local area network. Experts from the past, incorporated in the software based on real historical accounts, offer advice about routes to take and the decisions to be made.

Once the students have reached the West, they can try their hand at overcoming the difficult conditions that faced prairie farmers with the simulation, Go West! The Homesteader's Challenge (1997; see Figure 10-2). In this simulation, students must buy seed, plant and harvest crops, and deal with natural disasters, such as tornadoes and wildfires. Mathematics and decision-making skills are important. Local characters provide advice to the novice farmers. Steck-Vaughn/Edunetics' simulations were developed for native-speaking middle school students, but audio and text support make them adaptable to ESL students in, for example, a sheltered history course. The software shapes an authentic and absorbing set of tasks that demand hard choices as well as responses to environmental factors.

Another exciting history simulation is Sid Meier's Civilization II (1997), which provides scenarios from various historical eras, such as the days of the Roman Empire. Students can make diplomatic, political, and, if all else fails, military choices in an attempt to establish their own civilization while coming to understand historical processes.

Ingenuity Works' Crosscountry USA (1992) and Crosscountry Canada (1992), developed for the study of geography and the fundamentals of trade in elementary school, include maps and charts of products and the places

Figure 10-2. Scene From Go West! The Homesteader's Challenge (1997)

Note. From Go West! The Homesteader's Challenge [Computer software], 1997, Austin, TX: Steck-Vaughn/Edunetics. Copyright © 1997 by Steck-Vaughn Company. Reprinted with permission.

they are grown and manufactured. Students drive a truck across the country, pick up and deliver products, decide when to stop for rest and food, and follow the best route to arrive on schedule. A demo version of Crosscountry USA, suitable for use with students, is available from Ingenuity Works' Web site (http://www.vrsystems.com/).

As indicated in the thumbnail sketches of the programs above, simulation software gives students significant practice in higher order thinking skills, particularly those involving decision making in groups. However, for the most part it is entirely up to the teacher to write lesson plans that lead students through a successful exploration of the simulation and encourage them to practice the vocabulary specific to the content area and to the group decision-making process.

Tom Snyder Productions (TSP) is one of the few publishers that provide lesson plans for research-based decision-making activities. Although TSP's products were not developed specifically for ESL students, the visual and text support in the software allows advanced students to learn about a subject while employing critical thinking skills and acquiring the vocabulary of the content. The titles in Decisions, Decisions (1996; see also chapters 3, 4, 9, and 13), an excellent series of diskettes for high school students, focus on such historical issues as colonization, immigration, and revolutionary wars. For younger students, Choices, Choices (1994) features typical school and playground scenarios, such as a bully on the playground, in which students decide what to do. In another TSP product, Cultural Debates (1996; see Figure 10-3), students develop a position to take in a debate as they complete worksheets and watch the Mentawai people on video footage shot in the Indonesian rain forest. Students are encouraged to compare their own community with that of the rain forest dwellers.

Search and Research in the Sciences

Scientists were among the first professionals to realize the full potential of the computer in running "what-if" simulations, so it is easy to find software with which to explore chemical properties, wavelengths, subatomic particles, the behavior of light, and other phenomena, all without the danger of blowing up the lab. Advanced language learners at universities have little difficulty accessing such programs, as they are in relatively common use in academic departments. The programs mentioned below are mainly for Grades K–12 but are adaptable for adult learners. The best of these programs, although not developed specifically for ESL learners, have the multimedia support that makes them appropriate to a sheltered language context.

TSP, mentioned above, is a particularly good source of science materials. In Rain Forest Researchers (1996), an ecology program that uses footage

Figure 10-3. Screen From Cultural Debates (1996)

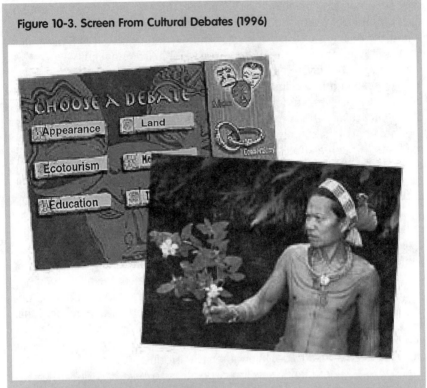

Note. From Cultural Debates [Computer software], 1996, Watertown, MA: Tom Snyder Productions. Copyright © 1996. Reprinted with permission from Tom Snyder Productions.

from the same region as Cultural Debates (1996; described above), each member of a student group at the computer has a different reference book and plays a different role on the scientific team—a kind of jigsaw learning. Students address research questions as they watch videos, analyze information, share results, and explore the use of biological resources.

Steck-Vaughn/Edunetics' science materials for Grades 4–8 contain large CD-ROM databases of video, photos, drawings, animations, and sounds. A presentation tool allows students to create their own multimedia presentations using art and text clipped from the software. Text resources and manipulatives accompany some of the CD-ROMs. Titles include Our Environment (1996; CD-ROMs plus a 14-book library, two audiotapes, bug-collecting bottles, and a tree-ring kit); Map Room (1996), in which students create and print their own maps; Violent Earth (1996; on volcanoes); and Light and Sound (1996; on physics). These packages could fully supplement a middle school curriculum or an English for science and technology course for older students. Again, although not created specifically for the ESL/EFL student, most of the programs present the option of having the computer read a text aloud, and most have a hypertext glossary (students point and click the mouse on a word for a definition or a link to an explanatory page), so they are adaptable to the needs of language learners.

In one particularly interesting Steck-Vaughn/Edunetics product, Message in a Fossil (1996; see Figure 10-4), young students become paleontologists and prepare presentations of their findings. Clicking the mouse on tools at a dig allows the students to unearth the bones of dinosaurs, which are then cleaned with a tiny brush and taken to the museum collection for identification. After comparing the find to other bones in the museum and reading about the habits of the creature, students create a diorama on screen by selecting elements appropriate to the setting and habitat and

Figure 10-4. Diorama From Message in a Fossil (1996)

Note. From Message in a Fossil [Computer software], 1996, Austin, TX: Steck-Vaughn/Edunetics. Copyright © 1996 by Steck-Vaughn Company. Reprinted with permission.

having the computer clothe the bones with flesh and skin until a tyrannosaurus rex or stegosaurus appears—and moves. Student can record their own voices describing the display as a presentation for others.

The Imagination Express series by Edmark, another producer of content-based CD-ROMs for middle schoolers, is a good way to launch research projects that may take students beyond the CD-ROMs and into the World Wide Web. The series combines the sciences, social sciences, and language arts in a whole language approach. Titles include Destination: Rain Forest (1995) and Destination: Ocean (1995). These CD-ROMs work well with ESL students because of audiovisual support: The computer can read all the texts aloud, and video and animation sequences explain key elements, so the software addresses multiple learning styles. The search features are easily accessed with tabs on the side of each page of information. On the opening screen (see Figure 10-5), a series of animal and human characters present creative writing ideas in the form of spoken story prompts. A click anywhere produces a new character with a new suggestion. After selecting one, students write their own stories by using a built-in word processor and follow links to reference pages to find facts and details on the rain forest habitat and its denizens. Students can also copy pictures of rain forest people, animals, and plants into a setting to illustrate the story and record

Figure 10-5. Suggestions for Writing From Destination: Rain Forest (1995)

Note. From Destination: Rain Forest (Imagination Express) [Computer software], 1995, Redmond, WA: Edmark. Used by permission of Edmark © 1997.

their own voices as part of the presentation. As a bonus, the CD-ROMs include an excellent video with tips to the teacher or parent on how to teach creative writing using the prompts and reference material.

Because of recent requirements for technology-related products in state textbook adoption codes, a number of school text publishers are entering the content software market. One of their strategies is to find existing software that relates to a particular content area, but some publishers have developed new CD-ROMs directly based on and supportive of the curriculum. In one such series of programs, Multimedia Literature, published by Macmillan/McGraw-Hill, highly motivating, technology-driven tasks have been devised based on a number of texts and stories in the upper elementary and middle school curriculum. The original text is enhanced by audiovisual support and apparatus that only the computer can provide, and the student's tasks replicate the behavior of scientists in the field. For instance, using the software Do Not Disturb (1996), which is based on the book of the same name (Facklam, 1989), the student enters a forest ranger's cabin and reads a note containing an assignment: Use a beeper and binoculars to track bears throughout several seasons. On exiting the cabin, the student chooses a season, activates the beeper to find the bear, and clicks on the binoculars. A video of the bear appears in a simulated binocular peephole, giving an almost startling realism to the observation task. In the boxes, students take notes using prompts that help them organize their observations. The notes taken during the field observation task then serve as the basis for other activities, such as typing what is known or predicted before reading a text, reading a short essay, examining a chart, and viewing other videos on screen. The student thus receives input in several different ways, using a variety of learning modes, and the text is always supported by visual and auditory enhancements. Once the student has located sufficient information, writing prompts appear on screen to help the student organize the notes into a full report.

The Arts

Music

Numerous software programs allow the computer to record and play music and even generate a written score. However, of more relevance to language instruction is the use of music and text to assist students in learning to read and pronounce a second language. Listening to singing and singing along seem to be very natural elements of learning a first language, so second language students might enjoy similar tasks, especially when the computer allows instant replay of any word, expression, or bar of music.

Theatrix/Sanctuary Woods Multimedia has developed a series of particularly delightful programs to take advantage of the music-to-words mode.

The programs, in English, French, and Spanish, are intended for elementary school learners aged 7–11 (I recommend these titles for preschoolers also, with parental assistance at the keyboard) and include Sitting on the Farm (1996) and The Cat Came Back (1996). The child can listen to a song illustrated with colorful mini-animations; to a variety of instruments, including some exotic ones, such as the Japanese *koto* (see Figure 10-6); or to a voice alone. Tasks include singing along while viewing either the text or the music only, with a bouncing ball to keep time and help students follow the notes on the staff, and composing additional verses with new creatures and situations. Picture prompts (with audio and sound effects) help the students create their own songs with their own words. It is easy to imagine the composing process as a group or dyad activity. Students can record their voices and play the result back for their peers. The Cat Came Back is also available on videodisc with animated video.

Older students also take great pleasure in deciphering musical lyrics, and a number of ESL/EFL teachers have reported using clips mounted by

Figure 10-6. Sing-Along Section of Sitting on the Farm (1996)

Note. From Sitting on the Farm [Computer software], 1996, San Mateo, CA: Sanctuary Woods Multimedia. Copyright © 1996 by Theatrix (SWMC). Reprinted with permission.

pop music groups on Web sites as a successful basis for this activity. Most rock groups and performing artists have their own Web sites, and MTV *Online* (http://www.mtv.com/) has an extensive archive of music clips and interviews with rock celebrities as well as a live chat area. Students can download audio files—usually consisting of only a stanza or so of a song by any of dozens of recording artists—to play repeatedly as they write down the words. (See Fantin, 1997, for a lesson plan using a text reconstruction program with song lyrics; however, having the students rather than the teacher figure out the words has considerable advantages.) This task has a high degree of authenticity, as it replicates what teenagers around the world do outside class. Newer push-pull or streaming technology allows music (and speech) to play instantly over the Internet, but having an audio file to replay is helpful for the language learner.

Skill-building activities such as transcription can be woven into assignments focusing on the larger cultural context of the music. Students can explore the place of music in the culture, the political and social impact of a particular artist or genre, or the importance of the work in the evolving history of music.

Art

The CALL environment demonstrates considerable power in the area of graphics. I have already mentioned multimedia tool software, which usually has some drawing capabilities built in. However, software designed specifically for graphic arts and photo montage is an exceptionally useful tool in the task-based curriculum. Students often spend considerable time and effort designing illustrations for their writing or creating artwork that serves as a stimulus for their own or others' oral and written production. Relatively inexpensive clip-art collections give weaker artists a starting point for their own designs, and a simple graphics program, such as Kid Pix (1997), works equally well with both older students and youngsters.

An interesting use of this program in a cross-generational language task comes from the Intensive English Program at Indiana University in Bloomington. Joy Egbert's ESL students worked in elementary classrooms in an elective course called Kids and Computers. The ESL students had to first learn how to use Kid Pix (1997) and then teach native-English-speaking children in an elementary school classroom how to use it. One side of the jigsaw task was to use English in communicative exchanges with native speakers. The other side of the task was to learn to use the drawing software. (See Egbert, 1996b, for the resulting artwork and students' comments.)

Another cross-cultural art project (associated with De Orilla a Orilla, described below) is the International Education and Resource Network (I*EARN), which regularly sets up art tasks and puts young artists from around the world in touch with each other. The I*EARN *Global Art Project Home*

Page (1996, http://www.vpds.wsu.edu/i*earn/global_art.html; see Figure 10-7), displays many projects and e-mailed comments from students about each other's work. The site holds much potential for linking art and language.

For the older student, most of the world's great museums and many small, local ones have mounted Web pages that are a rich resource for images to illustrate projects or as a content supplement to an art history course. For instance, middle and high school students producing multimedia projects were delighted to find art and architecture from Ukrainian and Romanian art museums and from archeological sites in the Yucatán (Hanson-Smith, 1997b). A number of museum sites (see, e.g., the National Gallery of Victoria, Australia's Web site, http://www.ngv.vic.gov.au/) include such details as analyses of brushwork, biographical backgrounds of the artists, interesting comments on art history, and even viewing tasks, based on assignment sheets accompanying the exhibits.

In a CALL task using art content, described by Lapp and Solé (1997), students in pairs view a modern abstract painting and, through prompts in a simple HyperCard® (1997) stack, comment on the work and their reactions to it. After sharing their joint effort with the class, students return to the computer to create and interpret their own designs.

Figure 10-7. Student Artwork on *I*EARN Global Art Project* Home Page (1996)

Note. Pictures by elementary school students (left to right) A. Karamova, Moscow, Russia; K. Volkening, Pullman, WA, USA; A. Eveleth, Pullman, WA, USA. From *I*EARN Global Art Project Home Page: A Sense of Family,* 1996, Washington State University, http://www.vpds.wsu.edu/i*earn/global_art.html. Copyright © 1996 by Washington State University. Reprinted with permission.

Literature

Many of the authors in this text note the enormous bank of resources for reading available on the Internet (see chapters 9, 13, and 14; see also Appendix F). For example, Michael Hart's *Project Gutenberg* (http://www .gutenberg.net/) collects and electronically publishes all written works whose copyrights have expired. This archive is a rich mine of sources for concordancing activities or the creation of an individualized reading program for the price of the ink and paper and the time invested in downloading and printing.

Other on-line sites provide activities to accompany reading. For example, *The Comenius English Language Center* (http://www.comenius.com/) offers a classic literary genre, Aesop's fables, followed by comprehension questions scored on-line and writing prompts to help students create their own fables. A bulletin board lets students read others' work and post comments. The interaction among readers and writers motivates beginning writers and provides an authentic audience for their compositions. Writing fables is a good way to come to an understanding of the genre and to make cross-cultural comparisons among similar tales.

The Internet has also allowed readers fascinating glimpses into the life and work of professional writers. Many authors now have their own Web sites, replete with interesting and often interactive items, such as pictures of the author's family, photos of locations for the stories, biographical tidbits, a bulletin board on which readers can exchange comments, and tips for would-be authors. Interaction with the author by e-mail can generate considerable motivation for the novice writer and the reader discovering literature in a new language. Students can be asked to research biographical information that aids in the interpretation of a story or query the author about the meaning of passages in a book. The author usually sends a very rapid electronic response.

Reference Software and Web Sites for Content Searches

The advantage of software like that produced by TSP, Edmark, Steck-Vaughn/ Edunetics, and Theatrix/Sanctuary Woods Multimedia is that the lesson plans are well developed, the content has been organized with the curriculum in mind, and the tasks are suggested within the software. In contrast, a number of excellent content CD-ROMs—and the World Wide Web—contain searchable information, but the teacher must develop lesson plans incorporating authentic tasks that will motivate students to seek that information. (See Appendix F for a list of Web sites offering content.)

Among the hundreds of excellent reference CD-ROMs are those produced from footage taken by the National Geographic Society (supported by exceptionally fine activities at its Web site, http://www.nationalgeographic .com/) and the Discovery Channel (see, e.g., Nile: Passage to Egypt, 1995). Some content CD-ROMs, such as Microsoft® Cinemania® 96 (1995) and the hypermedia Microsoft Encarta® 1998 World Atlas (1997), have gained great popularity in the commercial market, thus proving their potential appeal to students before teachers even try them. Many such CD-ROMs eventually are designated as remainders and sell for $10–$15. Among the remainders, teachers may find Space: A Visual History (1994) or the complete History Through Art (1994), a collection of thousands of photographs of the world's art treasures on CD-ROM. Bins of inexpensive software are found in office supply houses, in electronics stores, and even at supermarket checkout lines. Another way to find such titles is to search the Web for on-line software discount clearinghouses, many of which offer reduced prices to educators.

Content-Based Tasks for On-Line Learning

A variety of on-line sites, both commercial and free, are sources of authentic tasks. The World Wide Web is often referred to with dread as the "World Wide Wait," but patience and a high-speed connection can reward the researcher with enormous quantities of data, the teacher with ready-to-use classroom materials, and the student with fascinating on-line activities.

Producers of television programs, such as the Public Broadcasting System/WGBH (see NOVA Online, 1996, http://www.pbs.org/wgbh/nova/), the National Geographic Society (http://www.nationalgeographic.com/), and the Discovery Channel (http://www.discovery.com/) also operate Web sites offering lesson plans, additional study materials, and opportunities to chat with other student researchers. NOVA Online: Teachers (1997; http://www.pbs .org/wgbh/nova/teachers/) also provides full transcripts of NOVA television shows and notes for teachers to preview for upcoming TV broadcasts, as well as detailed lesson plans that teachers can download free of charge. The worksheet shown in Figure 10-8 accompanies a NOVA television program (or the video recording) concerning the use of a tyrannosaurus rex fossil found on private lands. The students are assigned various sides of a proposed debate and take notes as they watch.

The Quest Project of the U.S. National Aeronautics and Space Administration (NASA) offers many free curricular materials related to an amazing number of content areas in the sciences and the language arts. Links from the project's home page (http://quest.arc.nasa.gov/) lead to an almost bewildering array of engrossing adventures, such as the Web Interface for Telescience Simulation (WITS), in which visitors can tell the Mars Explorer how to move; Live From Mars, archives of footage downloaded directly from the red planet in the summer of 1997; photo archives of several space explora-

Figure 10-8. Activity From *NOVA Online: Teacher's Guide* (1997)

Part I

Fill in this chart as you watch the program, noting any other information that will support your group's claim.

Group	Reasons for collecting fossils	Methods of collecting fossils	Uses of fossils
Scientists			
Commercial Dealers			

Note. From "Curse of T. Rex: Digging Fossils," NOVA *Online: Teacher's Guide*, 1997, http://www.pbs.org/wgbh/nova/teachersguide/trex/trex_sp1.html. Copyright © 1997 by WGBH Educational Foundation. Reprinted courtesy of NOVA™ Science Unit.

tions now under way; a gallery for student work; and live chat sessions with NASA scientists and astronauts. The Smithsonian Institution supports another excellent site (http://www.si.edu/) featuring numerous content-based lesson plan archives, resource guides, partnerships with and outreach to schools—organized by the content areas of art, language arts, science, and social science—and links to related sites, including the U.S. national museums of space, history, and art.

Commercial publishers are beginning to promote on-line learning as a basis for authentic, content-based, multimedia-enhanced tasks. Fully developed Web projects involve a variety of action research, often on sites mounted for only a limited time and usually including two-way communication to researchers in the field. Participants in *Classroom Connect* (http://

classroom.com/) may, for example, ride with a team of long-distance bicyclists as they explore a Mayan city or follow an expedition to Africa or the Galapagos Islands. Access to parts of the Web sites is free, and supporting curricular materials both on and off the Web are available by subscription.

TSP provides texts and lesson plans to accompany three interactive Web pages at SitesALIVE! (http://www.oceanchallenge.com/), which involve Internet exchanges with native speakers studying at research sites around the world. One of these sites, Class Afloat Live '98 (1998, http://www.oceanchallenge .com/cal/98f/ca98ffin.htm), is a setting for adventurous tasks involving research on ocean life, meteorology, geography, cultures, and peoples. Individuals and families as well as classes may sign up for the site, and a demo package including newsletters and teaching activities is available free on-line. The fee-paid Class Afloat package includes a biweekly newsletter written by students aboard the tall ship Concordia; a tracking map, poster, and video; and an Internet address at which students e-mail the student crew of the ship. Instead of waiting weeks for surface mail, students contact their counterparts on board the ship within a few moments via satellite link. The student crew posts an ongoing text and photo record of their encounters with the climate, cultures, and geography of countries from the United States to Australia, North Africa, the Mediterranean, and northern Europe.

Other SitesALIVE! on-line projects supported by TSP materials include a rain forest camp in Australia and a Caribbean seashore research site. The number of such on-line opportunities will no doubt continue to grow; perhaps the best places to spot them are technology magazines, such as Electronic Learning (published by Scholastic) and publishers' catalogues. The great advantage of these projects is that someone else has detailed the Web links and the tasks to pursue, although there is a cost involved in joining the project, purchasing the texts and materials, and so on. However, at commercial sites teachers have access to help from the site's publisher, who has a responsibility to see the class through once the project fee has been paid. The teacher's main responsibilities are to ensure that the project fits into the curriculum and to see that students stay on task.

Other types of distance learning now taking shape allow students not only to study and practice language but to do a full university degree program (see chapter 26). These technology-enhanced opportunities may ultimately change the nature of the university as an institution.

Designing a Content-Based Multimedia Task

The by-now traditional I-search paper (see Macrorie, 1988), which guides students in formulating and researching their own topics, is one of the most valuable content-based tasks I have used with intermediate to advanced students. The content-based research paper and presentation support students in gathering information in their areas of interest or study (an authentic task). In addition, if the audience has the appropriate motivation and opportunity to listen and respond, this task can incorporate many of the other conditions for optimal language learning discussed in chapter 1, including interaction, authentic audience, exposure and production, and intentional cognition.

Each part of the project involves writing and has its own deadline; the result is a fairly lengthy paper that meets most requirements for a research paper in a content course. Although the I-search can be adapted to any level, I have encouraged ESL students at the university level to use this assignment to write a required research paper for a content course in their major. My grading rubric focuses on the search and writing process, which includes multiple drafts, the editing of grammar, an understanding of citations, and the avoidance of plagiarism; the grade in the content course depends on the content and on whether the paper satisfies the additional requirements of the content instructor (e.g., a higher minimum number of references, greater length, discipline-specific formatting and citation styles, and even a more specific topic).

In the project, the students receive the following instructions:

1. Define a topic, describing what you already know and what you hope to discover.

2. Perform research within certain parameters (set or approved in advance by the teacher); the search might include interviews with knowledgeable informants. Describe how and where you searched and what resources were most useful.

3. Present the results of the search. (I usually require both an oral presentation and a written paper.)

Often the search or its failure forces students to change or revise their topic, but almost invariably students become caught up in their hunt for information. Deadlines and peer reviews at each step along the way mean that the project does not become unmanageable, and the sharing of research produces interest among peers, tips on sources, and a chance to verbalize in ways that unblock the writing process. Very specific steps for each section and ongoing revision of drafts provide clear benchmarks that usually entail success and unflagging enthusiasm. Searches on the Web, alone or combined with searches on content CD-ROMs, bring the attractions of multimedia to the composition, for students can add audio interviews, photos, graphics, animation, color, and video to their final papers. The oral presentation of the paper, at any level, lends itself to the use of media-rich authoring software (see chapter 25).

Because the I-search paper is open ended and develops through negotiation with the teacher and with the resources available, it works best with intermediate to advanced language learners, although teachers can adjust the extent and depth of the search and the topics to the level of the students' ability. If students simply use multimedia content CD-ROMs, such as Microsoft Encarta Encyclopedia 98 (1997) or the media produced by the National Geographic Society, as sources, then the I-Search paper may be short and well illustrated, and a chief concern may be appropriate quotation and citation. If the search includes the Internet, the teacher must give some thought to where and how students can find appropriate sites and content. Even at the high school level, some of my students at first hoped to get by using commercials on the Web for references. Some practice with Internet search engines, such as Yahoo! (http://www.yahoo.com/) or AltaVista (http://www.altavista.com/), is extremely important, because each uses a slightly different format, some use Boolean operators, and each searches for slightly different things. As a result the teacher may need to narrow the research areas considerably and preselect a number of sites to make students' searches more efficient.

To present media-enriched research, students must learn to use one of the multimedia presentation programs they might use in their future careers, such as HyperStudio (1997) or Microsoft PowerPoint® 97 (1996). Students readily learn to add their own artwork, photos, video clips, and text to the cards or slides in such tools. Most presentation software programs include a Web interface that allows projects to be displayed on the Internet, and the creation of a Web site is itself a significant authentic task, as it sends content out to a global audience. For information on authoring software and on Web and e-mail projects, see chapters 6, 7, 9, 13, and 25; here I mention only a few of many sites displaying students' projects: *Email Projects Home Page* (Gaer, 1997, http://www.otan.dni.us/webfarm/emailproject/email.htm; see chapter 6), *Famous Personages in Japan* (Robb, n.d.-a, http://www.kyoto-su.ac.jp/information/famous/), and *Kyoto Restaurant Project* (Kitagawa, 1997, http://www.kyoto-su.ac.jp/information/restaurant/). In the *Kyoto Restaurant Project* (see Figure 10-9), the appetizingly illustrated buttons link to lists of restaurants in Kyoto; the site also has a clickable map so that users can choose dining establishments by location.

Curricular Exchanges at a Distance

Content-based multimedia presentations authored by students are an appropriate resource for the growing number of worldwide curricular exchanges. The De Orilla a Orilla/From Shore to Shore exchange program, under way for over 15 years (see Cummins & Sayers, 1995), began as an exchange of physical objects by post, primarily among schoolchildren. The project then incorporated the videotaping of the opening of packages, an exchange of the videos, and finally postal and e-mail exchanges between classes in different countries working on compatible curriculum projects

Figure 10-9. Kyoto Restaurant Project (Kitagawa, 1997)

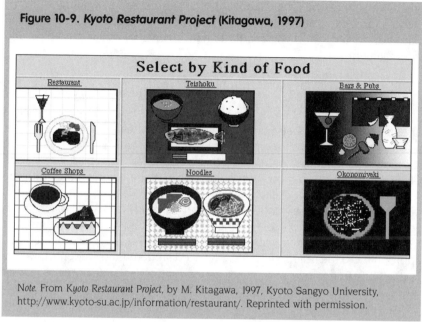

Note. From *Kyoto Restaurant Project*, by M. Kitagawa, 1997, Kyoto Sangyo University, http://www.kyoto-su.ac.jp/information/restaurant/. Reprinted with permission.

agreed on by the teachers involved. The success of the project depends less on the technology than on the teachers communicating clearly about goals, scheduling, and the content of the curriculum. (See the project's Web site, http://orillas.upr.clu.edu/, for more information.)

Unlike De Orilla a Orilla/From Shore to Shore, the HUT Internet Writing Project, based at Helsinki University of Technology, has operated mainly among adult classes in intensive and college programs. Students in different countries read the same texts, write essays about them, and exchange and critique the essays via the Internet. (See Vilmi, 1998b, http://www.hut.fi/~rvilmi/Project/, for information on taking part in the exchange and a list of currently participating schools and universities.) The King's Road 2001 Project (see Vilmi, 1997b, http://www.hut.fi/~rvilmi/King/), a visionary project for northern Europe that is under development at this writing, will bring together classrooms from St. Petersburg to Helsinki in virtual and real-time adventure tasks, including the exchange of cultural information and even the opportunity to ski on portions of the historic highway. The King's Road site also has links to similar projects in other parts of the world.

On-line curricular exchanges between ESL/EFL classes and classes of native English speakers, as well as exchanges among language learners around the world, are reportedly highly successful (see chapters 6, 7, and 26; also see, e.g., Boswood, 1997; Cummins & Sayers, 1995; Warschauer, 1995a, 1995b, 1996). The immediacy made possible by the electronic medium greatly enhances the long-distance exchange: Instead of waiting weeks or months for replies, students can interact frequently or even in real time and can take advantage of the media enhancements of voice recording and video camera.

Conclusion

The range of products and educational opportunities available shows that technology has given an interesting twist to the idea of *task* as a language learning strategy in the content-based classroom. Virtual reality, whether on CD-ROM or on-line, can be as gripping as a real-life environment, with the added advantage that, unlike real-time tasks or exchanges, one can put the task safely on "pause" until the student is ready to come back to it. Technology, unlike real-life interlocutors, tolerates tireless repetition of target structures and vocabulary. Learning can take place at a pace appropriate to the novice or to the advanced student, and students have the opportunity to deploy a wide variety of learning styles and strategies in their quest to understand content and language.

Chapter 11

CALL Issues: Instructional Aspects of Software Evaluation

Claire Bradin

One often hears that no "good" CALL software is available; in fact, this view is so commonly held that, true or not, it seems to have passed into conventional wisdom. In fact, hundreds of programs are available and are widely accepted. You as a responsible language teacher, however, must look at software as critically as you do textbooks and other materials. You should also keep in mind that materials are not inherently better just because they are on the computer.

Basic Considerations

Language teachers who are not accustomed to looking at CALL software may perceive its purpose very differently than those who are more experienced. Neophytes who believe that the computer is supposed to replace a human teacher may project human-type expectations onto a computer program, requiring the software to be able to perform exactly in the same way that a human being does. To the extent that teachers demand human qualities, CALL software will always fall short. Any appraisal of a particular software package should therefore be based on knowledge of what computers are capable of and what the inherent drawbacks of computers are. With this awareness in mind, you can ask, "What does the software do?" instead of focusing on what it does not do.

Another important aspect of software selection is an understanding of the *setting*, or how the software will be used. Will it be used

- for independent study in a lab where little or no help is available?
- at home?
- in a classroom where there are only one or two computers?
- in a lab setting where the entire class has been scheduled to meet periodically?

The setting in which the software will be delivered is an important consideration in determining its appropriateness in a given situation.

As with any good lesson plan, the *pedagogical goals* must be clear. Does the software further those goals? If so, how? You need to examine the software to determine the specific ways in which it will do so. For example, the knowledge that a certain software package deals with vocabulary at a certain level may not be enough, as two ESL vocabulary programs may be very different. You also need to know whether or not the software presents students with many new vocabulary words or reinforces the words they already know through practice and additional input. Additional questions to ask include the following:

- What is the ratio of new words to reviewed words?

- Are the lexical items used in context, and are a variety of examples provided? Are all the models isolated sentences, or are there also short passages or conversations to provide a larger background for understanding the words?

- Is the vocabulary presented in non-text-based modes?

- Are graphics or video included? If so, how well do these media illustrate and explain the vocabulary? (Do not assume that high-tech is best. A still photograph may convey meaning more effectively than a video can, and a simple black-and-white line drawing may serve to clarify the target language better than a color photograph does.)

- Is there audio reinforcement? If so, how is it implemented? Do learners hear the target vocabulary only as isolated words, or can the learners hear phrases or sentences? Are the sounds played automatically, or is audio an option chosen and controlled by the learners? (Audio may not be necessary or even desirable in all situations; indeed, if the objective is improvement of skimming, scanning, or test-taking skills, sound may prove to be a distraction.)

There are other concerns as well. For example, do students have an opportunity to incorporate the vocabulary items in producing their own examples? Because computers are not very good at handling answers to open-ended questions or freely composed language, be prepared to eke out more value from the computer program by providing tasks that enhance its use. Consider means—perhaps nonelectronic means—for students to use the vocabulary items in their own examples. Such supplementation might take the form of worksheets on which students note new vocabulary words and use them in sentences or an assignment in which students record examples onto an audiotape and hand it in. Computer-based reinforcement might involve having the students enter the words into their own database, spreadsheet, word-processed file, flash-card template, or word game or use them in an e-mail message to you, their classmates, or international pen pals.

The concerns mentioned are critical in examining vocabulary software, but considerations for choosing another type of software with different objectives might be altogether different. For example, if learners are expected to interact and collaborate with other language learners in using the software, you might ask how well a given program lends itself to pair or group activities. (See chapters 9 and 10 for examples of software that lends itself to interactive tasks.) A computer program that purports to "teach" in the sense that it explains and defines everything may receive high marks for completeness when used by students working alone, but it may be less successful when used by pairs or small groups of students, who can often help one another by supplying missing pieces. In these situations, the lack of information provided in the software may actually serve as a catalyst for communication among students. Here your skill as facilitator is a key factor, as students take their cue from your expectations of the role of the software in the activity.

Other issues include what outcomes you and the students expect, what tasks the students will perform, and how those tasks will be evaluated. Chapter 8 presents some methods of evaluating the language and authenticity of CALL tasks, and these questions are also discussed in more detail in this chapter.

Criteria for Software Evaluation

In general, the individual teacher or the institution decides on the underlying pedagogical approaches to and procedures for the use of software. It is worth some staff discussion to make these assumptions clear, as they will determine what software is used and how it is used (Hubbard, 1987, 1996; see also chapter 17 for policy considerations). Once the basic assumptions are on the table, evaluating the software is a two-step process: exploring feasibility and determining quality (Figure 11-1).

Step 1: Feasibility

The first consideration in software evaluation is whether it is possible to use the software in your particular lab environment. No matter how good the software is, serious consideration may be a waste of time until you settle issues of feasibility (see the box on p. 162).

Will the Software Run on Your Computer and Platform?

The only way to be absolutely certain that the software will work correctly in your environment is to obtain a review copy, install it, and try it

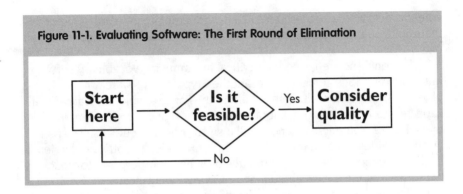

Figure 11-1. Evaluating Software: The First Round of Elimination

out. The manual or other promotional material probably lists specific requirements, such as the platform (machine type: typically Macintosh® computers or those running the Microsoft® MS-DOS® or Windows® operating system) and operating system version. Other requirements, such as the amount of random-access memory (RAM) and hard drive space, a CD-ROM drive, or a color monitor, may be mentioned. However, older software does not necessarily run on later-model computers, so view statements like "runs on System [X.XX] and later" with some skepticism. Conversely, because the development of ESL software tends to lag 2 or 3 years behind the appearance of state-of-the-art equipment, many programs run best on slightly older machines.

Does the software run on a type of computer that is readily accessible to your students and faculty? Regardless of your own preference or conviction that a particular platform is better, nobody will use the software if the right computers are not available. Further, if computers of the right type are at hand, do the teachers and students know how to use them? If they normally use another platform, and all their experience, orientation, and preferences lean in that direction, training them or convincing them to become familiar with a different type of computer merely to use a particular piece of software may not be worth the time and trouble.

Feasibility Considerations

- Will the software run on your computer and platform?
- Will the software run on your network?
- Can the software be made available to many students?
- Does the software require Internet access?
- Can you afford the software?

Will the Software Run on Your Network?

In a computer laboratory setting, issues other than platform come into play. If the computers are connected in a network through which software is distributed, will the software in question operate correctly on the network? Many programs are now shipped on CD-ROM, but if students cannot access the CD-ROM through a server, they must use it at individual workstations. Although sometimes both network and stand-alone versions of the same program are available, the storage and distribution of stand-alone CD-ROMs may prove to be a major headache.

Lab management policies may also be a factor. Does the network administrator allow software to be run from the hard drive, if necessary? If the software crashes on one workstation, can the program easily be restarted and reaccessed without interfering with the rest of the network? To answer these questions, there is no substitute for actually installing the software and testing it.

Can the Software Be Made Available to Many Students?

Can the software be installed in other labs or libraries on campus or in the community to extend students' access to it after class hours? Will individual students be able to purchase the software for use at home? As computers become more widespread and affordable, the possibility of home use becomes an increasingly important factor in the decision to adopt a certain program.

Does the Software Require Internet Access?

At this writing, software developers are starting to incorporate Internet capability into software that formerly ran only on local computers or networks. Through the use of *plug-ins* (applications that extend a World Wide Web browser's capabilities), interactive language lessons are now offered on the World Wide Web. Some examples of plug-ins are Shockwave (1995), as used in *Cutting Edge CALL Demos* (Duber, 1997), and LiveCard (1996); HyperStudio (1997) and other authoring software use plug-ins for Web capability (e.g., HyperStudio Web Browser Plug-In, 1996).

One obvious advantage of software that runs on the Internet is that users can access materials regardless of platform. However, the software requires a very fast connection to the Internet and a computer with a great deal of RAM. These types of programs are in their infancy and may perform slowly or erratically. Test them carefully in a particular lab setting before recommending them to or using them with students.

Can You Afford the Software?

Is the price right? Because budgets for software vary tremendously, there cannot be a simple answer to this question, nor can the relative value of various packages be easily determined. Sometimes discounts on software are available to educational institutions. Keep in mind that purchasing a single copy of the software gives you legal permission to install it onto one computer only. For software that will be used on several computers, you may be able to purchase a site license, which permits installation on multiple machines and which may be significantly cheaper than purchasing individual copies for each computer.

Cost is usually an important consideration; however, do not automatically buy or recommend software just because it is inexpensive. Your students' time is valuable and should not be wasted on a bargain that may not fulfill your objectives or their expectations. On the other hand, do not assume that the most expensive software is always the best; in fact, some of the most successful software can be obtained at low cost or as freeware or shareware.

Step 2: Quality

Once the software has passed the test of feasibility, think about quality and appropriateness. Is the software worth buying? Three aspects of software determine whether it is worth buying: the program's content, its format, and its operation (see the box).

Software Content

What is the goal of the software? Is that goal consistent with yours and that of your students? At this juncture, seriously consider the subject matter covered in the software in order to avoid being enticed by the embellishments of multimedia. Is the content relevant to other texts in use? Is the software adaptable or supplementary to your class or curriculum? On the other hand, expecting a very close fit between software and curriculum, as many teachers do, may be unrealistic. As with other types of materials, success in using a computer program may depend on your creativity in discovering ways to integrate it into classroom activities and individual assignments.

Is the level appropriate? Learners may not feel challenged if the language used in the software is too simple. At the other end of the spectrum, very complex language with many unknown words may prove frustrating for beginning or intermediate students. You may be able to use such software by providing the students with glossaries, worksheets, summaries, or preparatory sessions, but be sure to factor the time involved in developing these supplementary materials into the real cost of adopting the software. Higher level software may also work well in multilevel classrooms or in classes that use cooperative learning techniques. Also examine the program's "Help" screens to ensure that they are at a level appropriate to the learners.

Is the content accurate? Is it up-to-date? Has the text been proofread carefully? Many factual or editorial errors may indicate a sloppily made product. On the other hand, occasional typographical errors have always

---

Quality Considerations

- Content
  - What is the goal of the software?
  - Is the level appropriate?
  - Is the content accurate and up-to-date?
  - Is the material culturally appropriate?
  - Does the software accommodate the students' learning styles and preferences?
  - Is the software interesting?
  - How flexible is the software?

- Format
  - Is the interface consistent?
  - Is the screen display effective?
  - Are the motivational devices effective?

- Operation
  - Is the software easy to use?
  - Can the text and graphics be printed?
  - How much control are the learners allowed?
  - How interactive is the software?
  - Are the quality and degree of feedback adequate?
  - What kinds of records does the software keep?

---

been tolerated in printed materials, and it may not be fair to impose a higher standard on CALL software. Errors in fact or inconsistencies might actually offer a point of departure for discussions or an opportunity for students to hone their critical thinking skills.

Is the software culturally appropriate? Is it embedded with stereotypical images or inappropriate role models that run contrary to your general objectives and values? This concern may be particularly important with respect to some computer games, which have violent or sexual themes (see also chapter 20).

Does the software accommodate the learning styles and preferences of your students? For example, are they willing to read large amounts of text on a computer monitor? What is their attention span likely to be? Do not expect one computer program to serve all their needs and interests. A more realistic approach may be to purchase several software packages, each of which will meet the needs of a particular type of learner. For example, an analytical learner who wants to keep track of each move and is reassured by rules may appreciate a preparatory exercise for the Test of English as a Foreign Language that provides feedback on and explanations for each point. A learner who needs practice in listening and has the patience to play a sound repeatedly will benefit from software that offers this opportunity. Students who enjoy puzzles and merely seek confirmation that their own text is correct but do not need clarification can make advantageous use of a text reconstruction program, such as Storyboard (Jones, 1990) or Eclipse (Higgins, 1995).

Is the software interesting? Will the students enjoy using it? For the time on task to be spent profitably, the software must contain some spark of appeal for the learner. The content of the software must have some relevance, and the student must take pleasure in working through it (Chapelle, 1988).

How flexible is the software? Can the content be adapted? Can you add your own text, graphics, and sound? Some CALL programs are really shells or templates: They come with some preset text, but you can enter your own materials. (See chapter 25 on the use of authoring software, e.g., NewReader, McVicker, 1997; Rhubarb, Higgins & Higgins, 1987; Sequitur, Higgins, 1986; Storyboard, Jones, 1990; SuperMacLang, Frommer & Foelsche, 1996.) Assuming that you have time to enter the content, these applications allow you to create supplementary materials that fit exactly into your syllabus without having an advanced knowledge of programming.

Software Format

Is the format consistent? In general, the interface (the program's appearance to the user) should be consistent enough that learners can focus on the task and not the operation but varied enough that they do not become bored. In well-designed software, the technological interface becomes transparent and needs almost no conscious attention from the user. One of the best examples of such an interface is HyperACE Intermediate (1995), a program for practicing listening comprehension (Figure 11-2). Volume controls, an easy exit (by means of a "Quit" button), and simple navigation buttons ("Back" and "Next" are apparent on the screen) allow the student to maneuver through the software easily.

Is the screen display effective? Often visual effects are significant to a learner's concentration, so consider such questions as these:

- Can the text be easily read, or is it too small?

- If colors are involved, are they garish or distracting, or do they add to the attractiveness of the screen?

- Is the quality of the graphics sufficiently high?

- Are pictures used for appropriate pedagogical reasons? That is, do they clarify the language or add interest, or are they merely gimmicks?

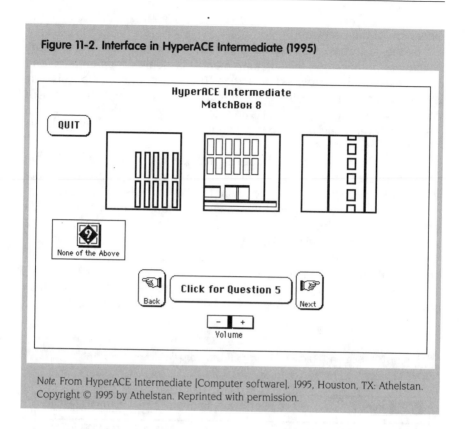

Figure 11-2. Interface in HyperACE Intermediate (1995)

Note. From HyperACE Intermediate [Computer software]. 1995, Houston, TX: Athelstan. Copyright © 1995 by Athelstan. Reprinted with permission.

How effective are the software's motivational devices? In drill programs, examples of motivational devices are the cheerful tunes and flashing screens that are triggered by correct answers and the angry buzzes or sad faces occasioned by wrong responses. Early research with drill programs (*computerized learning* or *programmed learning*) found that students deliberately made errors because the feedback for incorrect answers was much more interesting than that for correct ones. This situation has now been reversed in most software. Some students find that buzzes and trumpets add excitement to an otherwise boring exercise, whereas others have commented that they are annoyed or, even worse, embarrassed because they do not wish their classmates to know every time they make a mistake. Such contrivances tend to lose their charm after several repetitions, and students using software with audible feedback may require headphones so as not to disturb others in a lab. Especially in the case of audible feedback, the software should offer the option to disable the sound (and an easy control for sound levels, as in HyperACE Intermediate, 1995, Figure 11-2) if the software is to be used in a lab setting. Feedback should be appropriate to the age of the intended user. (See chapter 27 for more information on program format.)

Operation of the Software

Is the software easy to use? Are the task and directions clear? Regardless of how good the software manual is, some documentation and directions should be provided on screen. The best of printed manuals may be lost or may not be available when learners need them. Verb Professor (McVicker, 1995b; see Figure 11-3) is an example of software with clear screen directions. Everything the students need to complete their task is clearly explained or available.

When beginning language students or those whose computer skills are weak use the software for the first time, you may want to provide a handout with simple instructions and screen shots. You may also wish to demonstrate the program to the class by means of a liquid crystal display panel, a large-screen TV monitor, or another projection device. However, do not underestimate the students' ability to discover on their own how to use the software. ESL students are often more adept at figuring out computer programs than their teachers are!

Does the software allow you to print out text and graphics? Learners often appreciate the added security of being able to take home a printed

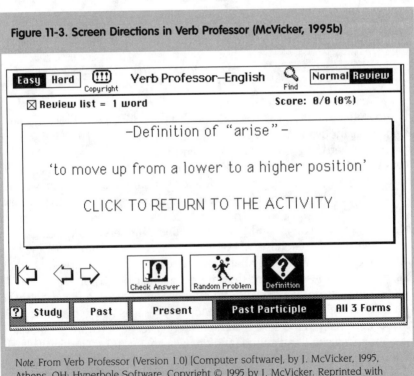

Figure 11-3. Screen Directions in Verb Professor (McVicker, 1995b)

Note. From Verb Professor (Version 1.0) [Computer software], by J. McVicker, 1995, Athens, OH: Hyperbole Software. Copyright © 1995 by J. McVicker. Reprinted with permission of the author.

copy of the materials viewed on screen. They can annotate the hard copy and use it for further review and reinforcement. The ability to print is not necessary, nor is it even desirable in all CALL software, but if a printer is available and you want to be able to print, consider this feature in the decision to adopt the software.

How much control are the learners allowed? At the very least, the option to "Exit," "Quit," or some other clear indication of how to leave the program should be readily available on every screen. Do the students have the freedom to change to a different activity in the middle of a sequence, or must they plod along to the end? Should they be permitted to do so? When learners are locked into an extremely limiting interface that permits few or no alternatives, they may feel frustrated. On the other hand, when confronted with too many options, they may become confused or fail to take advantage of the choices available. Some research (Chapelle & Mizuno, 1989; Robinson, 1991) indicates that a happy medium between these two extremes may be best. The issue of control is a complex one (see chapter 24), and you will need to use your best instincts to determine what is appropriate for your students. The simulation Immigrants (Brooks, 1988; see Figure 11-4) allows a variety of choices for activities that you could assign or the students could select.

How much interactivity does the program offer? At its very worst, so-called educational software presents screen after screen of text, and the

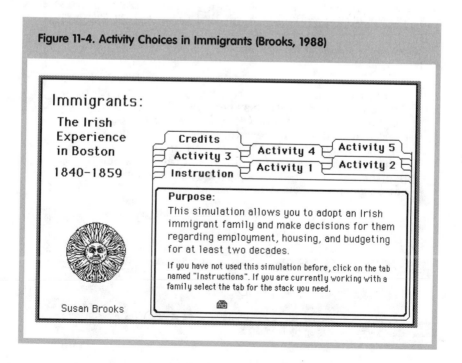

Figure 11-4. Activity Choices in Immigrants (Brooks, 1988)

Immigrants:

The Irish
Experience
in Boston

1840–1859

Credits
Activity 3
Instruction
Activity 4
Activity 1
Activity 5
Activity 2

Purpose:
This simulation allows you to adopt an Irish immigrant family and make decisions for them regarding employment, housing, and budgeting for at least two decades.

If you have not used this simulation before, click on the tab named "Instructions". If you are currently working with a family select the tab for the stack you need.

Susan Brooks

learner need only press the "Enter" key or click the mouse to proceed to the next screen. Such a design, often referred to as *electronic page turning*, reduces the user's role to such passivity that the material might be presented more effectively in a printed textbook.

Software should actively engage students by presenting tasks to them. Some typical tasks involve choosing an option by typing a letter or word or clicking the mouse on a given location on the screen, clicking on a button to hear a sound or activate an animation, selecting an object and dragging it to a new location based on textual or aural cues, or making a sound recording (Meskill, 1987); in Constructing the Paragraph (Hanson-Smith, 1997a), one of a variety of tasks involves identifying the topic sentence in a paragraph (see Figure 11-5). This software provides several different kinds of activities to test students' understanding of the tutorials.

Are the quality and degree of feedback adequate? As students interact with the software by performing the required tasks, the computer responds in various ways. *Immediate feedback* is often mentioned as one of the

Figure 11-5. Topic Sentence Exercise From Constructing the Paragraph (Hanson-Smith, 1997a)

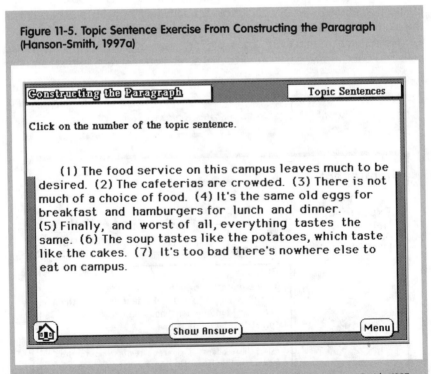

Note. From Constructing the Paragraph [Computer software], by E. Hanson-Smith, 1997, Sacramento, CA: Computers for Education. Copyright © 1997 by E. Hanson-Smith. Reprinted with permission of the author.

computer's greatest advantages as a learning tool. Instantaneous though the response may be, it cannot be intelligent in the sense that it understands the learner's input in humanlike fashion (Lian, 1992). Some drills do no more than display "Yes, you're right" or "No, you're wrong; try again" in response to various choices, giving no indication as to why the answer was wrong or right. This type of response may not be enlightening, but at least it signals whether learners are mistaken or correct, at which point they can seek an explanation from another source. Note that information about correct answers can also be useful to the student, especially when a correct answer is the result of a chance keystroke or a lucky guess. Other lessons include a range of possible wrong answers and attempt to supply item-specific feedback based on the individual answers given. This type of feedback can provide helpful information to the learner. However, when learners type in their own answers, it is beyond the capacity of computers to anticipate all possible incorrect answers and furnish explanations for them.

Given the inherent limitation of computers, expecting all the feedback to come from the software itself is not necessary or reasonable. You or other students working in pairs or groups can provide some input. Another common technique is to allow the learner a second or third try or even to give hints that lead the learner to discover the answer. Other options involve pedagogical decisions, such as whether to provide feedback on correct answers and whether to make the correct answer available all the time, only after a set number of tries, or not at all. In some authoring programs, such as Dasher (Otto & Pusack, 1994) and SuperMacLang (Frommer & Foelsche, 1996; see Figure 11-6), you can configure these options before you make the exercises available to the students.

What kinds of records does the software keep? Keeping score was an important component of many early CALL programs. However, because it has become associated with behaviorist schemes in which learners are tracked and programmed into various prescribed activities according to their performance, scorekeeping has been less popular in recent years. Nonetheless, software that keeps track of items missed in an exercise and presents them to the learner at the end—offering the opportunity to repeat only those items and not the entire exercise—can be of great benefit. NewReader (McVicker, 1997; see Figure 11-7), for example, records all the learner's actions in each exercise. The actions appear in a "Notes" section that can be saved as a separate file or printed out.

Some software that claims to have *artificial intelligence* (AI) may respond to each answer by increasing or decreasing the difficulty level of the following questions. Obviously, this type of program cannot account for random keystrokes, wrong guesses, or experimental or playful responses. Also, the total number of questions in the data bank will determine how refined the adjustment process can be. AI is often a part of software that is based on the programmed learning of discrete grammar points or vocabulary items,

**Figure 11-6. Authoring Options in SuperMacLang
(Frommer & Foelsche, 1996)**

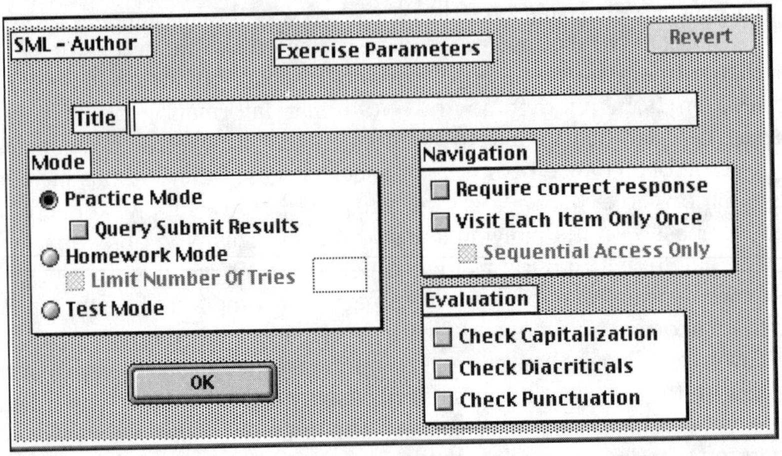

| SML – Author | Exercise Parameters | Revert |

Title |

Mode
- ● Practice Mode
  - ☐ Query Submit Results
- ○ Homework Mode
  - ▨ Limit Number Of Tries
- ○ Test Mode

OK

Navigation
- ☐ Require correct response
- ☐ Visit Each Item Only Once
- ▨ Sequential Access Only

Evaluation
- ☐ Check Capitalization
- ☐ Check Diacritics
- ☐ Check Punctuation

Note. From SuperMacLang [Computer software], by J. G. Frommer and O. Foelsche, 1996, Dartmouth, NH: Dartmouth College/Harvard University. Copyright © 1996 by J. G. Frommer and O. Foelsche. Reprinted with permission of the authors. This screen was constructed for pure functionality; the graphical interface will probably be revised in future versions.

so you must determine how appropriate the tasks are to the age and motivational level of your students.

Testing the Software

Regardless of the type of software under consideration, it is crucial to test the program before you purchase it. Many publishers, especially publishers of large, complex programs, will provide demonstration (demo) copies of their software or allow an institution to try out parts of the program for a limited time period.

If at all possible, have some students for whom the software is targeted actually try it out. Watch them carefully as they work with it. Using the Checklist for Software Evaluation (Figure 11-8), see how easily students are able to grasp what the task is and how they should use the interface. Is the way to use the software self-evident? If not, are the on-line instructions easy to understand? How much individual guidance do students need to get started? This is especially important if students are to use the software for

---

Figure 11-7. Student Record Kept by NewReader (McVicker, 1997)

```
• STUDENT: Gizmo
DATE: 10/10/97
CURRENT TEXT: 'Budget deficit debate'
2:29 PM-Started 'READ THE TEXT'...
  >Looked up 'economic' means: having to do with
money
  Example: "The country's economic problems are due
to its lack of natural resources."
  >Looked up 'control' means: to regulate or
dominate
  Example: "He is able to control his breathing
when he is excited."
  »Looked up 'presidential' - not in dictionary.
  »Looked up 'revenue' - not in dictionary.
2:30 PM-Started 'VOWEL SEARCH' (lines 1 to 4 of the
text)...
  Total score: 8 / 9    (89 %)
2:31 PM-Started 'VOWEL SEARCH' (lines 5 to 8 of the
text)...
  Total score: 2 / 2    (100 %)
2:31 PM-STARTED CLOZE PUZZLE; every 6th word is
missing ... first 30 lines
  • You tried 2 times; you used 'will' (??) in
place of 'would'    for problem #1 in phrase:"...
what [1] be needed to tame the [2] billion ..."
  Total score: 3 / 4    (75 %)
2:32:43 PM-STARTED PACED READING at 200 words per
minute.
```

---

independent study, whether at home or in a self-access lab where instructors are not readily available. Also consider how much time teachers will need to commit to lesson planning once the software is purchased.

Conclusion

The discussion in this chapter shows clearly that software evaluation can be quite time-consuming. Note, however, that you will rarely need to go through each point of the Checklist for Software Evaluation (Figure 11-8) in painstaking detail for every program under consideration. Very often one or two disqualifying factors appear early on in the process, and you can quickly eliminate a particular package from further consideration. As you develop skill in examining CALL software, you will be able to evaluate it more quickly.

Figure 11-8. Checklist for Software Evaluation

Step 1: Feasibility

_____   Will the software run on your computer?

_____   What platform (computer type) does the software require?

_____   Will the software run on your network?

_____   Can the software be made available to many students?

_____   Does the software require Internet access?

_____   Can you afford the software?

Step 2: Quality

Content

_____   What is the goal of the software? Is it consistent with yours and that of your students?

_____   Is the level appropriate?

_____   Is the content accurate?

_____   Is the material culturally appropriate?

_____   Does the software accommodate the students' learning styles and preferences?

_____   Is the software interesting?

_____   How flexible is the software?

Format

_____   Is the interface consistent?

_____   Is the screen display effective?

_____   In drill software, are the motivational devices effective?

Operation

_____   Is the software easy to use? Are the tasks and directions clear?

_____   Does the software allow text and graphics to be printed?

_____   How much control are the learners allowed?

_____   How interactive is the software?

_____   Are the quality and degree of feedback adequate?

_____   What kinds of records does the software keep?

Note. Adapted from an unpublished checklist developed by Claire Bradin and Macey Taylor, 1988.

With experience, you will develop a feel for what works best for your students and will become more discriminating in the selection of new programs. As your tastes develop, you will be able to discard even more rapidly those programs that do not fit your requirements. Regardless of the time involved in assessing software, the responsibility to be well acquainted with all software adopted rests just as clearly on your shoulders as the obligation to scrutinize textbooks and other materials does.

Once you have found some software that you really like and that you believe will work successfully in your program, do not be too surprised if other, non-CALL-enthusiast faculty members do not share your enthusiasm. They may need to see the program in action or hear the positive reaction from the students over a period of time before they are willing to use the software. Some faculty members may never develop an interest in CALL at all. However, once a CALL program is begun, students are likely to respond enthusiastically.

Explorations

Projects

1. Choose three software programs (or three software reviews) used in second or foreign language courses. For whom and in what contexts could the tasks provided by the software be considered authentic? What changes could be made or tasks added by teachers to make the software more authentic for specific language learning contexts?

2. Describe how you would design a grammar checker appropriate for second language learners. What features would it need to have?

3. Design a World Wide Web site (on paper or using a graphics package or HTML editor) to support a stand-alone, content-based software package. Include activities, lessons, graphics, or other elements that would assist your students in using this software package to meet their goals.

4. Based on the checklist in Figure 11-8, develop a software evaluation form for language teachers at your school. Which items would you leave in, take out, or add? Why?

Guided Research

1. What impact might new technologies have on the listening performance of second language students? Explore different types of research on these new technologies. Determine how listening practice with new technologies, such as computers and the Internet, differs from practice without technology or practice using older technologies, such as audio- or videotape.

2. What technologies and software are most often used to support authentic tasks? Which technologies and software best support

those tasks? In what kinds of settings? Examine recent studies describing technology used in content-based ESL/EFL classes.

3. Using the framework in chapter 8, design a longitudinal study of the impact of task type on student learning in several different kinds of classrooms. How does technology fit in these classrooms? Is it used as effectively as it might be? Who controls the use of technology: the students, the teacher, or lab personnel?

Questions for Further Investigation

1. Do student-created tasks have the same amount and kind of impact on language learning as teacher-created tasks do? What kind of impact do they have?

2. How does task affect other variables in the environment model that serves as a framework for this text (see chapter 1)?

3. What kinds of tasks do language students consider authentic? In which contexts does this definition differ?

 # PART IV

Opportunities for Exposure and Production

Chapter 12

Theory and Research: Input, Interaction, and CALL

Lloyd Holliday

Learning a language involves internalizing a very complex set of interlocking systems that allow the user to produce and interpret novel but culturally acceptable utterances in appropriate situations. As noted in chapter 2, to produce or understand such utterances, the language user or learner has to interact with other users of the language. No matter to what degree human beings are genetically programmed to acquire languages, humans need to interact in language environments (i.e., with language users) to learn or acquire a language (i.e., to become language users themselves). This interaction is not a simple process of identifying labels for things in the environment. A word is not an independent, preexisting item that transparently refers to a preexisting object, and people cannot learn a second language by simply learning new words for existing items, that is, by substituting new names for the first language names for things. Thus, a person cannot learn a language by being filled up with knowledge *about* a language.

As an illustration, consider that people may learn the laws of physics or chemistry but do not use that knowledge to produce the chemicals reacting in their bodies that make them living organisms. Knowing the laws consciously is not how human beings produce the chemical reactions that sustain their lives. In the same way, knowing about language does not turn people into language users and producers. Being taught the grammar rules of a language does not turn people into speakers of that language. To accomplish what can be called learning a language, people need to become like a cell in their bodies that knows how to read proteins that act as chemical messengers and knows how to produce new substances to build bodies and keep them alive. To have learned a language means to have become an interactive language user. A key component of modern second language acquisition (SLA) theory is, therefore, the study of the interactive processes that lead to becoming a language learner.

Language Acquisition Processes

There are many different views on which interactive processes are absolutely necessary for language acquisition. Supported by the framework of this text, I take the view that interaction in a social and verbal sense is necessary whether the second language is learned in a second or foreign language environment or under naturalistic or classroom-instructed conditions. I also take the view that second language learners can acquire a language through various levels of conscious attention to the language and that, for success, the language available in the environment needs to be enhanced or organized in such a way that learners can make use of these levels of attention, the more conscious of which can gradually become more automatic. Furthermore, I would argue, on the one hand, that feedback on learners' performance can under certain conditions be useful but, on the other hand, that the mere learning of rules and rote memorization of facts cannot lead to successful language learning.

This line of argument follows in part that of language acquisition researchers who employ a universal grammar (UG) approach. However, it extends far beyond the UG approach by arguing that, especially for SLA, learners need more than mere exposure to the language to be learned, or *primary language data*, as Schwartz (1993) calls it. (This disagreement between the UG theorists, often referred to as *innatists*, and the theorists who believe in interaction is complex and cannot be pursued further here, but I believe the positions are reconcilable.)

Again, to become a proficient user of a language or a participant in communicative exchanges in a second language, the learner has to actively interact with other speakers in the second language. In a way this interaction is like new employees being eased into a job, feeling their way, learning the new rules, and getting to know the quirks of their colleagues and bosses so that they can be fully accepted as new members of that society or, in language learning terms, become fully accepted, functioning members of a new speech community. Research into input, uptake, and negotiation investigates what this interaction looks like and how much interaction learners need if they are to be successful.

Input

Input in its broadest sense can refer to all the target language that the learner is exposed to and that potentially provides the learner with knowledge about the target language. (The term *input* does not mean knowledge about the language in the narrow sense of direct teaching about grammar rules.) The origins of research into input from the interactionist perspective commenced with Ferguson's (1971) concept of *foreigner talk* as a specific register of simplified input used by native speakers when talking with second language learners. Wagner-Gough and Hatch (1975) and Hatch (1978a, 1978b) studied the structural characteristics of foreigner talk discourse, and Hatch (1978b, 1983) proposed a discourse model of SLA, suggesting that by using conversational strategies in interactions to negotiate input, language learners are creating their own language learning syllabus (Snow, 1972) or *comprehensible input* (Krashen, 1978, 1980, 1985). Krashen (1978) has suggested a theory of SLA called the *monitor model*. Interactionists would not agree with all of Krashen's proposals, especially his suggestion that acquisition is a process relying totally on innate factors in the human brain and that deliberately learned language knowledge cannot become acquired knowledge.

Although I agree that knowledge about language and interactive language use itself are quite different, I would also make a distinction between knowledge about grammar rules and deliberately learned language knowledge (e.g., purposeful manipulation of or focus on a limited set of language structures at any given time during planned language instruction in a classroom situation). Nevertheless, most SLA theorists have no problem with the relatively obvious concept that comprehensible input is necessary for SLA. Where researchers working in the interactionist paradigm differ from Krashen is in stressing the additional necessity for negotiation during interaction to generate the comprehensible input.

Negotiation of Meaning

Interactionists formed the concept of *negotiation of meaning* by borrowing several constructs previously developed in the fields of ethnomethodology and conversational analysis, namely, *other-correction, self-correction, repair, feedback channel, side sequences,* and *negotiation.* Garfinkle (1967) pointed out that conversational interaction is an ongoing *negotiation process,* and Jefferson (1972) used the term *side sequence* to call attention to breaks from the main stream of the conversation. *Conversational analysis* reported on the negotiations occurring during conversational interaction, such as the opening and closing of conversations (Schegloff & Sacks, 1973), the turn-taking system within conversations (Sacks, Schegloff, & Jefferson, 1974), and the repair of trouble sources (Schegloff, Jefferson, & Sacks, 1977). Schwartz (1980) described these repairs in learner-learner conversations as "a process of *negotiation* [italics added] involving speakers conferring with each other to achieve understanding" (p. 151). During interaction, both learners and their native-speaker interlocutors have opportunities to check the comprehensibility of their own messages as well as to request clarification, confirmation, or reiteration of each other's messages. In this way they can achieve mutual comprehensibility by repeating or modifying their own messages (self-repairs) or suggesting repairs for each other's utterances (see Figure 12-1).

Pica, Young, and Doughty (1987) confirmed that negotiations of meaning

---

Figure 12-1. Typical Negotiation of Meaning

Native speaker	Nonnative speaker
I drew a vee-cee-r on the table. (Trigger)	Bee-cee ... um ... ? (signal of difficulty)
I drew a videocassette recorder. (response: modification)	Oh, yes, for TV. (closure)

(i.e., adjustments) during conversations between native speakers and nonnative speakers resulted in *comprehensible input*. This comprehensible input was input modified by the native speaker at the request of the learners as they negotiated to complete tasks—in their study, for example, to select and place items on a felt-board garden according to instructions given by a native speaker. One group of learners was allowed to negotiate in order to complete the task. The instructions were then modified to reflect exactly what the learners had sought as input during the negotiations. A second group then attempted to complete the tasks, listening to the input modifications made as a result of the interactions occurring in Group 1. Group 1, which was allowed to negotiate interactively to receive modified input, outperformed Group 2, which listened only to the modified input, by 19%.

Comprehensible Output

Interactionists have not, however, claimed that modified comprehensible input is the only factor that leads to acquisition. Swain (1985) pointed out that *modified comprehensible output* was also a requirement for complete, native-speaker-like acquisition of the target language, and several studies since (Day & Shapson, 1991; Lightbown & Spada, 1990) have also suggested that the acquisition of some linguistic features may require in addition a *focus on form* during feedback on learners' production. Swain (1985) argued that the ability of learners to comprehend input did not guarantee the acquisition of certain forms and structures, for even though learners were involved in attempting to process the meaning of a message, they might not necessarily have paid much attention to form. On the other hand, learners who were given opportunities to modify their output during spoken interaction as a result of feedback from native speakers about the doubtful comprehensibility of what they had first said would need to focus on the form of their message in order to produce more comprehensible utterances.

In slightly different ways, modified comprehensible input (i.e., input modified by the native or expert target language speaker at the request of the learner) and modified comprehensible output (i.e., output in which the learner has attempted to become more intelligible) may force learners to rethink their interlanguage system and adjust it so that it is more targetlike. In this process of constantly changing their interlanguage system or developing a more targetlike system, learners move along an interlanguage continuum from zero knowledge about the second language to a point at which they possess a usable competence in the second language comparable to that of an expert or first language speaker of that language.

Following Swain's (1985) *comprehensible output hypothesis* (p. 249), which states that learners need to be pushed through negotiations to produce comprehensible output if they are to achieve production mastery during SLA, Pica, Holliday, Lewis, and Morgenthaler (1989) and Pica, Holliday, Lewis, Berducci, and Newman (1991) examined the availability of opportunities for learners to modify their output toward greater comprehensibility. They came to the conclusion that, although ample opportunities were presented to learners, two important factors appeared to facilitate learners' negotiations of meaning. First, two types of tasks—information-gap tasks in which the learners rather than the native speakers held all the vital information needed to complete the task and, to a lesser degree, jigsaw tasks requiring an exchange of information—appeared to provide learners with more opportunities to produce modified comprehensible output (see chapter 8 for further consideration of tasks). Second, female native-speaker interlocutors tended to give both male and female learners more opportunities for negotiation than male native speakers did.

Research Findings on Input and Output

Input-output studies following an interactionist perspective (Futaba, 1994; Holliday, 1993a, 1993b, 1995c; Linnell, 1995; Mackey, 1995; Oliver, 1995; Pica, 1991a, 1991b; Pica, Lewis, & Holliday, 1990; Pica, Lincoln-Porter, Paninos, & Linnell, 1995) have introduced many new ways of looking in detail at how learners encounter their target second language and how the whole environment of exposure may facilitate or retard the language learning process. However, many factors still need much more careful study before definitive conclusions can be reached. Because interaction is a social phenomenon, research on interaction incorporates a multitude of social variables, all of which need to be taken into account as part of the total environmental system. Currently the research on input and output can be summed up as having investigated the following points:

- Learners are not equally ready for all aspects of the target language at the same time.

- Development occurs as a result of differing levels of attention to the input.

- Focusing on forms that are problematic in either learners' input or learners' output is more effective than presenting abstract grammar rules.

- Explicit teaching of grammar can assist fluency in production if the teaching is linked to learners' negotiation of communication.

- Flooding the input with target structures is useful but not sufficient to guarantee mastery of those structures.

- It is beneficial for learners to negotiate the modifications of the input.

- Corrective feedback on output has a role in language learning but is not universally the best strategy.

- The gender of the participants in the interaction affects the quantity and quality of the modifications likely to be made to the input and output.

- The nature of the activities or situations in which the interaction occurs affects the quantity and quality of the modifications to the input and output.

- Modifications made to input and output as the result of negotiations can highlight the syntax of the target language.

Applications to CALL and Computer-Mediated Communicative Language Teaching

The findings of the research on input and output are applicable to CALL, as computers influence the environment in which learners are exposed to the second language. The design of multimedia language learning products and methods, such as CD-ROMs and computer-mediated communicative language teaching, needs to take input and output factors into account.

Unfortunately, a great deal of software either does not use the computer for the best language pedagogy or does not exploit the potential of computers to use pedagogies that previously were not possible or at the very least were impractical in classrooms. In most software billed as interactive, as in *interactive multimedia*, the learner is in reality not interacting with another speaker or language user at all, and all of the computer's supposed interactive responses are in fact drawn from a limited data bank of preprogrammed, pre-audio-recorded, or pre-video-recorded items. Teachers and software developers need to give more thought to how CALL can promote interaction. (A number of ideas are presented in the Classroom

Practice chapters of this volume.) There is no doubt that the computer can be used for task-based activities that focus on form, but very often this focus does not offer much more than a paper-based grammar drill does, and it ignores the distinctive ways in which computers may be able to focus learners' attention on form while they are engaged primarily in other tasks.

In addition to CALL activities in which learners interact with multimedia software, learners can interact with other speakers of the target language via networked computers on the Internet. In a number of articles (Holliday, 1995a, 1995b, 1995d, 1996, 1997, 1998), I have described computer-mediated communication for language learning using e-mail lists. The repetitive nature of some e-mail, in which writers tend to copy portions of and comment on one another's messages, may generate distributional cues to syntax similar to those described in another study (Holliday, 1995c). And although Pinto (1995) obtained disappointing results in a preliminary investigation of the potential of synchronous, or real-time, multiuser object-oriented domains (MOOs; see chapter 22) in language learning, this environment may be more useful for more advanced learners; this idea needs investigation. One of the possible advantages of having computers mediate conversations in real time is that the productive output is available to learners not merely in a linear stream of utterances but also as text on the visual display unit for comparison in a fixed, written medium. Whether this feature helps learners focus on unknown forms and accelerates learners' language acquisition requires investigation.

An argument used against language mediated via computer is that it is an impoverished, nonstandard variety that cannot supply learners with suitable second language input. To investigate this argument, I examined the quality of a large corpus of second language learners' output taken from the SL-Lists (e-mail lists for second language learners; see chapter 6) and compared this corpus with two genres (namely, personal letters and telephone conversations) from Biber's (1988) corpus. In the comparison, I employed 32 of the 67 linguistic features that Biber used in his analysis to profile the discourse characteristics of various genres (Holliday, 1997, 1998). I was able to demonstrate that, by and large, the e-mail messages of second language learners do provide other learners with grammatical, targetlike input displaying a range of language features similar to those used by first language speakers of English in comparable genres. In the second language learners' messages in English, the frequency of various linguistic features that characterize genres or styles appears to coincide with that in telephone conversations and personal letters. Differences in frequency can be explained, first, by the medium of e-mail English, which is written but is more interactive than the English used in letters and thus approximates more closely conversations that are not face-to-face; and, second, by the fact that the addressees are largely unknown to the writers and subscribers to e-mail chat lists. In the 1997 study, I commented that

Overall there seems no reason to believe that the use of English features in computer mediated communications via e-mail are skewed from norms of use by first language speakers of English. And thus there is no reason to believe that second language learners do not benefit from the practice of producing output in e-mail messages nor that they cannot benefit from these same messages as second language input. (p. 8)

Summary

In CALL, the medium of learning should provide learners with ·

- opportunities for interaction to negotiate meaning
- opportunities to hear or read modified comprehensible input
- opportunities to produce or write modified comprehensible output
- input that allows for a focus on target features of the second language
- possibilities for optimal feedback either in the form of self-access windows or buttons or in the form of interaction
- a rich context in which the second language facilitates comprehensible input

Nonetheless, research into input and output has suggested caution in certain areas. For instance, the less context, the more linguistic coding that is required. In other words, if the situation and nonverbal signals are not rich in clues about the message, the speakers need to use more language to make their message clear. Conversely, too much context in interactive multimedia may detract from rather than promote increased attention to form, as learners will not need to focus on language to understand the message or interact with the program. Also, in CALL activities, the inclusion of buttons or windows offering corrections to learners' errors (i.e., modified comprehensible input about errors in the learner's production) may not be a particularly useful teaching strategy. Research has shown that learners often simply acknowledge such signal modifications but that the signal does not lead learners to produce further modified comprehensible output. Feedback in the form of such acknowledgments may not allow processing that is deep enough to lead to cognitive restructuring of the learner's interlanguage.

Chapter 13

Classroom Practice: Using Multimedia for Input and Interaction in CALL Environments

Elizabeth Hanson-Smith

Chapter 12 describes language acquisition or, perhaps more properly, language development, as a complex process involving far more than a passive exposure to input. The active negotiation of meaning, comprehensible output, and the cognitively based restructuring of the learner's interlanguage appear to play important roles in the development of fluency and accuracy. As computer software has evolved into the elaborations of multimedia, the teacher has to face a crucial question: How can the CALL environment best provide both (a) exposure to language (input) in a variety of modes and representations and (b) opportunities for interaction or negotiation with the language (output) in a variety of modes?

Multimedia in a CALL environment means that input from written texts may be enhanced by pictures, graphics, animations, video, and sound as well as hyperlinks to other, explanatory texts. Likewise, video and other visuals, as well as a scrolled or highlighted text, may support audio. Multimedia on the computer allows students almost complete control of the number of repetitions and the amount of nonlanguage media support, a choice of other languages for bilingual glossing, and instant replay from any point in an audio or video presentation. Likewise, students may respond to multimedia stimuli not just by hitting a key or button but by producing answers in the form of text, audio, and even video.

In this chapter, I examine a number of multimedia computer programs that provide opportunities for exposure and production and analyze their relative merits as means to developing the target language. The individual teacher must still decide how much weight to give each of these aspects and at which point in development the learner might benefit most from one or the other. The software mentioned might serve as models of the kinds of software many teachers choose for specific settings and students.

Focus on Input

Listening and Vocabulary

This section focuses primarily on listening as the major mode of computer-assisted input. Computers seem to have many advantages over the audio recorder: (a) Listening to voices in a visual context can create stronger memory links than voices alone can, and (b) instant, accurate playback should enable students to hear specific parts of a segment without a tedious search through an audiotape, which is quite difficult even on an audiotape player with a counter. Indeed, Thornton and Dudley (1996), in comparing computer- and audiotape-accessed versions of the same listening materials, found that students spent considerably less time on nonlearning tasks, such as rewinding, when using the computer-based materials. Ease of use does not mean, however, that students actually take advantage of a feature. The study also indicated that students in the computer-using group spent less time listening, although they scored just as well as the audiotape player–using group when tested. These results seem to imply that students can obtain input faster with computers than with older technology. Ease of replay and the student's control over replay make the CALL environment a very rich source of listening input, particularly with the full contextual support of multimedia.

Probably one of the earliest multimedia programs, The Rosetta Stone (1995), is popular both in schools and with tourists or casual language learners. The software starts by presenting individual words at the zero level (in any one of a dozen or so languages) in several display modes (photos, text, and sound), offering learners a recording option and a testing mode in which the students either type words or click the mouse on the appropriate photo or text (see Figure 13-1). As the learner progresses through the skill levels, full sentences are eventually introduced. Students can test themselves by listening (with or without simultaneously seeing the text) and clicking on a photo, or they can simply listen to the labels on the photos read in sequence. Test scores in the full school version are kept in permanent student files for the teacher to review.

The Rosetta Stone (1995) has enjoyed wide popularity, and teachers report that their adult students love it. Despite the beautiful photos, however, I have three very strong critiques of this software as an input device for language development:

1. The words and sentences are not contextualized beyond the photos, which are unrelated to each other; that is, there is no story line, character development, or coherent setting. The software therefore does not provide a means to create cognitive scripts, which many practitioners and pedagogical theorists feel is a crucial element in what Holliday calls the *restructuring* of

Figure 13-1. Testing Mode in The Rosetta Stone (1995)

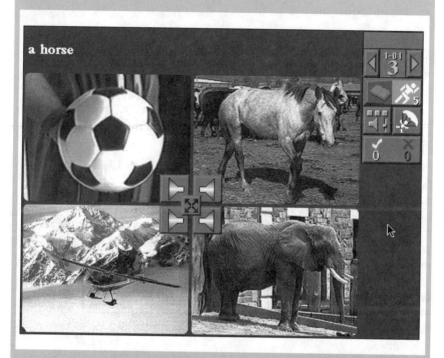

Note. From The Rosetta Stone (Version 2.0) [Computer software], 1995, Harrisonburg, VA: Fairfield Language Technologies. Copyright © 1995 by Fairfield Language Technologies. Reprinted with permission.

interlanguage (see chapter 12). Put more simply, photos and text assembled at random provide input, but not comprehensible input in the largest sense.

2. There is no social contextualization. Because The Rosetta Stone's photos are organized around the structures of a language—for example, the present progressive—the photos cannot model typical discourse interactions, which often include a wide variety of (sometimes quite advanced) grammatical structures, ellipses and contractions, and colloquialisms, as shown in the following example:

    A: Hi, how'r' ya?

    B: Hey, what's up? Ya goin' t' the show?

Students using The Rosetta Stone are learning textbook words and sentences, not real language (a problem many grammar textbooks also suffer from).

3. There is no built-in opportunity for interaction, as the computer is not (yet) a good conversation partner. Although learners can record their own voices and compare them with the machine's recording, this *interactivity* with the computer is not *interaction* in the sense that language theorists use the term. In language interaction, one speaker negotiates meaning with another speaker until both are satisfied that communication has taken place (or until one of the interlocutors walks away).

Why are learners so happy with The Rosetta Stone (1995) despite these flaws? Perhaps because no one walks away from the learners, frowns at their accent, or gives off the signals of impatience that even a trained teacher at times cannot suppress. The goal of learners may not be to negotiate meaning, a difficult and burdensome struggle, but to have a safe experience with learning, and The Rosetta Stone indeed offers a comfortable environ-ment for studying language. It is patient, impersonal, and impassive, features that can be a great advantage for adult learners who may be relatively self-conscious and socially aware and therefore relatively ill at ease in a new language environment. The Rosetta Stone might thus be particu-larly useful as a self-access program for one or two students who are at too low a level to benefit from classroom interaction or as a way of introducing the handwriting or written system of a language. When using the software with students, the teacher should be sure to write out clear directions so that students will use the input mode (listening as the photos are highlighted in clockwise sequence) before trying the self-test modes.

Another type of software favored for language input is the point-and-click environment, as, for example, in Community Exploration (1994; see Figure 13-2). One of the pioneer programs in multimedia language software, Community Exploration has worn remarkably well. Instead of showing unrelated photos on a screen, it presents landscapes and rooms with people, actions, and objects in naturalistic association. From an overview of a city, users click on a building to enter it. They click on figures on the screen to hear a word and one or more sentences related to the setting. Students zoom in from a city scene to specific neighborhoods and buildings that provide a context in which to explore words and sentences. Sound effects and short, sometimes humorous animations enhance the realism and motivate continued exploration. Students may record their voices, and scores on vocabulary tests are saved to a file.

The presentation of objects and actions in a coherent setting in Community Exploration (1994) results in far greater comprehensibility of input than that found in The Rosetta Stone (1995), although Community

Figure 13-2. Screen From Community Exploration (1994)

Note. From Community Exploration [Computer software], 1994, Lansing, MI: Hartley Courseware/Jostens Learning. Copyright © 1994 by Jostens Learning. Reprinted with permission.

Exploration is less comprehensive. Its humor makes it appropriate for beginning adolescent learners who might quickly become bored with the very dry presentation of words and structures in The Rosetta Stone.

A number of dictionaries or encyclopedias on CD-ROM also use point-and-click exploration to introduce reading vocabulary. One problem to watch for is the overuse of special effects, that is, exaggerated sound effects or animation that, despite their entertainment value, may keep students from learning the words. This problem most often presents itself in software targeting children. The latent assumption seems to be that children can only be amused or entertained, not taught, an approach that devalues the learning process. An example of this problem is found in the charming but occasionally fluffy Me and My World, a picture dictionary (1995; see Figure 13-3). For example, an octopus turns into a woman's head with Medusa-like hair. The image is amusing, but it is confusing for language intake because the animation has little to do with the ocean context.

Figure 13-3. "In the Ocean" Page From Me and My World (1995)

Note. From Me and My World [Computer software], 1995, Lincolnwood, IL: National Textbook Company. Copyright © 1995 by National Textbook Company. Reprinted with permission.

A Plan for Using Point-and-Click Software

To use the point-and-click environment successfully for student input, teachers should develop a careful set of lessons relating the software to course content. An example of what can be done is The New Oxford Picture Dictionary CD-ROM (1997; Figure 13-4), a fully contextualized multimedia dictionary. On the page called "The Market," students click on an item to hear its name, which appears in a text box below the picture. Submenus lead to detailed pictures of food items and more vocabulary. A button control panel takes the students to practice games, tests, and readings. In using this CD-ROM during a unit on foods, the teacher might

Figure 13-4. "The Market" Page From The New Oxford Picture Dictionary CD-ROM (1997)

Note. From The New Oxford Picture Dictionary CD-ROM (Bilingual Spanish ed.) [Computer software], 1997, Oxford: Oxford University Press. Copyright © 1997 by Oxford University Press. Reprinted with permission.

1. specify how to navigate to "The Market" or to one of the detailed food pages, giving specific directions on which buttons to click and when to do so

2. specify a minimum number of words to click (20 is the minimum to take a test in this program)

3. indicate which tasks to complete, such as Exercise 1, a reading passage and cloze test ("Read, Listen, and Speak"), and a Concentration-style memory game

4. as a follow-up, ask students to seek out all the foods needed to make a favorite recipe, or have them arrange the foods they have selected into the major nutritional groups and explain their choices to classmates

Discourse

Although Community Exploration (1994; discussed above) allows students to listen to words and sentences and easily record their own voices for comparison, the software does not focus on the discourse functions of language. Two CD-ROMs, Learning English: Home and Family (1994; see Figure 13-5) and Learning English: Neighborhood Life (1994) were developed at the same time as Community Exploration. They are based on dialogues and narratives appropriate to typical situations for the newcomer to the United States: A family moving into a new neighborhood, a visit to the supermarket, a shopping trip to the mall, and so on. In the software, a dialogue bubble pops up as characters speak. A small animation bubble explains vocabulary perceived to be difficult for learners.

The dialogues in the presentation phase of the software provide naturalistic language input punctuated by drawings, animations, and sound effects. The script is available for reading input. Testing in the software includes having students select items on sale in the market (which drop into

Figure 13-5. Presentation Mode in Learning English: Home and Family (1994)

Note. From Learning English: Home and Family [Computer software], 1994, Lansing, MI: Hartley Courseware/Jostens Learning. Copyright © 1994 by Jostens Learning. Reprinted with permission.

a shopping cart) and move boxes into a new home with the mouse. The heightened interactivity of the software (e.g., the dragging and dropping of objects) should not be confused with sociolinguistic interactions between people, although these are well modeled in the short narratives and dialogues in the presentation mode.

Two other interesting programs that present naturalistic settings, discourse, and human action for the adult learner are MacESL (1992; described further in chapter 25) and Accelerated English (1995; Figure 13-6). Both programs present narratives based on typical situations, such as finding employment, interviewing for a job, and renting a house, through sound and animated drawings and through text and sound. The presentations are followed by practice in completing cloze passages, matching sentence halves, ordering the story, and the like. Learners thus may access input in a variety of ways, for example, reading and listening to the text or viewing the animated drawings while listening to the script. Students can take advantage of their preferred learning modes while gaining entry into the language. In both programs, students can record their own voice and compare it with the model.

Figure 13-6. Screen From "Airplane Trip" (Dialogue With Media Support) in Accelerated English (1995)

Note. From Accelerated English (Demo version) [Computer software], 1995, Cupertino, CA: Courseware Publishing International. Copyright © 1995 by Courseware Publishing International. Reprinted with permission.

Although many software programs take full advantage of the computer's ability to handle sound and graphics, Quick English (1997; Figure 13-7) goes a step further by providing video-based dialogues that allow the high-intermediate to advanced learner to listen in on realistic-sounding (although fully scripted) conversations that take place in typical work or home venues (e.g., making a hotel reservation over the telephone or making a purchase in a store). Students may listen to and watch the video with or without seeing the text, read the script and review the video, and then take a test. An interesting feature of the software is that students can make the conversation branch to alternate versions of the videos; one might contain a negative response to a question whereas another might contain a positive response. Students can thus reuse the same video passage several times to practice different structures.

Authentic Language Sources for Advanced Learners

As an addition to stand-alone or networked multimedia software designed for ESL/EFL learners, the Internet provides a number of free, authentic

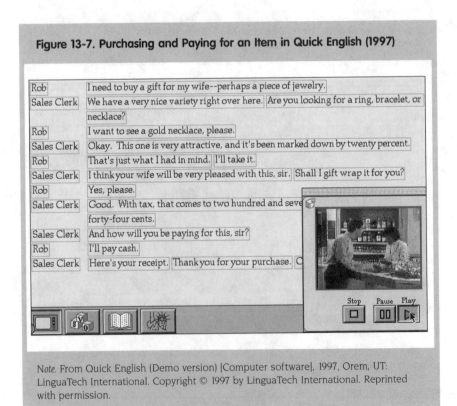

Figure 13-7. Purchasing and Paying for an Item in Quick English (1997)

Rob	I need to buy a gift for my wife--perhaps a piece of jewelry.
Sales Clerk	We have a very nice variety right over here. Are you looking for a ring, bracelet, or necklace?
Rob	I want to see a gold necklace, please.
Sales Clerk	Okay. This one is very attractive, and it's been marked down by twenty percent.
Rob	That's just what I had in mind. I'll take it.
Sales Clerk	I think your wife will be very pleased with this, sir. Shall I gift wrap it for you?
Rob	Yes, please.
Sales Clerk	Good. With tax, that comes to two hundred and seve[n] forty-four cents.
Sales Clerk	And how will you be paying for this, sir?
Rob	I'll pay cash.
Sales Clerk	Here's your receipt. Thank you for your purchase.

Stop   Pause   Play

Note. From Quick English (Demo version) [Computer software], 1997, Orem, UT: LinguaTech International. Copyright © 1997 by LinguaTech International. Reprinted with permission.

listening resources that are particularly appropriate as input for intermediate to advanced learners. At MTV Online (http://www.mtv.com/), students may listen to short audio files containing excerpts from the recordings of performance artists. World Wide Web sites for newly released movies feature short video clips from the film and audio clips of the dialogue (see also The Internet Movie Database, http://us.imdb.com/, and Appendix F).

News sites on the Internet sponsored by radio stations, television networks, and newspaper and magazine publishers, including Voice of America's home page (http://www.voa.gov/), CNN Interactive (http://www.cnn.com/), and USA Today (http://www.usatoday.com/), provide short videos, audio files, or photos accompanied by sound bites from speeches. These resources may be adapted to whole language activities, such as note-taking or research. (See chapter 9 for suggestions on using these sites for listening dictations.) Certainly, advances in push-pull or streaming technology, which allows the smooth play of audio files and live videoconferencing, will provide increasing opportunities to use the Web for both real-time and asynchronous listening activities and conversations (see Duber, 1997, http://www-writing.berkeley.edu/chorus/call/cuttingedge.html; Li, 1998, http://www.lang.uiuc.edu/r-li5/book/; Trickel, 1997, http://grove.ufl.edu/~ktrickel/teslmini/activity.html; and Appendix G). In addition, CD-ROMs are now being developed with Internet links—sometimes referred to as connected CD—so that students may watch a video on the CD-ROM and, by means of a hyperlink, see explanatory information stored on the Internet.

A Plan for Using Video or Sound Clips

Whatever the level of Internet connectivity in a CALL environment, the teacher must devote time to preparing activities or tasks that promote the learners' interaction with the material, with each other, and with native speakers. A simple plan for having students use a sound clip on a CD-ROM or a Web site for discourse activities might look like this:

1. In the classroom, the students review vocabulary found in the dialogue or sound clip.

2. In the CALL lab, the students listen to a specified sound clip, taking notes or downloading printed text, graphics, photos, or related materials.

3. In groups outside the lab, the students create a new dialogue using the same or similar vocabulary for a related situation.

4. The students present the dialogue to other class members, either live or on videotape.

5. The students analyze each other's use of vocabulary and social collocations, using a rubric prepared by the teacher or the learners.

Reading Holistically

The second major mode for language learning input is reading. Although ordinary conversation in English, for example, may involve only 50 or so vocabulary items, the educated native speaker has a vocabulary of 25,000–50,000 words. After learners know approximately 3,000 words, they will acquire most new vocabulary through reading. Of course, learning the language of written texts is crucial for students wishing to pursue higher education. A combination of skills, such as skimming, scanning, and predicting the meaning of words in context, is useful, but extensive reading for meaning and the ability to read large amounts of text at nativelike speed (over 350 words per minute) is also important. (See chapter 9 for a discussion of discrete reading skills in a CALL environment, including the use of the Internet and e-mail.)

Beyond skills, reading with a purpose—for example, to understand a communication from a keypal in an e-mail message—can provide beneficial target language input in an interactive setting (see chapter 12). However, for more holistic, extensive reading input, the computer has definite disadvantages:

- Reading from a monitor can produce serious eyestrain.

- The breaks between screens can disrupt the flow of reading far more than page turning can, as students must guide the mouse pointer to a button or scroll bar in order to advance to the next screen. In so doing, the eyes leave the text and must reposition themselves. By contrast, students can turn pages in a book without changing their visual focus.

- Pages are usually much smaller on screen than in a book and contain less text, further disrupting the cognitive work the mind performs in predicting and constructing larger meanings from words, sentences, and paragraphs.

None of these drawbacks is serious when the texts are relatively short, as they are in all the software mentioned earlier except Quick English (1997), which displays long passages of text on screen. And, despite these short-comings, the computer provides several clear advantages over written texts.

Sound Capabilities

Many multimedia programs, even those not written specifically for language learners, take advantage of the computer's sound capabilities to read the text aloud, often while highlighting individual words or sentences. For example, in Destination: Ocean (1995) and other software in the Imagination Express series (see chapter 10), which targets native-English-speaking middle school students, learners can click on the audio option to hear the text read; each word is highlighted as it is spoken. The reference material shown in Figure 13-8 contains a text-to-speech option (the loud-

Figure 13-8. Reference Material From Destination: Ocean (1995)

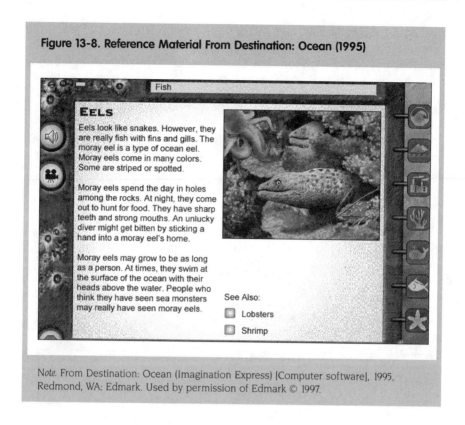

Note. From Destination: Ocean (Imagination Express) [Computer software], 1995, Redmond, WA: Edmark. Used by permission of Edmark © 1997.

speaker button) and additional, different oral input (the camera button), so that students may listen while viewing an animated sequence. Tabs on the right lead to other reference sections.

Whereas forcing children (especially language learners) to read aloud to the class can be traumatic for the reader and boring and painful for the class, being read to models the reading process, helping students associate typical sentence patterns and vocabulary collocations that they may recognize in oral language with the print counterparts. Being read to by adults and older siblings seems to be one of the chief factors in producing early reading mastery by native-speaking children, and in some adult literacy programs tutors read aloud to their students. However, this kind of dual (hear-see) input is difficult for adult learners to come by except in one-on-one tutoring, so the CALL environment can be an ideal medium for initial reading experiences, especially when large classes might prevent close attention to individual students.

Scrolling

A second advantage of the computer over written texts is that, in paced reading, the need to scroll rather than turn pages, which can slow down reading for meaning, can operate to the learner's advantage. That is, the computer can be set to scroll pages automatically at a certain rate. NewReader (McVicker, 1995a; see chapter 9) uses this function with any plain-text file imported into the software by the teacher or student. As shown in Figure 13-9, the student sets a pace on the slide bar at the bottom of the screen, and a line runs through the text, guiding the eye downward.

When using paced reading activities, the teacher should prepare several global comprehension questions to ensure that students do not become bored; however, even without follow-up, setting a reading pace of about 350 words per minute can give college-bound, motivated adult students a good idea of the reading speed an academic degree requires.

Hypertext and Hypermedia

A third advantage of using computers for reading is that hypertext or hypermedia links allow instantaneous glosses in the form of pictures, animations, video, and related reading material. At the advanced level, for

Figure 13-9. Paced Reading Activity in NewReader (McVicker, 1995)

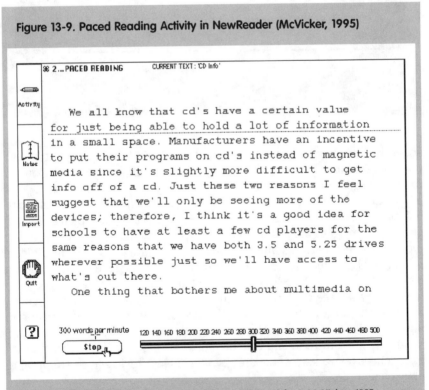

Note. From NewReader (Version 1.00) [Computer software], by J. McVicker, 1995, Athens, OH: Hyperbole Software. Copyright © 1995 by J. McVicker. Reprinted with permission of the author.

example, in HyperStory (May, 1995; an accompaniment to the short-story textbook *Fiction's Many Worlds*, May, 1993), hyperlinks point out metaphors and symbols and provide study questions and ideas for writing assignments. When a hyperlink is accessed, a simple word processor allows students to take notes and begin composing an essay. The student reads the text on paper first and uses the software version to review and prepare for the composition process.

Students at the early levels of language learning spend a great deal of reading time transferring the contents of a bilingual glossary or dictionary to the page being read. This lookup process considerably slows the real reading process and probably overloads short-term memory, thus interfering with the acquisition of vocabulary. A reference to a picture or a video gloss of a word may be less distracting to readers, in part because it can be accessed almost instantaneously and in part because it can assist memory more fully by creating multiple means to store and access the reference later. However, hypermedia may also prove a fatal distraction when students fail to use any prediction strategies at all or when they follow hyperlinks in several different directions and lose their way back to the original text, either metaphorically or literally. Several software packages, including NewReader (McVicker, 1995a), allow teachers to create their own hyperlinked glosses for texts, thus controlling and limiting lookups. Authoring software, such as HyperCard® (1997; for Macintosh® computers only) or ToolBook II (1996; for computers running Microsoft® MS-DOS® or Windows® only), makes the process so simple that students can create hypermedia-linked texts for each other as a means of learning and practicing vocabulary.

When using hypermedia, teachers should set up some guidelines for students to follow as they point and click. For example, the teacher needs to specify that the students should read the entire passage or essay and then return to the beginning of the reading before clicking on any links. HyperStory (May, 1995) almost demands a text reading first because the stories are relatively long. Additionally, teachers should encourage prediction by having students write up briefly what they expect to find based on the title of the story and any illustrations. Boswood's (1997) collection of lesson plan ideas for using computers devotes a section to the use of multimedia encyclopedias, such as Microsoft Encarta® Encyclopedia 98 (1997), a point-and-click multimedia reference work. Most such works now also come with a "homework helper" that maps out ways for a student to create a research paper using the resources in the reference work.

The Internet as a Reading Source

Teachers are coming to realize that the Internet is a marvelous source of free multimedia reading materials (see Appendix F), generally at the sixth- to eighth-grade native-speaker level. *Project Gutenberg* (http://www.gutenberg.net/)

collects copyright-free texts worldwide and places them in an on-line archive accessible on the Internet. The teacher (or the students) may download these reading materials and use them either as texts on screen or printed out on paper. In addition, the Web contains a vast array of media-supported reading. Sites on science, history, and culture are widely available and often not only come with audiovisual support but also relate to television programs—for example, those produced by the Public Broadcasting System (PBS)/WGBH (see NOVA Online, 1997, http://www.pbs.org/wgbh/nova/), the Discovery Channel (http://www.discovery.com/) and the Learning Channel (see the Discovery Channel's site). (See chapters 7 and 10 for a discussion of Web sites supporting television and video.) Travel and tourism sites on the Web are another good source of reading materials with visual support. News sites, such as CNN Interactive (http://www.cnn.com/) or USA Today (http://www.usatoday.com/), are particularly useful for intermediate-level learners of English, as the numerous photos, audio files, and videos give context to the written articles. CNN San Francisco: Interactive Learning Resources (1998, http://www.cnnsf.com/education/education.html) also provides reading materials prepared at a beginning level of English along with comprehension questions scored on-line and writing suggestions; Classline: The Daily Teaching System (1997, http://www.usatoday.com/classlin/clfront.htm) provides a daily lesson plan using USA Today's news, entertainment, and sports stories.

One interesting activity, suggested at LinguaCenter (http://deil.lang.uiuc .edu/), the home page of the Division of English as an International Language, University of Illinois at Urbana- Champaign, is to compare news stories on the same topic in each of several Internet news sites. LinguaCenter contains the necessary links. Also, a number of push services individualize Internet content for their customers and e-mail it to them. Usually subscriptions are free to users (paid for by advertisements), so students can select a number of topics they are interested in and receive updated news each time they go on-line. This individualized reading can be highly motivating, but the teacher may also specify one or more common news threads for the whole class to receive and then discuss together. The Yahoo! channel is one of the easiest such services to access and personalize (see Yahoo!, http:// www.yahoo.com/, for instructions).

Reading in Context

A clear advantage of the CALL environment is the computer's ability to provide contextual support in a wide variety of media to students attempting to read in a content area. Some CD-ROMs provide multimedia-based lesson plans as well. One of the best packages of CALL reading support is Macmillan/McGraw-Hill's Multimedia Literature series (described in chapter 10). Each of the software programs, intended for the middle-school-aged native speaker, is directly linked to and based on a fiction or nonfiction text in the curriculum. Because of the intelligent array of cognitive support, the software is readily adaptable to the intermediate-level nonnative speaker of the same age. For example, in Do Not Disturb (1995; discussed in chapter 10), the learner uses a simulated tracking beeper and binoculars to observe a bear while taking notes in a little journal on screen. Next, students use the textbook, a diagram of the bear, short videos, and their own notes to answer questions about bears' habits, specifying in the answer to each question where they got the information. Before accessing the diagram and video, students prepare a checklist based on what they already know or believe. While viewing the video and listening, they confirm or correct their initial predictions. Finally, students use their notes and the answers to their questions to write a paper based on a set of writing prompts. Papers are peer edited using another set of prompts for evaluation built into the software. The educational value of such a computer program is clear, and the cognitive skill-building and vocabulary development aspects of the software are well developed.

Another similarly well-designed series of software for somewhat younger students, Discoveries, by Houghton Mifflin, presents a very attractive 360-degree photo of a natural habitat. Discoveries: In the Desert (1995), for example, allows users to explore a desert scene of the southwestern United States, clicking on a number of animals and plants for reference information (Figure 13-10). A cabin set in the panorama is the entrance to the library, where further information about the desert and its inhabitants may be found. For example, a clickable map takes the user to other major deserts around the world; textbooks on the shelves open to reveal reference

Figure 13-10. Objects Leading to Reference Information in Discoveries: In the Desert (1995)

Note. From Discoveries: In the Desert [Computer software]. Copyright © 1995 by D.C. Heath & Company. Reprinted with permission of Houghton Mifflin Company. All rights reserved.

information, a notebook or journal for record keeping, and prompts for writing activities (see Figure 13-11). The software makes apparent the advantages of multimedia support for content-related vocabulary and reading input and writing activities.

Available on-line are Web pages by major producers of educational CD-ROMs and television programs. These pages include interesting reading material in a variety of content areas with appropriate visual support and on-line explorations. The National Geographic Society's *King Cobra* (1997, http://www.nationalgeographic.com/kingcobra/index-n.html; see Figure 13-12) is a good example; clicking on various parts of the snake on the right brings up the small inserts on the left, with text, animations, and video clips. Also included on many of these sites are lesson plans to use in school and tie-ins to the television programs. Sometimes, as in NOVA *Online* (1997, http://www.pbs.org/wgbh/nova/), the resources even include the transcripts of the related TV show for teachers to preview with their students.

As mentioned with regard to multimedia point-and-click environments, the teacher should clearly indicate a minimum number of objects for students to find and how many and which activities students should complete. In *King Cobra* (1997; Figure 13-12), for example, the teacher might

Figure 13-11. Reference Material in Discoveries: In the Desert (1995)

Note. From Discoveries: In the Desert [Computer software]. Copyright © 1995 by D.C. Heath & Company. Reprinted with permission of Houghton Mifflin Company. All rights reserved.

Figure 13-12. Reference to Support Television Show on National Geographic Society's *King Cobra* Page (1997)

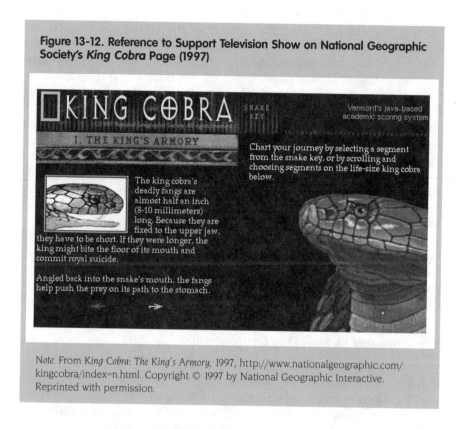

Note. From *King Cobra: The King's Armory*, 1997, http://www.nationalgeographic.com/kingcobra/index=n.html. Copyright © 1997 by National Geographic Interactive. Reprinted with permission.

specify that students should click on all the parts of the snake and reply to a set of questions about the reference material, first making predictions based on what they already know or believe.

Focus on Output

Speaking and Interaction

Ideally, listening and speaking occur together in an interaction that fosters such desirable social goals as giving strokes, maintaining friendships, group identification, and saving face as well as the exchange of information (see chapter 8; see also Wolfson, 1989). However, many language learners do not have the opportunity to interact with native speakers in a meaningful way; if they do, their efforts may be rebuffed or misunderstood because discourse conventions differ among cultures. The CALL environment may be an ideal safe haven for learners to practice interaction before plunging into the deep waters of real conversation.

Because of the limitations of the technology, early computer software focused primarily on non-oral output from the learner: clicking on the correct response to a question or moving a word or object across the screen to the right location. Increasingly, however, voice technology is allowing learners to give spoken responses as well. For instance, in the Triple Play Plus! series (Syracuse Language Systems/Random House), available for French, Spanish, and English, the learner orders food at a café. The computer responds only if it understands what the student has said. In a similar vein, in TRACI Talk: The Mystery (1997) the student helps solve a mystery by speaking to the computer.

Computers' speech recognition capability is still fairly limited, however, so users must choose one of several fixed answers for the software to recognize the spoken response. Also, speech recognition does not help with accent reduction, as the software recognizes even a very heavy nonnative accent as long as the whole utterance is comparable to the canned script. Even given these limitations, speech recognition technology can give learners a positive whole language experience that prepares them for interaction with conversation partners outside the lab. Talking to a machine can be far less intimidating than talking to a human.

The Computer as Speaking Environment

One of the most significant uses of the CALL environment is as a stimulus for classroom conversation—talking around the computer rather than talking to it. Many tasks formerly performed with paper and pencil can now be accomplished with the computer's power of data manipulation: Cities can be built, civilizations rise and fall, and whole ecosystems be constructed or destroyed with a keystroke. Learners can explore the magical world of Myst (1995), identify a mysterious stranger in Who Is Oscar Lake? (1996), or drive a covered wagon along the Oregon Trail (Oregon Trail II, 1997). Usually the experienced teacher allows a group or triad of students to work for a limited period of time on a simulation or adventure, often on a predefined task. Groups will then put the software in "pause" mode (or save the current state of the game) and reassemble away from the computer to compare notes and maps and write up directions for the next session, or for other users if they swap machines (see Baltra, 1984). Be sure to assign students definite roles, such as note-taker, keyboarder, timekeeper, and group leader, and have the students rotate roles as they work through a program. Especially at the low-intermediate level, students might benefit from the rehearsal of polite requests, suggestions, and advice—the social discourse needed for the group work; the teacher might wish to introduce and encourage students to use the vocabulary pertinent to the game's or simulation's content.

An interesting, ongoing study of simulations and the language they practice is being conducted by Wright (1998). Meanwhile, many teachers have seen the immediate advantages of computer simulations, as opposed to debates, board games, or even teacher- or textbook-created simulations: The computer does not require additional space to set up and store physical materials; students may return to the game at another time and pick up where they left off; and instructions and help screens are always accessible, sometimes in the native language. The level of complexity can be adjusted, and, especially in the sciences and social sciences, multimedia simulations provide experiences for students that are impossible or extremely difficult to come by in the classroom—a trip to the planet Mars, a journey back to the Babylonian kingdom, or a visit to the rain forest or deep under the ocean.

A Plan for Using Simulations

Another advantage of educational simulations is that some of them are packaged with lesson plans to help the busy teacher spark interaction. Among the most interesting of such simulations are those created by Tom Snyder Productions (TSP). This company's products (see also chapters 3 and 19) span a wide range of interests and age groups, beginning with Choices, Choices (1994), which asks elementary school students to form discussion groups on topics of importance in their own lives and the life of their community, and Decisions, Decisions (1996), which covers topics in U.S. history for high school students. The software gives directions for forming groups and asks students to take a stand, look at more than one side of a question, debate, and report back.

TSP's software is written primarily for native speakers; however, the instructional apparatus is excellent and readily adaptable to the language learner as well. The advantage of using such software is that the roles within the tasks are already well defined, so students will have ample opportunity to practice interactions and negotiate meaning. The same principles, however, may be used for any adventure or simulation software:

1. Place the students in groups, and give each participant a clearly defined role.

2. Limit the task to a specific time period: 15–20 minutes at the computer followed by 15–20 minutes to "download": organize notes, make maps, and write directions for the other teams. This stage is the one in which the best student interaction takes place. This strategy is perfect for the one-computer classroom, in which teams may rotate through the same application and later share their findings.

3. Make sure students understand how they will report back to the whole class. The reporting method may be as simple as giving a "hot tip" of the day or as complex as designing a new simulation.

4. Tie discussion and game activities to a written or oral follow-up for closure at the end of each session.

The principles apply when students are using educational videos, particularly those that ask them to debate or take a stand on an issue. The Web sites of the producers of several television series (e.g., *National Geographic Society*, http://www.nationalgeographic.com/; *NOVA Online*, 1997, http://www.pbs.org/wgbh/nova/, mentioned above) now have interesting materials that foster interactive use of television or video. PBS *TeacherSource* (1998, http://www.pbs.org/teachersource/) has tips and lesson plans to accompany PBS shows; A&E *Classroom: Classroom Materials Pages* (1997, http://www.aetv.com/class/teach/) offers materials designed to be used with A&E Television Network shows. Many of these Web sites also offer live chat on-line. Increasingly, the interactivity possible on the Web is being cross-linked with the more passive television broadcast system.

Writing as Interaction

One of the most significant advances in the teaching of language has been the extensive use of the word processor for composition. It is difficult to imagine writing as a process without the ease of revision and editing provided by the computer. When students must revise by hand, the teacher hardly dares request major revisions, particularly in longer compositions. When students are freed by technology to write at length and revise globally, the focus shifts from local corrections to communication, from recopying to reorganizing. Furthermore, when students find an authentic audience beyond the teacher and participate in peer editing, writing becomes a communicative act between reader and writer.

Chapter 12 explains the significance of interaction in the e-mail keypal setting. In the same way, software that encourages peer interaction in a more formal composition classroom has come to play an increasing role in the teaching of writing. Software like Daedalus® Integrated Writing Environment (DIWE, 1997), CommonSpace (1997), and Web-B-Mail (Pfaff-Harris, 1996) allows students to form small groups electronically (either within one classroom on a local area network [LAN] or across the world on the Internet) in order to brainstorm ideas, read and respond to each others' writing with comments in margin-windows, and assist in peer editing and evaluation. Although at first blush networking the writing group seems unnecessary, as students can sit in a circle face-to-face in a classroom, in fact the electronic network enhances the group's functions in surprising ways. The most verbally fluent participants cannot dominate the group, because each member has plenty of time to compose and type questions and responses before they are posted. Because each member's contribution is saved to a file or bulletin board for all to see, the teacher and the group leader can easily keep track of each member's contributions and maintain the direction of the discussion or review the previous discussion to pick up earlier threads. As shown in Figure 13-13, a student composes a response in the box

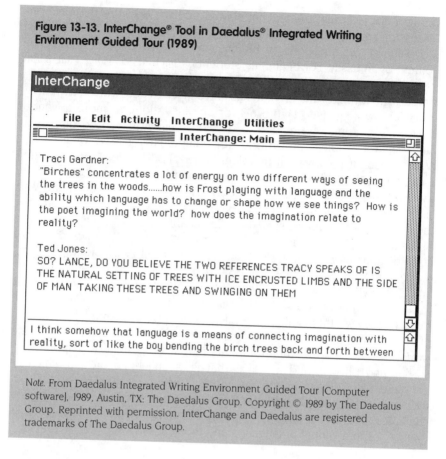

Figure 13-13. InterChange® Tool in Daedalus® Integrated Writing Environment Guided Tour (1989)

> **InterChange**
>
> File   Edit   Activity   InterChange   Utilities
>
> InterChange: Main
>
> Traci Gardner:
> "Birches" concentrates a lot of energy on two different ways of seeing the trees in the woods......how is Frost playing with language and the ability which language has to change or shape how we see things? How is the poet imagining the world? how does the imagination relate to reality?
>
> Ted Jones:
> SO? LANCE, DO YOU BELIEVE THE TWO REFERENCES TRACY SPEAKS OF IS THE NATURAL SETTING OF TREES WITH ICE ENCRUSTED LIMBS AND THE SIDE OF MAN TAKING THESE TREES AND SWINGING ON THEM
>
> I think somehow that language is a means of connecting imagination with reality, sort of like the boy bending the birch trees back and forth between

Note. From Daedalus Integrated Writing Environment Guided Tour [Computer software], 1989, Austin, TX: The Daedalus Group. Copyright © 1989 by The Daedalus Group. Reprinted with permission. InterChange and Daedalus are registered trademarks of The Daedalus Group.

at the bottom of the screen while the present state of the conversation is recorded in the scrollable window on top.

Another advantage of an electronic writing environment is that, instead of popping in to hear one student for a few seconds, the teacher can switch from group to group on-line and read the entire transcript of the discussion up to that moment—without making any learner self-conscious. At the end of the session, the entire transcript is saved, and each participant can get a printout to take home. This kind of interaction—which involves only a slight time delay and requires keyboarding rather than speaking—can produce considerable depth of thought and a sense of an authentic audience because the peer group, not the teacher, determines the course of discussion. One further advantage is that the peer group need not be physically present in any one geographic space. The technology of an electronic writing environment gives the remote student or the handicapped student who uses specially adapted equipment to operate the keyboard full access to opportunities for language exposure and production.

In a class setting, the teacher should perhaps organize the electronic discussion groups across generations and language differences and furnish a specific set of questions to brainstorm or to review and analyze the content of an essay. For beginning students, *Email Projects Home Page* (Gaer, 1997, http://www.otan.dni.us/webfarm/emailproject/email.htm) provides a simple form for reporting on readings and a place to post written comments on others' writings (see Figure 6-3 for an illustration). At more advanced levels, students may be guided to develop their own focused discussion questions for readings and rubrics for editing. HUT *Internet Writing Project* (Vilmi, 1998b, http://www.hut.fi/~rvilmi/Project/) offers ideas for discussion and composition either on the Web, as students across the globe read the same materials, or in a classroom if only LAN access is available. Many Web sites offer chat rooms or bulletin boards that allow students to interact at their own pace with native speakers. (See chapter 6 and Appendix B on the SL-*Lists*, in which students write to one another on set topics or follow conversations at will.) *Biography Magazine* (1997, http://www.biography.com/read/), for example, has message boards on movie stars, historical figures, and even mythical and fictional characters, a wonderful writing supplement to a reading unit or course. Also, *Heinle & Heinle Museum of Cultural Imagery* (1996, http://www.thomson.com/heinle/museum/welcome.html) has pictures of, for example, friends from different cultures in various settings around the world, a "schoolroom" where students may write poems or responses to stories and photos, and a "café," that is, a bulletin board on which to converse with others about the stories they have posted and about cross-cultural issues. (See chapter 7 and Appendix B for the names of other chat sites.) These sites provide many opportunities for students to express themselves in a variety of language and thought modes.

Multimedia Projects

Desktop publishing (DTP) and multimedia presentation software have become significant extensions of the word-processing tool, and they give students practice in tasks that they will use in the academic and business worlds. DTP software, such as Microsoft Publisher 97 (1997), allows students to lay out text and interweave text and graphics or photos as is done in a professionally produced newsletter or magazine. Presentation software packages (described more fully in chapter 25), such as HyperStudio (1997) or Microsoft PowerPoint® 97 (1996), are simple to learn to use and allow students to develop and expand their own writing and research with the addition of color, sound, video, graphics, and animation. Most such programs have Web plug-ins so that presentations can be posted on the Internet and viewed by others. Multimedia presentations are used throughout the business world, so teaching students to produce them jump-starts learners' career skills while allowing students to access their own creative strengths in a variety of learning styles.

For young, beginning-level language learners, software like Storybook Maker (1994) uses the Macintosh computer's built-in text-to-speech function to read aloud (in a robotic voice) what the student has written. Although the accent and stress are not necessarily good models of pronunciation, there is considerable satisfaction in hearing one's writing read aloud, and the learner may also find some delight in correcting the computer. Certainly, the software follows the tenets of the write-to-read approach. A number of the content-based programs described above, such as the Imagination Express series (e.g., Destination: Ocean, 1995; see Figure 13-14), also have modest multimedia authoring tools to help students create presentations using clips of the art and text in the software and allow students to record their own reading of the stories they have composed. In Destination: Ocean, students can clip art from reference material on the software, insert it over backgrounds, write their own text, and record their own voices reading it. (See chapter 10 for details on content-based software with multimedia production capabilities; see chapter 25 for detailed procedures for using multimedia authoring projects and software.)

Figure 13-14. Multimedia Presentation From Destination: Ocean (1995)

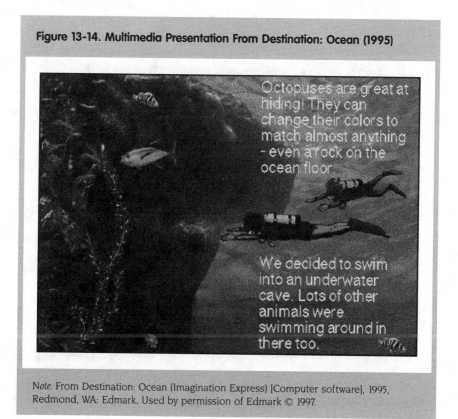

Note. From Destination: Ocean (Imagination Express) [Computer software], 1995, Redmond, WA: Edmark. Used by permission of Edmark © 1997.

In using DTP and producing multimedia projects, students must define a voice, target an audience appropriate to their project, and develop a plan to incorporate a variety of media into a satisfactory whole. Work in groups on relatively complex productions, such as a class newsletter, a Web page, a cultural investigation, or a science project, also requires the use of language for interpersonal communication and the application of higher cognitive skills in learning how to use the software and then in organizing and presenting the subject matter. In projects I helped students create, middle and high school language learners presented their work orally as well as interviewing each other, writing explanatory text, incorporating a variety of visual media, and creating short recordings of their own voices (Hanson-Smith, 1997b).

The following are some ideas for multimedia projects. (See Appendix F for examples of student projects and resources for content.)

- *hometown magazine*: Students research interesting facts about the city they live in. (See chapter 25 for similar projects; see Faulkner & White, 1993, for a model multimedia project on the National Zoo in Washington, DC.)

- *jobs and careers*: Students research the minimum wage, housing costs, and job prospects in their area, interviewing prospective employers.

- *where to find it*: Students create a multimedia guide to their school or their community, perhaps including a treasure hunt game.

- *multimedia journal*: Art and graphics come to life; students record interviews.

- *school newsletter*: Posted on the Web, it can be updated cheaply and easily and makes a good international advertising tool for intensive programs.

- *cross-cultural friends*: Students research typical greetings and social expressions in their own language and that of the target country.

- *travelogue*: Students research their home country or town as a place to visit.

- *I-search*: Students negotiate with the teacher to research a subject they have a genuine interest in; the project can be adapted to any level (see Macrorie, 1988).

- *curriculum exchange*: Teachers from classrooms in different parts of the world help students decide on complementary projects. (See Hanson-Smith, 1997b, for details on organizing these projects.)

Multimedia projects created for the classroom may also find a larger audience on the Internet, even if the school does not maintain its own Web site. Some Web sites are designed specifically to encourage the exchange of such projects, for example, *Email Projects Home Page* (Gaer, 1997, http://www.otan.dni.us/webfarm/emailproject/email.htm; see chapter 6). Also, most cities have Web sites and will help schools that provide interesting content, for example, a restaurant guide (see *Kyoto Restaurant Project*, Kitagawa, 1997, http://www.kyoto- su.ac.jp/information/restaurant/), a hometown "where-to-find-it" guide, or a jobs and career guide. For the adult academic class, HUT *Internet Writing Project* (Vilmi, 1998b, http://www.hut.fi/~rvilmi/Project/) supports the exchange of academic articles written by students. For the K–12 audience, the Orillas project (*De Orilla a Orilla*, http://orillas.upr.clu.edu/) helps classrooms exchange cultural projects across the globe. (See chapters 6 and 10 and Appendix H for details on these and other curricular exchanges on the Internet.)

Summary

The CALL environment gives students the opportunity to engage in many different styles of learning and to expand their relatively impoverished classroom environments with the excitement of contact with exotic environments and the global community. Although computer technology is at present still only groping toward ideal ease of use and interaction, many recent innovations—super-high-speed processors, digital videodisc, streaming, wireless connections, Web TV, and connected Web CD-ROM—will enhance the CALL environment further. In the future, multimedia may become as easy to use as the telephone and considerably simpler to use than the videocassette recorder or audiotape deck. In the meantime, both software and Internet sites give the language teacher an exceedingly rich set of resources to enhance input and output for students at any level.

Chapter 14

CALL Issues: Resources for CALL

Jim Buell

Just as learners need many modes and sources of input and many ways to produce language, teachers in computer-enhanced environments require many types of resources and ways to share what they have learned or created. The land-based and electronic resources for computer-enhanced language education are amazingly rich and diverse. Whether you like to provide a great deal of guidance for your students or prefer to set them free to discover and learn for themselves, there are hundreds of on-line and off-line resources to choose from, including thousands of language-specific and general-interest World Wide Web sites that might have just the information you are looking for. (See the Appendixes for land-based addresses of organizations mentioned in this chapter.)

Remember that Web sites are set up by ordinary people. Many of the sites mentioned in this chapter are maintained by classroom ESL teachers, whereas others are set up by language programs, small- and medium-scale software design firms, and students themselves. In fact, one of the most important aspects of good educational use of the Web is to develop a critical stance toward the material you will be examining. In an age of information overflow, perhaps the most significant questions about any medium are, "Why are they telling me this?" "What use is it to me?" and "How does this fit in with what I already know?" These questions are particularly crucial in a medium that has no editors—anyone with a computer and an Internet connection can put up a Web page, and anyone else in the world can locate it through an electronic key-word search.

A Framework for Resource Use

Chapter 1 introduces conditions for optimal learning environments that structure this book as a whole. Learning comes about through interaction and negotiation; it is enhanced via authentic language use, tasks, and audiences; it demands opportunities for exposure and production; and from the teacher's perspective, it often centers on providing proper time and feedback to support the development of learner autonomy.

Although no single educational methodology unites Web users, and although no one point of view unites all teachers of ESL/EFL, the framework of this text encourages you to

- give learners experience in the knowledge construction process
- give learners experience in and foster their appreciation for multiple perspectives
- embed learning in realistic and relevant contexts
- encourage ownership and a voice in the learning process for learners
- embed learning in social experience
- foster the use of multiple modes of knowledge representation
- foster awareness of the knowledge construction process (Honebein, 1996, pp. 11–12)

ESL/EFL teachers are using the Web and other CALL resources today to help their learners in all these areas. Even without your involvement, electronic resources can give students immediate access to a world of authentic language samples, tasks, and audiences. But it is up to you to help learners by structuring activities and projects that promote authentic and meaningful interaction with these materials and with each other. With the right mix of resources, instruction, and opportunities for local and distant collaboration, learners even in foreign language settings can overcome the constraints imposed by narrow textbook-based study and break into the real world of English language interactions. In particular, for students with access to the necessary technology, the World Wide Web offers unprecedented opportunities to communicate unencumbered by geographic limits, whether the locus of communication is one to one, one to many, or many to many.

In this chapter, I examine a variety of CALL resources, focusing especially on World Wide Web and Internet resources. The chapter looks in turn at

- the variety of tools and information resources that exist
- the kinds of problem-solving activities teachers and learners are doing
- ways that CALL resources are helping English learners work together and support each other
- ways that you can guide students toward their learning goals using these resources

The uniform resource locators (URLs, or Web addresses) for the Web sites described here were checked repeatedly during the preparation of this chapter. Owing to the dynamic nature of the Web, however, some sites will inevitably have moved or disappeared by the time you read this. Search engines such as *AltaVista* (http://www.altavista.com/) or *Yahoo!* (http://www.yahoo.com/) can help you locate sites if their URLs have changed (see Appendix C for the URLs of other search engines). You can also learn about changes, and much more, at my Web page (Buell & Rule, 1997, http://lrs.ed.uiuc.edu/students/jbuell/construct_ESL/).

Language Teachers' Organizations

Many professional organizations can be contacted on-line (see Appendix A for other contact information). Some especially useful ones are

- TESOL (http://www.tesol.edu/; see Figure 14-1)
- TESOL's CALL Interest Section (*Computer-Assisted Language Learning, a TESOL Interest Section*, 1998, http://darkwing.uoregon.edu/~call/)
- the Japan Association for Language Teaching (JALT, 1997, http://langue.hyper.chubu.ac.jp/jalt/; see Figure 14-2)
- the Computer-Assisted Language Instruction Consortium (CALICO, http://www.calico.org/)

Figure 14-1. *TESOL Online* (http://www.tesol/edu/)

Teachers of English to Speakers of Other Languages, Inc.

TESOL Online

[What's New? | Association News | Membership Information | TESOL '98: Connecting our Global Community | Interest Sections and Affiliates | Career Services | TESOL Publications | TESOL Academies | US Advocacy | IEP Accreditation | ESL Standards | TESOL White Pages | Download Central | Sign or View our Guestbook | TESOL Fax-on-Demand | Contact TESOL]

Teachers of English to Speakers of Other Languages, Inc.
1600 Cameron Street, Suite 300
Alexandria, Virginia, 22314-2751 USA
Tel. 703-836-0774, Fax 703-836-7864

Note. From TESOL *Online*, http://www.tesol/edu/. Copyright © 1998 by TESOL, Inc. Reprinted with permission.

Figure 14-2. Home Page of the Japan Association for Language Teaching (1997)

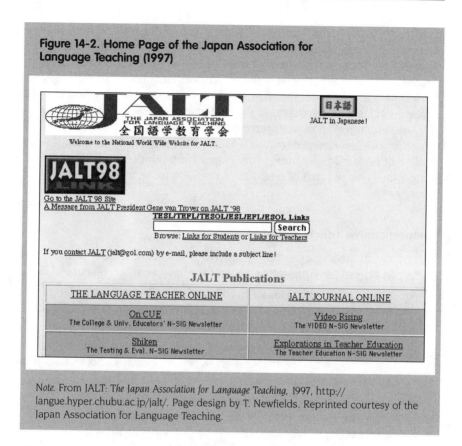

Note. From JALT: The Japan Association for Language Teaching, 1997, http://langue.hyper.chubu.ac.jp/jalt/. Page design by T. Newfields. Reprinted courtesy of the Japan Association for Language Teaching.

- the International Society for Technology in Education (ISTE, http://www.iste.org/)
- Linguist List (http://www.linguistlist.org/)

On the Web sites, you may join the organization, link to catalogues of publications for sale or subscription, obtain information on conferences, and read on-line papers and electronic magazines. Linguist List's Web site contains many links to other home pages and resources for a number of different languages.

Links to Links

There may be no better place for you to start looking for resources on the Web than ESLoop (see ESLoop Index, n.d., http://www.webring.org/cgi-bin/webring?index&ring=esloop; one starting point is Kristina Pfaff-Harris's Linguistic Funland, http://www.linguistic-funland.com/). ESLoop is a ring network, a collection of Web sites that are linked so that visitors can jump from one to the other with the click of a button. ESLoop contains a great collection of sites developed and maintained independently by ESL professionals around the world. As of October 1997, 54 sites were on ESLoop; by October 1998, over 90 sites were linked. Visitors can choose to view only the names of the sites or the names plus descriptions provided by the developers. Developers may add their own sites to ESLoop at any time.

An even larger set of annotated links is *Online Resources and Journals: ELT, Linguistics, and Communication* (Kitao & Kitao, 1997, http://www.ling.lancs.ac.uk /staff/visitors/kenji/onlin.html). This page offers hundreds of links to ESL-related sites and the text of a complete book on using the Web with English learners.

Comprehensive Teacher-Made Sites

Dozens of outstanding and comprehensive Web sites have been prepared by English teachers (see Appendix C). Six of the very best are discussed here.

- *Computer-Assisted Language Learning@Chorus* (Duber, 1998, http:// www-writing.berkeley.edu/chorus/call/) has experimented regularly with the latest technology for CALL.

- *Dave's ESL Café* (http://www.eslcafe.com/), by Dave Sperling, has many interactive features, such as on-line quizzes and a bulletin board called "Graffiti Wall."

- *LinguaCenter* (http://deil.lang.uiuc.edu/), the Web site of the Intensive English Institute and the Division of English as an International Language, University of Illinois at Urbana-Champaign, contains many interesting ESL/EFL activities, including audio files and transcripts of situational conversations.

- The pages at *Linguistic Funland* (http://www.linguistic-funland.com/) are so comprehensive they've been called the *Yahoo!* of ESL sites.

- *OPPortunities in ESL* (Opp-Beckman, 1997a, http://darkwing .uoregon.edu/~leslieob/) features several teacher-designed and student-created projects.

- *Volterre-Fr: English and French Language Resources* (Thalman, 1997a, http://www.wfi.fr/volterre/) is a comprehensive EFL-related Web site based in France (see Figure 14-3).

Search Engines

Among the most useful general tools for you and your students alike are the many search engines that let users find nearly any site on the Web through key-word searches. Host computers for the search engines spend their time scouring the Web for sites, archiving their pages, and indexing the full text of

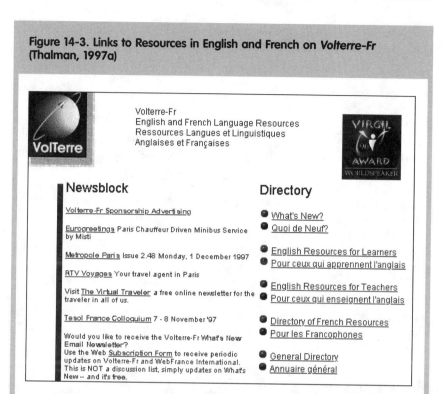

Figure 14-3. Links to Resources in English and French on *Volterre-Fr* (Thalman, 1997a)

Note. From *Volterre-Fr: English and French Language Resources*, by L. Thalman, 1997, http://www.wfi.fr/volterre/. Copyright © 1997 by WebFrance International. Reprinted with permission of the author.

the pages. However, effective searching is something of an art because so many pages are available. You may find it useful to write out a list of likely key words ahead of time and to type in different combinations as individual words and as phrases until your search results in the kinds of links you are looking for. As you find sites, be sure to bookmark them in your browser for future reference.

Four of the most popular general search engines are

- *AltaVista* (http://www.altavista.com/)
- *Excite* (http://www.excite.com/)
- *HotBot* (http://www.hotbot.com/)
- *Yahoo!* (http://www.yahoo.com/)

Each of the search engines has somewhat different features, so try several before settling on a favorite (see Appendix C for a list). Be sure to check the search features of each engine carefully—some allow Boolean searching, which results in faster and more specific searches.

Software on the Web

Downloadable software programs are one of the most popular resources found on the Web. There are at least four distinct types of downloadable software: *public domain software, freeware, shareware,* and *demos.* Programmers rarely release their programs into the public domain, explicitly giving up all rights to what they have created. More often, they retain copyright but permit certain uses of their software free of charge (freeware) or in return for a fee (shareware). Demos are generally feature-restricted versions of off-the-shelf commercial software. They might stop operating after a certain date or a specified number of uses, or they might lack certain essential features, such as the ability to save files.

Thanks to the ease, low cost, and increasing popularity of Web distribution, the lines between the four types of downloadable software are becoming more blurred all the time. Netscape Communications, for instance, sells its popular Web browser software, Netscape Navigator® (1997), in stores and also allows users to download the program themselves.

Software Archives and Sites

There seem to be almost as many ways to locate software on the Web as there are programs available. Descriptions of several useful resources follow (see Appendix D for others).

- A popular searchable resource is *Download.com* (http://www.download.com/), a site produced by CNET: The Computer Network, which has links to tens of thousands of shareware, freeware, and demonstration programs, along with software reviews and feature articles.

- A much smaller but more focused resource for language instruction is the IALL *Foreign Language Software Database* at Dartmouth College (Foelsche, 1995, http://fldb.dartmouth.edu/fldb/), with instant searching for ESL and foreign-language educational software reviews.

- One large collection of shareware, freeware, and demos for ESL instruction is CELIA *at La Trobe University: Computer Enhanced Language Instruction Archive* (Holliday, 1997a, http://chiron.latrobe.edu.au/www/education/celia/celia.html), accessible by file transfer protocol (FTP) and Gopher (see Figure 14-4). A collaboration between CELIA archivist Lloyd Holliday and

Figure 14-4. Home Page of *CELIA at La Trobe University* (Holliday, 1997a), an Archive of Freeware, Shareware, and Publishers' Demos

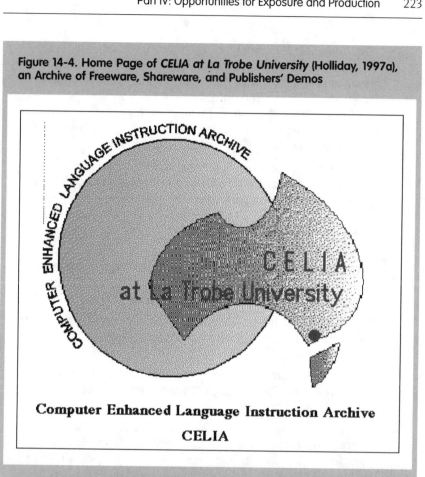

Computer Enhanced Language Instruction Archive

CELIA

Note. From CELIA *at La Trobe University: Computer Enhanced Language Instruction Archive,* L. Holliday, 1997, http://chiron.latrobe.edu.au/www/education/celia/celia.html. Reprinted with permission.

members of TESOL's CALL Interest Section led to the compilation of TESOL/CELIA '96 (1996), a somewhat dated but perhaps still useful CD-ROM collection of several hundred redistributable programs for English learners that has been marketed by TESOL. Many of the programs archived at CELIA are also accessible from the CALL Interest Section's Web site (*Computer-Assisted Language Learning, a* TESOL *Interest Section,* 1998, http://darkwing.uoregon.edu/~call/)

Some additional sites feature software that is especially useful for English instructors and students:

- *The Virtual CALL Library* (1997, http://www.sussex.ac.uk/langc /CALL.html) offers links to ESL shareware and freeware by Martin Holmes (n.d., http://www.net-shopper.co.uk/creative/education/ languages/martin/); see especially the Evil Landlady Action Maze (Holmes, 1997b), a simple but innovative set of pages written in Hypertext Markup Language (HTML), and Clozemaker (Holmes, 1997a), which creates cloze exercises from texts.

- *Updates for Software* (Higgins & Higgins, 1997, http://www.stir.ac.uk /epd/celt/staff/higdox/software.htm) offers dozens of free and low-cost programs, most for text-reconstruction exercises that run in the MS-DOS® operating system. Titles include Double-Up (Higgins, 1994a), Eclipse (Higgins, 1995), Sequitur (Higgins, 1994b), and Switch (Higgins, n.d.).

- The Comenius Group, which sells over 100 ESL programs from various sources, has reviews of these programs on its site, *The Comenius English Language Center* (http://www.comenius.com/).

- *Linguistic Funland* (http://www.linguistic-funland.com/) includes an extensive collection of links to publishers, resellers, and authors of ESL software.

- *Volterre-Fr: Software* (Taber, 1997, http://www.wfi.fr/volterre/ software.html) contains ESL software resources compiled in June 1997.

- A database version of the 1996 TESOL CALL Interest Section Software List (Healey & Johnson, 1996) can be found in the "teacher-utils" folder in both the "mac" and "win" subdirectories within CELIA's English directory (see Holliday, 1997a, http:// chiron.latrobe.edu.au/www/education/celia/celia.html). The 1997 edition (Healey & Johnson, 1997) is available only as a printed publication.

- Compiled by a graduate student at the University of Queensland, Australia, *Links to Sites With Public Domain EFL/ESL CALL Freeware and Shareware* (Chantrill, 1997, http://www.cltr.uq.oz.au:8000 /~richardc/pubsoft.html) also includes directions for downloading files from various archives.

Software Publishers and Distributors

Below is a sampling of companies that create and sell software for English instruction. Almost all of these companies make downloadable demos or sample screens from products available on-line (see Appendix E for other contact information).

The Web sites of several publishers of educational software are worth visiting.

- Brøderbund Software (http://www.broderbund.com/) is the creator of the Living Books series of children's readers.

- A branch of the Learning Company, Creative Wonders (http://www.cwonders.com/) publishes multimedia educational software programs, including those related to *Sesame Street*.

- Davidson & Associates, which publishes many educational programs, also operates a Web site (http://www.davd.com/).

- DynEd International (http://www.dyned.com/) specializes in language instruction software.

- *Heinle & Heinle Museum of Cultural Imagery* (1996, http://www.thomson.com/heinle/museum/welcome.html) contains hundreds of photos useful for multimedia projects, lessons for writing, and a chat room for students to discuss their work, as well as links to the publishing house.

- MVP Software (http://www.mvpsoft.com/) produces relatively inexpensive shareware games that might be useful for vocabulary development.

- Tom Snyder Productions (http://www.teachtsp.com/), which designs software for Grades K–12 and provides Web-site-based curriculum support, gives a free CD-ROM to visitors to the company's Web site.

- Wida Software, which publishes ESL text-reconstruction and test-creation software, also sponsors a Web site (http://www.wida.co.uk/).

Distributors and resellers of ESL/EFL software include the following:

- *Agora Language Marketplace* (http://agoralang.com/) bills itself as "an on-line index of companies offering language related publications, products and services. An information source for the foreign language professional" (n.p.); the index is quite comprehensive.

- *Athelstan Online* (http://www.athel.com/) offers a range of software for ESL students and instructors.

- For ESL-related materials, the Comenius Group sponsors *The Comenius English Language Center* (http://www.comenius.com/; mentioned above), home of the "Fable of the Month" and purveyor of commercial software for ESL instruction.

- Royal Software (http://www.royalsoftware.com/; formerly Heizer Software) specializes in distribution of software for language instruction.

The publishers of two popular authoring programs operate Web sites:

- Pierian Spring Software (http://www.pierian.com/) produces Digital Chisel (1996), a very reasonably priced multiplatform and Java-based multimedia authoring program, as well as other software especially for teaching and testing.

- Roger Wagner Publishing (http://www.hyperstudio.com/) is the creator of HyperStudio (1997; see chapter 25), a multimedia authoring program that runs on both IBM-compatible and Macintosh® computers. A free CD-ROM is available from the Web site.

Links to Printed Publications on the Web

Thousands of nonelectronic periodicals and books, many of which address issues in language learning and CALL, have made their way on-line (see Appendix F). Indeed, some publishers even post entire books on the Internet in the hope of attracting sales. It might seem strange to give something away in order to sell it, but experience is showing that it works—reading on-screen and printing out are both just inconvenient enough that people who find something they like on the Web often buy the paper version, too. The growing number of publications on-line is especially good news for the many teachers and learners who live far from well-stocked English-language bookstores and magazine shops.

- One of the largest on-line bookstores, *Amazon.com* (http://www.amazon.com/) offers on-line reviews of many of its items.

- Most publishers of academic texts, such as Cambridge University Press (http://www.cup.cam.ac.uk/) and Oxford University Press (http://www.oup.co.uk/), are reachable on-line; the latter maintains an on-line searchable catalogue of its offerings, which includes such publications as the *Oxford Picture Dictionary* (1998).

- MIT Press (http://www-mitpress.mit.edu/) has put selected chapters from many of its academic textbooks on-line.

- *Project Gutenberg* (http://www.gutenberg.net/) offers the complete texts of several hundred classic works that are copyright free and thus in the public domain.

- Along the same lines, *William H. Calvin's Books and Articles* (http://www.williamcalvin.com/) is well worth a mention for the content of his many books—he writes about cognition, brain function, and language—and for the fact that he has put the complete texts of nearly all his works on his Web site, a practice I hope others will emulate.

- Ziff-Davis, a company that specializes in books and products related to the world of computing, operates the site ZDNet (http://www.zdnet.com/).

- Newspapers on-line, such as *Mercury Center* (http://www5.mercurycenter.com/), the on-line version of the *San Jose Mercury*, offer a great deal of knowledge at a keystroke.

Sources for Student Activities

Lesson plans, content-based units, and opportunities to practice the skills of writing, listening, speaking, grammar, and test taking are all abundant on the World Wide Web. In each of these areas, you may wish to go beyond the information given by the authors of the sites mentioned here. For instance, you might encourage learners to write additional exercises of the various types represented at a site and even to put their own efforts on the Web, as suggested in chapters 6, 10, 13, and 25.

Writing and Grammar

English learners with an Internet connection anywhere in the world can visit at least three Web sites to get personal assistance with their academic writing:

- *The University of Maine Writing Center Online* (1998, http://www.ume.maine.edu/~wcenter/)

- *Online Writing Lab* (http://owl.english.purdue.edu/) at Purdue University (see Figure 14-5)

- *UVic Online English Writing Course* (Holmes, 1997c, http://web.uvic.ca/hrd/OLCourse/) sponsored by the University of Victoria's English Language Centre

On-line labs are often staffed by graduate or undergraduate students who are fulfilling requirements for peer tutoring or teaching ESL composition. They will not rewrite papers for students but will make suggestions for revision. Some sites also contain links to on-line grammar rules or even grammar practice. One worth a look is *Grammar Safari* (Mills & Salzmann, 1998, http://deil.lang.uiuc.edu/web.pages/grammarsafari.html), which uses Web search functions to help students find a sufficient number of occurrences of words or collocations to understand grammatical relationships. Another site offering a variety of help with grammar-related questions is

Figure 14-5. *Online Writing Lab* at Purdue University
(http://owl.english.purdue.edu/)

228 Heavilon Hall
West Lafayette, Indiana 47907
(765) 494-3723
owl@cc.purdue.edu

———————— **Search Our Website** ————————

Our Writing Lab
- Our hours, schedule, and staff
- About our Writing Lab
- The Writing Lab Newsletter

Online Writing Labs (OWLs)
- About our OWL
- About other OWLs
- OWL resources

Internet Search Tools
- Collection of Search Engines
- Advice on Searching the WWW
- List of Starting Points for Internet research

Resources for Writers
- Over 130 Instructional Handouts
- Help with English as a Second Language (ESL)
- Links to relevant sites for writing resources

Resources for Teachers
- Overview of teacher resources
- Materials for language arts and English teachers
- Suggestions for teaching ESL students
- Materials for using writing in any discipline

Purdue Resources
- The Purdue University homepage
- Other writing-related resources at Purdue

Note. From *Online Writing Lab*, 1998, Purdue University, http://owl.english.purdue.edu/.
Copyright 1998 by Online Writing Lab. Reprinted with permission.

*grammar*ONLINE (Lieu, n.d., http://www.crl.com/~malarak/grammar/; see Figure 14-6).

Listening and Speaking

Your Web browser can work like a radio that pulls in stations from all over the world if you use RealPlayer™ (1998), a free software plug-in for Web browsers Netscape Navigator (1997) and Microsoft® Internet Explorer (1998). RealNetworks™, the producer of RealPlayer, sells streaming audio, video, and presentation software to Web site operators. The streaming process enables broadcasting to begin within a few seconds of a user's request for an audio file, no matter how large the entire file is; one segment plays as the next is being pulled in. Competitors to RealPlayer exist, and some sites are already using streamed video. College campus radio stations, commercial stations, and National Public Radio network programs are among offerings available on-line for RealPlayer. All of these sites are linked to sites from which you can download the free software easily.

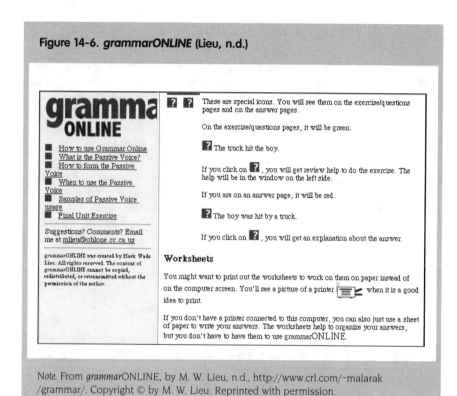

Figure 14-6. grammarONLINE (Lieu, n.d.)

Note. From grammarONLINE, by M. W. Lieu, n.d., http://www.crl.com/~malarak /grammar/. Copyright © by M. W. Lieu. Reprinted with permission.

Two other sites are well worth a listen (see also Appendix F):

- Learning Oral English Online (Li, 1998, http://www.lang.uiuc.edu/r-li5 /book/) offers RealPlayer files of several situational dialogues that are compatible with Netscape Navigator (1997).

- Voice of America's Web site (http://www.voa.gov/) contains archives of newscasts and features in both fast-paced and slow, clear "special English" from the U.S. government–supported radio network.

Testing

- The TOEFL, the Test of Spoken English, and the Test of Written English are among the most important hurdles for would-be international students at U.S. colleges and universities. Each test is a creation of Educational Testing Service, whose site, ETS Net (http://www.ets.org/), can help demystify these important tests by providing thorough familiarity with the test procedures and practice questions.

- *The Internet TESL Journal* (1998, http://www.aitech.ac.jp/~iteslj/; see Figure 14-7) offers access to over 350 simple ESL quizzes created by Charles Kelly and many other authors using Java (1998), a scripting language for Web browsers. Users of these tests can guess which of a set of answer choices is correct, then see the answers.

- More elaborate tests that make use of a browser plug-in for Director (1998) authoring software can be found at *Computer-Assisted Language Learning@Chorus* (Duber, 1998, http://www-writing.berkeley.edu/chorus/call/) and at *Dave's ESL Café* (http://www.eslcafe.com/). Explanatory answers, rather than just a score, are provided as feedback.

Figure 14-7. Links to Teacher-Created On-Line Tests From *The Internet TESL Journal* (1998)

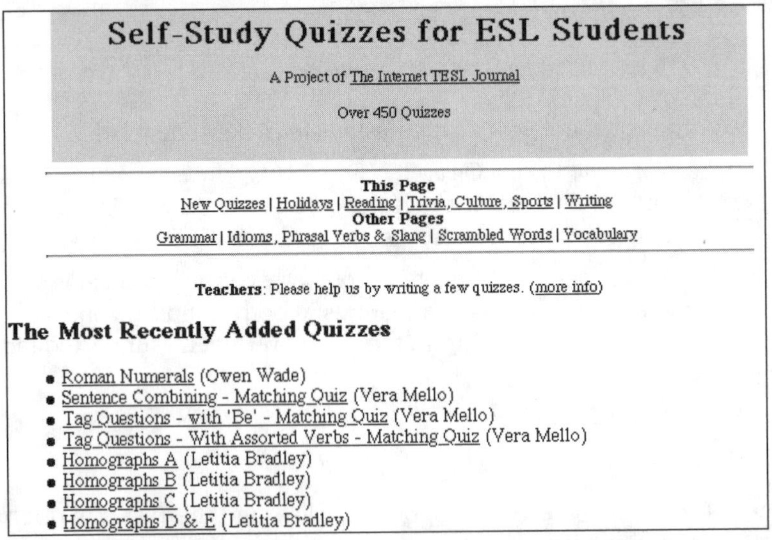

Self-Study Quizzes for ESL Students

A Project of The Internet TESL Journal

Over 450 Quizzes

This Page
New Quizzes | Holidays | Reading | Trivia, Culture, Sports | Writing
Other Pages
Grammar | Idioms, Phrasal Verbs & Slang | Scrambled Words | Vocabulary

Teachers: Please help us by writing a few quizzes. (more info)

The Most Recently Added Quizzes

- Roman Numerals (Owen Wade)
- Sentence Combining - Matching Quiz (Vera Mello)
- Tag Questions - with 'Be' - Matching Quiz (Vera Mello)
- Tag Questions - With Assorted Verbs - Matching Quiz (Vera Mello)
- Homographs A (Letitia Bradley)
- Homographs B (Letitia Bradley)
- Homographs C (Letitia Bradley)
- Homographs D & E (Letitia Bradley)

Note. From *Self-Study Quizzes for ESL Students*, 1998, http://www.aitech.ac.jp/~iteslj /quizzes/. Copyright © 1998 by The Internet TESL Journal. Reprinted with permission.

Content Units

Many teachers have used the Web as a place to explore content-rich issues and to showcase their classes' learning. Among the many examples of their work are the following:

- *Web Classes* (1998, http://www.uno.edu/~webclass/) is a set of content-based units for ESL students in the 8-week Intensive English Language Program at the University of New Orleans (see Figure 14-8).

- Content-based lessons for the independent learner are also offered by the Comenius Group at *The Comenius English Language Center* (http://www.comenius.com/).

- Finally, students aged 12–19 who would like to try to win a share of $1 million in awards by creating an innovative educational Web site should visit *ThinkQuest* (1997, http://io.advanced.org/thinkquest/), which hosts an on-line competition and provides links to outstanding sites from past years' contests.

Figure 14-8. *Web Classes* (1998)

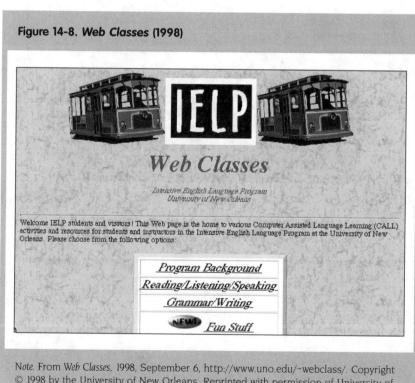

Note. From *Web Classes*, 1998, September 6, http://www.uno.edu/~webclass/. Copyright © 1998 by the University of New Orleans. Reprinted with permission of University of New Orleans, Intensive English Language Program.

Support for Collaborative Learning

The World Wide Web also features sites that support collaborative learning (see Appendix H). The sites, which might fit into other sections of this chapter and are mentioned in other chapters as well, are placed here partly as a matter of convenience but also to illustrate important aspects of Web-based learning.

Schools and Programs

Higher education is making use of the Web in nearly every area imaginable:

- Learners in every field will find it worthwhile to visit *World Lecture Hall* (1998, http://www.utexas.edu/world/lecture/), the premier archive of links to Web-based university courses (see Figure 14-9).

- To get a sense of the number of U.S. universities with home pages, and to visit them, see the links at *College and University Home*

Figure 14-9. Classes Offered On-Line Listed by Topic Area in *World Lecture Hall* (1998)

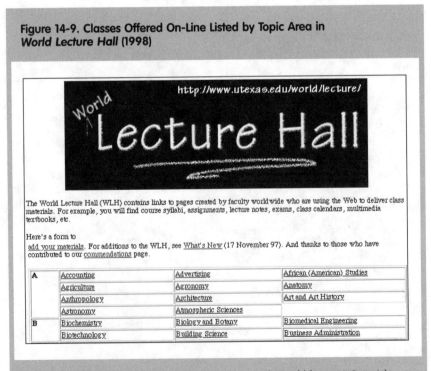

http://www.utexas.edu/world/lecture/

World Lecture Hall

The World Lecture Hall (WLH) contains links to pages created by faculty worldwide who are using the Web to deliver class materials. For example, you will find course syllabi, assignments, lecture notes, exams, class calendars, multimedia textbooks, etc.

Here's a form to
add your materials. For additions to the WLH, see What's New (17 November 97). And thanks to those who have contributed to our commendations page.

A	Accounting	Advertising	African (American) Studies
	Agriculture	Agronomy	Anatomy
	Anthropology	Architecture	Art and Art History
	Astronomy	Atmospheric Sciences	
B	Biochemistry	Biology and Botany	Biomedical Engineering
	Biotechnology	Building Science	Business Administration

Note. From *World Lecture Hall*, 1998, http://www.utexas.edu/world/lecture/. Copyright © 1998. Used with permission of University of Texas at Austin, TeamWeb and Academic Computing and Instructional Technology Services (ACITS).

Pages—Alphabetical Listing (DeMello, 1996, http://www.mit.edu:8001 /people/cdemello/univ.html).

- International students can find information about U.S. universities at *American University and English as a Second Language Information Service* (AUESLIS, 1997, http://www.iac.net/~conversa /S_homepage.html).

Quite a few intensive English programs at U.S. universities have their own home pages and support Web pages created by students. An unrepresentative sampling includes

- CESL *at* SIU-C (1997, http://www.siu.edu/~cesl/), the home page of the Center for English as a Second Language, Southern Illinois University at Carbondale
- *LinguaCenter* (http://deil.lang.uiuc.edu/), the home page of the Division of English as an International Language, University of Illinois at Urbana-Champaign
- *Ohio University CALL Lab* (1998, http://www.tcom.ohiou.edu /OU_Language/OU_Language.html), which contains many language teaching resources

Exchanges

Collaborative learning can be centered squarely in cyberspace, as two Web sites based at the University of Illinois show:

- At *Impact! Online* (Page & Sugimoto, 1995, http://lrs.ed.uiuc.edu /Impact/impact_homepage.html), ESL students can learn together about many aspects of the language.
- *Exchange* (1997, http://deil.lang.uiuc.edu/exchange/; see Figure 14-10) is an on-line journal in which ESL students can publish their writing.

E-mail exchanges are often coordinated and archived via Web pages:

- Two windows onto one exchange between ESL tutors at the University of Oregon and students at Senshu University in Japan can be seen at the tutors' site, *Senshu/University of Oregon*, AEI (Opp-Beckman, 1998b, http://darkwing.uoregon.edu/~leslieob /senshututors.html) and the students' page, *Oregon-Senshu Project* (Iwabuchi, 1998, http://gkk.senshu-u.ac.jp/~tiwabuchi/o-sproject /sthomepage.html).
- A site offering to link e-mail correspondents is *E-Mail Key Pal Connection*, at *The Comenius English Language Center* (http:// www.comenius.com/).

Figure 14-10. *Exchange* **(1997), an Electronic Magazine for Students**

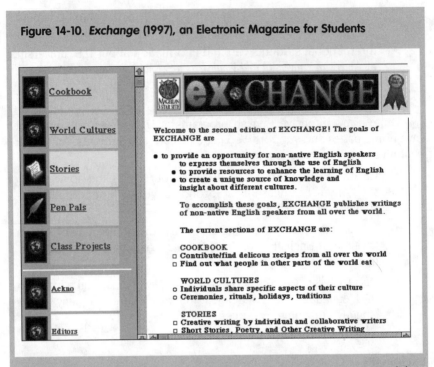

Note. From *Exchange*, 1997, University of Illinois at Urbana-Champaign, Intensive English Institute and Division of English as an International Language, http://deil.lang.uiuc.edu/exchange/. Copyright © 1997 by the Board of Trustees of the University of Illinois. Reprinted with permission.

- The SL-*Lists* (see Holliday & Robb, n.d., http://chiron .latrobe.edu.au/www/education/sl/sl.html) are e-mail discussion lists for ESL students (see chapter 6 and Appendix B).

At least two sites provide links to English classes that "meet" on the Web:

- the home page of the CALL-ED discussion list (Wong, n.d., http:// tiger.coe.missouri.edu/~cjw/call/call-ed.htm), which contains an archive of files, including requests for exchanges
- *Interactive Internet Language Learning* (1997, http://babel .uoregon.edu/yamada/interact.html), at the University of Oregon

Guides for Teachers

What use do you and your students have for the Web? That question has a world's worth of answers, as this chapter has shown. But with so many possibilities, how can you know which to choose? This section discusses sites that will help you wade through the information logjam (see Appendix I).

Several educators have created resources to introduce the Web to their colleagues and to recommend uses for the medium:

- On his home page, Robb (n.d.-b, http://www.kyoto-su.ac.jp /~trobb/) describes several kinds of projects that ESL teachers and students can create on the Web and displays his students' work.

- A *Language Professional's Guide to the World Wide Web* (Fidelman, 1996, http://agoralang.com/calico/webarticle.html) offers a comprehensive set of recommendations on where to browse and how to get started with authoring.

- At *LinguaCenter* (http://deil.lang.uiuc.edu/), one finds WWW *Activities That Work (and Why!)* (Hegelheimer, Mills, Salzmann, & Shetzer, 1997). On this page, which is a document based on a presentation at the 30th Annual TESOL Convention in 1996, four ESL instructors at the University of Illinois discuss uses of the Web for writing, grammar exploration, communication, and collaboration.

Going beyond these how-to guides are sites that consider how Web use might relate to wider issues of pedagogical approach and methodology. Two sites are especially relevant for educators who favor a *constructivist approach*, which is centered on content-based and project- based discovery learning.

In *Harnessing the Power of the Web: A Tutorial* (1998, http://www.gsn.org /web/), the Global SchoolNet Foundation states its basic principles as follows:

> Throughout our thirteen years of serving telecomputing teachers, we here at the Global SchoolNet Foundation have always espoused an old-fashioned, student-centered, project-based learning point of view that is well supported in traditional literature. In this Tutorial we apply the World Wide Web to this proven learning context where the Web becomes a total information gathering, multimedia presentation, and a global communications tool of enormous power to engage and challenge your students to learn and to excel. (n.p.)

See also the Global SchoolNet Foundation's home page (http://www.gsn.org/; see Figure 14-11).

Figure 14-11. Global SchoolNet Foundation's Home Page (http://www.gsn.org/)

Note. From *Global SchoolNet Foundation: Linking Kids Around the World*, 1998, http://www.gsn.org/. Copyright © 1998 by Global SchoolNet Foundation. Reprinted with permission.

A site with a similar purpose is *Apple Classrooms of Tomorrow* (ACOT, 1997, http://www.research.apple.com/go/acot/). As the developers see it,

> ACOT's mission is to advance the understanding of teaching and learning in global, connected communities of educators and learners. This includes investigating how teaching and learning change when people have immediate access to technology as well as helping people better understand how technology can be an effective learning tool and a catalyst for change. (n.p.)

What these sites have in common is an overarching vision that situates Web use in the context of classrooms in which teachers assist learners in locating, understanding, and creating meaningful content yet do not attempt to control access to what can be learned.

Conclusion

The organizations and products mentioned in this chapter are only a small number of the great many resources available both on- and off-line to the language teacher working in a computer-enhanced environment. By far the most important resource is colleagues, who can be reached through electronic discussion lists (see chapter 6 and Appendix B), through their Web pages (see Appendix C), or through many professional organizations (see Appendix A). More recently, on-line and on-site courses addressing CALL issues have become available through universities and other educational organizations, and these, along with conference presentations and continued discussion among computer-using educators, promise to be a rich source of information and sharing in the future.

Explorations

Projects

1. Visit some of the language programs in your local schools and describe what language students are doing with technology. Write a summary of what you find, and share it with your colleagues. Optionally, organize this project as a group effort, with each person on a team visiting a different site and adding data to the joint analysis.

2. Create external documents to enhance the input and output opportunities provided by a software package or World Wide Web site. For example, supplement a visual or aural program with a reading, or enhance a text-based program by adding a piece of music and a graph for students to fill out.

3. Choose two content-based software programs for your content area, and write a brief review, focusing on the type and amounts of exposure and production in the target language afforded by each piece of software.

Guided Research

1. Observe learners working with a variety of software packages. How does the language exposure (input) they receive relate to the language they produce (output) in either form or content?

2. A possible advantage of conversations that are mediated via computers in real time is that the productive output is available to learners not merely in a linear stream of utterances but also as written text on the visual display unit. Design a study that would help determine if this feature facilitates learners' ability to focus on unknown forms and accelerates their language acquisition.

3. Examine a software program that language learners use. Do you find instances where the language used in the software is

inauthentic? If possible, take notes as you observe learners using the software. Do your recorded notes indicate cases in which students have acquired computer-induced errors? Find further research on this subject to support the results of your observations.

Questions for Further Investigation

1. What combination of media is the most useful for language learning? Why? Does music enhance or detract from the language learning experience?

2. How much input do learners actually acquire, and at what speed do they acquire it? Can technology assist learners in acquiring language, culture, pragmatics, or content more rapidly?

3. What forms of language production are the most useful for language acquisition?

PART V

Time/Feedback

Chapter 15

Theory and Research: New Emphases of Assessment in the Language Learning Classroom

Chin-Chi Chao

Assessment, as a form of feedback, is a critical component of the language learning classroom, but most former language students still remember the nightmarish assessments in which they took part. My memories of foreign language learning include long lists of vocabulary words and multiple-choice, fill-in-the-blank, and discrete-item tests. Every week I took at least one vocabulary test, which normally included a long list of lexical items. The teacher would stand in the front of the classroom, carefully and slowly uttering the foreign words one by one. The girl sitting next to me would write furiously on her paper, but, unable to think of anything to write, I could only stare at the white piece of paper. I was supposed to spell all the words correctly in less than 2 minutes, but the words did not ring a bell in my mind because they were completely out of context; it was extremely difficult to spell them correctly. The best strategy that I could think of for learning the words was to use mnemonics, but remembering 10–20 different mnemonic devices was also difficult! The teacher assessed our communicative competence by having us recite memorized paragraphs, articles, and dialogues word for word.

Most of the assessment methods used in my foreign language learning years involved no skills other than memorization and testwiseness, that is, picking up an answer based on the clues revealed by how the question was structured. Other people's experience with language learning and assessment might have been better than mine, but many are probably like me in believing that there must be a better way to conduct assessment. Just as the computer has brought about many new possibilities in other aspects of life, it might also bring about new ways of conducting assessment in the language learning classroom.

The Purpose of Assessment

To discuss how the computer might change the way language learners are assessed requires an understanding of why assessment is necessary. Most teachers would probably say right away that the purpose of assessment is to document students' achievement. But why do teachers want to document students' achievement?

First, employers want to know how well teachers teach and how well the students learn. *Employers* in a broad sense include the head of the educational institution, the board of the school corporation, the ministry of education, and other offices or personnel that have the power to decide on language education policies. For these people, the most useful kinds of information result from comparing different groups of teachers and learners based on discrete criteria. In English language teaching, the Test of English as a Foreign Language (TOEFL; Alderson & Hamp-Lyons, 1996) is one of the instruments most often used for this purpose. Communicative skills are often assessed with the ACTFL interviews (American Council of Teachers of Foreign Languages, 1986) and some newer approaches, such as having the test-takers work on cooperative tasks. For the convenience of comparison and for an assessment to be objective, standardized questions as well as carefully observed procedures for administering these tests are absolutely necessary. The test constructors have to be very careful about obtaining high reliability and validity ratios, and language learners have to outperform a large number of others to be considered favorably and to honor their teachers.

On the other hand, the teacher, the learners, and the learners' families also want to know how well the teacher and the students perform. For this purpose, however, comparisons among students or teachers are not necessary. What teachers need is information that shows the learner's strengths, weaknesses, and progress (or lack of progress) in learning so that appropriate instructional support can be provided. For teachers, as opposed to employers, in other words, assessment has instructional purposes. For such purposes, the goals of classroom assessment are to help learners

- move ahead and improve
- gain familiarity with the content being taught
- become aware of their own position in the learning process
- fine-tune their understanding of the target language and culture
- set goals for the next stage of learning

The classroom assessments that language teachers use often consist of self-developed discrete-item questions with a focus on lexical or grammatical knowledge. Many teachers also include functional language use assessments, such as oral interviews with students. However, to accomplish the goals listed, assessment must (a) be integrated into the classroom activity, (b) be learner centered, (c) guide the learner toward improvement, and (d) encourage reflective and conscious learning. Assessment has to focus on the learning process itself, not the product. The information collected should cover all facets of language learning, including grammar and lexical knowledge and use, learning strategies and styles, and communicative competence. Perhaps assessment can also provide teachers with some data on which to base a learning diagnosis. Useful forms of assessment might include projects, portfolios, cooperative tasks, and even self-assessment tools.

Having begun the chapter by describing a situation in which only one kind of learning and assessment was used, I emphasize that it is not my intention to say that language learning classrooms and curricula should exclude memorization activities, vocabulary testing, or discrete-item questions. Most standardized and objective tests are efficient sources of information that help teachers understand the student's mastery of structural and functional knowledge in relation to other learners'. Even though there are many problems with standardized tests, they are still widely used and are efficient for administrative decision making. However, no single assessment tool can tell teachers everything about the learner and the learning process (Woodward, 1994); what is important is to understand the reasons for using a particular type of assessment and to use one that can generate useful information. In other words, teachers need to know which assessment method to use in which contexts, for what audience, and for which purposes (see Table 15-1).

New Emphases of Assessment

The kind of classroom assessment that I experienced during my language learning years is most often used to assess lexical, grammatical, and structural knowledge similar to what the TOEFL assesses. This type of assessment, perhaps the most common type of achievement test in ESL/ EFL classrooms, has several shortcomings: (a) The test questions appear out of context; (b) the test does not require students to use the language as it appears in normal, everyday life; and (c) the test may not show a complete and correct picture of the learner's proficiency level, strengths, and weaknesses. According to Spolsky (1989), functioning well in a second language requires the coordinated and integrated use of not only linguistic knowledge of structural forms but also functional abilities and general proficiency. To help learners become fluent language users, then, teachers need not only to address the problems with structural form that knowledge assessment can reveal but also to use other evaluative methods to assess learners' growth in the integrated use of the target language. This idea is the basis and rationale

Table 15-1. Overview of Second Language Testing and Assessment

	Formal testing	Classroom assessment
Audience	Educational institutes, administration, researchers	Teachers, learners, parents
Purposes	Support administrative decisions by comparing group achievement or identifying a learner's relative position in a group	Support learning and facilitate instruction by identifying each learner's strengths and weaknesses
Forms Assessment of grammatical or lexical knowledge	Standardized tests (e.g., TOEFL)	Teacher-created, discrete-item tests
Assessment of functional language	Tests of communicative competence through interviews (e.g., ACTFL interview, 1986; performance assessments)	Tests of language knowledge as a functional whole, including grammar and lexical knowledge, learning strategies and styles, communicative competence, and general learning problems through projects, portfolios, tasks, and self-assessment tools

for a recent shift in the emphases of assessment in communicative second language learning.

A trend in educational assessment that has been observed in classrooms of all subject areas (see, e.g., Farr, 1992; Haney & Madaus, 1989; Moya & O'Malley, 1994) incorporates five principles:

1. integration rather than isolation
2. learner autonomy rather than teacher control
3. guiding rather than mere grading
4. critical thinking rather than testwiseness
5. process as well as product

Embedded in these new emphases of assessment is the most current educational philosophy: Learners should take responsibility for their own learning. According to this philosophy, all classroom activities are to bring about initiative and mindful and reflective learning on the part of the learners, and assessment is no exception. The scenario below exemplifies the five principles.

Mr. White's Class

Learner Profile

Mr. White's ESL students in the United States are 18–22 years of age. Their proficiency in the target language is intermediate, which means that they can use English fairly well in everyday situations. The students are from different countries and have varying native language backgrounds. Most of them have college degrees and are preparing for graduate study in the United States as the next stage of education. Their length of stay in the United States ranges from 6 months to 1 year.

The Activity

Using World Wide Web pages that they design and create, the students are to introduce one aspect of the city that they are now living in to people from their own countries. The aspect can be food, customs, school life, traffic, or any topic that they think a new or prospective international student would be interested in knowing about. The class has 2 weeks to complete the project.

The students agree that they will use a friendly tone in their Web pages, as if they are talking to a friend face-to-face. After they have finished creating the Web page, each of the students will do an oral presentation in class in the target language, stating their rationales and designs; a question-and-answer session will follow.

Criteria for Assessment

Mr. White and the class jointly create an assessment rubric for the project. The students will critique each other's work based on this rubric. Grades will be determined as follows.

- Language accuracy: 30%. The class decides that accuracy of language is very important. The students will especially attend to the way future tense (e.g., *you will see . . . , you will need to . . .*) and subjunctive mood (e.g., *If you have trouble, be sure to . . .*) are used. For the Web page, correct spelling is a must.

- Presentation: 30%. Presentation includes the way information is displayed on the Web, in the oral presentation, and in the question-and-answer session.

- Richness and usefulness of the information provided: 20%.

- Feedback to classmates: 20%.

Learners are encouraged to cooperate with and support each other in carrying out the project. All students are to use the rubric to evaluate their own work and to give feedback to other members of the class. Mr. White will also evaluate the students' work and, as necessary, provide suggestions using the rubric.

Student Tasks

1. Students decide on a topic to work on. They need to reflect on their own experience of living in the United States and possibly talk to friends who have experienced coming to a new country.

2. Students search for information on the topic in the local library or other information sources (such as local government databases or the World Wide Web). A lot of reading is involved, leading to discussion and decisions about which information to use.

3. Students design and develop the Web page, with attention to key grammatical structures and vocabulary. Help with computer skills comes from an aid provided by Mr. White and from peers.

4. After feedback from Mr. White and peers, students revise the Web pages as necessary; they examine other class members' work and give feedback.

5. Students present the Web page to the class and conduct a question-and-answer session.

Teacher's Role

1. During the development stage, Mr. White guides the students as well as helps solve problems with (not for) the students. When the students can solve problems by themselves, Mr. White stands aside, carefully observing the students' activity. From time to time he may encourage the students or provide help with and feedback on language, Web page development, research strategies, and project ideas and direction, but he lets the students make decisions for themselves. Outside class, he maintains contact with each individual through e-mail.

2. During the presentation, Mr. White ensures that the discussion flows smoothly (e.g., by helping with timing), helps students facilitate discussions or form questions and answers, and provides feedback.

3. At the end of the activity, Mr. White conducts a class discussion in which students reflect on the process of this activity. He asks

> such questions as how they performed; what problems they
> had; and what Mr. White, the class, or the individual student
> could have done to make the project better.
>
> 4. Mr. White writes a descriptive report of each student's
>   achievement, strengths, and weaknesses based on the rubric as
>   well as the effort that he has observed in class and in e-mail
>   interactions.

This scenario reflects the five new emphases of assessment listed above. I now look more closely at how to implement these principles.

Integration Rather Than Isolation

The concept of integration includes two ideas:

1. Language should be seen as an integrated construct, and its use and assessment should be treated as such.

2. Assessment should be part of the classroom activity rather than something set aside to do separately.

Many educators believe that language is no longer language if it is not maintained and treated as a whole. As the framework for this text does, Gomez, Parker, Lara-Alecio, Ochoa, and Gomez (1996) suggest that language assessment should always be situated in a meaningful, realistic situation over extended periods of time and within a range of social situations involving two-way communication. This list sounds daunting, but with careful project management, integration is possible.

For example, Mr. White's Web page project involves the integrated use of the target language in a context that is meaningful to the students. The language is used as a whole construct; students read in order to select appropriate content for their project, write in order to present their thinking on the information presented, speak in order to inform the audience of their rationale and design, and listen in order to understand questions asked during the presentation. The students also use English when they negotiate the rubric, give and receive feedback and support, and consult Mr. White for ideas and various kinds of help. Even the reflection at the end of the activity is a meaningful use of the target language in context. In other words, language use itself is not the purpose of the activities; rather, language serves as a tool for real-world purposes, just as it does in everyday life.

As for the second point, that assessment itself should be made an integral part of normal classroom activities, Rivers (1973) describes how testing can be a part of learning:

The test is, as it were, a source of information or a set of instructions that enables the learner to keep up his efforts till he has matched the criterion, testing and retesting to see how close he is coming to the desired performance. Each time he falls short he makes a further effort to reach the criterion; each time he achieves his aim he moves on to the next phase of activity. In this way the testing is an integral part of the learning process. (pp. 3–4)

The process that Rivers describes has the overriding intention of helping learners improve and fine-tune their own learning. To do so, learners must be engaged and reflective. For an assessment activity to implement this principle, its design has to be based on a learning goal. Pearson and Berghoff (1996) have shown that the appropriate interweaving of assessment and teaching can encourage students to participate actively in their own learning. Herschensohn (1994) also suggests that assessment should be consistent with classroom procedures: It should measure growth and breadth, and use authentic language materials and a variety of evaluation techniques.

However, because the goal of instruction is often embedded in the activity, students may find it difficult to see the goal and therefore to reflect on it. Mr. White may choose to discuss the goal when negotiating the rubric with his students. A rubric or a list of evaluation criteria is helpful both in his assessment of the learners and in the students' self-assessment. Both parties should understand and agree on how the final product will be evaluated (Tuttle, 1996). In the process of developing the project, Mr. White should emphasize the goals and objectives through feedback and discussion. He should also take debriefing as another opportunity for students to become conscious of their weaknesses, appreciate their strengths, fine-tune their understanding, and move ahead in the learning journey.

Learner Autonomy Rather Than Teacher Control

Because assessment is part of learning, and learning is basically a very personal endeavor (i.e., nobody can really make people learn if they do not want to), it should follow that learners' autonomy must be honored in assessment, too (see chapter 24 for a discussion of autonomy). Teachers should therefore respect students' opinions regarding the structure of the assessment and leave room for students to show their individual strengths. Portfolios containing an ongoing evaluation of student progress, self-assessments, and peer reviews are a means of empowering and motivating students in this way (Newman & Smolen, 1993).

In Mr. White's Web project, the students are given many opportunities to exert control over their learning. For example, in creating the assessment rubric, students negotiate with him to determine the weight of each criterion. They have a say in the items on which they are to be evaluated. In addition, based on their own experiences students can decide on the project theme that they feel is the most urgent for newcomers. The students also have to make many design and development decisions in the process of the activity, including the kind of feedback that they will give to their peers. They help each other learn new computer skills and acquire language knowledge. Furthermore, the question-and-answer session during the presentations is another opportunity for the students to "control" the class—if Mr. White is willing to leave the floor open to them.

Empowering students, however, is not an easy thing to do from either the teacher's or the learners' perspective because both must change their attitudes and the way they interact with each other in conventional classrooms. In providing opportunities for learner control, Mr. White has to be willing to give up the traditional authority that teachers enjoy. As described in the scenario, Mr. White still has many critical roles to play in the assessment process. He needs to probe and guide the students, encourage them, provide help and feedback, sustain interaction with them by e-mail, retain the management of the classroom, facilitate discussions, organize learning events, and give detailed descriptive reports on the learners based on his careful observations. If Mr. White is not willing to share some of the classroom authority and support learner-centeredness, the students will not be able to assume responsibility for their own learning.

This principle involves some hidden concerns. For example, some students might not appreciate the opportunity to have so much power or might not have enough experience to handle it, and Mr. White might find it difficult to stand aside and watch the students making their own way at a very slow pace. He should explain to students the importance of having them take on some of these responsibilities and the kind of support that is helpful to them. He should also show them that he is there to support them whenever necessary in becoming independent learners. His actions and attitudes must be consistent and definite; Mr. White himself needs to be mindful when giving feedback and interacting with the students. Following these assessment principles and supporting learning in a learner-centered project is an art that has to be learned. Fortunately, with the convenience of e-mail, the interaction between teacher and student can be more frequent and more timely and can allow more time for careful thinking.

Guiding Rather Than Mere Grading

In the scenario presented above, Mr. White is to give a descriptive report of each student's achievement, strengths, and weaknesses at the end of the activity. These descriptions should help the learners and their parents understand the learning that took place more clearly than numbers and letter grades could, and the report should also indicate a concrete direction for future improvement. This step supports the idea that assessment is a part of learning.

In fact, the teacher's guidance is not limited to the final report. In the scenario, Mr. White does not just give the students questions and let them struggle in the dark; he is always present to help and guide them. Because assessment is part of the learning process, appropriate feedback during the process is critical. Bonk and Kim (1998) have identified 10 ways of providing guidance:

1. modeling
2. coaching
3. scaffolding and fading
4. questioning
5. encouraging student articulation and application
6. pushing student exploration
7. fostering student reflection
8. providing cognitive task structuring
9. managing instruction through feedback and reinforcement
10. giving direct instruction only when absolutely necessary

Guiding emphasizes leading students to reach a decision by themselves. Students must not only be required to do the task well but must also be shown how. Guidance should lead every student to be successful and allow the assessment to contribute to learning.

For large classes such as Mr. White's, general guidelines, job aids, or graphic organizers may be useful in guiding students in the development process. Students should also be encouraged to help each other. A good support system that has been successfully built up within a class promotes good interaction among class members and leaves the teacher free to work with those who need more help.

Appropriate feedback generally cannot be prepared ahead of time, and giving just-in-time guidance certainly takes some planning and management skills. The CALL classroom provides some help with this. For example, the use of e-mail keeps the interaction between the learners and the instructor immediate, rapid, and also secret. The learners do not feel the threat of exposing their weaknesses to the rest of the class, and the instructor and the learners are encouraged to maintain constant interaction with each other. Also, computer databases can keep records of the teacher's interaction with each individual, which certainly can help to make guidance efficient and effective; keeping records in a database makes it easy for Mr. White to compose descriptive reports. In addition, because work produced on the computer is generally easy to change, the learners are more likely to revise and improve their work in response to feedback. Feedback is then much more useful to the learner than if the computer is not available for projects and assessments.

Critical Thinking Rather Than Testwiseness

As mentioned, traditional methods of assessment, such as standardized multiple-choice or fill-in-the-blank tests, often encourage testwiseness; students who can figure out what the logic of test questions is or what is in the teacher's mind can accurately guess the correct answer. What students learn is how to appear smart without rigorous study and thinking. Students waste reflection on approximating what other people (especially the teacher) think rather than seek real and meaningful understanding for themselves.

Teachers need to design tasks well enough that there is little room for testwiseness and a great deal of demand for critical thinking during the assessment. Critical thinking, generally defined as the ability to interpret, analyze, evaluate, infer, explain, and self-regulate (reflect), is often related to the concept of problem solving. It can also be defined as the ability to think about one's thinking in such a way as to recognize its strengths and weaknesses and, consequently, the ability to recast the thinking in an improved form (Paul, 1995). The biggest difference between testwiseness and critical thinking skills is that tasks requiring critical thinking—but not those that are open to testwiseness—leave room for creative problem solving, self-assessment, and deeper understanding of the use of the target language. Many times there may be more than one correct answer to an assessment task that requires students to think critically about solutions to real-world problems and use the target language creatively. A detailed explanation of critical thinking skills can be found in Browne and Keeley (1990). In addition, the Questioning Kit (McKenzie, 1997), which distinguishes 18 question types, is a good resource for any teacher who would like to ask thought-provoking questions in assessment tasks.

In Mr. White's Web project, students have little need for testwiseness but many opportunities to use reflective and conscious thinking skills. When students decide on a theme for the project, they need thinking skills to read, analyze, select, and organize the information. Because accuracy is weighted heavily during evaluation, the students have to consciously monitor their own language use, especially in the area of structural forms. The feedback provided to other class members also demands good critical thinking skills. The most obvious opportunity for reflection is the class discussion at the end of the activity. Students are asked to reflect on how they did, what problems they had, and what they could have done to make the project better. This is a time for students to evaluate their use of language, learning strategies, learning styles, use of communication skills, and many other factors related to the project and to language learning. Mr. White can also give his own feelings, experiences, and observations at this time. It is important to show that the purpose of the debriefing and reflection is improvement, not criticism. If the class has been interacting quite well in the process of carrying out the project, a friendly and supportive classroom atmosphere can be expected, and reflection is more likely to be useful and helpful to class members.

All kinds of computer tools can promote the goal of encouraging learners to think critically. For example, new word-processing tools automatically highlight typographical or spelling errors as they are typed. While writing for assessment, students should be encouraged to try to correct these errors themselves before looking at the suggestions provided by the software. The prompt and the immediate feedback provided by the software help students become aware of the mistakes they most often make and encourage students to make a conscious effort to avoid these errors. In this way, the requirement to correct their own spelling errors could contribute to students' awareness, learning, and improvement rather than just function as a means of assessment.

Process as Well as Product

In the past, most classroom assessment methods strongly emphasized the product of instruction, that is, what the student could produce after instruction. More recently, the process, that is, how the student accomplishes the task, has become more important in evaluating students' achievement. The concept of *process* is most used in writing instruction, in which students or students and teacher brainstorm writing topics, draft pieces, share and confer on writing, revise, edit, and publish (see Rotta & Huser, 1995, for a review of techniques for assessing the writing process). In the workshop atmosphere in which these steps occur, reading, writing, and speaking are often integrated and support each other. Process-oriented activities and assessment in fact work very well in projects that require students to use computer applications such as authoring or presentation software.

Again, putting the focus on the learning process leads to more concern about how people think, solve problems, reflect on their own learning, and set the next goal. A process orientation encourages learners to think and to reflect constantly; students are guided to think deliberately and modify before coming to any decisions on their actions. An emphasis on process also fosters the deliberate integration of critical thinking functions, such as abstracting, generalizing, defining, and comparing. These processes allow the learner to make an evaluation or judgment and not to respond purely intuitively or without a basis for connecting ideas constructively (Schön, 1983). Reflection, which is important to a focus on the learning process, thus assists understanding, develops self-awareness, enhances the ability to analyze, encourages deeper thinking, and promotes independence (Miller, Tomlinson, & Jones, 1994).

An assessment that encourages reflection during the learning process does not require that the student be corrected or be perfect during the first attempt at a task. The idea is that it is great if students can do a task perfectly but that the experience is also useful if students can think for themselves about what they did well, what they did not do well, why they did certain tasks well or poorly, and what they should do to make the work better the next time. Being aware of what decisions one makes during the task and of why and how one makes them is a critical factor for self-improvement and is greatly valued in the new assessment paradigm.

In the new assessment paradigm, process as the support of learning becomes the focus of attention. The purpose is not to label students by the work they produce but to understand what difficulties they have so that the necessary help can be provided. And that is also why teachers should value learner-centeredness; guidance rather than instruction; critical thinking; reflection during the assessment; and the integration of language use, instruction, and assessment.

How Does the Computer Help?

The five new emphases of assessment discussed above apply to learning environments with and without the computer. However, with the help of the computer, educators now have more tools than ever to create language learning assessments that fit the new emphases of integration, learner control, guided learning, critical thinking, and process orientation. For example, authoring software, word processors, presentation software, graphics packages, spreadsheets, and database applications all allow learners to create new information for assessment purposes using the target language in an authentic, meaningful, and holistic way.

The thinking skills required for integrated projects are much more varied than those required for traditional pencil-and-paper, discrete-item tests. In the process of creating, the teacher and the learners can see the development of thoughts easily. The teacher can give learners guidance and feedback with the expectation that the learners will take advantage of the ease in making corrections that the computer allows. Communication tools such as e-mail can promote interaction among learners as well as between the teacher and the learners. In addition, with the convenience of management or database software, teachers can now easily trace each student's language learning development, making it easier to provide personal help, feedback, and descriptive reports. The result is an environment that supports learning, which is exactly the purpose of classroom assessment.

Conclusion

This chapter has presented recent emphases in educational assessment. The ideas of integration rather than isolation, learner autonomy rather than teacher control, guiding rather than mere grading, critical thinking rather than testwiseness, and process as well as product help teachers focus on promoting better learning from second language instruction. The convenience of computers gives teachers more tools than ever before to make these ideas work.

As seen in Mr. White's Web project, these principles do not dictate the use of any one particular form of assessment (see chapter 16 for practical ideas for implementing the principles in the CALL environment). Mr. White's project is just one example that employs several computer tools. Many different projects and tasks based on these tenets of classroom assessment can be designed around the computer. I certainly hope that, if I learn a new language, I can avoid the assessment nightmare I experienced. I also hope that my instructor understands that classroom assessment is a part of the learning process that belongs to me as a learner and that it should be treated as such.

Chapter 16

Classroom Practice: Practical Assessments in the CALL Classroom

Joy Egbert

Learners need both enough time to complete their tasks and sufficient feedback to succeed. Classroom feedback has many components; traditionally, teachers might think of feedback as providing answers to learners' questions or making a qualitative statement such as "You're right" or "That's good." However, if feedback is seen as information that helps the learner understand just-completed tasks or assists with present or future tasks, then assessment that gives information to the learner is an important type of feedback in the language learning classroom.

Assessment includes two complementary elements that can help learners succeed: (a) the assessment of process, as mentioned in chapter 15, including the metacognitive, cognitive, and procedural operations learners use as they complete the task; and (b) the evaluation of progress or outcomes (in other words, determining where learners were and where they are now). In computer-assisted language classrooms, technology can also play two overlapping roles in the process of assessment. First, the computer can play the role of an integrated tool that supports the assessment of what happens during or as a result of CALL tasks. In this case, the technology is used not directly as an assessment tool but as support for activities that are assessed. Second, the technology can be used to prepare or perform the assessment, as, for example, in computer-based testing.

The general principles of assessment remain the same regardless of what tool students are using to learn—whether they are reading from a book or from the computer screen, or speaking into a stand-alone microphone or into a computer-based video camera. This chapter presents practical ideas for assessing learners' process and progress in the CALL classroom using the following guidelines, which are based on the principles discussed in chapter 15:

1. Assessment takes place in multiple contexts.

2. Both process and outcomes are assessed.

3. Assessment is spread out over time.

4. The method of assessment fits the content and method of what is taught.

Most of this chapter focuses on assessing process because the literature contains far less about this area than about outcomes testing. The techniques mentioned here are only a few of the many possibilities for providing feedback in the language learning classroom; these tools and activities should be used not in isolation but in conjunction with each other, as none of them can fully do the job of demonstrating learners' knowledge and skills.

Techniques and Methods

Testing

Testing has been the most common way for teachers to evaluate student outcomes or products in the language classroom, and much has been written about how and why to use tests. Cloze, multiple-choice, true-false, and fill-in-the-blank tests are very popular evaluation tools, used to test discrete grammar points and specific vocabulary items, check reading and listening comprehension, and evaluate other discrete linguistic tasks. As noted in chapter 15, there are advantages and disadvantages to using these types of tests in the classroom. They can be used in multiple contexts, and retesting can take place over time, but it is difficult to see learners' processes from this kind of outcomes testing. Teachers also need to make sure that the teaching and testing match, that is, that testing helps measure outcomes based on the goals set for the task or activity and that the test is appropriate to the method through which the learning took place.

For example, in teaching vocabulary from authentic texts, it would probably be invalid to test learners' knowledge of vocabulary through an uncontextualized multiple-choice or fill-in-the-blank test. A more useful way might be to ask the learners to do a verbal report using an authentic reading passage, as outlined below in Scenario 2. If, on the other hand, the learners have studied grammar items using drill-based grammar software, a drill-like test would be appropriate. As another example, if students are to choose their own topics for and create a World Wide Web home page, employing integrated skills as in the scenario in chapter 15, it would probably not be profitable to give students a standardized test on discrete vocabulary items.

Creating tests that match teaching and learning methods and that actually do test what teachers want to test is a very difficult task even for seasoned educators. Although technology cannot really help in the design and content of tests, computers can make the administration of tests very easy. Various computer-based testing software exists to help teachers construct and score tests that students can take on the computer; teachers and students can receive scores instantly. Adaptive testing software allows the teacher or student to set the initial test level and allows students to progress through various levels of self-testing as they show their competence at one level. Adaptive testing software programs are available from many Internet-based software archives (see Appendix D).

Verbal Reporting

One goal of an activity in the language learning classroom is to help students learn how to think about how they learn, for example, how to approach unfamiliar vocabulary in context or how best to approach problematic situations. Verbal reporting, one component in a powerful set of assessment tools available to teachers, helps learners understand their metacognitive and cognitive processes and helps teachers understand where students are in this skill development process. In verbal reporting, students speak or write; it has also been called a *think-aloud protocol*. During verbal reporting, the teacher is assessing how learning is taking place (the process) rather than what specific items have been learned (the product).

Verbal reporting can take a variety of forms and can be used to assess learning that takes place at the computer. The computer can also be used as part of the assessment, as, for example, in Scenarios 1 and 2.

Scenario 1

During a project that involves finding information on the World Wide Web about rain forests, Ms. Rivera asks her students to use Web directories (indexes) rather than search engines, in which only key words are entered. Having observed several students experience trouble performing the same operations during other assignments, she wants to check on the processes that students are using to find information from the index and make hypertext links. Ms. Rivera sits next to Maya, one of the students who seemed to be having trouble previously, and asks her to describe the process as she performs the task. Ms. Rivera finds out that although Maya knows the names of all of the letters of the English alphabet, she has an incomplete grasp of alphabetical order. Ms. Rivera develops lessons to help Maya and her classmates with this essential skill.

Scenario 2

One of the goals of the week has been to help students discover ways to uncover the meaning of unfamiliar words through the use of context clues. To assess her students' progress with the concepts involved in using context clues, at the beginning of the week Ms. Howard asks the students to read a passage that she has provided and to write in their electronic journals their thoughts and processes when they come to words that they do not know (she has modeled this process for the students prior to this assignment). During the week, the students work on a variety of exercises emphasizing the use of context clues. At the end of the week, Ms. Howard assigns a reading passage with several new words and asks the students to complete another written report in their electronic journals. She accesses the journals and compares the two reports to determine what progress the students are making made toward the goal of applying the strategy she has taught. She can then prepare further lessons based on the information collected from this assessment.

Observation

Teachers observe their students all the time. In fact, many teachers do it constantly but barely give it a thought; others consider observation a valuable way to assess students. Observation is one of the most reliable tools for determining how students are progressing in class and can be purposefully employed to gather information about a wide variety of learners' abilities, skills, and competencies. Observation over time, in a variety of contexts, helps teachers understand their students' needs in ways that they cannot with one-shot assessment methods such as tests. Observation is integrated into the language lesson and is most profitable when done with guiding questions in mind. Teachers may even prepare a formal or informal checklist to guide their observations in the classroom. For example, teachers might compile from their resources a short list that includes the characteristics of good language learners and gather useful data about learners by observing over time which of these characteristics they display.

Although technology can play a role in observation, the computer itself cannot "observe" in the true sense of the word. However, in tandem with video or audio recording, technology can make it easier for the teacher to record what is going on in class and to have a chance to observe and reflect on the classroom outside of class time. Computer technology might also capture aspects of students' performance that otherwise might be overlooked. Scenario 3 suggests one way to use observation.

Scenario 3

Based on his observations of learners in group work over the years, Mr. Long has put together a checklist of what learners need to do in order to achieve the language goals of group tasks. These actions include active participation, clear preparation, the use of the vocabulary of turn taking, and others. During a computer-assisted problem-solving task in which students must unanimously decide how to proceed in the software program, Mr. Long walks around the classroom mentally checking off students who are meeting the goals in the checklist and noting those who do not seem to be employing one or more of his guidelines. Mr. Long repeats this procedure over the course of the first several weeks of class, determining which students need more assistance in working successfully on this type of task.

Written and Oral Retelling

How well do students understand what they read or listen to? Can they understand the rhetorical devices? Do they grasp the main ideas, the key subtopics, and the subtle nuances of a text? Can they use the text's structure to help them gather information about what they read or hear? Teachers may try to answer these questions with a test that involves comprehension questions, perhaps with short-answer or fill-in-the-blank items, but this type of test has several crucial disadvantages in this context. Because a discrete-point test cannot easily cover an entire reading passage, it is difficult to tell from this type of evaluation where the students are having difficulties in comprehension and what students really understand of the passage as a whole.

Retelling, an assessment tool that has been around for a very long time but has not been the focus of much recent attention, can provide a holistic idea of what students understand and why they do not understand certain things. In retelling, students write or tell what they remember in their own words, including main ideas and relevant details, without looking back at the reading or listening to the text again. For oral retelling, which requires the teacher to meet with individual students, Brozo and Simpson (1995) suggest that the teacher use a checklist to record the kinds of ideas that the student mentions in the retelling, whether they are main ideas, significant details, or insignificant details. The teacher might also note whether significant vocabulary from the text has been used appropriately. Reading or listening instruction can then center around the skills that the student needs to improve. A more detailed analysis of the retelling might involve audiotaping the learners' responses.

Computer technologies can help with this assessment process in several ways, such as by presenting a passage through text or audio within a limited time frame and not permitting learners to look back at it. The computer could then provide a place for students to record their retelling orally or in writing. Such a system could be created fairly easily using any of the authoring software packages mentioned in chapter 25. Scenarios 4 and 5 use retelling for classroom feedback. Note that in each of these scenarios retelling is not used in isolation but instead adds information about students to a growing set of assessments compiled in a variety of ways.

Scenario 4

Using the software VersaText (Woodbury & Smith, 1990), Ms. Campion has presented students with a brief reading passage dealing with immigration, a subject that they have been exploring in class. She has set the reading speed at 150 words per minute, the curricular goal for reading speed at the students' level. After the students read, Ms. Campion asks the students to use a simple word processor, already open on their computers, to retell the passage in their own words. From this exercise, she finds that some of the faster readers need help understanding how to find main ideas and that some of the slower readers need to focus less on details. After discussing these points with her class, she creates lessons to assist all of her learners in gaining the skills they need to meet the reading goals of the course.

Scenario 5

For her part in a group project, Hai's assignment is to write a summary of Martin Luther King, Jr.'s "I Have a Dream" speech, and she asks her teacher for assistance in finding computer-based resources. Mr. Chen shows Hai how to use Microsoft Encarta Encyclopedia 98 (1997), which contains a video clip of the speech. Mr. Chen knows from recent verbal reports that Hai's metacognitive processes for listening have been improving and decides to take this clear opportunity to assess her understanding of the speech. Mr. Chen sits beside Hai as she listens to parts of the clip and asks her to retell what she understands of the passage during periodic breaks. Mr. Chen sees that, although Hai does not understand the nuances of the speech, she is applying the skills that have been practiced in class and is making a concerted effort to be a good listener. He discusses Hai's progress with her and encourages her to continue applying the skills she is learning.

Using Graphical Organizers

The use of graphical organizers, especially for content-based activities and lessons, is becoming more popular as alternative methods of assessment take hold in language classrooms. Graphical organizers, including Venn diagrams, grids, pictorial representations, tree diagrams, tables, charts, figures, concept maps, and webs, help teachers see how students understand the relationships between concepts, ideas, and words.

Graphical organizers can be constructed by students or teachers, either freehand, by using a simple electronic graphics package such as Microsoft Paint 95 (1995) or Kid Pix (1997), or even a simple word processor (see Figure 16-1). As Scenario 6 shows, the software can be used during the assessment of tasks.

Scenario 6

Dr. Flinker believes strongly that peer review is a critical component of assessment both to help writers assess themselves and to give peer reviewers exposure to others' writing. During the writing and revising stages of his unit on process essays, Dr. Flinker routinely has his learners review other students' essays using graphical organizers as their comment sheets. During this process, each student sends an essay via e-mail to another student for review. The peer reviewers either use a flowchart template that Dr. Flinker has created (see Figure 16-1) or create their own flowchart that shows what they understand as the steps in the process described in the essay. Breakdowns in the process are signaled by broken arrows, and missing steps are signified by a blank shape. The author, the reviewer, and Dr. Flinker can clearly see where the essay does not work and which areas need to be clarified. During the next round of reviews, all of the interested parties can see where changes have occurred and what still remains to be done.

Role Plays

Many language teachers employ role plays and simulations to provide learners with language practice, but fewer use them as the effective assessment tools that they can be. Role play can be used (a) to prepare students to deal with issues before doing a task (e.g., assess prior knowledge and competence) or (b) to demonstrate an understanding of the basic concepts of a completed task, as in Scenarios 7 and 8. The teachers in these scenarios could evaluate students on the basis of the outcomes of the activities and assign a letter grade to individual students, but they choose

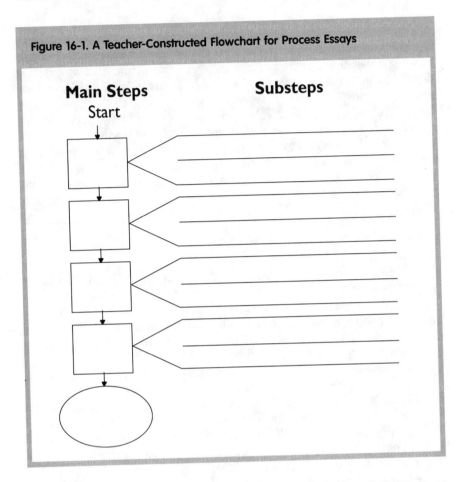

Figure 16-1. A Teacher-Constructed Flowchart for Process Essays

instead to use the opportunity to explore their students' learning processes and to use the assessments as feedback to students and as a basis for developing lessons focused on the students' needs.

Scenario 7

Dr. Mickuleski will soon start a content-based unit on U.S. culture with her students. One of the topics that she will include in the unit is prejudice and discrimination, and she will use the software package Decisions, Decisions: Prejudice (1994) as a learning tool. First, she needs to find out how much her students already know about the topic, including vocabulary, content knowledge, and appropriate grammatical structures, so that she can accurately plan the type and content of lessons. She gives her students cards asking them to act out a situation in such a way that the other students can guess what it is. For example, one student is asked to portray how it might feel to see a bumper sticker denigrating her home country, and another is asked to show how it might feel to be an immigrant coming through Ellis Island alone. Through the portrayals and the audience's responses, Dr. Mickuleski can judge where students might have a gap in knowledge and what their related experiences have been, and she can start to develop her plan for the unit.

Scenario 8

Students have been asked to consider the current situation in the simulated town that their group has built using SimTown (1995). There is a water shortage in their town, the food supply is low, and unemployment is high. The town's limited funds can be used to solve only one of these problems for the time being. Students role-play different members of a town council, each with a different set of priorities and an individual agenda. As a member of the town council, each student must present a recommendation for the use of the limited funds at the next council meeting.

One of the goals for this project, and one emphasis of the teacher-directed parts of the activity, has been to help students understand good decision-making processes. To assess whether her learners have integrated good decision-making skills into their metacognitive repertoire, Mr. Jones asks the learners to describe aloud the process they use as they formulate their recommendations during the role play. The students use computer-based audio or video software to record their choices and their thought processes as they consider their options. Mr. Jones can then listen to these recordings and decide which, if any, concepts need to be reinforced. After the town council has made its decision, the class discusses the problem-solving process in which they have participated.

Academic Journals

To obtain accurate information about students, teachers need to help some students overcome a reluctance to demonstrate ignorance in front of the class or provide a way for everyone to participate equally. Academic journals are one way of obtaining more information than an outcomes testing can provide. A subset of or complement to communications-based dialog journals (Peyton, 1990a), academic journals contain information based on course content. Students summarize, write questions, tell what they do not understand, explain how a lecture or an experience relates to what they have read, or respond to a statement about their writing. Students can write in their academic journals as a 5-minute exercise at the beginning of class, or the teacher can assign a question to be answered in the journal as homework. Students can complete their journals in a variety of electronic forums (using the computer as part of the assessment) or be asked to write about a computer-assisted task in which they participated (assessing an activity supported by the computer), as in Scenario 9.

> Scenario 9
> Mr. Crider's class has just completed a unit on prepositions, and in addition to giving a standardized computer-based test and having the students perform role plays, Mr. Crider asks his students to explain in writing in their electronic (e-mail) academic journals what they understand about preposition use in English. He expects that, because his students know that only he will read their messages, they will be open about what they understand and what they do not. He provides feedback to the students via e-mail, answering questions and explaining the kinds of problems that he reads about. He will use the information that he obtains from the journal entries to integrate information about prepositions into future lessons.

A computer-based outcomes test alone cannot provide Mr. Crider with the same kind of information that a variety of assessment measures can. The additional measures greatly enhance Mr. Crider's understanding of the problems his students are having with prepositions.

Self-Assessment

The teacher should not be the only member of the class to use assessment results to help students learn. Students themselves can be taught not only to assess themselves but to take advantage of ongoing assessment in the language classroom. There are many tools that teachers can use to help learners gain information about their own processes and progress toward their goals while providing teachers with a variety of information about learners. For example, at the beginning of a unit or lesson, learners using a pretest-posttest model can note what they know at the beginning of a lesson and what they want to know by the end. At the end of the unit or lesson, learners can look back at the pretest and note what they now know and whether or not they have learned what they wanted to learn. They can also note why they may not have learned it.

Alternatively, students can be asked how much they think they understood of a reading or a lesson, or they can construct an assessment tool for the lesson, administer the assessment, and then evaluate how successful the tool was. These and many other methods can be used in the language classroom to help students learn how to help themselves. Computers can play a central role in self-assessment, as in Scenarios 10 and 11.

Scenario 10

Students in Ms. Gunawan's class have been using the authoring software HyperStudio (1997) for a variety of assignments over the course of the school year. Ms. Gunawan has asked teams of students to build an assessment tool that will measure how well their classmates have mastered HyperStudio. The tool may take any form on which the team members agree.

At the completion of this task, Ms. Gunawan has the teams exchange assessment tools and complete whatever task the tool demands. The tool creators then comment on how well the assessed team performed. Ms. Gunawan then has the teams do a self-assessment, indicating what skills and knowledge they needed to build their assessment tools in the first place. Both the teacher and the students have several ways to see not only what students think was important to learn about the program but also how well they progressed toward these goals.

Scenario 11

After previewing a set of grammar mastery CD-ROMs that students will use throughout the session as a complement to their in-class work, Mr. Jessop and his students develop the outline for a pretest that Mr. Jessop will create. The students note the kinds of questions that should be asked, the topics about which they should be asked, and the format of the questions. After Mr. Jessop creates the test using test-making software, he and the class check to make sure that the test has the correct content and format. The students then take the test. At the end of the session, students take the test again. In class discussion, they note why the test does or does not

> accurately reflect their grammar knowledge and explain how they would change the test to make it reflect more accurately what they think they know.

As explained in chapter 15, it is important for students to have a hand in their own assessment. With computer technology, teachers can help learners control their learning by involving them in the process of ongoing assessment.

Portfolios

Portfolio assessment, addressed briefly here, is another way to involve students in their own learning (see chapter 15 for a brief discussion of the benefits of portfolio assessment). There seems to be a great deal of confusion among language educators about what should go into a portfolio, how it should be used, how to grade it, and who should see it. Fortunately, many texts and other guides are available to assist teachers in using portfolios successfully in different situations. However, the what, how, and who of the portfolio are up to the teacher, the students, or both. It is important first to have a goal for the assessment and then to decide what it will contain. There is no minimum set of requirements, nor is there a set of standard guidelines that must be followed.

Portfolios can be used in any number of authentic ways. For example, if the portfolio is meant to measure student outcomes across a school year, it can be a compilation of the student's products, including tests, quizzes, and final drafts of papers. If the goal is to assess students' progress or process, the portfolio can include multiple drafts of essays with self-assessment reflections, exercises and activities leading up to a test, and so on.

If necessary, the students and teacher can compose a formal rubric (see below) to help them assign a letter or number grade to the portfolio. This rubric could include, for example, five critical skills or concepts that students must show they have mastered, whether the skill is accuracy in using English articles or a clear understanding of the water cycle. For bilingual education students, the portfolio could be developed in either language so that progress in content-area studies can continue in spite of language difficulties.

Regardless of the goal of the portfolio, technology can help students organize and present their work. Electronic portfolios, created with simple authoring software such as Kid Pix (1997) or HyperCard (1995; see chapter 25) are easy to save and revisit, save storage space, are more durable than paper portfolios, and integrate computer skills throughout the process of building the portfolio. Electronic portfolios can contain links to Web pages and other electronic documents created by the students, and including audio and video clips gives a more holistic view of a student's performance than a collection of papers in a folder can.

If electronic portfolios are not an option, technology still has a role to play in portfolio development. Students can use word-processing software to record their reflections about their work; they can print e-mail messages and include them in the portfolio to demonstrate a variety of concepts such as brainstorming, revising, and assistance-seeking strategies; and they can incorporate screen dumps from software packages used in class in explanations of the activities that they have completed and the learning that has occurred.

Rubrics as an Aid in Assessment

The techniques and methods mentioned above are only a few of those that teachers can use to meet the goals and employ the principles of ongoing assessment. The techniques can be used informally or systematically, depending on the objective of the assessment. In both cases, rubrics can help quantify the results of these assessments when necessary.

Rubrics, in forms such as checklists or charts, can be used to assess CALL projects that might not have standard outcomes, such as multimedia portfolios and other computer projects (e.g., building a Web page or participating in a group simulation). Rubrics can also be used to formalize observation, retelling, and the other techniques mentioned in this chapter. Rubrics come in many shapes and sizes; some specify the exact criteria for successful completion of each objective and assign grades for each level of performance, and others are more holistic, informal lists of expectations. The rubric in Figure 16-2 could be used for a group presentation; teachers might use the format in Figure 16-3 as they observe students' spoken grammar during group work.

Rubrics aid the teacher and students in clarifying goals, organizing lessons and tasks, and assessing the extent to which students have met the goals during the lesson or task.

Summary

Assessment is an important but often overlooked component of feedback in the language learning classroom. Standardized tests, although useful in specific contexts, often do not account for the kinds of task-based activities that occur with and around the computer in the CALL classroom. This chapter has described practical ways to assess both the processes that students use while engaged in computer-assisted activities and the outcomes of these activities. It has also mentioned the role of computer-based

Figure 16-2. Presentation Evaluation Form

I. Delivery

Planning: Prepared and rehearsed presentation but did not write it in detail or read it from a script

Voice: Used appropriate volume, pace, articulation, pronunciation, variety, and verbal "noise"

Participation: Promoted and managed effective audience participation

1............2............3............4............5............6............7............8............9............10

II. Visual Aids

Appearance: Used simple, clear, large, easily seen, consistent, spell-checked, and error-free aids

Use: Aligned and focused aids, did not block aids, pointed to screen, and replaced aids quietly and carefully

1............2............3............4............5............6............7............8............9............10

III. Organization

Structure: Evidenced logical flow, clear introduction, agenda, body, conclusion, and summary

Transitions: Used smooth, logical, and informative transitions between speakers or sections

Audience awareness: Tailored speech to audience's needs, wants, knowledge, and skills

Time Management: Used time effectively; stayed within the time constraints

1............2............3............4............5............6............7............8............9............10

IV. Quality

Support: Addressed relevant issues and provided support for major points

Accuracy: Demonstrated sound, in-depth understanding of relevant issues

Creativity: Presented materials in an innovative, interesting manner

1............2............3............4............5............6............7............8............9............10

V. Teamwork

Collaboration: Showed evidence of individual participation, group understanding and agreement

Cooperation: Showed support for all team members

1............2............3............4............5............6............7............8............9............10

Figure 16-3. Simple Rubric for Spoken Grammar

	Alone	With help
Forms sentences		
Uses past tenses		
Uses future tenses		
Forms simple sentences		
Forms complex sentences		
Errors prevent comprehension	____ Yes	____ No

testing and adaptive testing as an integrated part of the assessment process. There are many more assessment techniques that can be used in a variety of ways in the CALL classroom; the point is that, whether in a CALL environment or not, language teachers must consider the assessment of both process and product as an integral and ongoing activity in their classrooms.

Chapter 17

CALL Issues: Setting Policy for the Evaluation of the CALL Environment

Ana L. Bishop

Setting policy and using it to implement the highest standards of instruction are not the first concerns in planning and implementing a CALL center or using computers in an ESL environment. However, without a policy and high standards for evaluation, it is not possible to understand the potential impact of a CALL environment on the teaching and learning of English. If policy is defined as standards of conduct in light of which individual decisions are made and coordination achieved, then setting CALL policy early in the design of the environment is even more important. If the standards are models to follow or imitate, implying a degree of quality, a level of achievement, or another measurement of success, then policies and standards for both the CALL center and the curriculum can be well coordinated and mutually supportive.

Whether you have been working within a CALL environment for some time or are in the process of expanding your ESL instruction to include computer enhancement, you should decide on a mission for your use of CALL and the policies appropriate to accomplishing your overall ESL instructional mission. Although you may not be starting from scratch and will have to make adjustments to accomplish your objectives, a basic policy should state (a) when and how you upgrade hardware and software, (b) who is allowed to download and upload files, and (c) where information on policy is kept and what is it used for. To accomplish more than the most fundamental goals, however, you will need a more global policy for the CALL environment. Setting such a policy has three components:

1. Know the mission of the CALL center or computer-enhanced environment.

2. Understand which aspects of the CALL environment require policies.

3. Apply policy so that it facilitates the results expected of the CALL environment. In the process of evaluating the environment, therefore, teachers and administrators may also improve, change, and adjust policy until the best possible results are achieved.

This chapter considers each of these aspects in turn.

What Is the Mission of the CALL Environment?

There are three crucial questions to answer in regard to the mission of the CALL environment:

1. What is the instructional rationale for the use of CALL?
2. Are the computer applications appropriate, effective, and intelligently applied?
3. What student results are expected?

In regard to the instructional rationale for the use of CALL, first question your own motives: Do you really need technology to help you teach language better? Some acceptable reasons for instituting CALL are

- Classes are too large for teachers to monitor their students' individual progress.
- Students in the same class are of varying levels and therefore need more individual attention.
- The students need CALL to prepare for their real-life business environment.
- The students need more one-on-one practice than they can get in the classroom.
- You want students to do collaborative projects as a means of enhancing communicative skills.
- You want enriched, alternative means of communication.
- You want to provide practice in a skill or an introduction to concepts that cannot be offered otherwise.

Some poor reasons for establishing a CALL environment are

- CALL is enjoyable.
- It's available (e.g., your institution got a grant to establish a CALL center).
- You have always wanted to try CALL, and everybody's doing it.
- The students want to play on computers.

- Computers keep the students busy.
- You want the teachers to have some extra preparation time.

Assuming you have a good reason to establish a CALL center and you do need the technology, be very specific about how you are going to use it. In other words, define the mission of the CALL environment (see the good reasons to use CALL listed above). In 1997, a question on how to justify technology sparked a long debate on the e-mail discussion list TESLCA-L (see Appendix B). The technology literate-teachers and writers who participated espoused most of the above reasons, including the poor ones, which shows just how much policy is needed and how often it is not used in a CALL environment.

The need for a good rationale for using CALL applies not just to lab settings or even pull-out ESL classroom models but also to itinerant ESL and foreign language teachers serving large school districts. These teachers often need to move from school to school, as they may be the only ESL professionals serving multiple schools, and they need to leave behind materials and resources that the students can use to strengthen the lessons that are delivered face-to-face.

In What Areas Is Policy Necessary?

A CALL environment needs to set policies for (a) curriculum and pedagogical support, (b) hardware use, (c) software selection and use, (d) staff, and (e) students.

Curriculum and Pedagogical Support

The most important issue in the list of policy areas is curriculum. A CALL center's main purpose is to support and advance the instructional objectives of a language teaching and learning curriculum, whether for ESL or for another language. Every piece of software in the CALL center must have a direct, positive impact on and relationship to what is being taught elsewhere in the school. CALL's relationship to the curriculum must therefore be clearly stated. Curriculum issues also imply pedagogical support: Do the hardware and software comply with the teachers' notions of good pedagogy? Are the students willing to use the technology even if it doesn't completely match their notions of how they learn?

Hardware Policy

The least important policy area is hardware (e.g., computers, printers, networks, and telephone connections). Hardware policy does not involve deciding which models or specific equipment you will use. This type of policy is usually set at the district or campus level and should be followed by the classroom or lab CALL environment. Only in smaller, private labs, which buy their own equipment, does hardware policy cover the selection of hardware. (For resources on hardware selection, see the organizations listed in Appendix A.)

The reason hardware is so unimportant for CALL policy is that you should choose hardware after you select the right software for the curriculum and students. The choice of hardware therefore depends on everything else that goes on in the CALL environment, even though a common way to make decisions about using computers or technology has been the reverse. Selecting the hardware first may limit unnecessarily your ability to choose high-quality software that meets your specific needs.

If the hardware for your CALL center has not already been chosen, you can start with a clean slate. In most cases, however, the hardware is already in place, and you have to live with it until funding allows you to change it. Policies should be fairly similar for both situations. (For information on evaluating software, see chapter 11.)

How you develop hardware policy is determined by your situation: whether you operate an isolated computer laboratory or have computers available in the classroom (as is often the case in the K–6 environment). Hardware policy also depends on whether you have a fully functioning network or use stand-alone equipment. Because my focus is not on the computer environment per se but rather on its function in enhancing language learning, I do not dwell on such policy issues as whether to allow food or drink in the room, who has the access to the keys for security purposes, or how many people have administrative or system-operator-level control over a network or equipment (see, e.g., McClure & Lopata, 1996, on administrative policy issues).

Software Policy

Generally, staff development should not take place until the hardware and software are in place. If you have the opportunity to build a CALL environment from scratch, however, an early round of training allows teachers to be involved in and learn from the software selection process. Policies regarding teachers and software may include

1. *periodic recommendations from teachers on new software*: You might set two or three times of the year when you will accept recommendations to purchase software teachers have observed at locations comparable to their own, or you might decide that you are always open to recommendations. Just keep track of the recommendations and the reasons given for them (see Item 2).

2. *a software evaluation form*: This form is usually developed in-house, but forms obtained elsewhere can be adjusted to fit your needs (see chapter 11 for a sample form; see also Bishop, 1997). Keeping a file of the forms the teachers fill out as they use software—and maybe even publishing the results in-house periodically—can prevent the duplication of recommendations and can give teachers ideas on how to use software that the lab already owns or is considering for purchase.

3. *a minimum 30-day trial of any software considered for purchase*: Sometimes software that sounds good is not so in practice. The only two ways to know this are (a) personal experience and (b) observation of success in another, comparable location. Most reputable software companies provide free trials of software ranging from 30 to 60 days and sometimes even 6 months, depending on the complexity of the content. And the companies can refer you to schools that have been using their software for a while and can attest to how it works. Be aware, though, that companies will direct you only to their model sites. If you do not do exactly what the model site has done to achieve its current success and do not have the same level of support to offer your center, you might not have the same results.

4. *the linking of software with learning objectives*: This effort ensures that you don't waste money or time considering software that will not directly benefit your students and curriculum. If the software doesn't fit your pedagogy and students, don't buy it.

5. *no installation of software in the CALL center without the approval of the center's administration*. This provision not only avoids a hodgepodge of software on the machines but also prevents the intrusion of viruses into the network or the individual machines and ensures compliance with copyright and licensing requirements.

If your university, school system, or institution already has a computer technology policy, you should adhere to it. Besides talking to the technology coordinator in your organization, you might try searching for information in such places as the *Switched-On Classroom* (1994), a World Wide Web site put together by the Massachusetts Software Council. Another excellent way to get answers to questions and see trends in CALL is to subscribe to the electronic mailing list TESLCA-L; a resource for those using the Internet for teaching is NETEACH-L (see Moody, n.d., and Appendix B). Also, either joining or requesting information from organizations that focus on broader technology issues can help (see Appendix A), especially if no one in your organization, such as a district technology person, can serve as a local resource.

To evaluate software as it is actually used in the CALL center or at the workstation, ask these questions:

1. Does the software accomplish the goals it is supposed to fulfill?

2. Does using the software have a positive effect on the students? If not, can the software be adjusted? If so, how much of an effect does using the software have?

3. How open-ended is the software, and how much trial and error will you allow a student before providing direct instruction, which entails additional investment on the part of the teacher?

4. Can the software be readily adjusted to a learner's level of language ability or preferred learning style?

These policy-related questions can be answered only with reference to your teaching philosophy and learning objectives. For instance, I highly recommend considering Factor 4, but some language educators do not feel it is important.

A major factor to consider is whether the software's purpose matches your educational purpose. In other words, does the software provide lots of pronunciation practice when what your students really need is grammar or conversation practice? If you are stressing verbal skills, does the software have, for instance, the ability to record the students' voices and play them back? Can the students hold dialogues—written or verbal—with another person or just with the program itself? Do the students have to give exactly the answers expected, or can the answers vary? This type of evaluation is preliminary to selecting software but also is relevant to setting policy for future software additions that will strengthen your CALL offerings.

One example of mismatched purposes involved a project that required math and science content in addition to ESL instruction. The educators who were to implement the project were not consulted on the curriculum, so the software that was ordered had nothing to do with either math or science; the titles sounded scientific, but the software was entertaining rather than instructional. Fortunately, a consultant to the project caught this error in judgment early on, and the software was exchanged for some that was more appropriate to the curriculum. Setting and following the policies described above could have saved a tremendous amount of time and effort, not to mention shipping costs and administrative headaches.

Staffing Policy

Communication among teachers and between the teachers and the CALL instructor (if there is separate technology-trained staff) is crucial to a strongly functioning CALL center that meets all policy requirements. Therefore, time for such communication must be an aspect of CALL policy implementation. Even if the CALL environment consists of a single ESL/EFL teacher alone in a school or college, communication with peers is important and can be achieved through participation in electronic mailing lists, such as TESLCA-L and NETEACH-L (see Appendix B), and through professional associations, such as TESOL's Computer-Assisted Language Learning Interest Section (see Appendix A).

Often, because of a lack of trained personnel or even a shortage of personnel, the instructor in the CALL environment has little or no knowledge of how to make a CALL center work effectively. And, even more commonly, the other teachers in the program have no idea why the CALL environment is needed or what role it can play in accomplishing their instructional objectives. Therefore, a major policy issue is to make sure that all the staff members involved understand the objectives of CALL. This means a heavy investment in staff development.

The staff development policy for CALL must allow for joint preparation time (or, as it is known in some circles, time for articulation). Preparation time is often the first element to go when budgets are tight, but teachers who want to make a CALL center work for the good of the whole language program especially need time to prepare. They must plan together and understand the software well enough to help determine what the students will do at the computers when they are not in other classes and what follow-up students will need. The solitary ESL/EFL instructor who works with many teachers or schools in rotation can involve those teachers in the planning process.

To understand the software, all teachers (even those who do not teach ESL/EFL) must be trained in the basics of the programs—their purpose, objectives, and content. Then teachers who will be the CALL leaders should receive further training and learn to do turnkey training (teaching other teachers their new skills right after learning them) for the rest of the staff when necessary. Staffwide training is crucial to an effective CALL center. Too many beautiful CALL centers have good software but only one person who knows about it. Such a center is not a CALL environment; it is just a room full of computers.

One example of the problems caused by lack of training is the situation in a K–6 school that had a brand-new lab, new software, and a full network, but the CALL teacher had gone on maternity leave. The students went without the use of the computers for a full year until she returned. If all the other teachers who had ESL students had been trained in using the CALL lab, they could have cooperatively drawn up a schedule for their students to use the computers or set up special projects in the CALL room to take advantage of all the hardware and software there. Instead, dust collected in both the room and the students' minds. The students were exposed to English, but they had one less important resource available to them for another year.

Student Policy

Determining who gets to use the computers, when, and for what purpose is a crucial aspect of CALL management. If the mission of the CALL center is to allow students to use the computers whenever they need access, then the policy must call for open hours at the center as well as the continued presence of a teacher, technical staff, aide, or peer tutor to answer questions or help solve technical problems. If the mission is to use technology seamlessly while teaching language, you must also carefully integrate the content of the curriculum with the software used in the CALL center so that students using the software on their own can go directly to the lessons assigned and not waste time trying to find an appropriate place to begin. Everything that goes on in the computer-enhanced environment, then, must relate directly to something that the students are being taught in other curricular areas.

The ultimate test of the computer environment, whether it consists of one computer in a classroom or a lab full of the latest gadgets, is the progress of the students in learning English. Many software programs include systems for recording pretests and posttests, and some can even place students at what are considered appropriate levels. Are you as the teacher allowed to circumvent the settings because you may know more than the software knows about a particular student's needs? If not, do you want to have that option in order to assess students' progress accurately? Other types of software collect notes on tasks attempted and time spent on tasks. The staff will need some way to sort through this information meaningfully.

How are students evaluated in the CALL center? Is the software-driven test checking what the software has taught the student or what the student already knows? This can be a fine line to draw, but in many cases software tests that it functioned as it was supposed to, that the student completed what was assigned, and that the student can reproduce the lesson. However, these tests might not be related to actual learning. (See chapters 15 and 16 for a discussion of assessment.)

What about self-assessment? Does a particular application or software program that you want to use strengthen students' ability to judge their own performance in the target language? Even advanced ESL/EFL students have difficulty evaluating themselves, so any way that the software can help (e.g., by enhancing their skill in comparing their own recording of a passage to a native speaker's version) will be an asset. Some language schools build in a contract system in which students can determine a course of progression through the software with the advice of the teacher or staff.

Also important is for students to evaluate other students' work. Using CALL for this purpose might mean considering collaborative writing software, such as CommonSpace (1997), which keeps a record of peer editing or collaborative work on idea development. Does the software allow you, other students, or a distant correspondent either to react to or further exercise the student's learning, or can the software itself do so?

How Can Policy Facilitate the Goals of the CALL Environment?

Remain Flexible

Once you have set policies in each of the above areas to support your mission, your staff must adhere to them—otherwise, why bother setting them? However, a policy does not have to remain a policy forever. Because the situation, the teachers, the student body, or notions of pedagogy may change, each policy must be reviewed annually to ensure that it still serves its intended purpose. If it does not, it is time to ask whether the policy is really necessary. Should it be revised? Is it enforceable? If so, how? Even a policy that does not relate strictly to instruction could affect the operation of the CALL center or classroom.

An unusual opportunity offered to the New York City public schools in 1997 illustrates the need to review policies periodically. With special funding from the business community, middle schools, starting with Grade 8 and working downward, began to install hardware and undertook teacher training in at least 10 classrooms per school. Project Smart Schools, as the effort was called, offered stand-alone equipment only, as some of the school buildings in New York were too old for electronic networks without extensive retooling. The project initially offered computers that would run the Microsoft® Windows® operating system only (because the sponsors came from the business community, where Windows is fairly standard). But the New York City school computer coordinators protested and eventually won the right for each school district to choose either Macintosh® computers or those running Windows. Most chose Macintosh. This decision raised the issue of how to set policy that not only covered hardware but also ensured the acquisition of software that cut across both hardware platforms while serving the city's large numbers of limited English proficient students (then 16% of the total student population). This was done by selecting only dual-platform software (software that ran on both Macintosh computers and those running Windows) and by specifying that content-area software be bilingual whenever possible to broaden its use.

Both of these hardware- and software-related policy issues had to be dealt with in a rather fluid way, even in as large a school system as New York City's. If the New York City school system can change its policies based on the needs expressed by the end users (the teachers and students), so can any individual CALL center.

Collect and Interpret Evaluation Data

Good uses of a computer environment also imply regular and thorough data collection and evaluation. Most software allows you to collect a great deal of data about your students' use of that software, but what do you do with the information that the software gathers? Information for its own sake, or for the sake of pretty charts and tables, is worthless. But information that allows you to adjust the teaching or the software to a student's learning style or to change the CALL center so that it serves the students better can be invaluable. The evaluation process contemplated here should be a continuous cyclical process (see Figure 17-1).

Evaluating students' progress is important, but so is evaluating the effectiveness of the teaching. After all, if all or most of the students have not mastered a concept or a skill after it has been taught, is it the fault of the students, the software, or some other factor? Explore how you can adjust the software to improve the results, and if the software cannot be adjusted, figure out ways to compensate for it by changing the task, the goals, or the assessment.

Another question to answer is, Who sees the data that are collected? How public or private are those data? The policy must deal with the students' and teachers' right to know and right to privacy.

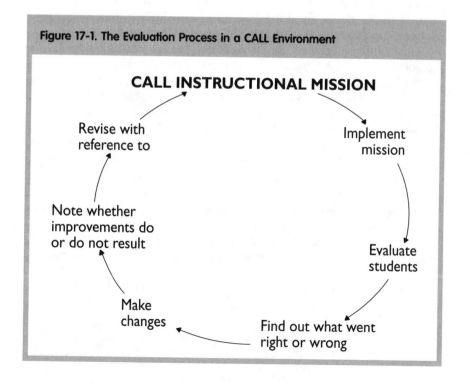

Figure 17-1. The Evaluation Process in a CALL Environment

CALL INSTRUCTIONAL MISSION

Revise with reference to

Implement mission

Note whether improvements do or do not result

Evaluate students

Make changes

Find out what went right or wrong

An important policy involves deciding what to do with the data you collect. Are they for internal, self-access learning purposes only? Are they collected to prove the effectiveness of the program in order to obtain continued funding or to enhance the learning process within the curriculum? Be careful what you do with what you've learned. Some teachers may get so carried away with the numbers, charts, and results produced by a data-collecting computer environment and with the research possibilities that they forget the humanity of the students they are teaching. Others may be too concerned with making the data say what they want to hear. The data collection policy should assist teachers in reading the data honestly and should encourage teachers to use the data to improve the CALL center and its service to the students. The data can also be used to examine teachers' strengths and encourage and develop more positive methodologies. In other words, data collection should help teachers learn what works and explore it with others.

One way to collect data effectively is to train the teachers to read what the data say about each student and about their teaching, and what they can do to improve the results if they are not happy with them. For example, a computer-based test may reveal that several students are having trouble with a particular grammatical form. Is this because the form has not been taught by the software or in the classroom, because those students were absent or occupied with other activities when the form was covered, or because the students are not at a level to benefit from that instruction? Whatever the reason, a teacher can pull those students aside and focus on the cause of their problems. By the next test, the teacher should be able to see some improvement in the students' performance.

The most difficult part of setting an evaluation policy is deciding what to change, what to retain, and what to throw out. Often, because of budget cuts and other funding problems, teachers live with second-rate software because they have little choice. Teachers may know that a software program does not really do much for their students or that a particular type of activity does not enhance language development, but they may continue to use the software or activity because they are used to it or because someone paid good money for it. However, there is no excuse for continuing to use something you know doesn't work. It is better to switch to simple e-mail or word processing than to waste time on useless software.

For example, you may inherit software that has been used without being evaluated. If you evaluate its effectiveness and find that using the software is a waste of time for your students, what do you do? As suggested in chapter 3, you can add external documents, use the software in a different way, or develop alternative tasks. You may have the students come up with more creative ways to use the software or specify how useless it is. In that case, they are at least using their brains (and their language skills). If nothing else, you can stop using the software in the hope that you can replace it with something more useful in the future, when you will have a much better idea of what you are looking for.

Summary

Setting policy for a CALL environment takes foresight, research, and time. You need foresight to know what the students' needs are and will be, what skills teachers will need to develop, what curriculum and content will need to be supported, and what could possibly go wrong and why. Research shows you what is in place, what possibilities exist, what resources are available, and what resources you can pull from local or remote sources to help achieve the ultimate learning objective. And finally, you need time—time to ensure that a policy set to foster high standards in a CALL center actually is a useful policy, time for teachers to absorb the policy and implement it, time for students to benefit from the policy, and time to rethink and review the policy whenever major changes occur in the CALL environment.

Ultimately, policy in computer environments should be fluid and set to make the situation better for all concerned. It is not a rigid code to be followed to the detriment of learning.

Explorations

Projects

1. Visit some ESL quiz sites on the World Wide Web (see chapter 14). What kinds of feedback do the sites provide? What kinds of learners would benefit most from this kind of feedback? What problems, if any, are there with this kind of feedback?

2. In electronic portfolios, students put together a variety of projects that demonstrate different ideas, mastery levels, or skills at various stages of their learning in the CALL classroom. Develop an outline for an electronic portfolio for your learners. What are the goals of the portfolio? What elements should be included, and in what form should they be included? How will the portfolio be assessed and counted in the final course grade?

3. For a group of learners that you select, design a CALL task that focuses on a communicative function. Your goal is to ensure that the students attend to the accurate use of the past tense in English. Examine the design of your task with the five emphases of assessment in mind (see chapter 15).

4. Review a local school's or district's mission statement. Is there a policy statement on computer use? If so, how does it support the mission of the institution? If not, what elements should be changed?

Guided Research

1. What do learners do with feedback? Design a study that will help answer this question. Be sure to include interviews with students to ascertain their understanding of the feedback they have received and what they have attempted to do with it.

2. If you have responsibility for a class, implement the portfolio concept you developed in Projects, No. 2. Include an exit

interview with your students to obtain their views on portfolios as an assessment tool. Be sure to consult the many articles written on portfolios and electronic portfolios.

3. How are language learners currently assessed? To answer this question, develop a study involving local teachers and learners.

Questions for Further Investigation

1. What are the lasting effects of specific kinds of assessments?
2. How can teachers determine what appropriate feedback is?
3. How can technology assist in providing students and teachers with the amount of time and feedback they need?

PART VI

Intentional Cognition, Learning Styles, and Motivation

Chapter 18

Theory and Research: Learning Styles, Motivation, and the CALL Classroom

Keng-Soon Soo

People are fundamentally different from one other. Obvious areas of difference are ethnic origins, clothing, food, languages, and even ways of learning. On a broad level, these differences stem from the societies, cultures, and families that individuals come from. On a more personal level, individuals are born with different genes and dispositions.

For language teachers, these differences are important when they influence students' learning, and research shows that they do. Differences among learners affect the learning environment by either supporting or inhibiting their intentional cognition and active engagement. Specifically, the teaching styles employed may be at odds with the students' learning styles, and the resulting clash can adversely affect students' learning and attitudes toward language learning. For example, a teacher may like to explain a lesson orally to the students, whereas they may prefer to read the information from a book or off the chalkboard. Expecting such students to learn according to the teacher's style is a little like asking right-handed students to write using their left hand. The goal is to produce writing that conveys the students' ideas; whether the right or left hand produces the writing should have no bearing on the task as long as the result is legible. However, when the teacher's style and the students' learning styles differ, the students are often judged on how well they learn using the teacher's style. The students may perceive the instruction as boring or difficult to comprehend. They become discouraged because the effort required to get at the task may exceed the effort required to carry it out; as a result of low motivation, less language learning may occur.

Research on learning styles has highlighted this problem, showing that failing students did significantly better "when they were taught with strategies that complemented their learning-style preferences" (Dunn, Griggs, Olson, & Beasley, 1995, p. 353). If some students are not performing as well as they could because their style does not match the teacher's, then the teacher needs to understand the differences causing this clash and turn them to the students' advantage. In this chapter, I define learning styles, explore why they are important to language teachers, review the types of learning styles, and consider their implications for the computer-assisted classroom.

What Are Learning Styles, and Why Are They Important to Teachers?

The concept of *learning style* has its origins in the beginning of modern education. Johann Pestalozzi, who pioneered the progressive instructional method in the 19th century, and Maria Montessori, who initiated the Montessori school system in 1907, both believed that education should take learners' differences into account. In fact, one of the main reasons for the enduring success of the Montessori schools is that they allow their students to learn according to their preferences. Today, learning-style theory suggests that "individuals process information differently based on either learned or inherent traits" (Dunn & Griggs, 1995, p. 15). Following Reid (1987), I define *learning style* here as "an individual's natural, habitual, and preferred way(s) of absorbing, processing and retaining new information and skills" (p. iix). Learning styles are generally discussed in four domains—cognitive, affective, perceptual, and physiological (see What Types of Learning Styles Are There? below). However, it has always been assumed that learning styles are heavily influenced by culture, and recently this assumption has crystallized into discussion about *cultural learning styles*, which are the common preferences of an entire people.

Note that *learning style* refers to how students approach learning, not how well they learn. As Dunn (1996) puts it, "No single style is better or worse than any other. Everyone can learn; we just learn differently" (p. 2). Language teachers who can match their students' learning experience to their learning styles or help them understand new ways of learning can ensure that the students have an opportunity to learn optimally even though they may learn differently.

Reid (1987) notes that, even if two siblings were to attend the same class, one might do well whereas the other might perform poorly. Under the circumstances, it would be easy to hold up the successful sibling's style as good and blame the other sibling's poor performance on a bad learning style. This explanation is not defensible for two reasons. First, in spite of the expected performance curve, the sibling who does poorly may have more company than the sibling who does well. In an egalitarian educational system, it is very difficult to justify catering only to some students and failing to meet the needs of others. Theoretically, some students may actually be doing well in school because their learning style coincides with the instructors' teaching style (Eliason, 1995). Cooper and Miller (1991) found that faculty in a business college taught in an *intuitive* manner whereas most students preferred to learn in a *sensing* style. Students expressed their dissatisfaction with this mismatch in course evaluations. Although studies (e.g., Rush & Moore, 1991) have shown that the longer students are exposed to a certain teaching style, the less problematic it is for them, the assumption that students will accommodate to the teacher's style is particularly objectionable when no one style has been proven to be intrinsically more worthwhile than another. Put another way, it is problematic to penalize the majority of the students for preferring learning styles different from those targeted by their teachers. Teachers must ensure that their teaching style enhances rather than interferes with learning, and they should be able to teach to the many different learning styles that exist among the students in a class—a difficult if not impossible task.

A second problem with teaching to a particular learning style is that styles can change with time and context (Kinsella, 1995a). Learning styles are assumed to be fairly persistent, even habitual, but, given time, they may change or stretch. Good learners may use different learning styles for different kinds of tasks. In fact, learning may be a cyclic process in which the effective learner uses several styles—thinking, doing, watching, and feeling—in succession. If this is the case, then learners should possess and use all four styles, although the level of these styles and learners' preferences for their use may vary. For students to use all the styles, then, as Hinkelman and Pysock (1992) suggest, teachers have to not only teach to the primary styles of their learners but also reinforce their teaching by targeting their students' secondary styles. In fact, some learners may have more than one preferred style in a given context. Hinkelman and Pysock found that "learners with mixed modality strengths may have a better chance of success than those with a single modality strength because they can process information in whatever way it is presented" (p. 32). Research has also shown that learning styles are influenced by maturation. The learning styles of children change as they grow older. However, such changes occur very slowly, and the effort to change a person's learning style often distracts both teacher and learner from the real task at hand—learning. The practical solution is to identify the learner's primary style and teach to it while also giving learners opportunities to experience different ways of learning (Kinsella, 1995b). Stretching the students' learning styles in this way is necessary, as the second language learner cannot expect to operate successfully in different contexts with only one style.

What Types of Learning Styles Are There?

Cultural Learning Styles

Recent studies indicate that different cultures are dominated by different learning styles. In a large-scale survey, Lim (1994) found that Singaporean 16-year-old students were less extroverted than a similar sample of U.S. students. Using the Myers-Briggs Type Indicator (Myers & McCaulley, 1985), he also found that Singaporean female students were mainly of the sensing/thinking/judging type whereas U.S. female students were mainly of the sensing/feeling/judging type. Simmons and Barrineau (1994), using several learning-style tools to study a college freshman class, similarly found that significantly more Native Americans were of the sensing type than were their same-sex counterparts from other cultures.

Many of the differences between peoples originate in societal institutions. One function of these institutions is to establish norms for such activities as learning; from the day of birth, individuals are socialized into doing things in the normal (acceptable) way through the silent example and overt teaching of family and friends. One of the first things individuals are shaped for is "learning how to learn" (Nelson, 1995, p. 6). As Oxford, Hollaway, and Horton-Murillo (1992) put it, "Although culture is not the single determinant, and although many other influences intervene, culture often does play a significant role in the learning styles unconsciously adopted by many participants in the culture" (p. 441). Singaporeans, for example, in general are much better than Americans at abstract conceptualization, but Americans are generally better than Singaporeans at active experimentation (Yuen & Lee, 1994). In a broader sense, some societies value individualism whereas others exalt conformity. In other words, "in every society, [there exist] unstated assumptions about people and how they learn, which act as a set of self-fulfilling prophesies . . . a kind of unintentional hidden curriculum" (Singleton, 1991, p. 120). As a result, learners from one society may have quite different ways of doing things from those from another society. Nelson's (1995) research in Hawaii, Oregon, China, and Japan suggests that students acquire their cultural learning styles before they begin formal schooling and that these styles persist despite efforts of the school systems to change them.

Cultural learning styles can affect learners in a variety of ways. First, international or immigrant students may be at risk because their preferences may "often differ significantly" (Reid, 1987, p. 99) from those of native students. Nonnative students may not understand the learning styles prevailing in the countries in which they are studying, and the learning styles that have proven effective in their home countries may yield significantly different results in their countries of study. For instance, Confucian societies tend to value rote learning, but students who excel in this style may find the going rough in societies that place a higher value on discovery and questioning.

Second, teaching approaches and methods developed in one society may have unexpected effects when transplanted to foreign soil. For example, collaborative learning is predicated on a learning culture that values collectivism. In more individualistic societies, where education may contain strong elements of competition, collaborative learning may be more problematic. In such societies, education also serves as a filtering system to identify desired characteristics, and collaboration may not be one of them. Therefore, the effectiveness of the language teaching methods used is, in some ways, circumscribed by the learner's affinity with those methods, which in turn depends in part on the cultural style that the learner is accustomed to using.

Individual Learning Styles

If everyone (or almost everyone) in a society learned in the same way, it would simplify matters greatly. One would have only to discover the dominant learning style of a society to guarantee that almost everyone in that society would be taught optimally. Yet until very recently, discussions of learning style have focused on differences among individuals—for a very good reason: The norms set by society are sufficiently broad to accommodate significantly different learning styles at the individual level. In other words, a cultural learning style is a continuum, making it relatively difficult to define. Therefore, discussions tend to center on the different learning styles of individuals from the same society, under the assumption that these individuals are heavily influenced toward certain learning preferences by their culture.

Students' learning styles can either help or hinder the students themselves and the language teacher. Hence, helping students learn is a matter of understanding what learning styles are and taking advantage of them. For example, Ehrman and Oxford (1990) suggest that learners described as introverts, intuitives, feelers, and perceivers have an advantage in language learning. However, more than 20 styles have been identified, and research indicates that individual learners can have 6–14 strongly preferred styles at the same time. These styles can be categorized into four broad domains—cognitive, affective, perceptual, and physiological.

Cognitive Dimension

The cognitive dimension includes the dichotomies of *field independent/field dependent*, *analytic/global*, and *impulsive/reflective* (Ehrman & Oxford, 1988, 1990; Witkins, Oltman, Raskin, & Karp, 1971). Early learning-style research focused on the field-independent versus field-dependent dichotomy. Learners were classified according to their abilities to pick out significant information from a confusing overall picture. In time, this research evolved into descriptions of analytic versus global learners (see Table 18-1).

Related to this dichotomy is the notion of <u>impulsive versus reflective</u> learners established in *conceptual tempo* research in the 1970s and continued in recent inquiry. Impulsive learners tend to accept initial hypotheses uncritically, which can make them more error prone, whereas reflective learners tend to be more systematic and analytical and therefore usually achieve greater accuracy (Oxford et al., 1992). The overlap among the analytical, field-independent, and reflective dimensions is apparent here.

Is one type of cognitive learning style better than another? Not generally; the effectiveness of a learning style depends very much on the context. Some situations are better suited for learners who tend to be

[handwritten margin note: impulsive not saved / question / or CALL?]

Table 18-1. The Cognitive Dimension of Learning Style

Analytic types	Global types
Begin with details to gradually build an understanding of the overall concept	Begin with the overall concept and fit in the details gradually
Prefer analytic strategies such as contrasting and finding cause-effect relationships	Learn through actual communication
Process information sequentially	Process information simultaneously
Learn to achieve accuracy through drills	Look for patterns; prefer holistic strategies such as guessing, predicting, and searching for main ideas
Prefer working alone or with a few others of like mind	Prefer working in groups whose members have diverse viewpoints
Are intrinsically motivated by self-set goals	Are extrinsically motivated by goals set by others
Can structure their own learning	Require others to structure their learning
Prefer learning without guidance or modeling and are not as affected by criticism or praise as global types	Require guidance, modeling, and praise from the teacher
Prefer multiple-choice and cloze tests	Prefer open-ended tests

analytical, whereas others are more suited for global learners (Chapelle, 1995a). The analytical learners do relatively better if learning is individualized and rule based, such as in the audiolingual tradition of language teaching. The global learner might shine in the communicative classroom. Teachers should be able to teach both analytically and globally to cater to both types of learners.

Affective Dimension

The affective dimension encompasses the aspects of personality—such as attention, emotion, and valuing—that influence what a learner will pay attention to in a learning situation (Keefe, 1987). These affective learning styles are "the learner's typical mode of arousing, directing, and sustaining behavior . . . [which] have to be inferred from the learner's behavior and interaction with the environment" (James & Gardner, 1995, p. 21). Some of the features normally investigated under this category are conceptual level and locus of control. *Conceptual level* is the degree of structure that a person needs to learn effectively. For example, learners with a low conceptual level may need a highly structured learning environment. However, all learners are deemed capable of developing a high conceptual level as they pass through the unsocialized, dependent, and independent stages successively.

Locus of control describes whether "an individual's perceptions of causality may be internal or external" (Keefe, 1987, p. 21). Internal or introverted learners feel responsible for their own behavior and prefer to explore on their own. They dislike continuous group work. External or extroverted learners feel that responsibility is collective. They base their perceptions on events and on what other people say and do. These learners like interactive activities, such as group work and role plays.

Perceptual Dimension

The perceptual dimension refers to one or a combination of up to three possible perceptual channels—auditory, visual, and kinesthetic (tactile)—through which learners extract information from the environment (see Table 18-2). This dimension is most closely aligned with the behaviorist perspective on teaching and learning (James & Gardner, 1995). As many as seven perceptual elements have been proposed. However, at the risk of overgeneralizing, I state only that perceptual learners may prefer to learn by listening, seeing, or using a hands-on or whole-body-movement approach.

School learning and assessment are heavily biased toward the auditory and visual learning styles. This bias is undesirable because "most adolescent males are not auditory . . . . As a result, lectures, discussions, and listening are the least effective ways of teaching males" (Dunn & Griggs, 1995, p. 20). Learners who are mostly visual and kinesthetic tend to underachieve in school because the teaching style does not match their perceptual strengths, and other ways of learning are not specifically addressed. Tests usually include written and aural elements, characteristics that favor auditory

Table 18-2. The Perceptual Dimension of Learning Style

Auditory types	Visual types	Kinesthetic types
Prefer learning by listening and speaking	Prefer learning from written texts and graphics	Prefer learning by doing and hands-on experimentation
Are strong in discussions and verbal responses	Are strong in reading and writing	Are strong in laboratory and project work
Tend to ask questions and vocalize what they read	Tend to highlight important passages, rereading notes and outlining	Tend to take notes but rarely read them; understand and remember by doing something physical

and visual learners. Teachers can reduce this problem by designing learning activities that address a variety of learning styles.

Physiological Dimension

The physiological dimension refers to learning preferences predicated by biological differences, such as gender and reaction to the physical environment. Several studies have found that female students employ more learning strategies, employ strategies more effectively, or both (Nyikos, 1990; Oxford, Nyikos, & Ehrman, 1988). Learners have different tolerances for noise, temperature, and even light. An incompatible physical environment, such as a room with too much noise or a temperature that is too low, will distract some learners, making it difficult for them to learn.

Which Learning Styles Should Language Teachers Cater To?

The profusion of learning styles can be overwhelming to teachers who want to promote cognitive engagement in their students. The natural question is which learning styles teachers should most attend to in encouraging intentional cognition and active engagement on the part of learners. Perhaps the proper perspective is to view learning styles as highlighting different aspects of a very complex entity. Like the proverbial blind men feeling different parts of the elephant, each of whom claimed he had the correct answer, teachers should understand learning styles as pieces of a jigsaw puzzle. For example, a global learner is probably also an auditory and extroverted one. The affective learner explores the social setting, too; this social characteristic is also central to cognitive learning styles. The different learning styles are not different phenomena but different aspects of the same phenomenon in the learner. Therefore, students benefit most from a teacher's understanding of learning styles when as many domains as possible are integrated into the instruction. Researchers have long recognized this, and many learning-style instruments are designed to measure multiple domains.

The Myers-Briggs Type Indicator (Myers & McCaulley, 1985) measures both the cognitive and the affective dimensions. This tool goes beyond learning styles to measure personality preferences, one of which is learning style. Kolb's Learning Style Inventory (1985), which was created for business management, measures cognitive, affective, and sensory factors. The learning-style inventory developed by Dunn, Dunn, and Price (1989) also measures multiple factors in the cognitive, affective, and physiological domains and is widely used in schools. The underlying principle of such instruments is to capture as many domains as possible in order to create as comprehensible a picture as possible of the learner's particular style.

It would be nearly impossible for teachers to achieve the flexibility necessary to change their teaching styles and instructional materials so that they cater to all the different learning styles in a class. The most common suggestion is to identify and cater to the two or three most common styles in a class. Although this strategy is certainly better than adhering to only one method, in principle it still does not solve the problem of abandoning a perhaps significant minority of the students who do not prefer the dominant styles.

How Can Computers Help Teachers Address Multiple Learning Styles?

When computers were first introduced into the language classroom, they were expected to be flexible enough to cater to multiple learning styles. That hope proved overly optimistic for two reasons—inadequate hardware and inadequate software. The computer hardware of even the late 1980s was not flexible enough to support audio or video playback of any degree of sophistication. In CALL, interaction was often limited to text-based functions, such as turning pages or flashing the correct words or phrases on the screen. Today, computers come with multimedia features built in. Laser disc–quality audio and video playback are standard features. Hypertext interaction comes complete with sound and full-screen, full-motion video. In fact, except for cost, which seems to be dropping rapidly, hardware capabilities have ceased to be a central issue.

Don't Blame the Computer

Some researchers claim that hardware capability should not have been an issue to begin with. As early as the mid-1980s, Sanders and Kenner (1984) warned that "unless people in CAI [computer-assisted instruction] move away from their present obsession with hardware and begin to focus more critically and imaginatively on the courseware offered, CAI may suffer a similar fate to the [audiotape] language lab" (p. 34). The main reason for the demise of the audio language laboratory was the poor quality of the courseware. Most consisted of structure-oriented, drill-oriented, stimulus-response, habit-formation-based materials following the audiolingual method that was in vogue at that time. Repetitive drills of small chunks of language structures cater to only a portion of learners, specifically those with analytic learning styles. Students with other learning styles may find such learning materials discouraging. Although these materials definitely have their place—even today, particularly for remediation and building background knowledge—the current communicative view of language learning has left such courseware far behind.

What is worrisome is that the pedagogical assumptions of audio language laboratory courseware, described above, also characterize much of today's computerized language learning software. In other words, current CALL courseware caters overwhelmingly to one learning style. Language educators seem curiously to ignore the fact that the computer is just another medium of presentation, albeit an extremely versatile one. What and how the computer teaches depends on the software used and the tasks set for its use. Even the most sophisticated multimedia computer will do no more than display page after page of text or present rote memorization drills ceaselessly if that is what it is programmed to do.

However, the multimedia computer can present language games, simulations, and problem-solving activities, too. The CALL environment can be highly motivating (some would even say addictive) for students of all learning styles (Pennington, 1996). Blaming the computer for inadequate communicativeness in a language classroom is as senseless as blaming the chalkboard or the textbook for its inability to teach fluency. The people who determine the success or failure of CALL are those involved in its development and use: the software designers who design their courseware based predominantly on one instructional method (owing either to lack of innovation or to the ease of following a well-traveled path) and the teachers who buy these software packages and use them unimaginatively. In other words, the problem is not that the computer cannot cater to different learning styles but that programmers and perhaps even teachers are not using the computer to the extent of its capabilities.

Nevertheless, there are grounds for optimism. The computer-assisted language classroom represents a far bigger market than the language laboratory of the past, a situation that will attract more and better instructional designers. There is already "a trend away from the rather drab CALLware of the 1970's and 1980's toward a more open-ended, interactive approach that takes advantage of the computing muscle available today" (Cunningham, 1995, p. 16). The explosive growth of the World Wide Web has revealed the true power of the computer in open-ended interactive learning, and this power has barely been explored. Assuming that high-capability hardware is supported by high-quality software on or off the Web, language learners may finally be able to learn language according to their preferred modalities.

Take Advantage of Multimedia

As noted throughout this text (see especially chapters 13 and 19), multimedia is one very good answer for teachers looking to address their students' many learning styles. Multimedia is defined as "a program or information environment that uses computers to integrate text, graphics, images, video, and audio" (Shih & Alessi, 1996, p. 204). All of these media have been used separately in classrooms for a long time, and their individual benefits to learning have been well documented. However, when integrated, the whole appears to be greater than the sum of its parts; each medium reinforces the effectiveness of the others in what has been dubbed the *dual modality advantage* (Najjar, 1996). According to dual-coding theory, "Learning is better when information is . . . processed through two channels than when the information is processed through one channel" (p. 134). Simply put, students learn more when information is presented in two or more modalities simultaneously. Because the multimedia computer has only recently come of age, research into the medium is scant, but the findings so far are encouraging.

Burger (1985) reported that no single learning style benefited learners more than another when used in computer-assisted instruction in medical terminology. Hinkelman and Pysock (1992) and Soo and Ngeow (1996), in studies with research assumptions based on perceptual learning styles, explored the effects of multimedia on different learning styles. Hinkelman and Pysock found that, for Japanese university students, a multimodality lesson achieved almost 20% better retention of vocabulary than a lesson catering to a single modality did. In a semester-long study in Malaysia, Soo and Ngeow found that a multimedia English proficiency program benefited learners with all three perceptual learning styles—auditory, visual, and kinesthetic—equally. Multimedia lessons appear to be able to address the modalities of a large number of learning styles simultaneously; in other words, a single multimedia program can cater to many learning styles simultaneously because the software teaches in auditory, visual, and kinesthetic media.

These results may be the harbinger of a very exciting time for the computer-assisted language classroom. Because the multimedia computer is so versatile, the possibility exists that students could learn the same content according to their individual learning styles by using software that has been appropriately customized. Well-designed software could teach by integrating several media—auditory, visual, and tactile—simultaneously, something human teachers might be hard put to do on their own. The use of the computer in this way may necessitate less face-to-face teaching and more individualized learning than is common today.

Does that mean the computer may supplant the teacher eventually? The answer is no, because software that can cater to all learning styles can be created only by designers who understand the styles, and many of those designers will be teachers. The design of good software depends on the findings of good research, which comes mostly from concerned and dedicated teachers. Good software is not effective unless teachers select it and use it properly. In time, the computer may supplant other means of presentation, such as books or chalkboards, just as the automobile supplanted the horse. Yet the advent of the automobile did not supersede the need for a guiding entity; the rider merely became the driver.

Can teachers cater to their students' different learning styles without the computer? The answer is certainly yes, but why would anyone want to continue riding horses to work when it is possible to drive or ride in cars instead? Teachers would be doing themselves and their students a disservice by insisting on doing things the hard way. In time, computers will permeate all aspects of teaching and learning, and although "computers will not replace teachers, . . . teachers who use computers will—inevitably—replace teachers who do not" (C. Bradin, personal communication, March 1996, cited in Hanson-Smith, 1997c, p. 14).

Conclusion

Research shows that students have significantly different language learning preferences. These preferences make any instructional environment, method, or resource more effective for some learners and less effective for others. This research makes it easier to understand the pedagogical swings of the past 40 years from the audiolingual method, to the notional-functional syllabus, to communicative methods. All these methods initially showed great promise. Once their use became widespread, however, teachers probably encountered students whose learning styles clashed with these approaches. When considered in the light of new research findings, the clash between students and methods caused disillusionment with the methods' apparent ineffectiveness and the students' lack of active engagement.

The answer to dealing with differences in learning style among language learners does not lie in finding one supermethod that can cater to all learning styles; there can be no such method. The key to teaching all learners as effectively as possible lies in identifying the needs and preferences of each learner and not only fulfilling learners' needs according to their preferences but helping them develop new ways to learn. Practically, this is impossible without a medium of delivery whose versatility matches the variety of learning styles. The computer seems versatile enough to be such a medium—if it is driven by well-designed software and properly utilized by well-trained teachers. The trend is only beginning, and for those teachers who dare take up the challenge, a brave new world awaits.

Chapter 19

Classroom Practice: Enhancing and Extending Learning Styles Through Computers

Karen Yeok-Hwa Ngeow

As demonstrated in chapter 18, a current concern of language teaching professionals is to provide a wide range of language experiences that can meet the challenges posed by students' diverse learning preferences. Learners who are capable of studying their own ideas and strategies in dealing with a problem are more likely to look for guidance and facilitating strategies that promote their learning and to be cognitively engaged (see, e.g., Mia & Walter, 1995; Wenden & Rubin, 1987). If learners are to enhance their *mindfulness* (Salomon, 1990), it is useful for them to realize for themselves, as well as to share with their peers and others, the different ways in which they learn language and to understand and practice new ways of learning.

Many educators feel that strategy training is a crucial factor in helping students reflect on and share their learning preferences and strategies (Dunn, 1996; Oxford, Hollaway, & Horton-Murillo, 1992; Reid, 1995b). This training is important in raising students' confidence because it allows them to take on and learn from a multitude of learning activities. Training learners to be mindful is a way of helping them be aware of their individual strengths and weaknesses in learning.

This chapter explains three complementary principles for addressing learning styles and strategy training in the CALL classroom and discusses ways to apply the principles to the planning and design of learning activities that enhance and extend students' learning strategy repertoires.

Addressing Learning Styles

Principle 1: Learners who are more conscious of their learning styles make better use of learning opportunities. Helping students become more conscious of their learning styles is a concern of many language educators who work with

302

learners from diverse learning and cultural backgrounds. In practice, this principle means first helping students understand their preferred ways of learning. Teachers can then design activities so that students can work on various aspects that best cater to certain aptitudes, abilities, and learning styles.

Principle 2: *Learners learn better when they are provided with learning opportunities that enhance and extend their learning preferences.* Teachers who are cognizant of enhancing learning by taking their students' learning styles into account can create a range of activities from which students can select those that best fit their preferences. At the same time, it is just as important for students to recognize the significance of other learning styles and strategies and share successes and failures with other learners. Activities designed to expose learners to others' preferences will encourage mindfulness in exploiting learning opportunities, including the opportunity to learn from each others' strengths and weaknesses.

Principle 3: *Learners work better with new learning styles when they are given guided opportunities to practice them.* After students understand their own learning preferences and have had opportunities to discuss and explore other preferences and strategies, they should be presented with opportunities to use a variety of strategies in their learning. Activities can be designed so that students must apply strategies not currently in their repertoire; the teacher must take care to give enough guidance and feedback in the use of these strategies so that frustration does not take the place of intentional cognition.

Applying the Principles

Computers can play several roles in helping language teachers address learning styles. For example, multimedia writing software can support authentic language learning activities (e.g., creating a class newspaper) that address a variety of learning styles. Other software tools, such as information organizers, help students present ideas in different ways. In these instances, the computer supports students in learning about and practicing different ways of learning. Computers can also help teachers record information about individual students and create challenging learning activities that enhance and extend students' learning styles.

The activities described in this section involve the computer in its role as an activity tool or a teacher's tool and demonstrate the application of one or more of the principles stated above. Note that there are many other ways to apply both the technology and the principles in teaching learners strategies that enhance and extend their learning styles.

Creating Learner Profiles

One way to better understand what activities work for students is to help them develop individual profiles of their preferred ways of learning. Learner profiles have several purposes. With the information in the profiles, the teacher and the students are better equipped to make learning more challenging by creating activities that whet the students' interests, focus on their abilities, and generally make them more aware of the possibilities for learning. Profiles can sensitize teachers and students to individual differences in learners' approaches to learning. In addition, teachers can use learner profiles to help students understand more about their own preferred learning styles. Teachers can also encourage students to discover more about each other's learning preferences by getting them to talk about the ways they prefer to learn. This type of discussion is especially useful in a class in which students come from different cultures and may not have been exposed previously to a variety of learning preferences.

To create learner profiles, students can fill in a self-rated questionnaire on learning-style preferences, such as Kinsella's (1995a) Perceptual Learning Preferences Survey, either on their own or as a class. An important follow-up activity aimed at making students more aware of their learning styles is to have students discuss their learning profiles. Students with the same learner profile descriptions can form groups to discuss how they approach a certain language task (e.g., organizing information). In this way, students explore how learners with similar learning preferences may organize information using different strategies.

The Internet has some resources for teachers and students who are creating learner profiles. One useful learning-style indicator, the Keirsey Temperament Sorter (Keirsey, 1984), includes a computer-based scoring device that allows students to arrive at a score and a description of their learning profile after completing the questionnaire. Doing this activity on the Internet has several benefits. First, students can create, review, or compare their learning profiles at different times in their learning experience. Second, the computer-generated scoring allows users to see their profile descriptions immediately instead of having to wait to discuss the results; immediate feedback helps maintain students' interest in the activity.

Using Information Organizers

Another tool that helps students become more aware of their learning preferences and strategies is the information organizer. Within other activities or as the focus of a lesson, the teacher can introduce several software programs that students can use to organize data, such as graphic outliners (e.g., Inspiration, 1988), word processors (e.g., Microsoft® Word, 1997), database applications (e.g., Microsoft Access, 1997), and hypertext systems (e.g., Microsoft FrontPage® 98, 1998). Students then use the software to organize information and explore the choices that they made during the activity. The computer-supported activity described below specifically emphasizes learning styles and the organization of information.

Note-Taking

1. Read aloud or play an audiotape of an article about language learning strategies to the students; have the students take notes using one of the software tools (e.g., Microsoft Word, 1997). (It is assumed that most students will take notes linearly, based on habit.)

2. Present a concept map (using a graphic organizer) based on the article read to the class.

3. Have the students compare and contrast the concept map with their own (linearly organized) notes.

4. Read the students another article. Have the students choose between the two different ways of taking notes.

Group Presentation

1. Ask the students to discuss in small groups their ideas regarding the 10 most effective ways of learning a foreign language (e.g., the use of e-mail to improve writing skills) and their reasons for choosing these ways. Printouts from an electronic discussion forum (see chapter 6) might be useful here.

2. Have the students compare the different ways that the groups present the information.

Reflection

1. After the activity, give the students a guide sheet (see, e.g., Figure 19-1) that helps them to reflect on their experience in organizing information in these two different ways.

Figure 19-1. Reflection Guide: Analyzing Preferences in Accomplishing a Language Task

1. How did you organize your information?

2. What did you like about organizing information this way? What did you find easy to do? Why?

3. What did you dislike about organizing information this way? What did you find difficult to do? Why?

4. How effective do you think this method of organization is in helping you present the information? Did this method make it easy for your audience to understand your presentation?

5. In which other situations do you think organizing information in this way is useful?

6. What have you learned about organizing information using two different methods? Compare the two ways of presenting information. Which one do you prefer? Which method would you use the next time? Can this method be used all the time?

7. Do a class survey to find out which method most students in the class prefer. Discuss the reasons for the class's preference.

Internalizing the Multiple Intelligences Theory

Stuart (1997) describes an activity in which students learn to enhance and extend their learning styles by developing a better understanding of *multiple intelligences* (MI) theory (Gardner, 1983, 1993). Instead of simply introducing the theoretical framework of MI to her students, Stuart lets the students experience for themselves how they learn best and see that each student possesses a different set of learning preferences and abilities. A CALL adaptation of the activity follows.

Introducing MI Theory With Multimedia Projects

1. Capture the students' curiosity by introducing a wide range of software (see Table 19-1). Have the students choose the software that interests them most (e.g., a creative activity application, a concept-mapping tool, or a multimedia resource). Although students may not know it, this stage is an introduction to MI theory.

2. Do a hands-on activity. Have the students work alone or in small groups to outline a miniproject in which they use the software to learn a language. Because the project taps into the

range of intelligences, encourage the students to use the ideas that are most appealing to themselves as learners. (For younger learners, Stuart suggests that the teacher compile a list of activities to choose from.)

3. Share and discuss project ideas. Using the students' projects as examples, talk about attractive learning features and the fact that students are inclined toward different activities because of their learning preferences.

4. Introduce and explain the concept of MI. Lead a discussion about learning styles, the terminology of MI, and the way the intelligences relate to students' learning. For example, explain that a project using SimTown (1995) demonstrates a spatial preference and that a decision to learn language using debate groups in Choices, Choices (1994) shows an inclination toward interpersonal and linguistic learning. In this discussion, make sure the students realize that language activities very often involve more than one form of intelligence—and that, for this reason, the students might want to work on extending as well as enhancing their learning strengths or abilities.

The broad range of software shown in Table 19-1 can enhance and extend students' learning styles in the classroom. These applications have been rated among the best educational software by the Association for Supervision and Curriculum Development (1997). Although I have categorized the software by the types of intelligence enumerated in MI theory (Gardner, 1983, 1993), in designing learning tasks for students, teachers must remember that these intelligences very often work in concert, not in isolation.

Integrating Software Use for Different Learning Styles

Table 19-1 includes both content-based (e.g., Choices, Choices, 1994) and content-free (e.g., Microsoft PowerPoint® 97, 1996) software. CALL teachers can combine two or more software programs to create a meaningful language learning activity for students with different learning preferences; in these activities, learners benefit from working together.

In one project, the students use the simulation Choices, Choices: Kids and the Environment (1994) and Microsoft PowerPoint 97 (1996) presentation graphics software.

Table 19-1. Software for K-12 Learners of Different Learning Styles

Type of learner	Likes to	May benefit from using software of this type:
Linguistic	Read, write, tell stories, create presentations	• Authoring program (e.g., HyperStudio, 1997) • Interactive simulation (e.g., A House Divided: The Lincoln-Douglas Debate, 1994)
Logical-mathematical	Work with numbers, classify and categorize, ask questions, reason things out by exploring patterns and relationships	• Information organizer (e.g., TimeLiner, 1994) • Application requiring problem solving with critical inquiry (e.g., The Lost Mind of Dr. Brain, 1995)
Spatial	Draw and design things, think using images, work on puzzles, watch movies, play with machines	• Concept mapping tool (e.g., Inspiration, 1988) • Planning- and design-oriented simulation (e.g., SimTown, 1995) • Tool for graphic presentation of knowledge (e.g., Microsoft® PowerPoint® 97, 1996)
Musical	Listen to music, sing and hum tunes, play an instrument, use rhyme and rhythm to aid memory	• Music-oriented electronic library (e.g., Juilliard Music Adventure, 1995) • Interactive software with music (e.g., Opening Night, 1995) • Creative multimedia tool (e.g., The Multimedia Workshop, 1994)
Bodily-kinesthetic	Move around, touch and talk, use body language, be involved in creative role plays	• Adventure simulation (e.g., The Amazon Trail, 1994) • Exploration-invention software (e.g., Widget Workshop, 1994) • Software involving hands-on exploration (e.g., Interactive Nova: Earth, 1994)
Interpersonal	Talk to people, develop social skills, work in groups, share ideas and experiences	• Decision-making simulation • Software involving exploration of social issues (e.g., Discovering America, 1993) • E-mail keypal activities (see chapter 6)
Intrapersonal	Work alone, work at own pace, pursue own interests	• Electronic library (e.g., The Electronic Bookshelf, 1984) • Self-paced tutorial (e.g., The Amazing Writing Machine, 1994) • Reflection on and exploration of relationships (e.g., Culture and Technology, 1996)

Using Presentation Software With Simulations

1. Have the students work in groups to make decisions based on the simulation and discuss the consequences of their decisions.

2. Have the students use a presentation tool to create professional-looking slides for an oral report in which the students must justify their choices

3. Arrange for the students to present their projects to an authentic audience, for example, a school-community board comprising parents and teachers.

Combining the use of the software with these activities allows learners who are more linguistically inclined as well as those who are more spatial or musical to contribute to their group's success in the project.

In another activity, students create and stage a live performance for a holiday pageant or a similar occasion. Software like TimeLiner (1994) provides a framework in which students document and organize data obtained from research, readings, and discussion. Software like Opening Night (1995) assists students by providing writing prompts with which to create original scripts and develop staging effects. Students then perform their own plays, either videotaping them or presenting them to a live audience.

Using Scripting Software With an Information Organizer

1. Have the students look up (on the World Wide Web or reference CD-ROMs) historical data on different aspects of the Victorian English lifestyle: the events, customs, attire, and occupations of people living in that particular era.

2. Have the students use an information organizer, such as TimeLiner (1994) to arrange and share the information gathered. Have the students choose from the various methods of presenting data (e.g., a list, a table, graphics), which represent the various preferences for learning and organizing information.

3. Have the students use Opening Night and the information they have gathered to write their scripts.

4. Have the students perform their plays for the class or at a school event. Videotape the productions if possible so that the groups can see their own work.

Thematic Activity

Creating a newsletter for the class requires the use of more than one form of intelligence or learning style. Many aspects of creating a newsletter bring out students' potential in a language learning environment, and the use of multimedia enhances this potential. Software that promotes creativity and lends itself to projects is readily available, but it is up to the teacher to design activities in which students learn not only from the work they engage in but also from their peers' learning styles in accomplishing certain tasks.

Many software packages that allow students to use their creativity, such as Creative Writer (1993) and the Writing Center (1991), have some of the features of a word processor, such as a thesaurus; design tools, such as animation and sound; and creativity tools, such as templates for cards and newsletters. In the project shown in Figure 19-2, students created a neighborhood newsletter by interviewing their neighbors, writing up the news, and designing news columns with Creative Writer. In another project, students researched a topic and worked together to create a children's encyclopedia entry using The Writing Center.

Another activity using software like Creative Writer (1993) or The Writing Center (1991) shows how multimedia software can enhance students' learning preferences and at the same time promote collaborative behavior among students.

Creating Theme-Based Projects

1. Establish the thematic framework. For example, the teacher reads an article in the newspaper about a very sick 8-year-old boy (vary the age based on that of the students) in Mexico (or another country) who needs a heart transplant. The class decides to do something that will cheer him up while he waits in the hospital for a yet-to-be scheduled operation.

2. Ask the class to form small groups and work on a project that they think may interest the boy. The projects could involve the following: making a get-well card, writing a humorous story, writing and animating short jokes or riddles, or making a banner. The class may come up with other ideas.

3. Have the students create the projects using one of the software applications suggested above. At the end of the activity, put the projects into a package to be sent off to Mexico (or wherever the recipient is).

4. Discuss with the class the various learning preferences they employed in their projects.

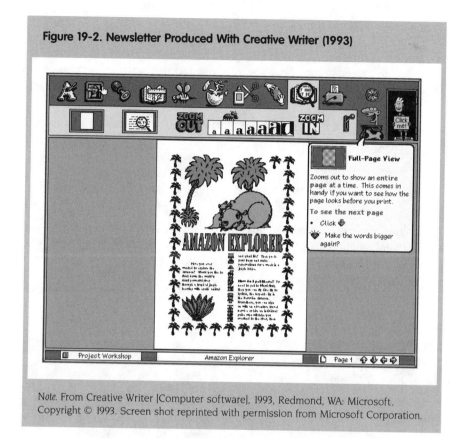

Figure 19-2. Newsletter Produced With Creative Writer (1993)

Note. From Creative Writer [Computer software], 1993, Redmond, WA: Microsoft. Copyright © 1993. Screen shot reprinted with permission from Microsoft Corporation.

This sort of class activity allows students to work on aspects of the project that best meet their abilities and interests. The imaginative student who is good with words might opt to work on storytelling, whereas the artistic and visual learner may wish to begin a graphic design project. The teacher guides the learners in realizing how to use their abilities to the fullest in contributing to a group effort.

At the same time, because the activity is based on a theme, the class works collaboratively to make the venture a success. Students can first work on one team and then move to contribute to another team's efforts or to help and ask for help from other team members. All these good learning behaviors can help learners reflect on different ways to learn and, if encouraged by the teacher, practice new ways of learning.

Learning Cooperatively in Role Plays

Many language teachers in CALL classrooms find it necessary to have students work in groups in order to increase the time spent at the computer during a task. A good reason for encouraging group work at the computer is that it leads learners to use their individual learning styles to the group's advantage. To optimize the benefits of a task and at the same time cater to individual learners' needs, however, the teacher needs to design tasks that allow differences among students to be accepted and appreciated. Such tasks should include

- thoughtfully and clearly designed roles for individual students
- conditions of positive interdependence as well as accountability
- clear social and academic goals
- opportunities for students to process and assess their work (Hooper, 1992)

Assigning a role (e.g., summarizer, checker, observer, timekeeper) to each group member is one way to allow for students' individual differences.

A software application that requires problem solving and lends itself well to cooperative learning and role play is The Factory (1995; see Figure 19-3), in which learners manufacture a product by visualizing the types of

Figure 19-3. One Learner's Solution in The Factory (1995)

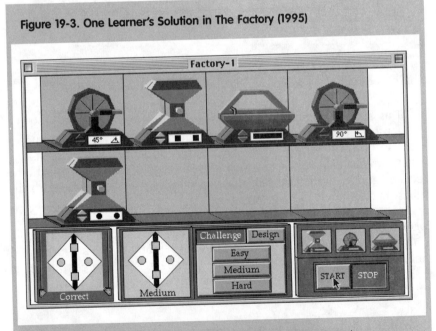

Note. From The Factory [Computer software], 1995, Pleasantville, NY: Sunburst Communications. Copyright © 1995 by Sunburst Communications. Reprinted with permission.

machines necessary and the order in which they must perform their functions. This software, originally designed for a mathematics curriculum, can be used with learners spanning a wide range of abilities and focuses on improving spatial visualization as well as problem-solving skills.

The following activity (from Antommarchi, Ngeow, & Yajima, 1996, using The Factory, 1995) is designed to facilitate group learning in the collaborative computer-based classroom. It can also help students become aware of their own styles and work on extending their learning preferences.

Organizing Collaborative Learning

1. Prepare role sheets, one for each student, that contain clear instructions and language cues:

   - The *director* instructs the group members on the steps they should take to accomplish the task in the software.

   - The *controller* works the computer mouse, listens to the instructions given, and may also make suggestions on the steps to take.

   - The *guide,* who is in charge of the language forms and functions needed for the task, helps other group members clarify the language they use.

   - The *morale booster* motivates and supports group members and sees the group through the task.

   (For groups of three, combine the roles of the guide and the morale booster.)

2. Have the students form groups of three or four, and ask each student to choose the role that feels most comfortable. For instance, linguistic and kinesthetic learners may wish to take on the role of the director or controller. On the other hand, students who prefer being the guide or the morale booster may be visual and perceptive learners who wish to view the proceedings before actively participating. Encourage the students to discuss the different reasons for their role preferences.

3. To help the group members extend their learning styles, have the students take turns performing different roles and, later, discuss reasons for preferring certain roles.

Initially, students may not feel comfortable taking turns at roles other than their chosen ones, but in this kind of cooperative learning activity, students can depend on other group members for help and support. For instance, students who are not comfortable giving instructions as the director can perform the task with the support and cooperation of group members. Taking on different roles that may be in contrast to the student's individual preferences for learning is much easier in a role play than in real life, particularly if all the group members accept the responsibilities that come with each role and support one another.

Participation in activities like the one described here leads to a deeper understanding of how different learning styles complement one another so that the group reaches a higher level of achievement. The activity also allows students both to experience and perceive how other students use their capabilities to learn successfully and to practice using unfamiliar strategies.

Role plays are particularly helpful with novice computer users, who grapple with mastering computer skills and language at the same time. Such students are bound to experience some level of anxiety about learning, and handling only one aspect of an activity or one role at a time (e.g., manipulating the mouse or giving instructions) may help alleviate this anxiety. (See chapter 21 on the role of stress and anxiety in language learning.)

Conclusion

Whether students work individually or together at the computer, they need to be aware of what their learning styles are and how they can become more successful learners by extending their learning preferences. Bickel and Truscello (1996) point out that the challenges for the ESL teacher in the computerized language classroom are not very different from those in the conventional classroom. The focus is still on enhancing students' learning by facilitating and assessing their learning processes in the best way possible. As pointed out in chapter 18, the teacher's overall instructional goal is to make sure that students learn optimally, even if they are learning differently. To do this, teachers need to provide their students with learning opportunities that encourage various means and modes of language learning and use so that learners can develop styles suited to their needs.

Diversity in learning needs and preferences calls for flexibility in teaching and learning approaches in the CALL classroom. Teachers need to be insightful and sensitive in creating opportunities for various kinds of computer-enhanced activities, and students need to take responsibility for their learning by enhancing and extending their learning preferences to meet the challenges of different contexts.

Chapter 20

CALL Issues: Multicultural Considerations in a CALL Environment

Ana Bishop

We increasingly live multiculturally. With little contact with other nations and their cultures, unicultural education could be excused, chances being that most contact would be with people from the same culture, even from the same local community. Even teaching the national, usually meaning the dominant, culture and language was going far, literally speaking. This is no longer so today. Unicultural education is insufficient preparation for life in a multicultural reality, not only at the world level but also in the local social practice of an increasing number of people. (Johan Galtung, quoted in McInnis, 1996, n.p.)

What does an educator need to know in order to ensure that software and computer communications projects in the CALL environment take into account relevant multicultural elements of either the target language or the target student population? This chapter poses many questions like this one, and many have no answers. You as an educator will have to adjust to a certain level of uncertainty because the issues raised here have no simple answers. The purpose of this chapter is to explore multicultural considerations for CALL, increase your awareness of what you can and cannot do to deal with them, and promote the use of creativity—with fluidity—to come up with workable answers yourself or in collaboration with other teachers or even with your students.

This chapter first defines multiculturalism and multicultural elements in CALL contexts. I then examine the multicultural considerations involved in evaluating software, Internet applications, or other technologies for use in the language learning classroom. Finally, I discuss the benefits of sensitivity to multicultural elements in the CALL environment.

Multiple + Culture = Multicultural?

The word *multicultural* is bandied about quite a bit, but few people know what it really means—or perhaps the meaning varies with the context. For instance, in human resources departments of corporations, *multicultural* has come to be synonymous with diversity, a variation on affirmative action with all its political overtones. As such, it constitutes mostly a reference to race and, in some cases, sexual preference. A survey conducted in San Francisco, California, on the issue of multiculturalism produced this reaction:

> When we use "multicultural" we are using it to say many, to stress diverse, and to pose against the idea of mono-cultural expressions. This term caused discomfort in almost every community we touched. Interviewees had an almost universally negative reaction to the word, calling it a rip-off, unfortunate, divisive, and misunderstood.
>
> The problem is the word [multicultural] has come to mean everything and nothing at the same time. On the one hand it has become a euphemism for non-European, thus a company that exclusively presents Chinese cultural statements is considered "multicultural" whereas on the other hand, a Polish organization is labeled as Eurocentric and pressured to become more "culturally diverse" or "multicultural."
>
> A phrase conceived with such promise, multicultural has come to signify all of the suspicion and mistrust that revolves around the issue of cultural expression in this society. Because the term multicultural does not have significant value in the context of this discussion, it is used only as a reminder that when we are talking about culture, we are always talking about more than one. (California Confederation of the Arts, 1994, n.p.)

For the purposes of CALL, I define *multicultural* as the element to consider when teaching a language to students from a variety of linguistic and cultural backgrounds; or, conversely, when teaching a language that may integrate a variety of cultural elements to students who are homogeneous in language and culture; or some variation thereof.

Context = Students + Teachers + Target Language Objectives

Multicultural elements that form the teaching context include such characteristics of the student population as

- the students' ages
- the students' grade level
- the students' level of competency in their native language

- the environment in which the students will use computers while learning the second or foreign language or in the future
- the degree of homogeneity of the student body

Two other areas of multicultural impact involve

- the teacher's English language ability and
- the level of competency expected in the second language by the course's end

These elements, of course, need to be evaluated in any language learning environment. The only difference in a CALL environment is the additional consideration of the effect of computers, telecommunications, and other technologies on students' learning. Here I focus briefly on only a few of these factors.

Age becomes a multicultural factor when students of a certain age and culture exhibit differing reactions to technology. For example, in New York City, the *Chinatown/Manpower Project* (1997) found that Chinese students who were over 40 years old had a much harder time accepting computer instruction than did under-40 Chinese clients. As a result, the project had to give over-40 students more teacher-centered instruction before introducing them to the computers. This difference may not seem at first glance to be a cultural factor; however, similar literacy projects among, for instance, Hispanics have not faced the same difficulty in attracting the over-40 age group to the computers.

The English language proficiency of teachers is a multicultural factor only if other local sources of native English are unavailable or limited. Often a group of students learning English speak the same native language and have the same cultural background. In some ways, this homogeneous group is the easiest of all groups to teach, except that in many cases no fully fluent, native-speaking teachers of English are available. This condition may occur either because the class is conducted in a country that lacks local teachers who are fluent in English or because the teacher acquired English as a second language relatively late in life. The teacher's lack of fluency in English may cause a greater reliance to be placed on the use of computers and related technology to provide native language models that would otherwise not be available to students

Target learning objectives may affect the use of CALL when the administration or teachers push the use of software that has appropriate linguistic objectives but does not match the cultural expectations, learning styles, or background knowledge of the students. In addressing learning objectives, you should ask, at a minimum:

1. What is the specific learning objective for this class? Is it to stress grammar? To teach writing? To focus on pronunciation? To provide practice in spoken English?

2. Am I teaching to a textbook or to a specific curriculum required by the local government or educational agency? Is my computer learning environment supposed to support such a curriculum?

3. Is my students' goal
   - more in-depth language studies?
   - a cursory knowledge of the target language?
   - fluency in the target language?
   - a working knowledge of the target language for business use?
   - something else?

Once you have answered these preliminary questions, the kinds of software that will be most appropriate will be clearer to you. You will then need to evaluate the multicultural sensitivity of the electronic media you intend to use.

Questions for Cultural Sensitivity in the CALL Environment

The level of cultural sensitivity of software is a rather broad area to assess. All you can do is ask a lot of questions about the electronic media that you are considering and about the CALL environment. The questions below are a starting point and by no means represent a comprehensive list. They simply give an idea of software characteristics that might pass unnoticed if they are not examined with an eye toward cultural sensitivity.

1. Is the software in a dialect? Does it utilize regionalisms that may not be relevant to the students?

For example, when studying English, will the students need to know American English, British English, Australian English, another dialect, or all the variations of the language? Does the software present these variations or, at least, allow you to add variations in diction, pronunciation, and emphasis?

To reach the broadest possible audiences, television—and now software—has attempted to establish a standardized form for every language, such as Broadcast English for U.S. television, BBC English in Europe, and other official or unofficial versions of pronunciation and vocabulary in English. However, some languages lack words for concepts or items unknown in native countries and cultures and therefore may require a little more explanation before they can capture the meaning of words in English; conversely, the native language may be richer in vocabulary for certain words and concepts than English is. This difference among languages is a problem, because, as Fillmore (1996) notes,

> Just as readers must apply their linguistic knowledge to the interpretation of the texts they read, so too must they make use of their knowledge of the world and their prior experiences in reading . . . . The ideal reader . . . is one who has the cultural background, experience, and linguistic knowledge to do just what the writer hopes the readers of the text will be able to do when they read it . . . . That fact presents a special problem to educators who are concerned with finding or preparing appropriate instructional materials and texts for children from diverse cultural and linguistic backgrounds. (n.p.)

These warnings concerning instructional materials apply to any form of software, multimedia, or telecommunication. Electronic materials and media should all exhibit some basic awareness of cultural elements and should clarify their meaning. The teacher must have sufficient sociocultural and linguistic knowledge to do this, too, and should not simply narrow down or lower the level of information presented to students. The best course to take is to be aware of the software's country of origin so that you can note similarities to and differences from the locally favored language variant. You should also be aware of native variants (e.g., in Indian English) that may not be received vocabulary in world English settings.

2. Does the software contain human characters or graphics simulating humans? If so, what variations in race, ethnicity, religion, and culture are presented?

The required cultural presentation of humans may vary according to where and whom you are teaching. You should look at the software with an eye to how appropriately different cultures are portrayed and whether the voices heard use inflections that are accurate for that language group or geographical region. If the presentation is inappropriate in some way, you will notice early enough to forestall it—either by not buying the software in the first place or by maneuvering around objectionable portions. Good software should allow you to do the latter.

3. What system of measurement does the software use? Why?

The problem of different systems of measurement occurs in a learning environment without computers but is often forgotten in software evaluation. Ideally, software that offers both the U.S. and the metric system is best. If the software offers only one system, choose the one that best fits your needs.

Even the monetary system used in software can become a problem. For example, one software package developed by a U.S. company used only the U.S. dollar system, but when the application was translated into Spanish for use in Mexico, the local user could choose either the U.S. dollar or an international monetary marker that could be interpreted as the currency of any Latin American country. Of course, the market for the converted software determined this need, but at the same time, it made the software a better seller in the United States for students learning Spanish as a native language who had come from other countries and who could initially work with a familiar currency. The option to use the international marker also helped ease the transition for English speakers in the United States who were learning Spanish and who were planning on living or studying in a Latin American country.

4. Does the software offer multiple chances to answer a question correctly, or must the learner answer perfectly the first time?

This question becomes a multicultural one when you teach students from a culture that does not tolerate a wrong answer or, conversely, from one that encourages dialectic discussions. In examining software, as in examining the rest of your teaching, be sure to ask yourself how much deviation or risk taking you as a teacher allow.

5. Does the software allow students to work on their own?

If you are teaching in a culture that discourages independent work, that tradition should be respected. However, if you are teaching students to function in a country where independence is valued, then you should gently introduce the degree of independence that is appropriate there as part of the acculturation that accompanies language learning. As Kitao and Kitao (1996) note, "Learning about the people who speak a language can help the language seem more real to the students as a means of communication, not just an object of study. Studying culture can give students a more positive attitude toward the people who speak the language" (n.p.).

6. Does the software provide assistance in the students' native language?

Even students who are quite fluent in the second language can use some help in their native language. They can also use some hints as to what is acceptable, appropriate, or discouraged in the cultural context of the second language. An example is the question of the way to recognize and the most appropriate way to address an adult or someone of superior rank in cultures and languages that recognize these differences.

7. Does the software allow special accommodations to deal with the grammatical or pronunciation issues raised by students from different language groups?

In sophisticated applications, students specify their native language when they first use the software, and the software presents exercises on grammatical or pronunciation problems in the second language that are common to students with that native language background. However, this feature does not address the cultural issues that many students face when working at the computer. For example, students from certain cultures may expect questions to have only one answer or, conversely, may expect a dialectic or discussion that leads to learning. Knowing this learning bias or learning style is critical to helping students make the best use of their capabilities.

8. Does the software allow for differences in learning styles?

Gardner's (1993) theory of multiple intelligences (see chapter 18), roughly stated, holds that every person has strengths in different areas of personality or intelligence and that learning should therefore be structured to approach students from different angles. The seven intelligences that Gardner proposes are (a) logical-mathematical (math smart), (b) linguistic (word smart), (c) interpersonal (people smart), (d) intrapersonal (self smart), (e) spatial (art smart), (f) bodily-kinesthetic (body smart), and (g) musical (music smart).

How does the theory of multiple intelligences apply to multicultural issues? Simply stated, the language people speak natively may well influence or direct how they think. For example, a culture associated with a melodic or tonal language may produce students who excel at music or at mathematics. International Business Machines (IBM), in fact, used to recruit programmers and engineers from among music and math majors in college. IBM's managers had discovered through experience that these learners had an affinity for the logical-mathematical thinking required in specialty areas.

9. What age group is the software aimed at, and what assumptions does it make about the learner?

Many times, software designed and aimed at elementary school children is used with students in middle school (ages 12–14) because software developers (at least those in the United States) do not put an emphasis on middle school English language learning. For example, I had a heated discussion with the late Dr. John Henry Martin (of Writing to Read fame) about the need for ESL software for the middle grades. His response was, "Let them use the early childhood software" (akin to "Let them eat cake"). In software development, the middle grades have not until recently received the attention that they so badly need. In particular, the content of software designed for second and third graders is usually not appropriate for pre- and early teenage students. Such content is not only insulting to their intelligence but also boring. The same could be said for adults using software designed for children. Is the ritual repetitiveness accepted and even loved in early childhood acceptable or even palatable to teenagers? Do adults relate well to music and graphics aimed at teenagers? You should keep these questions in mind when selecting software and determining how it is going to be used.

10. Do you address people the same way in person as you address them in electronic media?

Forms of address—whether in the native or a second language—have begun to change under the influence of the Internet. Because students often do not know whom they are addressing electronically, the tendency is to use the familiar form of the language (e.g., given names only). Spanish, French, Hoch Deutsch, and Japanese have seen recent changes in the application of forms of address on the Internet. Why and when these sociolinguistic shifts are appropriate culturally is an issue to discuss, if not resolve, in a truly multicultural environment.

11. How flexible are the topics and content?

Are the topics and content in the software, Internet source, or World Wide Web source flexible? Should they be flexible, given the culture of the language being taught and the native language of the student? Another way to phrase these questions is, How transparent is content? Can the software or application survive the vagaries and variations of culture to accomplish its language teaching task?

Cummins and Sayers (1995) discuss a joint project taken up by K–12 classes in Maine learning French and in Quebec City learning English. These students became target language mentors to each other. One cultural element that was unknown to the Maine group was that their French language mentors were deaf. This example points out that two elements that at first seem antithetical to foreign language acquisition—distance and asynchronous communication—instead became key elements in the development of language:

> Distance, in the context of class-to-class exchanges, creates the possibility of collaboration with an unknown but knowable audience, principally through written communications. The inevitable cultural differences that exist between distant groups require clarity of written communication in

disclosing local realities. Distance also provides multiple occasions for receiving questions from distant colleagues concerning these written communications as well as for querying their culturally bound, "home-grown" versions of reality. (Cummins & Sayers, 1995, p. 32)

Asynchronicity through e-mail, Cummins and Sayers continue, allows second language learners the time they need to reflect on their responses and to produce more carefully constructed communication. Cummins and Sayers, after exploring eight situations different from yet similar to the Maine-Quebec e-mail learning project, conclude that "computer-based networks have the potential to greatly magnify the reach and impact of intercultural learning across both cultural and geographic distances" (p. 79).

12. Does the software or electronic communication assume that the learner is monolingual, bilingual, or multilingual?

In Europe and on other continents, it is assumed that students will emerge multilingual from the school system. In the United States, this is not usually the assumption. In fact, more emphasis is placed on teaching ESL—with the ultimate objective that it will become the students' only language—than on producing students who can speak at least two languages. In a CALL environment serving a bilingual program in which English is taught along with the native language, it is particularly important for software to allow the students initially to use the language they are most comfortable in, learn the basic concepts of any subject in that language, and then transfer the higher order thinking skills that they develop into English. Once they know the software in the native language, the transition to the English version is easy. Plenty of Spanish-English software is available now, and some software coming onto the market presents at least three languages, such as English, Spanish, and French, as well as other language combinations. One of the most exciting features of this kind of software is that it is available for almost any content area, from math and science to social studies, language arts, and basic literacy (Bishop, 1996).

13. Can you add or alter any features that may enhance learning for students with particular background knowledge?

This question is separate from the linguistic assistance provided by the software. The issue is whether you can add visual tips or references to topics recently covered in other classes that the students are taking or to topics they have been exposed to in the past.

14. What will you do if students from cultures that do not encourage individual or personal expression are hesitant about certain projects?

How does a teacher working on, say, an autobiographical project engage students in it without threatening this cultural proclivity? Is the desire for privacy necessarily culturally bound? This topic is often addressed in teachers' e-mail forums, such as TESLCA-L and NETEACH-L (see Appendix B). Teachers report that students may be reticent about putting personal information, such as a résumé, on the Web, but it is unclear whether this hesitancy is culturally or personally determined. I recommend observing students' response to computer work to determine whether their native culture is affecting their interaction with the technology or whether their reaction is an individual one.

Benefits = Respect + Sensitivity

Considering the needs of the individual learner is the ultimate objective of a good teacher. The ultimate objective of a CALL environment is to support language learning beyond what the teacher can offer and to assist the teacher in meeting those individual needs. Computer enhancement provides additional benefits if multicultural elements are taken into account.

One major benefit of CALL is self-confidence. Software and technology in general can adjust to the level of proficiency of each student, thus enabling some individualization of learning and allowing students to work side by side at different competency levels. Students accomplish individual goals in learning English as they work together or separately. These accomplishments can translate into a feeling of confidence for the learner in both the process and the product of learning.

Another benefit is more subtle: Awareness of one's own culture can come rapidly through electronic media. As Kitao and Kitao (1996) note,

> Learning about another culture can help students not only understand that culture better but understand their own culture better. People who have not been exposed to other cultures are often not very aware of their own culture, partly because it seems natural to them, and they do not have to think about it. However, if they learn about another culture, they can compare and contrast that culture with their own culture and thus become more aware of their own culture. (n.p.)

Summary

Multiculturalism in the CALL environment encompasses three elements: (a) the multiple cultures reflected in the language taught through the technology; (b) the multiple cultures reflected in the students' learning of English through technology; and (c) the multiple cultural ways that, while learning and teaching English, the instructors, the software, the Internet, the technology, and the students interact. Awareness of these multiple aspects of multiculturalism not only yields heightened sensitivity to individual students' learning but may produce a more student-oriented and therefore more effective CALL environment.

Explorations

Projects

1. Have your students or classmates complete the Myers-Briggs Type Indicator (Myers & McCaulley, 1985). Discuss the results with them, and summarize the results of your discussion.

2. Examine various learning-style surveys. What modifications would you make for your students? What would you need to change to use the surveys in a CALL environment?

3. What makes your students pay attention in class? Are they extrinsically or intrinsically motivated? Devise a questionnaire for your students in order to ascertain their motives.

Guided Research

1. Why is technology motivating to some students and not to others? Develop or find a questionnaire that allows you to determine your students' (or classmates') attitudes toward technology. Pilot your survey with an appropriate sample, and administer it to your students or classmates. Correlate these questions with the Myers-Briggs Type Indicator (Myers & McCaulley, 1985) or another learning-style survey that is appropriate for the participants in your study (see Projects, No. 1). What kinds of patterns in attitude emerge? What cultural factors might play a role in your students' preferences and attitudes? Do other studies support your findings?

2. How do differences in CALL materials relate to how learners with different learning preferences use them? Examine at least two different kinds of software, characterizing their differing approaches and predicting their use by learners with different learning styles. Form a hypothesis concerning the roles they will choose and the types of answers they will give. Test your

hypothesis by observing while students use the software and correlating your observations with data from an appropriate learning-style survey.

3. What is the relationship between teaching style and students' learning styles in the CALL classroom? To research this question, (a) use the Myers-Briggs Type Indicator (Myers & McCaulley, 1985) or a similar learning preferences survey on both teacher(s) and students, and (b) define the type of CALL environment (e.g., self-access lab, learning center) and the tasks under study. Are the environment and the task conducive to the preferred teaching and learning modes of the participants in the survey? Do the environment and task(s) emphasize one group's preferences over another's?

Questions for Further Investigation

1. Do learning styles cross cultural boundaries? Does teaching new learning strategies to learners make a real difference in how much and how quickly they learn language?

2. How closely do previous learning experiences and schooling relate to personal learning preferences?

3. What processes cause learners to be motivated and cognitively engaged?

PART VII

Atmosphere

Chapter 21

Theory and Research: Classroom Atmosphere

Bill Johnston

Perhaps the greatest truism in late 20th-century education is, "There has to be a good atmosphere in the classroom." When all is said and done, this belief may be one of the most important ways in which values in education have changed over the past 100 years or so: Whatever changes in content and curriculum have occurred, educators now recognize that fear, coercion, punishment, threats, and other forms of negative psychological manipulation do not represent the best way of going about educating people.

What is true for education in general, of course, is also true for language teaching. The central importance of affective factors in language learning, including appropriate stress and anxiety levels and a good classroom atmosphere as one of the eight conditions for optimal learning, is noted in chapter 1. Spolsky (1989), too, included motivation/affect as a crucial element in the equation for second language acquisition (SLA).

Yet in the field of language learning and teaching, little theoretical or empirical work has investigated what exactly classroom atmosphere is and what exactly about it ought to be good. This omission is a pity, because even though teachers themselves hold this value dear, confusion often exists over how best to realize it in class; perhaps precisely because good classroom atmosphere is taken as a universally understood principle, the concept has not been critically examined, and teachers do not have a common language in which to discuss and think about the central issues.

The aim of this chapter, then, is to offer the beginnings of a vocabulary with which to address the question of what *good classroom atmosphere* means and the related question of the teacher's roles and responsibilities in creating such an atmosphere in the ESL class. My emphasis is on atmosphere as it relates to technology and specifically to computer-assisted learning, but most of what I write here applies to classroom atmosphere in general.

Stress and Anxiety: Focus on the Individual

In the 1960s and 1970s, a fair amount of research tried to identify the exact influence of certain affective factors, like stress and anxiety, on language learning. Researchers looked at a range of affective and personality factors in SLA, including anxiety, introversion-extroversion, motivation, attitude, degree of risk taking, and self-esteem. (For reviews of this literature, see Ellis, 1994, pp. 479–523; Larsen-Freeman & Long, 1991, pp. 172–192; MacIntyre & Gardner, 1991.) One classic study in this vein is that of Guiora, Beit-Hallahmi, Brannon, Dull, and Scovel (1972), who investigated the effect of progressively increasing doses of alcohol on second language pronunciation. Their findings, however—that small doses of alcohol improved pronunciation—have been called into question, for example by Ellis (1994, p. 519).

In fact, this literature as a whole has not really fulfilled its promise and has been less prominent in the field since the early 1980s or so, even though the topic is clearly an important one. Although certain general conclusions were possible—for example, that anxiety was indeed "an important factor in L2 acquisition" (Ellis, 1994, p. 483)—taken as a whole, the studies have produced "mixed results" (p. 482). Some studies (e.g., Parkinson & Howell-Richardson, 1990) found no correlation between anxiety and rate of improvement in a study of adult ESL learners in Scotland, whereas MacIntyre and Gardner (1991) report that in some studies anxiety was positively correlated with language learning; that is, more anxious learners learned more.

Anyone who has experienced a language learning situation knows that Ellis (1994) is right to say that anxiety plays an important role. Yet the studies he reviews are problematic in a number of ways, not because they are wrong to focus on anxiety but because they do so in ways that distort basic truths of the situation.

Above all, in the surveys of research referred to above, anxiety was included in a group of other affective and personality variables, such as motivation, attitude, extroversion, and self-esteem. The underlying assumption is that, like the other members of this category, anxiety is an inherent characteristic of the learner (in the same way as, e.g., aptitude or intelligence is). In reality, however, anxiety is obviously likely to vary considerably and to be to a large extent a product of a given situation (relations with a teacher or peer, the stress of exams, or other factors) rather than a personality constant. Indeed, many theories of stress are transactional in nature in that they take into account the interaction between personality and stressful events or situations (stressors) found in the outside world (see, e.g., Lazarus & Launier, 1978). Linked to these problems is the fact that the studies assume anxiety to be an individual trait; they focus on the state of individual learners and pay scant attention to the social setting.

An additional problem is that the relation between, for example, anxiety and language learning is conceived in terms of simplistic, linear, causal relations. Such an approach belies the complexity of the language learning situation, a complexity that any practicing teacher knows only too well. Furthermore, in the tradition of quantitative social scientific research, investigators have attempted to quantify and measure anxiety in numerical terms, and, as with any form of psychometric measurement, researchers cannot be entirely sure that what they are measuring is what they intend to measure.

Nevertheless, this research at least has put affective notions such as stress and anxiety on the table, acknowledging their importance and making them part of the *educational conversation* (Garrison & Rud, 1995) in ESL teaching. It is unfortunate that the problems listed above have seemed insurmountable and that new ways have not yet been found to look at these old and enduring issues. In fact, given the way the research tradition described here has largely petered out, new research in this area is urgently needed.

The Class as Community

In contrast to the focus on the individual that characterized the research on atmosphere outlined in the previous section, other approaches to teaching methods and to conceptualizing the language classroom have emphasized the class as group and, further, as community. For example, chapter 1 names "opportunities to interact and negotiate meaning" as the first of eight conditions for optimal language learning. In addition, the themes of cooperation, collaboration, and class as community are found in approaches as diverse as the Silent Way (Gattegno, 1972), community language learning (Curran, 1976), whole language (e.g., Rigg, 1991; Weaver, 1990), cooperative learning (Johnson, Johnson, & Smith, 1991), and communicative language teaching (e.g., Brown, 1994).

Although these various approaches obviously differ considerably in many aspects, the idea of community tends to be realized in the classroom in similar ways: students collaborating on tasks, an emphasis on cooperation rather than competition, students learning from other students, peer feedback on written and oral assignments, and a sense of the class as an audience for students' work. In general terms, community means respect for all students and for what each one brings to the class, more active student participation (i.e., engagement) in the class, and a recognition of the importance of collaboration in a learning situation.

The aforementioned classroom conditions are admirable goals or ideals. In addition, although they have not always been implemented, they represent a general tendency in many educational settings and have made classrooms less stressful places to be. In many educational and sociopolitical contexts, however, other forces have continued to militate against the widespread adoption of a cooperative approach to teaching. In thinking about the role of community and its influence on classroom atmosphere, teachers must be aware of these forces and recognize practical and perhaps also theoretical limitations on the extent to which language classrooms can rely on community as a factor in promoting student growth.

Three practical limitations (or, better, restrictions or constraints) in particular present themselves. One is that, even in many situations in which collaboration and cooperation are prized over solitary work, strong remnants of the latter remain—for example, grading tends to be done individually. When it is not—for instance, when a grade is awarded to a group as a whole—the students themselves often perceive this practice as inequitable.

The fact that students often want to be assessed individually leads to a second, related point. The broader context in which collaborative teaching takes place is often opposed to this form of teaching. Systems as a whole (e.g., programs, schools, universities) are generally set up in ways that favor individualism and competition over community and cooperation. In my experience, many teachers who have elected to take a whole language approach have found themselves relatively isolated within their schools and at odds with the prevailing values and methods supported by the administration and the other teachers. This barrier in itself is an insufficient reason not to pursue cooperation in learning, but it is a factor that teachers must take into account when trying to introduce cooperative modes of working as a way of enhancing the classroom atmosphere. In addition to these systemic constraints, many individual language learners, especially those from cultures in which education focuses on discrete individual accomplishments, are consciously and often volubly opposed to alternative forms of assessment.

The third major limitation on the notion of the classroom as community is crucial to acknowledge: In its traditional use in fields such as anthropology or sociology, communities are groups of people who live together for extended periods of time. Geertz (1973), for instance, talks of a community as a group of people who "grow old together" (p. 53). Yet classrooms are not really like this. In the U.S. system, the longest any group of learners stays together is usually 1 year, and that happens only up to sixth grade (around the age of 12). After that, classes become even more fragmentary groupings of people. They may come together for an hour or two a day and may stay in this configuration for a year. At the tertiary level, even these parameters are curtailed. A typical college class meets perhaps three or four times a week over 15 weeks. Unified cohorts of students of the kind found, for example, in central European secondary and tertiary education systems are rarely encountered. ESL classes are generally no exception: Two intensive

English programs with which I have had extensive contact, for example, offer courses that run for 7 weeks and 10 weeks respectively. Furthermore, because of their diverse backgrounds, ESL learners have even less in common with each other than students from a single culture do.

Under such conditions, speaking of community in the conventional sense is rather difficult. Rather, these groups resemble more the kind of *instant communities* sociologists have observed springing up in the United States, for example, in retirement communities. Americans are particularly skilled at this kind of group formation, perhaps because of the high level of mobility found in U.S. society. People brought up in other cultures (as ESL students by definition always are), may find the process of community building more difficult given these time constraints.

Additionally, permanent communities have a broad range of interests and concerns in common and extensive shared knowledge to draw on. Language classes, on the other hand, bring together people who may have little in common other than their desire or need to learn the target language—and they may have widely differing reasons, motives, and interests even in that sphere. The language class could be said to create a desert island situation, in which a small number of people with little in common are thrown together by little more than chance and for a limited period of time.

In fact, the typical "getting-to-know-you" games that many teachers play in the first few classes are arguably a response to the difficulty of forming a sense of community in such a transient situation. Teachers are, in a way, acknowledging the desert island situation mentioned above. One wonders, though, how nonnative speakers feel about these attempts to create instant, ersatz communities in the precious time they have available to learn the language.

Finally, the desire to talk about the class as a *community of learners* (an axiomatic phrase of the whole language movement) also reflects something of a romanticized notion of community—that communities are necessarily good things. This is not always the case. Communities can be indifferent to their members; they can be constraining and conservative, and sometimes downright unsupportive. Research in group theory (e.g., Hare, Blumberg, Davies, & Kent, 1994; Witte & Davis, 1996) demonstrates clearly that in small-group interactions, conflict, power struggles (or, technically, "power exertion"; Scholl, 1996, p. 138), and attempts to impose agendas are the rule rather than the exception. Thus, the equation of *community* with *cooperation* may also be misleading. (For a fascinating critique of whole language from the perspective of the orthodoxies of classroom interaction that it engenders, see Tobin, 1995.)

The Responsibilities of the Teacher

The problems and limitations outlined in the previous section raise a critical question: What are the responsibilities of the teacher in establishing and maintaining a desirable classroom atmosphere? This question is no less important for rarely being addressed directly in the literature on language teaching.

Brown (1994), one of the few writers to give prominence to affective issues, says that the teacher needs to create a "warm, embracing climate" (p. 255) and that "all second language learners need to be treated with affective tender loving care" (p. 22). He makes certain recommendations for teachers, including the following for teachers working with young children: help your students laugh with each other at various mistakes that they all make, be patient and supportive, and elicit as much oral participation as possible from students (p. 93).

Brown (1994) proposes a set of affective principles for teaching, including

- The fragility of *language ego* in the second language must be recognized.
- Learners' *self-confidence* is a crucial element in ensuring their success.
- For success, learners must be able to *take risks*.
- The language learner's encounters with the *culture* of the target language are a vital part of the language learning process. (pp. 22–26)

Finally, Brown argues that group work promotes a positive affective climate for learning (p. 174).

Other writers on language teaching methodology (e.g., Nunan, 1989b) and classroom interaction (e.g., Malamah-Thomas, 1987) also mention such matters but tend to relegate them to the categories of "affective-humanistic activities" (Nunan, 1989b, p. 241), perhaps in line with Oxford's (1990) identification of affective strategies as one of the six categories of learning strategies. Writers like Nunan and others who have written about language teaching methods (e.g., Richards & Rodgers, 1986) take what might be termed an *instrumental* approach to what teachers do in classrooms. In this view, teachers' work is technical in nature and aimed primarily at making students learn faster and more efficiently. Affective techniques are simply one way of achieving this.

An alternative position, however, is that teaching is much more than influencing the cognitive processes of students. According to this view teaching is first and foremost a *relational* activity. The relation between teacher and student, and among students themselves, is the foundation of all that goes on in classrooms. Learning springs from these relations. Thus, so-called affective factors in fact represent the very core of teaching and learning.

Such a view of teaching is set out by Noddings (1984). For her, at the core of the occupation of teaching is the relation between teacher and learner, which she characterizes as a *caring relation*. Yet her account of this relation goes far beyond the warm and fuzzy "caring and sharing" that was supposed to occur in the humanistic classroom. Rather, Noddings recognizes "human encounter and affective response as a basic fact of human existence" (p. 4). In other words, affective issues are not an add-on that will help students learn better but a fundamental part of what is happening in the classroom.

Noddings (1984) describes the caring relation as comprising two unequal persons, whom she designates as the *one-caring* and the *cared-for*. The archetypal relation of this kind is mother-child; the teacher-student relation is comparable. The central characteristic of the one-caring is what Noddings calls *engrossment*—"I must see the other's reality as a possibility for my own" (p. 14). Engrossment refers to the ability of the one-caring (the teacher) to see things from the perspective of the cared-for (the student). In an example significant for teachers, Noddings talks of a math teacher with a student who isn't doing well in her class. Noddings suggests that rather than saying, "I must help this poor boy love mathematics," teachers should put another question to themselves: "How would it feel to hate mathematics?" (p. 15). Likewise, ESL teachers, instead of asking, "Why can't Khalid form questions properly?" might ask themselves, "What does it feel like to have difficulty with question formation in English?"

The notion of the caring relation as Noddings (1984) describes it offers a number of advantages in terms of thinking about classrooms and the teacher-student relation. First, it captures the unequal power and status inherent in the relation without making this imbalance the central issue. Second, Noddings recognizes the potential conflict in the way a class, with its many students, can make competing demands not just on teachers' time but on their emotional resources. Third, Noddings emphasizes the relational nature of teaching and indicates that, whereas the primary responsibility lies with the one-caring (the teacher), the cared-for (the student) also has a part to play in the relation. Finally, Noddings acknowledges that, because of the "uniqueness of human encounters" (p. 5), it is not possible to talk in general terms of a "universal caring" (p. 18); rather, "to care is to act not by fixed rule but by affection and regard" (p. 24), and thus teachers' relations with different students will themselves be different.

At the same time, the particular character of language teaching means that some features of the caring relation are peculiar to the language classroom. Above all, the practice of engrossment is more difficult because the teacher must cross profound cultural, social, and linguistic boundaries in seeking to understand the student's perspective. Indeed, a typical ESL class, with students from different native cultures, may evidence multiple sets of boundaries of this kind. Engrossment is not impossible, of course, but the imaginative leap is much harder with students from different cultures than with students from one's own country or culture.

One central pedagogical point that emerges from Noddings' (1984) theory is that teaching is not and cannot be a technical and mechanistic activity that relies on generalized knowledge generated by research. Learning takes place from the point at which a particular student is at the time and can best be facilitated if the teacher focuses on the learner, not the material. As Noddings says, "The learner is infinitely more important than the subject" (p. 20). This statement should give considerable pause to any teacher who has ever worried about "covering the material." Noddings argues that the teacher can help make real learning take place only from the attempt to engage with specific learners at the point where they find themselves.

The rationale that Noddings (1984) has developed clearly has major implications for classroom atmosphere. Above all, it suggests two things. First, each group of learners is unique, just as each individual learner is unique; therefore, the resulting relations between teacher and student will also be unique. In other words, a teacher's human response to each class will differ; overall guidelines may be of some use, but classroom atmosphere will depend on the particular relations in a particular setting. Given the diversity of ESL classrooms, differences between classes are likely to be dramatic.

Second, Noddings' (1984) view strongly indicates a specific role for the teacher in developing a desirable classroom atmosphere. By Noddings' account, the teacher-student relation is two-sided, and therefore part of the responsibility lies with the students (in other words, the teacher is not 100% responsible for the atmosphere in the class). However, the unequal nature of the relationship between the one-caring and the cared-for—an inequality all the more marked for learners from authoritarian cultures, who are accustomed to having less voice in educational settings—means that it is primarily the teacher's job to attempt engrossment, to see things from the perspective of the students, and to nurture learning from that perspective. According to Noddings, classroom atmosphere depends largely on the teacher's ability to meet the students where they are and to lead each student to greater knowledge and skills in ways that are best for that student.

Optimal Learning Conditions

As mentioned earlier, one much-overlooked truth in education is that stress in itself is not necessarily a bad thing. Psychologists (e.g., Rice, 1987) talk about *eustress*, a desirable form of stress that leads to heightened alertness, improved performance, and greater engagement with whatever one is doing. In fact, as Rice shows, it has long been known that with an increase of stress, performance levels constitute an inverted U-shaped curve (see Rice, 1987, p.

19). As stress increases, performance increases proportionately—to a point. When stress becomes too great, performance falls and continues to fall as stress increases.

Perhaps the clearest framework in which to develop and convey this idea is psychologist Csikszentmihalyi's (1991, 1996, 1997; van Lier, 1996) notion of *flow*. The basic concept of flow is that optimal experiences (which in educational settings are intimately linked with optimal learning) take place in a zone that lies between anxiety and boredom: That is, as in the relation of stress and performance, some stimulation—what Csikszentmihalyi (1991) calls *challenge*—is required for an optimal experience to be attained.

Flow, however, is a dynamic process. As an example, imagine Akiko, a student learning ESL. Akiko has a low level of ability, so activities or tasks requiring a low level of skill (e.g., simple linguistic and pragmatic actions like giving her name or ordering coffee in a coffee shop) provide the right level of challenge for her. At this point, an increase in the level of challenge (say, making small talk at a party) will lead to anxiety or frustration. Conversely, if the level of skill required by different tasks remains the same but Akiko's command of English improves, the result will be boredom. What Akiko needs is an activity that requires greater skill and represents a greater challenge. For Akiko, this activity may be writing a short personal letter or having a brief conversation about a movie she has seen. As Akiko's fluency and vocabulary develop even more, appropriate kinds of activities will be located further along the flow channel.

Csikszentmihalyi (1991) has documented accounts of flow experiences recounted by a wide range of people and involving a huge variety of activities, including reading, raising children, rock climbing, playing professional football, dancing, and appreciating art. From these instances, he observes that flow experiences typically contain at least some of the following elements:

1. They occur "when we confront tasks we have a chance of completing" (p. 49).

2. We can concentrate on what we are doing.

3. The task undertaken has clear goals.

4. There is immediate feedback.

5. We act "with a deep but effortless involvement that removes from awareness the worries and frustrations of everyday life" (p. 49).

6. We have a sense of control over our actions.

7. Concern for the self vanishes, yet "paradoxically the sense of self emerges stronger after the flow experience is over" (p. 49).

8. Our sense of the passage of time is temporarily altered: Time seems to pass more quickly.

Summing up, Csikszentmihalyi says, "The key element of an optimal experience is that it is an end in itself" (p. 67).

These elements of flow are remarkably consonant with the eight conditions for optimal language learning outlined in chapter 1. Four points of similarity are particularly noteworthy. First, Csikszentmihalyi's (1991) emphasis on tasks that can be completed, that have clear goals, and during which there is adequate feedback is reflected in Condition 5 ("Learners have enough time and feedback to complete the task"; addressed in Part V). Second, the effortless involvement and absence of concern for the self that Csikszentmihalyi writes about seem to be another way of describing the *mindfulness* (Zellermayer, Salomon, Globerson, & Givon, 1991) discussed in chapter 18. Third, Csikszentmihalyi's mention of control is clearly equivalent to Condition 8, which concerns the importance of learner autonomy (discussed in Part VIII). Lastly, at a more general level Condition 3, regarding authentic tasks (see Part III), seems to echo Csikszentmihalyi's overall point about optimal experiences constituting an end in themselves.

Clearly, as van Lier (1996) has also suggested, Csikszentmihalyi's (1991, 1996, 1997) model of flow provides a wonderful stimulus for thinking about classroom atmosphere and the classroom experiences of language students. Although it would be unreasonable to expect to replicate flow experiences for all students all of the time (or even for most of them, most of the time) as an ideal and a goal, the description of flow given above offers certain guidelines for the design of activities for language teaching.

Csikszentmihalyi (1991) argues that it is no accident that many flow experiences occur in activities such as games and sports:

> What makes these activities conducive to flow is that they were *designed* to make optimal experience easier to achieve. They have rules that require the learning of skills, they set up goals, they provide feedback, they make control possible. They facilitate concentration and involvement by making the activity as distinct as possible from the so-called "paramount reality" of everyday existence. (p. 72)

Yet at the same time, Csikszentmihalyi notes that flow can be achieved in "an almost infinite range" (p. 6) of activities.

Put briefly, Csikszentmihalyi's (1991) challenge to language teachers is to create activities for students that push them to perform better and better without overreaching themselves. Language learning, surely, is a skill like those Csikszentmihalyi describes. He suggests that to maximize positive stress, activities need to have clear rules and clear goals, offer rapid feedback, be clearly delineated, allow the students to feel in control, and, above all, have a purpose. Additionally, and crucially, Csikszentmihalyi's emphasis on student control supports Noddings' (1992) argument that learning must be related to the individual and the individual's stage in his or her own development. Each person's flow channel looks different; the design of learning experiences needs to recognize this fact. With these principles in mind, Csikszentmihalyi suggests, teachers have a chance of providing an optimal learning experience for their students.

Technophobia

For CALL environments, one form of anxiety requires close examination: *technophobia*, or the fear (distrust, dislike) of technology. Other terms for this concept, used with more or less precision, include *computerphobia* (Hudiburg, 1990), *computer anxiety* (Howard, 1986), and *techno-stress* (Weil & Rosen, 1997).

The notion of technophobia rarely surfaces in discussions about CALL, except in passing (although see Davidson & Tomic, 1994). In other fields, however, notably psychology, management, and to a lesser extent education, some attempt has been made to pin the concept down; to ascertain how many people it affects, to what extent, and in what ways; and finally to consider what to do about it.

Weil and Rosen (1997) refer to a range of studies and surveys suggesting that 30–80% of people report some sort of anxiety about using computers. Given the notorious problems associated with self-reported data and survey research, a large part of this variation is probably related to research methods. Nevertheless, the results suggest strongly that technophobia is a widespread phenomenon; most scholars agree that it will not go away. (The 11-year gap between the books by Howard, 1986, and by Weil and Rosen, 1997, would seem to support this premise.)

What exactly is technophobia? As it relates to computers, it covers a range of negative attitudes, beliefs, and emotions concerning computers in general and one's own interaction with them in particular. Recurrent issues in the literature include

- confusion caused by computer jargon
- a sense of being left behind as everyone else turns to computers
- a fear that learning computer skills is too difficult
- a fear of making mistakes that cannot be corrected later
- a more generalized anxiety about the role of computers in everyday life
- the everyday hassles of computer use, such as crashes and the loss of data
- the dehumanizing effect of computers
- a feeling of lack of control (Dukes, Discenza, & Couger, 1989; Hudiburg, 1989, 1990; Kernan & Howard, 1990; Marcoulides, 1989)

Technophobia, then, appears to be a complex, pervasive, and persistent phenomenon.

Howard (1986) suggests that psychological resistance to computers is both deep-seated and rather vague; as such, it may be difficult to affect. On the other hand, guided experience under the right conditions can address what he calls *operational* anxieties concerning the actual use of the computer. In other words, actually using computers in an environment where help is available may go some way toward dealing with this part of the problem (see chapter 23).

Howard (1986) also acknowledges the usefulness of being aware of one's feelings about computers. This theme is taken up by Weil and Rosen (1997), whose book, interestingly enough, is shelved in the self-help section of my local bookstore. Weil and Rosen stress the importance of the computer user's taking control, including carefully reflecting on what exactly the computer is for and what purposes the user needs it for. Such reflection clearly relates to the theme of autonomy running through this book (see chapter 24).

A third, contrary position is taken by Yeaman (1993). He claims that "computer anxiety is a label that blames the victims" and challenges the "myths of computerism" (p. 19)—pointing out, for instance, that the biggest obstacle to learning about computers is not computer anxiety but restricted access to computers. He argues that computer anxiety is a perfectly normal (not pathological) reaction to computers as they are presented and used in society. Finally, he lays the blame squarely at the feet of those who design the software and hardware with their often "opaque and mysterious" (p. 23) technologies. (See chapter 28 for a discussion of similar issues.)

In any case, technophobia is clearly a force to be reckoned with. In the language classroom, the elements of computer anxiety are compounded by language problems and may also be exacerbated by cultural unfamiliarity with a range of features of software, from the language of commands to the iconography employed. Like it or not, computer-assisted learning adds computer anxiety to the other sources of anxiety and stress that learners may be experiencing.

Computers and Classroom Atmosphere

This chapter has focused mainly on classroom atmosphere in general with the aim of considering how research and theory in this area might affect CALL. It is also instructive to turn this question on its head and ask, How is the use of computers in education likely to affect classroom atmosphere?

Speculation on this topic is rife. Here I draw on a single study because of the rich material it offers: Schofield's (1995) study of computer use in a large urban high school, one of the best and most thorough empirical investigations available. Schofield conducted a yearlong qualitative study of the use of computer technology and computer-aided instruction in a number of classes in one U.S. high school. Her research questions were

1. What is the effect of the instructional use of computer technology on students and on social processes?

2. How does the social context in which computers are used for instruction shape their use? (p. 8)

Although the study is complex and reveals a great number of interesting facts, Schofield's (1995) overall findings include the following:

*   Computer use "enhanced student enjoyment of, interest in, and attention to classroom activities" (p. 192). Schofield speculates on the reasons for this and reports research suggesting that "computers are motivating to the extent that they increase challenge, control, curiosity, and fantasy that allows for personalization of one's work" (p. 196). Note that the themes of challenge, control, and individualization echo the discussion above of the work of both Noddings (1984, 1992) and Csikszentmihalyi (1991, 1996, 1997) as well as the conditions for language learning presented in chapter 1.

*   With increased use of computers came a change in the role of the teacher "from that of the expert who presented information . . . to that of a coach or tutor" (p. 201) assisting students.

*   In some classes, peer interaction increased when computers were used. However, this change was not as widespread as has been claimed elsewhere in the literature (p. 207). In some cases, the use of computers did not have a demonstrable influence on interaction. In others, interaction was competitive rather than cooperative. Additionally, girls who developed an interest in computers found themselves socially isolated and even ostracized (p. 208).

*   On the subject of the influence of computers on education, Schofield found that computer use increased "the disparity between the 'haves and the have nots,'" in that, for example, "the academically more advanced students had more access to computers than did their peers" (p. 214). Schofield notes that this tendency has been observed in many other settings (p. 215).

*   Generally, there was a failure in this school setting to realize the "transformative potential of computers" (p. 217), for example, in enhancing individualized instruction, fostering collaboration, promoting critical thinking skills, and connecting the classroom with the real world outside; Schofield says that this, too, is "not

an idiosyncratic finding" (p. 217). Speculating on the causes of this failure, she suggests that relevant factors include the fact that teachers' values are often in conflict with the views of proponents of computers in education (p. 219). Furthermore, the traditional classroom format (e.g., lecture-style teaching) is at odds with computer-based teaching (p. 221). Finally, standardized tests have a strong tendency to "inhibit the innovative use of computer technology" (p. 222).

Taken together, Schofield's (1995) findings provide fascinating food for thought about the use of computers in schools and other educational settings. Her overall conclusion is twofold: Computers inevitably affect classroom atmosphere ("social processes," p. 8) in varying and unpredictable ways; existing social and political structures in turn shape computer use in educational contexts.

Summary

In this chapter I have offered a vocabulary and a set of concepts that might help open a dialogue on classroom atmosphere in language teaching. I suggest that, although stress and anxiety clearly play a role in language learning, thinking of them as individual traits or states may not be helpful, for they are critically linked to contextual features. On the other hand, although collaboration and community in the language classroom are admirable goals, there may be significant practical and theoretical constraints on the extent to which they can be realized.

Perhaps paradoxically, although I question the validity of the notion of community, I propose Noddings' (1984) notion of the *caring relation* as the best way of conceptualizing the teacher's role in establishing, promoting, and maintaining a desirable classroom atmosphere. Noddings' work suggests that classroom atmosphere may most usefully be thought of not in general terms but in light of relations between the individuals concerned. Further, classroom atmosphere may to a large extent depend on teachers' abilities to perceive the learning situation from the perspective of their students.

Noddings' (1984) emphasis on the individual learner and on the teacher's response to that learner's unique situation is echoed in Csikszentmihalyi's (1991, 1996, 1997) concept of *flow*, which I put forward as a way of capitalizing on the positive elements of stress in promoting an optimal learning experience. The principle of flow offers a provocative framework for teachers striving to provide the best possible learning experience for each of their students; it is also remarkably close to the conditions proposed in chapter 1.

Finally, *technophobia*, or *computer anxiety*, is a force to consider in the language classroom. Schofield's (1995) detailed study of the impact of computing on learning and social relations in a high school supports the notion of the social component of stress and anxiety and suggests strongly that classroom atmosphere and computer-assisted learning will affect each other in ways that are as profound as they are unpredictable. Specifically, her study supports the emphasis on individualization and on learner control that is noted by Noddings (1984, 1992) and Csikszentmihalyi (1991, 1996, 1997) and is a major theme of this volume.

Chapter 22

Classroom Practice: MOO, WOO, and More—Language Learning in Virtual Environments*

Lonnie Turbee

A MOO is a novel written and read by its characters.—*Harold Jones*

Where did you learn to speak a second language? Were you sitting in a class trying to think of what the teacher wanted you to say, or were you sitting in a café on a busy street sipping a cup of strong coffee or a glass of hearty red wine? Were you worrying about grades, or were you concentrating on getting taxi driver to understand which hotel you were going to? Chances are that learning took place in all of these and many other environments. In some of them you felt anxious, nervous, or even afraid. In others, however, you were aware of the hard work of communicating, but you were so engaged, or the need to communicate was so pressing, that you didn't really notice how much you were learning.

Go back in your mind to an environment where you recall using a second language effectively, maybe gloriously if not perfectly. What country were you in? What objects could you see? What sounds could you hear? What did the environment smell or even taste like? Who was with you? How did you feel? If you can answer these questions, you are ready to describe your first room on a language learning MOO (see the definitions below). It may look like this:

*This chapter is dedicated to Harold Jones, chair of the Department of Languages, Literatures and Linguistics at Syracuse University, New York, from 1988 to 1997. I am grateful for his vision, enthusiasm, and support.

```
THE MAIN STREET CAFE

This café has a few booths inside and,
spilling out over one corner of the plaza,
a number of small white metal chairs
pulled up to round, white tables. There
are people sitting at many of the tables,
sipping espresso from tiny white cups or
frothy cappuccino from large cups. Most
people are nibbling on pastries or scones.
The smell of the coffee and sweet treats
combines with a sensation of relaxing
warmth on your face from the bright
sunshine. You look forward to settling in
here for a while and wonder if a friend
will come by.
```

Some Technical Background

The Internet is a vast network of millions of computers connected to each other through telephone lines, satellite signals, fiber-optic cable, and the like. The World Wide Web is, put rather simply, the information found at some of the destinations along the routes of the Internet. You can access that information through a *browser*, such as Netscape Navigator® Gold (1997) or Microsoft® Internet Explorer (1998). Web sites and the other Internet-based environments mentioned in this chapter can be accessed by anyone anywhere in the world who has a computer, the necessary software, and a connection to the Internet, usually through a telephone line to an Internet service provider or a direct connection at work or school.

E-mail is an example of *asynchronous communication*, as response time is anywhere from a minute or so to days, depending on when the recipient decides to respond. A growing variety of computer applications allow people to connect with others via the Internet and communicate *synchronously*, that is, in real time, with little or no delay in response. Users of such applications report a sense of place or presence that is virtual rather than physical (Towell & Towell, 1997). Although they may all be seated at far-flung individual computers, users of a given environment have, quite literally, a meeting of the minds.

This chapter discusses a number of applications used for synchronous communication: what they are like, how to use them, how to choose from among them, and how to incorporate some of them into the language learning classroom. I also touch on pedagogical issues as they apply to the use of such applications. Finally, I look at the future of these tools for language learning.

Virtual Environments for Real-Time Communication

Web Chat

Chat is one of the easier synchronous formats to use because it requires only a Web browser and a uniform resource locator (URL, a Web address) to use it. Some sites, like the *WebChat Broadcasting System* (http://pages.wbs.net/), require you to register. You then use a user identification (*userid*) and password to access the chat rooms. Web chat has some disadvantages for the language learner: None of the sites are designed specifically for the learner; other users' language or graphics may be unpleasant, vulgar, or rude; and screen refreshes, slow graphics downloads, or other delays may make the reading of the conversation difficult and disjointed.

Internet Relay Chat

There are a number of ways to connect to Internet Relay Chat (IRC), one of the best being the mIRC client program, through which it is relatively easy to find or open a channel (see Vonck, 1998, http://geocities.com/~mirc/). Usually you can find target language channels by typing the # sign followed by the name of a country where the language is spoken. A favorite for Spanish, for example, is #*espana*. When you join a channel, you will likely find others already talking in it, some in the main public area and others off in "rooms" that have been created (in seconds) by users for private conversations. When the last person leaves the channel, it closes.

The world of IRC is, for the most part, as wild as that of Web chat areas. IRC has the advantage of being easy to access and read: Text rolls up the screen at a conversational pace, and there are no screen refreshes. However, teachers bringing students to existing public channels run the risk of exposing the students to superficial or inane conversations at best and risqué or abusive language at worst. The advantages and disadvantages of IRC relative to MOOs for language learning are discussed below.

MOO, WOO, and GMUK

MOO, an acronym that actually contains another acronym, refers to a MUD, a *multiuser domain* or *dungeon*. MOOs are *multiuser domains* that are *object oriented*. MUDs began as dungeons-and-dragons-type games on the Internet, and some MOO terminology reflects those beginnings.

MOOs have evolved from their game origins to become host to some of cyberspace's most fascinating and engaging on-line communities. Like IRC channels, MOOs are social environments, many of them akin to local bars, pubs, cafés, or corner coffee shops where people gather to chat, exchange news, and meet new people. Each MOO has its own theme, ranging from wild role-playing games to serious academic topics. An example of the latter, *Café MOOlano* (http://moolano.berkeley.edu/) offers an environment in which distance-learning students at the University of California at Berkeley can interact with professors and classmates. Among the courses offered for credit at this writing are Freshman English, Chinese Law, and Malay/Indonesian.

A visit to a MOO shows clearly that it is not just another chat room. Everything in a MOO is known as an *object*, each of which can be programmed by the user to represent anything that exists in reality or in the imagination. Users, also called *players* or *characters*, can create rooms, objects, and programs that recreate in text anything imaginable—from books of poetry, to artificial intelligence robots, to MOOmail (asynchronous communication, like an internal e-mail system). A great deal of "MOO-space" development is done by people who have no programming skills at all. Table 22-1 outlines the various levels of users in the social and programming hierarchy of a typical educational MOO.

A WOO is essentially a Web-enhanced MOO. The underlying structure is a MOO, but it is accessed through the Web and uses the Web's graphical interface to make the experience more pleasant. A good example of this is *The Sprawl* (1998, http://sensemedia.net/sprawl/). Multimedia virtual worlds are also known in some circles as *graphical multiuser konversations* (GMUKs), a term used here for ease of reference. They all require more memory (data storage space), a faster central processing unit (CPU, the part of the computer that controls all the other parts), and a faster modem (hardware for connecting to the Internet through a telephone line) than are necessary for IRC and MOOs. To detail how each one works is beyond the scope of this chapter. Some GMUKs available at this writing include *The Palace* (http://www.thepalace.com/), *Active Worlds* (http://www.activeworlds.com/), *Worlds Chat* (1998, http://www.worlds.net/wc/), *PowWow* (http://www.tribal.com/), and *PuebloLindo* (http://pueblolindo.heinle.com/). A list of chat environments can be found on *Webcrawler: People and Chat* (1998, http://Webcrawler.com/Chat/chat.worlds.html).

Atmosphere and Role-Playing Games

As stated in chapter 1, an ideal atmosphere in which to learn a language provides an optimal level of stress or anxiety. If the learner is not challenged enough, boredom sets in and the learner does not reach the stress level necessary to force attention (see chapter 21). However, anxiety about a

Table 22-1. Hierarchy of Educational MOO Users

User	What the user can do (in addition to the privileges at the previous level)	How to attain this level
Guest	Talk, page, use MOOmail, move from one virtual room to another	Log onto the MOO using the words *connect guest* at the log-in screen
Permanent character	Have password access, name and describe self, set gender, add features	Request a permanent character by sending e-mail or MOOmail to the registrar (often the MOO owner)
Builder	Create and describe own room, exits, and other objects; write messages; does not need to know MOO programming language	Describe yourself, set your gender, become known on the MOO, have good ideas for objects that contribute to the theme of the MOO
Programmer	Write programs in the MOO programming language	Convince a wizard that a program you have in mind would contribute to the theme of a MOO
Administrator	Use commands that allow users to create new characters, see where users are logged on from, disconnect unruly guests from the MOO, help the wizards with social and pedagogical issues	Usually, be a teacher or a very helpful programmer who connects often and who is vitally interested in the well-being of the MOO
Wizard	Use the full set of MOO commands (dozens of them) to shape the MOO according to its theme (Wizards are essentially omnipotent.)	Demonstrate to the archwizard outstanding ability in programming or the management of administrative duties
Archwizard	Create and compile the MOO, run the MOO from outside as well as within, be ultimately responsible for the MOO	Start your own MOO (Rarely, this role is shared by more than one person, as on *MundoHispano*, Turbee, 1997b.)

number of issues—performance or cultural differences, for example—can raise affective filters so high as to preclude any useful production or even reception of the target language. Giving learners a measure of control means allowing them to participate in the design of an atmosphere in which they are most likely to learn.

Because many of the virtual worlds mentioned above have their origins in role-playing games that are played either on or off the Internet, the reasons for their popularity may be relevant to the language learning environment. The three most outstanding features of role-playing games are the high degree of creativity required of players, interaction with other players, and the high stress and eustress levels achieved during the game.

> Role-playing games are really just an advanced form of regular board games. In fact, they are so advanced that they no longer use a board. Some of the elements are still the same . . . . But the main thing you need to play a role-playing game is IMAGINATION. (Siembieda, 1995, p. 31)

Players in virtual worlds create "an imaginary individual that is [their] playing piece in this game. Just like an actor assuming a role for a movie, [they] play a fictitious character in the game" (Siembieda, 1995, p. 31). In the most basic of text-based worlds, the only avenue for creativity may be the character's name, such as *Dreamy* or *MetalHead*, and the utterances and described actions of the character. In MOOs and GMUKs, text and (in GMUKs) graphics are used to describe or show what a character looks like, what it is feeling, how it reacts when spoken to, and what objects it has created. *Rooms* in the environment, contexts in which the conversation and actions of the characters take place, are similarly described, as in the Main Street Café description at the beginning of this chapter. In almost all educational virtual environments, individual players have nearly complete control over these descriptions.

Like on-line role-playing games, on-line virtual environments are meeting places for any number of players who log on from anywhere in the world. In the role-playing games, a player is likely to be pitted against other players in fierce competition for goods (objects) or status in a hierarchy. In the social environments—including most educational MOOs and GMUKs—the interaction is much more similar to the discourse and behavior of people gathered anywhere for the purpose of socializing. Conversation, the formation of personal and professional relationships, and cooperative work or play are the goals. The average MOO has enough interesting places to entertain the solitary wanderer, but most users agree that there is nothing as stimulating as the unpredictability of human interaction.

In just about any game, competition with other players is the driving motivation for playing. In a role-playing game, the opportunity to overcome and win is ever enticing, and the constant threat of loss (in some cases, virtual death) sharpens the wits and makes intense attention to the game a necessity. The role-playing nature of MOO use can lead to experiences that cause the heart to pound and the real world to disappear (e.g., a MOO user may wonder, "Will Rosa like the box of chocolates I just made for her?"). Stress experienced this way is not only eustress (discussed in chapter 21) but can become an optimal experience. As Csikszentmihalyi (1991) notes,

> We have seen how people describe the common characteristics of optimal experience: a sense that one's skills are adequate to cope with the challenges at hand, in a goal-directed, rule-bound action system that provides clear clues as to how well one is performing. Concentration is so intense that there is no attention left over to think about anything irrelevant, or to worry about problems. Self-consciousness disappears, and the sense of time becomes distorted. An activity that produces such experiences is so gratifying that people are willing to do it for its own sake, with little concern for what they will get out of it, even when it is difficult, or dangerous. (p. 71)

Interestingly, this description fits a rather typical MOO experience if the player has learned the commands and knows how to get around fairly well. With good training in the technology and sound pedagogical underpinnings provided in class, language learners report similar experiences, as in this e-mail message from a student:

> I'm really enjoying the Moo. I haven't figured out all the commands, but I keep playing with it. When I first started I was hooked. I almost forgot to go to class and another time I was late to a class because I was on Moo. Whenever I get into a good conversation I like to stay and chat. Its great to see how fluent Spanish speakers speak or in this case write. I had to cut down my time on it just because its so addictive!!! I could easily spend an hour on it a day, but I have four other classes to think about! Sorry I was late! (V. Hughart, personal communication, September 30, 1995)

MOOs and the Learner-Centered Classroom

All the virtual environments described above have been or can be used for language learning. They all share the three elements that make role-playing games so much fun: a need for players to be creative, interaction with other players, and an intensity of play that raises stress levels in a pleasurable way. The rest of this chapter focuses on only one of the environments, MOOs, for several reasons:

1. IRC as a language learning environment is not contextually rich enough. MOO users experience a sense of place, a setting in which communication takes place:

   > There are a couple of problems with IRC. First, the content is often superficial garbage. More important, the chat has no context other than the conversation itself. Looking at schema theory, you can

understand how helpful it is to anchor a conversation in a larger context. (Backer, 1997)

2. A MOO, unlike IRC, is a relatively permanent environment. It can be programmed, compiled, and saved while still running, so virtual spaces and objects that users create in a MOO remain constant. Both the feeling of object ownership and the permanence of the environment motivate users to return for continued conversation and community building.

3. The use of GMUKs expressly for language learning is still in its infancy. As of this writing, the only one being developed for language learners is *PuebloLindo* (http://pueblolindo.heinle.com/), an experimental Spanish language environment that includes the use of rolling text, sound files, and photographs for navigation and object depiction. Other sites, such as Diversity University's (http://www.du.org/), offer Virtual Reality Modeling Language (VRML) versions as an enhancement (e.g., Diversity University's *Student Union Lounge*, n.d., http://moo.du.org:8000/99anon /anonview; see Figure 22-1). This GMUK environment and others

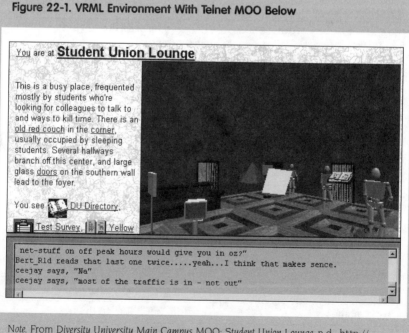

Figure 22-1. VRML Environment With Telnet MOO Below

Note. From *Diversity University Main Campus MOO: Student Union Lounge*, n.d., http:// moo.du.org:8000/99anon/anonview. Copyright © by DU Educational Technology Services. Reprinted with permission.

should be explored as potential language learning environments, as they all provide, to varying degrees, something for every learning style. To what extent the graphics and sound capabilities enhance rather than interfere with language learning is still quite unknown. All GMUKs require technology (i.e., hardware, software, bandwidth) that is not yet readily available in many areas of the world, so some native speakers of, say, Spanish or learners of EFL might find it impossible to connect to or fully utilize them.

Language learners connecting to a MOO seek primarily to converse with others in the target language. They know who is in the room by looking at the room (using the *look* command; see Table 22-2) and seeing who is listed as being "here." They can look at anyone in the room by typing *look* followed by the person's name. They can also "walk around" the MOO by typing the name of the exits they see in any room. Look, for example, at the Main Street Café and one of the characters in it through the eyes of a language learner,

Table 22-2. MOO Commands

Type this command:	To make this happen:
`telnet moo.syr.edu 8888`	Connect to *MundoHispano* (Turbee, 1997b; Telnet required)
`telnet schmooze.hunter .cuny.edu 8888`	Connect to *schMOOze* University (Falsetti, n.d.; Telnet required)
`connect [name] [password]`	Get into the MOO
`@who`	See who is connected to the MOO
`page [person] [message]`	Talk with someone else in the MOO
`" [message]`	Talk with someone else in the same room
`: [subjectless sentence]` (e.g., `:smiles`)	Show actions or emotions (e.g., "Colegia smiles")
`@join [person]`	Join someone elsewhere on the MOO
`@who [person]`	Look for a specific person
`look [person]`	Look at someone in the same room
`look here`	Look at the room you are in, find exits
`[exit name]`	Get from one room to the next
`news`	Learn what's going on in the MOO
`@quit`	Leave the MOO

called Jeanne. The short phrases are commands that cause certain texts to appear on the screen.

```
look café

THE MAIN STREET CAFE

This café has a few booths inside and,
spilling out over one corner of the plaza,
a number of small white metal chairs
pulled up to round, white tables. There
are people sitting at many of the tables,
sipping espresso from tiny white cups or
frothy cappuccino from large cups. Most
people are nibbling on pastries or scones.
The smell of the coffee and sweet treats
combines with a sensation of relaxing
warmth on your face from the bright
sunshine. You look forward to settling in
here for awhile and wonder if a friend
will come by. You see Scott, Ruth,
Armando, and Dave here.

Obvious exits:

west to the Plaza

south to Come Back Inn

look Dave

A tall, slender guy with short dark hair
and a friendly smile, he is wearing black
pants and a dark purple shirt. He looks
like he's just been laughing at a joke. He
is awake and alert.

Carrying:

guitar            amplifier

muscle mag        water-filled watch
```

The choices here are all in the hands of the player (in this case, Jeanne). She can interact with the other players in a number of ways: by looking at them, talking with them, asking Dave for an explanation of what a muscle mag is, or asking him to give her the water-filled watch. When she types

> "Dave, could I look at your watch?

she sees

> You say, "Dave, could I look at your watch?"

But everyone else in the room sees

> Jeanne says, "Dave, could I look at your watch?"

If Dave wants to give her the watch, he types

> give watch to Jeanne

Now Jeanne has the watch. She can look at it:

> look watch
> This is a silver watch of the old-fashioned style that hangs from a large silver clip. Oddly enough, it appears to be filled with water, for small watch parts float just under the surface of the glass face.

Jeanne and others can tell that she is holding the watch simply by "looking" at her (that is, by typing *look Jeanne*). The watch will appear in the list of objects she is carrying, and if the other players look at Dave, they'll see that he no longer has it in his list. Objects can be created so that they hold other objects, and programs can be written that cause lines of text to appear on the screen at certain intervals:

> Sparky wags his tail at you.
>
> . . .
>
> Sparky runs over to you and barks again.
>
> . . .
>
> Sparky sits up and begs for a treat.

The ability to interact and create contributes to the atmosphere of play in a MOO, and the choices outlined above are only the beginning of the possibilities, for just about anything imaginable can be written or programmed into a MOO. Given that no knowledge of programming is necessary, even novice-level learners of the target language can use simple commands to build themselves rooms, create objects, and have hours of fun with other players.

Most important, the interaction takes place primarily when the teacher is not even connected. Learners can choose to converse in a café, on a beach, in a toy store, or in a jungle. One of the last places they choose to talk in, interestingly, is a classroom. Educators diligently create libraries, lecture halls, and administrative offices, but learners generally go where the fun is, such as the Scrabble Room at *schMOOze University* (Falsetti, n.d., http://schmooze.hunter.cuny.edu:8888/) or the Bar de Mejillones at *MundoHispano* (Turbee, 1997b, http://web.syr.edu/~lmturbee/mundo.html).

Getting Started With Language Learning MOOs

In a learner-centered environment, the teacher's expectations are reasonable, and goals are attainable. However, if the environment is new to the teacher as well as the students, no one can possibly know what to expect, as Higgins (1988) relates:

> When we try to use computers in education, we could be said to be transferring acts of teaching and learning to a new medium. Like the child or the untrained layman, our first attempts will reflect our preconceptions or common-sense ideas about learning . . . . When a predicted learning event does not take place, we are forced to conclude either that the machine is unsuitable, or that our model of how to use it was based on a misconception. (pp. 1–2)

Most teachers who decide to investigate MOOs and use them in their classes focus first on the machine. They want to know

- What kind of hardware and software do I need?
- How do I get connected?
- How do I get an account on a MOO?
- What are the MOO commands?
- How do I talk to people on a MOO?

All these questions have readily available answers. Sadly, many teachers become only partially acquainted with the technological issues before bringing classes onto a MOO, thus dooming the foray into cyberspace. Perhaps more damaging, however, is a lack of understanding of the pedagogical model on which the use of MOOs is based. For this reason, I briefly outline the technological issues and point you to more detailed resources before turning to the model for language learning that works best in a MOO.

The Basics of MOOing

The Teacher

Plan on spending 20–40 hours in a MOO before introducing it to your students. Even though beginning MOO use can be quite simple, the possibilities for both technical and social complexity are nearly limitless. Become aware of how virtual communities work, what their joys and pitfalls are, and what you can expect your students to master in the time available. Arm yourself with MOO stories to tell before your students first log on, and make sure a good in-MOO support system is available for you and the learners. (For more information, see Batson & Williamson, 1998.)

The Computer

You can use a computer with an Intel 286 processor and a slow modem for MOOing, but unless you have access to a Unix account on which you can run the TinyFugue client software (Keys, 1996), it is best to use a faster computer and a graphical interface. The ability to use the Telnet protocol is essential unless you are using client software that connects you directly. More information on Telnet is available from *Big Dummy's Guide to the Internet: Telnet* (Gaffin, 1993, http://www.hcc.hawaii.edu/bdgtti/bdgtti-1.0210.html).

Client Software

Client programs make it easier to read incoming text, edit output before it is entered into the environment, and log (save to a file) and print MOO sessions. More information on client software can be found at the MOOs (see Appendix B).

MOOs

There are currently three sizable MOOs that were created with the language learner in mind:

- *sch*MOO*ze University* (Falsetti, n.d., http://schmooze.hunter.cuny.edu:8888/)

- *Mundo*Hispano (Turbee, 1997b, http://web.syr.edu/~lmturbee/mundo.html)

- MOO*francais* (Kain, 1997, http://moo.syr.edu/~fmoo/fmoo/)

The one GMUK for Spanish learners is *PuebloLindo* (http://pueblolindo.heinle.com/). Other MOOs exist in a variety of languages. A list of MOOs, including non-English ones, can be found at *Rachel's Super MOO List*:

Educational MOOs (Lindsey, n.d., http://moolist.yeehaw.com/edu.html); also see Appendix B.

Expert Help

Virtual communities of your MOO-using colleagues are there to help. See the following sources to learn how to connect with them:

- NETEACH-L (Moody, n.d., http://www.ilc.cuhk.edu.hk/english /neteach/main.htm; see Appendix B)

- NETEACH-L: MOO *Sessions* (Younger, n.d., http:// spot.colorado.edu/~youngerg/netmoo.html)

- *Epiphany Field Guide*: MOO *Resources and Professional* MOO *Meetings* (Keenan et al., 1996, http://mason.gmu.edu/~epiphany/docs /dointhemoo.html#resources)

- WWW *Virtual Library* (Schneider, 1995, http://tecfa.unige.ch /edu-comp/WWW- VL/eduVR-page.html)

- *Virtual Reality in Education: Education and Moo, Mud, Mush* (angus1@cris.com, 1998, http://angus.interspeed.net/eduvr/)

More information on the basics of getting connected and starting to use educational MOOs can be found in *Educational MOO: Text-Based Virtual Reality for Learning in Community* (Turbee, 1997a) and in the chapters on MOOs in Warschauer's (1995b) *Virtual Connections* (Falsetti & Schweitzer, 1995; Gölz, 1995; Sanchez, 1995; Turbee, 1995a, 1995b; Turner, 1995). Several teachers who have used MOOs with their students have written simple directions and have posted them on the Web (see Frizler, 1997, http://thecity.sfsu.edu /~funweb/schmooze.htm). As always, Web sites such as those cited above can become obsolete or cease to exist, so the best way to find current information is to do a key-word search of the Web using any of the common search engines (see chapter 14 and Appendix C).

The Learners

Plan on at least three in-class sessions during which you teach your students to use the MOO. Ideally, assign no more than two students to a computer. At novice levels, it is a good idea for one student to use the keyboard while the other reads and helps with commands; both students contribute to creating the conversation. Students who have never been involved in a virtual community, such as a bulletin board, a newsgroup, an e-mail discussion list, or IRC, would benefit from the use of an in-class e-mail discussion forum before MOOs are introduced. (Check with your computing center to see if you can set one up; a small list is easy to use.)

Most important, remember that you, too, are a learner: You will learn about the technology of MOOs and about the target language. Some of your own students may already be avid users of virtual communities, and even native-speaking teachers can learn more about their own language from native speakers who connect from other countries.

The Pedagogical Model

By now, many teachers have shifted their teaching style from that of the giver of knowledge to that of the facilitator. Understanding that knowledge is socially constructed, they have rejected the model of education in which knowledge is treated as a commodity that can be poured from the full vessel of the teacher or books into the empty vessel of the student's mind. What is needed, however, is a greater understanding of the changes that take place in the teacher's role when the students take more responsibility for their own learning. As access to the Internet and its flood of information increases, teachers must become more like librarians, guiding students to information sources, opportunities to create knowledge, and the interactive experiences that can be found on the Internet.

MOOs are truly learning environments of the Information (or digital communication) Age. Although anyone who has embraced the communicative approach can easily recognize the objectives it serves, a MOO's demand for learners to make the decisions driving the learning process may confuse students who are more accustomed to passive reception than to active involvement. Teachers using MOOs for language learning therefore need to be clear about why they are teaching and why their students are learning a language.

If the objective is to produce grades, then MOO use may seem an odd choice, as it does not lend itself to traditional assessment—hours of live communication by each student could never be graded as tests are. However, if the objective is to be able to receive, process, and produce in the second language at relatively normal speed, then, aside from a homestay in a country where the target language is spoken, there is nothing like a MOO. No amount of study of grammar, reading of texts, repetition of taped phrases, or interaction via e-mail will approach the MOO's ability to give students an experience so similar to face-to-face conversations with native speakers. Students would do well to continue the activities already common to language classes, but, ideally, half the time allotted to language study should be dedicated to the use of those skills.

What can your students do in a language learning MOO? The best answer comes from teachers who have used MOOs, who know the course objectives, and who have done some creative thinking. The many teachers who connect regularly to MundoHispano (Turbee, 1997b) and schMOOze University (Falsetti, n.d.) can help the new user devise tasks for students to carry out in the MOO. Below I describe just a few examples of the many tasks that such teachers have used and might suggest for your students:

- Find someone to talk to and ask three questions.
- Interview a native speaker at some length.
- Gather information from other users or from items in the MOO, and write a report.
- Log and print out a conversation, highlighting new vocabulary or idiomatic expressions.
- Build rooms in response to an in-class reading.
- Hold a party in the MOO; invite on-line friends.
- Start a MOOmail correspondence with someone you meet in the MOO.
- Design your own tasks, as individuals or in groups.
- Keep a journal of MOO activities.
- Write a simple program that helps others learn the language.

A Look Into the Future

At the current rate of change, it is nearly fruitless to attempt any serious predictions about the world of technology. Multimedia environments are already being developed. With increased bandwidth and more powerful computers, top-quality sound via the Internet will soon be a reality. Costs will continue to fall; much of the equipment now considered expensive will become inexpensive and as ubiquitous as the telephone.

Technology, however, is only part of the picture. The more difficult question is, Will educational institutions keep up with the rate of change? As lifelong learning, just-in-time learning, and distance education become the norm, will methodology keep up? Teachers who began their careers before the computer entered the world of education will either find immense opportunity or baffling changes just around the corner. Text-based MOOs are simple by current standards, yet pioneering educators are just beginning to fully understand its educational uses. Teachers who wish to understand the oft-mentioned paradigm shift taking place would do well to experience and come to understand the attractions and pitfalls of the MOO, a deceptively simple program that brings teachers, learners, and native speakers together in intense interaction.

Chapter 23

CALL Issues: Introducing Students to Computers

Sheryl Beller-Kenner

After months of planning, you are the first teacher in your school to take your language students into the new multimedia lab. Each student finds a seat in front of a blank screen, ready to work on the new listening comprehension software you've selected for the class. After briefly explaining the goal of the activity, you instruct the students, saying, "The software is very easy to use; just boot up the machine, use the mouse to double-click on the icon of the CD-ROM, and follow the directions from there." The students look around, bewildered, until one brave student finally raises her hand and asks, "Where's a mouse? What's an icon?" Even though you may have worked very hard to select an activity and software that would be appropriate for the language level of your students, it immediately becomes obvious that you have misjudged their ability to use the technology. Can this language lesson be saved? What else do you need to know so that you can avoid problems of this type?

Although the numbers vary from country to country, statistics show that computers have infiltrated classrooms and homes. More than two thirds of all U.S. students in Grades 1–12 used a computer in 1993, with 59% having used them in a school, a number that almost doubled between 1983 and 1993 (National Center for Educational Statistics, 1995). Because so many elementary and secondary schoolchildren get some training in computers and use them for their schoolwork, you may think that all your students will enjoy using technology. However, not everyone accepts the idea that technology actually improves the quality of life or learning; for example, students who are jaded by arcade-quality video games may not want to use the same (or lower level) technology for reading text. And, in fact, a significant number of administrators, teachers, and students still resist using computers and believe that computers can complicate classroom life. Teachers ready to try CALL should be aware that, according to Roger's

Rules of Computing Misery, at each point in the training sequence at which something can go wrong, it probably will—for at least one person.

When training language learners to use computers, I have found that about 25% of the students become lost, for some reason or other, after Step 1, which is to start up the machine. As the lesson progresses, another 25% become lost because they haven't heard, they haven't understood the language, they have done something wrong, the hardware or software has not been set up properly (or was changed), equipment has been moved around or removed, equipment is defective, or they have experienced any of a number of other unforeseeable problems. Even students who are computer literate may not be familiar with the procedures necessary to run a particular type of computer or software, and they tend to race ahead, ultimately to a dead end that you will have to help them out of. In a lab like mine, packed with 32 students, this translates into 8 students at any given moment who need my immediate attention. The need seems to increase exponentially with each step.

The solution may seem to lie only in trying out the software first and giving proper instructions; however, an effective and engaging lesson takes more than that. This chapter first explores the institutional and curricular aspects that set the larger environment for CALL and that will directly affect your success in getting students ready for technology-based activities. I then focus on how to introduce your students to computers in a low-stress atmosphere and how to avoid situations that can change a 50-minute class from an exciting language learning opportunity into a discouraging waste of time.

The Institutional Aspect

Whether and how much you use computers will depend in part on your institution's point of view. Your administration or chairperson may pressure you to use the computers this semester, like it or not. In my program, most students are scheduled to meet in the CALL multimedia lab for 1 of 3 class hours every other week, so the assumption is that instructors are to use the computers. However, during lab time, some teachers conduct communicative activities using tape recorders or give paper-and-pencil exams; the message students get is that their teachers are convinced that the computers cannot help them improve their language skills. Because classroom space at most schools is usually at a premium, if you are scheduled to be in the computer lab but choose not to use the computers, perhaps you can exchange rooms with another teacher who would make better use of the machines. (Clear the exchange with the lab director and your department head first.)

In the opposite case, some school administrators still do not support the integration of computers into school life, and you may find that there isn't any money in the budget for computers or software. Don't let that stop you. In my determination to bring computers to my students, on many occasions I have transported my machine from my home or office and set it up in the classroom. My students have used freeware (see Appendix D) instead of the more powerful but expensive software that I use at home so that they can do the CALL activities easily and without having to spend any money for the additional materials.

If the majority of the faculty members in your department are computer users, they may put pressure on the administration (and the other faculty members) to budget some money for hardware and software and try to incorporate them into the curriculum. If the impetus to incorporate computers into the curriculum comes from you alone, you will need the support of others in your institution. Seek out those who are interested in using computers for teaching, even if they are in other departments. You might be able to share already available resources, thereby saving time and money and increasing the presence of computer-using faculty.

If your school competes for students, the administration may yield to pressure from students (and their parents) or future employers to provide computers or CALL courses in which students can update their language skills as they learn about the technology. Be sure to make your voice heard so that you, too, can influence the choice of equipment and materials. How much support—in terms of equipment, training, and other resources—you get for having your students use computers depends on where the pressure is coming from.

The Curricular Aspect

The quantity and type of computer enhancement also depends on who sets the curriculum. In most elementary and secondary schools, a school board, ministry, or local committee works on the program guidelines and writes course goals and objectives. The curriculum may be so specific that it details the daily lessons the teacher is to follow. At the other end of the spectrum, you may have complete control of the content and methods of delivery in your course.

Whether you decide on the curriculum or not, you can be very creative in finding opportunities and activities for computer enhancement. My program receives course guidelines from the Quebec Ministry of Education, but I was able to quadruple the 7 hours per semester allotted by the college to CALL activities by offering one of my weekly office hours in a small computer lab instead of in my office and by assigning students to go to the free-access lab to get publications in English from the Internet.

The key factor in the above example was that I was self-motivated and willingly increased my students' time with the computers. However, teachers often resent the fact that many programs mandate a set amount of time per semester for the use of computers. This requirement usually means that students and teachers may be evaluated on how well they use the technology. You can adapt to this situation more easily if you understand how technology can enrich the teaching and learning experience and if you use technology only in appropriate instances. You cannot force children to eat their vegetables, and, likewise, you will not have much success with a lesson if you force students to use computers just because they will need to use them in the future. If the students are not successful, neither are you. However, both you and your students can change a poor attitude that will hinder learning into a positive attitude that will enhance it. A curriculum that mandates the amount of time computers are to be used in your classroom will influence your freedom and the number of hours your students can use the computers for their work, but it will not prevent you from using the best application or software for a particular job. Listed in the box are some ways to cope with institutional and curricular limitations on computer use.

Training Variables: Finding Comfort Zones

You might assume that computer use has a positive effect on students' learning, and although some studies show this to be the case, students who are uncomfortable using computers can have a difficult time learning.

Quite a number of variables can make students uneasy about learning to use computers. As noted in the discussion of flow in chapter 21, students who have just become comfortable at a particular language level may

---

Coping With Institutional and Curricular Limitations

- Exchange rooms for a day or a period with a non-CALL teacher.
- Bring a computer from home or the office.
- Place one lab computer on a rolling stand.
- Use freeware.
- Share resources with other departments.
- Find a support group of other computer-using teachers.
- Hold office hours in the lab.
- Use CALL activities only when they provide a clear instructional advantage.

become uncomfortable when forced to use a computer, and this discomfort may negatively affect their perception of their communication skills or cause them to become passive rather than active learners. This is especially true of adult learners, who may be quite accomplished in other areas of their lives and as a result are discomfited by being put into the role of beginner when they sit down at a computer screen.

Student Technophobia

I try to avoid the possible negative effects of the CALL environment by putting students in groups and giving them roles in which they will be successful. For example, in a group of three, one student can be assigned the role of keyboarder, one the secretary for recording the steps and the results, and another the decision maker and tiebreaker. When the students are ready, they can switch roles.

Students' discomfort levels may also rise when they leave their safe language classroom to go into the lab, which may be shared by all the students in the school and where there may be nobody who is sensitive to their language needs. Avoid this problem by giving the students tasks on software you know they are familiar with (accompanied by clear directions you have presented in class), by sending them to the lab at times when someone who is sensitive to second language learners' needs (you, a student monitor, or a sympathetic lab director) is available, or by having them go to the learning center with a partner.

To raise students' comfort level, make sure that you open lines of communication between you and your students (see the box). At the beginning and end of some semesters, I have students fill out question-naires designed to elicit information about their computer expertise and attitudes. Sometimes I have the students evaluate their activities during the term in the form of checklists or 1-minute messages to me. Also, students can contact me through my World Wide Web page even if they can't send e-mail. I find that the most valuable approach is to have students write in a weekly guided journal. In it, I sometimes have them answer questions designed to elicit their feelings about a particular piece of software they have used or are about to use, and I have them write about their feelings on

---

Lines of Communication Between Teacher and Student

- Questionnaires about computer use
- One-minute evaluation messages
- Weekly interactive guided journal

technology in general. When the students know that their feelings are important, they are more apt to share with me the obstacles that I have put in the way of their learning, and I can better adapt my CALL assignments to their needs.

English Language Proficiency

You can't assume that everyone who speaks English well can use computers, just as you can't assume that a student who doesn't speak English well isn't more familiar with the computers in your lab than you are. Because beginning students lack sufficient English language skills to follow the directions for much software, even that written specifically for beginning users, you may need to prepare simplified directions that students can keep in their notebooks. Make sure that the students know how the software expects them to register answers (e.g., by pressing the space bar, the "Enter" key, or a letter key). Tell them how to erase (e.g., with the "Del" key, with the "Backspace" key, with the left arrow, or by highlighting) and exit from the software (e.g., by pressing the "Esc" key, typing *quit* or Q, or pressing a function key) at any time. None of these commands is as intuitive as some people say.

The Internet, about 80% of which is in English, is another place where students with limited English proficiency can have problems. Your students may lack sufficient English language skills to surf the Web. In an EFL setting, even with a browser in the students' native language, this language barrier creates complications. In the past, my students could choose to use a Web browser in their native French. Unfortunately, the browser actually prevented them from learning to use the Internet quickly because they had to translate the words on the menu from the English I was using to the French that they wanted to use. When I included both the French and the English words and pictures on an overhead transparency or handout, the extra text cluttered the page and gave the students twice as much text to read. In addition, in commercial software the labels for shortcut keys are translated into French so that the software can be sold in Quebec, but the keystrokes are still based on the English words. For example, the English version of a particular software application uses the easy-to-remember shortcut keystroke Ctrl + P as the print command. In the French version of the same software, one taps the same keystroke, even though the word for *print* in French is *imprimer*. Only by using many illustrations—either graphics or real-time demonstrations—can I keep the session completely in English and the students together (see Figure 23-1). The message is that teachers need to be consistent and clear. If there are three different ways to print an assignment, pick and teach only one.

Figure 23-1. Graphic Used to Illustrate the Print Function in Netscape Navigator® Gold (1997)

Assignment for Unit 1 Outstanding Athletes
Printing the Web Page Version of Your Paragraph
Directions: Using *Netscape Navigator,* print your file **ul.html**

- At the top of the *Netscape* window, **single-click** on the **Print** button.

Computer Experience

Another variable in students' training and comfort levels is the wide range of prior computer experience. Some of my students had never used a computer; others are studying computer science and have taught me a thing or two about designing good Web pages.

Personal and Social Factors

A number of personal and social factors affect a person's computer exposure, most notably age, socioeconomic status, and gender. These factors also affect students' attitudes about computer use and their receptiveness to activities that are technologically enhanced. Although you cannot change a student's age, finances, or gender, you can make sure that you provide all students computer access in an equitable fashion. For example, I have allowed low-income students who need to work during open-access lab hours to use my personal computer in my office, and I have been able to open the lab myself for before- and after-hours computing sessions. Move older students who may be hard of hearing or nearsighted closer to you and your audiovisual aids. Make sure that both males and females do a variety of tasks, such as keyboarding and decision making. Don't promote the old stereotypes; help all students be successful at CALL tasks.

Learning Styles

CALL activities offer the possibility of using a variety of teaching methods and therefore may accommodate students with various learning styles, another training variable. By providing your students with many kinds of materials and enough information that they can choose which ones to use and how best to use them, you encourage independent learning. You can move away from a curriculum that is teacher centered and teacher structured toward activities that are learner centered and learner structured. You can also guide students to select activity types—for learning as well as for evaluation—that they prefer according to their learning styles and for which they take full responsibility.

Teacher Technophobia

Teachers must be considered a training variable, because they can affect their students' attitudes toward computers. Just as you can see students passing notes or dozing off in the back of the room, students, too, perceive the signals you give. Any negative attitudes you have about computers will be passed along to the students.

Coley, Cradler, and Engel (1996) found that only 15% of U.S. teachers reported having at least 9 hours of training in educational technology. Teachers who attempt to use CALL activities must be very comfortable with networks, computers, and software. Things always go wrong in CALL labs, and in most cases you are the only one around who can fix it quickly or decide that a student has to move to another computer. If you are not sufficiently trained to be comfortable with computers, your students may become uncomfortable as well.

Among the factors that cause teachers to have a negative attitude toward CALL, Schofield (1995) has identified doubt about the value of computers in education, the view that computers disrupt normal classroom organization, a lack of initial and ongoing training, and a perception of computers as a threat to the teacher's authority. Classroom teachers have told me that other reasons include a perceived lack of high-quality language learning software, a sense that the technology is too complex for their students to use, resentment at being required by their supervisors to use computers, and their own computer anxiety.

General Training Guidelines

Remember that your primary goal is always to create an optimal language learning environment in which the language is used in authentic, interactive situations that provide much practice and feedback and in which learners take much of the responsibility for their learning. Other goals are secondary.

Guidelines for Training

- Make the computer center inviting.
- Vary the computer activities.
- Use humor.
- Make objectives meaningful.
- Teach technical elements on a need-to-know basis.
- Demonstrate all software.
- Choose an appropriate level of challenge, or let students choose the level.
- Don't let technology become a barrier to learning.
- Give students feedback.
- Provide additional resources for independent learners.
- Give students enough time to practice.

Keep in mind the general guidelines listed in the box above as you prepare your students to use computers for learning.

Prepare the Environment

Make the computer area a warm and comfortable place. A room filled with high-tech equipment can look very cold and uninviting. Combine high tech with human interaction: Let the students know that you are there, and interact with them; circulate constantly to ask students how or what they are doing; don't sit at the front of the room reading a manual. Stay around, stay involved, and know when to observe.

Pair students whenever possible, and encourage them to interact with each other. Most activities designed for one can be modified for two. For example, when each student has to type a document using a word processor, pair the students up and direct one to type and the other to proofread simultaneously. Inevitably, they have grammar or style questions for each other, and the task seems to take less time to complete. For listening comprehension and pronunciation practice, if computer stations are configured so that two students can hear the same passage and record their voices onto the software, two students can alternate giving responses after agreeing on the answer.

Some students take longer to warm up to the technology, and some never do, so make sure there are tables and chairs in the room for students who prefer to work with paper and pencil.

Vary the Activities

Most teachers view an electronic activity as a change of pace from regular classroom work. This may not be the case for students. Also, a new learning situation, whether language learning or tool learning, can be fatiguing, so keep activities that involve new material short, and recycle previously taught information to make sure students are comfortable using what you have already taught them. For example, in teaching students how to use text reconstruction software for the first time, use as the content a passage they have already seen, with vocabulary and structures that are familiar to them.

Use Humor

I have a collection of cartoons on overheads that make fun of the common anxieties people have when using computers; students get some relief in knowing that I'm aware of their feelings.

Make Objectives Meaningful

Although each student comes into the language learning class with different goals or purposes in mind, all students share the need to do well in your class. Making all students see how a particular lesson will improve their overall language proficiency is admittedly difficult, but you can increase motivation by showing the students how an activity meets a particular objective of the course and relates to what they are doing in class.

Teach Technical Elements Selectively

Teach computer skills and operation of equipment on a need-to-know basis. At one institution where I worked, the lab director insisted on teaching the students how to use all the equipment in the room—computer, CD-ROM player, tape recorder, videodisc player, videocassette recorder (VCR)—in a single session the very first time the students came into the lab. In about 20 minutes, using no visual aids or written directions, he explained orally how to use every piece of equipment. Most of the students lost interest after 10 minutes, and the week after not one student could remember how to start up the equipment.

The second semester, I made him change his procedures radically. During the first lab session, the technician explained the lab procedures for free access and distributed the current schedule. When he was finished, I walked the students through the start-up procedure for the computers, had them do a short tutorial on using the computers, and told them how to shut the computers down properly. The next time the students were in the lab, I reviewed the previous functions and then taught them how to launch a software application from the CD-ROM player. To this day, the lab director is still angry that I didn't teach the students how to use the videodisc player, but because my students never needed to use it, I couldn't see the purpose in their learning it.

Lab orientation sessions in which students are told how to use all the equipment before they can do anything with it are a waste of time. Focus only on those skills needed to effectively complete the language task at hand. Give students cheat sheets for operations they won't use often, and tape sheets of directions to the desks.

Demonstrate Software

For software that is new to the students, demonstrate it from beginning to end, as many students do not know what to expect from computer applications. Show the students what happens when they get an answer wrong as well as what happens when they get one correct. Let those who are ready begin, and demonstrate again for the small group of students who are still not comfortable.

Don't count on having all the students do the activity correctly the first time or even finish the activity in the allotted time period. Once I planned to do an activity in the second hour (of a 3-hour class) based on what the students had found on the Internet in the first hour. However, some students had so many problems—some with the browser, others with the search engine, and still others with printing—that I could not move on to the next hour's activity. Provisions have to be made for alternate lessons.

Choose an Appropriate Level of Challenge

Many software programs permit students to select the level of difficulty of an activity. I find that the students usually select the level that I would have chosen for them and that those who select lower levels than they can handle soon become so bored that they increase the level of difficulty themselves.

Because much software is not written specifically for ESL students, familiarize the students with the necessary (and only the necessary) vocabulary, review the language needed for the directions or exercises, and demonstrate the software before the students use it. Also be wary of using software designed for children with adults who have a low level of English proficiency; they do not necessarily appreciate pictures and sounds designed to appeal to children.

Another note of caution: In the late 1970s, many teachers learned to choose lesson content containing grammatical structures that were slightly easier than the students could handle; in this way students would feel a sense of success and be able to build up confidence in their second language abilities. Studies by Krashen (1982) and others have since shown that it is better to present content and language structures (but not directions for using the equipment!) at a level just a little more difficult than the students can easily understand. Challenge students by increasing the vocabulary load of a CALL reading exercise, the speed at which a text moves across the computer screen, or the weighting of points given for answering more difficult questions.

Don't Let Technology Become a Barrier

Don't let the hardware or software become a barrier to language learning. The more time students spend on getting the software to run, the less time they will spend on the language task. Avoid making technology a barrier by selecting user-friendly software and giving clearly written directions. If students must struggle in the language learning classroom, it should be with the language itself and not the tools.

Make the computer seem easier to use by avoiding the jargon of salespeople and techies. Demonstrating before requiring your students to use the equipment provides a model for them to follow, and they will be more at ease when they see that you are comfortable using the technology.

Teach the students good computer habits. Don't assume that students, even ones who are experienced with computers, know, for example, the correct start-up and shutdown procedures on the platform you are working with. Also teach students to press the "Return" key when nothing else is happening and the "Esc" key when things are going awry. Teach them to save their work every 10 minutes or so and before all memory-devouring operations, such as printing or opening another application.

Give Feedback

Make sure students get feedback, either intrinsic or extrinsic. More and more software applications have record-keeping options, and students and teachers vary in their opinions on the importance of keeping a score. From the teacher's perspective, whether to do so or not may depend on whether the CALL activity is optional or required. When the activity is optional, let the students know and decide for themselves whether to keep score. (Don't forget to show the students how to change the software options.) Whether I require students to keep score or not, at the beginning of the semester I usually give them a feedback form on which they can keep a record of what they have done and whether or not they thought it was helpful (see Figure 23-2).

Figure 23-2. Feedback Form for CALL Activity

Checklist for Unit 1: Outstanding Athletes Essay

Step	Date completed	Date submitted to teacher	Feedback to Teacher (Answer questions on the back of this page after doing each step.)
1. Write first draft.		(Do not submit.)	
2. Peer edit with partner.		(Do not submit.)	a. Were your partner's comments helpful? Why or why not?
3. Do first revision.		[date provided by teacher]	
4. Do second revision.		(Do not submit.)	b. Did any of your partner's comments help you get a better score? Explain.
		[date provided by teacher]	c. Were the directions for this assignment clear? Why or why not? d. What did you like the best about this assignment? Why? e. What did you like the least? Why? f. How would you have changed the assignment to make it more interesting?

Allow for Further Practice

Provide resources for further practice, either as review or as enrichment, so that students who choose to do further work can do so independently. If, for example, you assign work on multimedia courseware to practice the past tense, provide the names of other accessible software that students can use for further practice. Because in many programs the lab technician or monitor is not familiar with CALL software, make sure that the students can find and use the software they need to complete an assignment independently. Make sure you specify what the title of the lesson is, what type of exercise it is, how long it will take the students to complete a lesson, whether it is best done individually or in pairs, who can help them if they have a problem, and how they should do the exercise. Let the students know that you will be glad to review anything that puzzles them during the extra practice.

Allow Enough Time for Practice

Students need adequate and regular practice. Don't let poor performance with a particular tool negatively influence a student's grade. Don't try to measure the effectiveness of a tool until you have allowed ample time for students to become very comfortable with the software and hardware.

Suggest strategies for continued learning. Tell the students how much time they will need to set aside in order to do the practice exercises, what other skills they can use the software for, where and from whom they can get additional help if they need it, and how they can get access to the materials outside of class.

Presentation and Delivery Methods

You can provide a nonthreatening CALL atmosphere in which students can ask questions and get answers about computers, software, and computer issues. Let students know that there is no such thing as a dumb computer question, and if you decide that you cannot answer a student's question immediately, promptly make an appointment with the student to supply the information. Basically, you should use the same presentation methods for CALL activities as you would for activities in a non-computer-enhanced classroom.

Because an expanded treatise on teaching techniques is beyond the scope of this chapter, I discuss in detail only those approaches that pertain specifically to technology (see the box). Remember that the aids mentioned are meant to accompany or follow up, not to replace, a complete presentation by the teacher and that, although the ideal CALL training session is

Teaching Aids for CALL

Less useful	Useful	More useful
Books and manuals	Paper handouts Quick reference cards	Screen shots for illustrations (on overhead projector)
	Computer projection	Peer demonstrations
	Wall posters	Posters made by students
	Video tutorials	Classroom-produced videos
	On-line help via e-mail	Peer help via e-mail
	Pairs and teams	Identification of peer experts
	Alliances with other departments and community groups	Speakers who are trained in sensitivity to ESL students

hands-on, you may have to explain all or part of an application without access to the computer. In those cases try to make the presentation as realistic as possible by using audiovisual aids.

Help for your students can come in many different forms, and I recommend that you provide students with a wide choice of formats.

Paper Handouts

Provide simple directions, outlining basic procedures in the first section and advanced procedures at the end. Most students do not read directions completely; neither do I. Because I prefer the quick reference cards provided with many applications, I try to make one available for each piece of software the students use during the semester.

Number steps only if they are sequential. Take screen shots (pictures of the screen) after each step in a procedure, and use them to illustrate your paper directions (see Figure 23-1). If you can't attach a projection panel to a computer, you can make overhead projection transparencies of the screen shots to simulate what students will see.

Computer or Projector

If the group is very small, even one computer is enough for an effective demonstration. A large computer monitor or a TV monitor link permits you to work with a larger number of students at once, but students will find it difficult to see the screen, especially if it contains text, from any farther away than usual television-watching distance. By using an electronic overhead projector (OHP), you can significantly increase the projection area. Like television monitors, electronic OHPs come in black and white or color, but color monitors are far more expensive. As with regular OHPs, the lights must be dim; this hardware is very sensitive to extraneous light. OHPs are thus not the presentation method of choice for teachers who don't like to have their students sitting in the dark.

The pedagogical advantage of using a projection panel is that you are demonstrating in real time, and the students can see the results of any keystroke or response exactly as they will see it on the computer. You can also call students up to do parts of the demo and get a feel for the software.

Posters

Display wall posters of basic procedures, such as starting up the computer, shutting it down, and printing. If you share a lab with teachers from other departments, they, too, may find the posters helpful. If your lab director is against the posting of any signs, hang them just before class and take them down at the end of the period, or tape directions on the computer tables, on the sides of the computers, and next to the printer. Your computer-literate students can help you make posters.

Books and Manuals

Most students don't read manuals—and they shouldn't have to! I have trouble understanding most manuals myself. Second language students should not have to wade through an 862-page word-processing manual to complete any part of their assignment for your class. In other words, don't use manuals as teaching aids.

Electronic Tutorials

Many applications have interactive, hands-on tutorials that lead a student through all parts of the software. For each piece of software, I do the tutorial before trying the software so that I use it armed only with the information presented in the tutorial. When vocabulary items are difficult and descriptions of important features are missing, I prepare a vocabulary list (on paper, in a text file, or in a help file) and a second part to the tutorial with directions that are specific to the equipment in my lab, emergency escape procedures, and so on.

If you are comfortable with word processing, you can type your directions and save them as text so that students can open them with any word processor on any platform. A self-running presentation created with Microsoft® PowerPoint® 97 (1996) or a help file that can be called on at any point will take more work on your part. If you want your work to be truly interactive, use more elaborate authoring software or Hypertext Markup Language (HTML, the formatting language used to create documents for the Web). If you use HTML, students can even take the demos home and use them with their Internet browsers.

Classroom Video

Videos can be a supplement to or the main vehicle for student training. Some software comes with a video tutorial. For other software, you may be able to borrow a training video from a local business, a public library, or a university collection. You might also consider producing a classroom video with your students to be used by students at a lower level of proficiency. Students who are working on reading and writing skills can write the dialogue, consulting with you and the more computer-literate students to work out procedures and explanations. Students focusing on listening and speaking skills can narrate, and students who need computer practice can be the models. More proficient students can work on production, and lower level students can pilot the material and give feedback.

On-Line Help

In addition to the other aids suggested above, students can e-mail you about problems, but the number of questions (especially oft-repeated ones) can get overwhelming unless you set up an electronic discussion list or forum (see your computer administrator on how to do so). Students would then submit technical questions to be answered by you and posted for all to see. Even though some students may feel stupid posting questions, this system is easier on you than having to wade through individual e-mail messages.

If you wish, recruit students with some expertise in technology to help you answer the questions. Over time, you can collect the most common questions and responses and distribute them to students on a home page as *frequently asked questions* (FAQs) archives and direct students to other sites containing directions and demos. (See, e.g., those suggested in chapter 22; see chapter 2 on the pitfalls of electronic discussion lists.)

Peer Presentations

Students make good teachers; use their talents and energy. When students teach their peers, you gain an assistant, the students confirm their mastery of what has been taught, computer-literate students develop even more advanced skills, opportunities for second language use increase, and students' self-esteem rises. Students who are too embarrassed to ask the teacher for help may more readily turn to other students; these students can then help others in the class. Use your powers of observation, or have students fill out a questionnaire at the beginning of the semester to see which ones are computer savvy.

Pairs and Teams

Students may also teach each other in teams organized across computer skill levels, differing native languages, or generations. I'll never forget the look of pride on a student's face when, weeks after the semester began, he spoke up for the first time in class to explain to his partner, a more advanced speaker, a word-processing function that she was not able to grasp. He was empowered by the role of knower of English for the first time, feeling confident that he understood what was going on in the class and could make a useful contribution. The students soon conferred the title *computer guru* on him, and his self-esteem and class participation soared. Newell (1996) describes another instance, a cross-age program in which fourth graders tutored second graders in computer literacy skills.

You could also appoint roving class monitors who make sure that other students are following the software or ask computer-savvy students to make a presentation either for credit or extra credit. I really enjoy learning from some of my more computer-experienced students, as do the other students. All student presenters work with me outside of class, and they benefit from the increased contact.

Alliances With Schools and Other Organizations

Bringing community groups into the training process gets other people involved in training and frees up some of your time for other language activities. You might contact a local computer users' group and invite some computer techies to do a training session. The presentation would also expose your students to accents and intonations other than yours. You will probably need to go over the content and language with untrained speakers in order to sensitize them to your students' language needs.

Training Content for the CALL Class

Computer Skills

It is easy to deflate students' egos in class by assuming that all students know nothing about computers. After ascertaining students' true abilities, use those students who are already computer literate in a way that will keep them participating in your lessons: as class experts. Because computer literacy includes the ability to search for and evaluate information, help students find and judge the appropriateness of particular software for their own needs. To minimize the learning curve, have students use macros or quick-keys to simplify lengthy procedures. Keep help close at hand in the variety of forms described above.

Computer skills lessons can later be used as the focus of grammar, reading, or (with videos) listening lessons. Having learners make posters or other training aids for these skills, as described in the previous section, is another way to ensure good language practice.

Computer Safety

Decrease the anxiety of students who are afraid of breaking the computer. Demonstrate that no key combination they can hit will blow up the machine. Show and then post correct procedures for handling hardware and software, and show students how to start up and shut down the computer. Show them the quick escape keys for each application you introduce (as well as the system commands for *forced quit* and *stop printing*) so that they are confident that they can bail out at any time.

Parts of the Computer

Teach students the parts of the computer that they can touch or break. Then show them that a wrong keystroke will not break the machine. You can use the names of computer parts as a vocabulary lesson or word game, but unless the computer is the content of the unit, don't make the students memorize the terms. Instead, make wall posters so students can refer to specific parts in case of problems or computer malfunctions.

Mouse and Keyboard

Don't assume that students know how to use the mouse or other important peripherals. Generally, I create an introductory task that covers all the computer skills learners need to successfully run the machine and put one copy of the task at each station before the students go to the lab on the first day. I walk around taking the names of students who are breezing through the task, and when they finish, I send them to sit with students who are having a harder time with the equipment. The slower students are more apt to ask other students questions they would be too shy to ask me, and the faster students are acknowledged for their high level of expertise. This activity, which is a quick assessment of the students' computer skills, also permits all the students to get their hands on the computer from the first class, gives them opportunities to interact, and permits me to see who knows what.

Saving to Save Students

To avoid disappointment, anger, and unfinished assignments, regularly remind students to save their work (e.g., give verbal reminders, flick the lights, sound a beep from the server), or have them use an autosave program. Teach the students to save their work as soon as they stop typing or before they go on to a new activity.

One of my students came to me in tears, insisting that she had saved her essay onto her diskette but that it had disappeared. She was angry at me and the machine and ready to get a zero for the assignment rather than have to do the whole thing again. When I recreated the steps she said she had taken, I realized that she—and all the other students in the class—were saving their work in the word-processing software's program folder on the network because I had neglected to show them how to change the *save* destination to their own diskettes. I have since modified my teaching to show learners how to save their work to the appropriate folder or directory. This problem notoriously occurs with word processors and CALL activities that result in a score. Let students know if you want them to save the score on the hard drive on which the software is located, in a teacher's file, or onto their own diskette, especially if you use the results for grading.

Tasks for CALL Skills

In training students to use CALL software, student-driven, as opposed to teacher-driven, tasks are more motivating for learners even though such tasks are more difficult to organize. (See chapters 8, 9, and 10 for a full discussion of tasks.) By creating appropriate student-driven tasks, you can integrate useful content and language learning activities with increasingly sophisticated computer skills.

In my English for the Social Sciences class, at least 25% of a student's work is supposed to be in the major field, but students in any one class are pursuing degrees in fields as diverse as psychology, dietary science, nursing, library science, and police science, making it particularly difficult to have the class work together on tasks with a common goal. As a result, when I present the Web as a research tool, I first have the students find an article in their major field. I then give them a focused task, for instance, to locate a few past tense sentences in one paragraph of the article. The whole class then can work on past tense question formation together. Even though I decide on the tasks, the students choose the content, which increases their motivation and participation.

Typing

In most cases, students do not really have to know how to type in order to complete an activity. Much CALL software requires the students only to highlight a correct answer, drag a word into a box, or click the mouse on the intended response. Some CALL software requires learners to type their names, classes, and so on, but these tasks do not require much in the way of typing skills. Even students who need to browse the Web do not have to know how to type quickly, not even to use the search engines that help them find information. For those students who insist on improving their typing for other reasons, many labs keep typing software on hand for students to use on their own time.

Word Processing

The simpler the word processor or text editor, the less chance there is for students to get distracted from the task. A fairly inexpensive word processor is therefore good enough for most purposes. Provide templates that will help students prepare a nice-looking document without having to spend class time learning about formatting.

For example, if you want students to type a short paragraph, you can make a template, entitled Paragraph 1, that looks something like the one in Figure 23-3. In that template, the heading is right justified and single-spaced, the title is centered and in boldface, and the body of the paragraph is left justified and double-spaced, all in 12-point Helvetica type. What is invisible is that the top, bottom, and side margins are set; a header will print out the time, date, and page; and the correct printer has been selected. Since I started using templates, students have prepared their work in the exact format I want, and I have saved the time I might have spent teaching students about formatting or printer drivers. They only have to know how to delete, type, and print.

Avoid potential problems by giving each student or group leader a prepared disk containing templates for all activities. Include handouts,

---

Figure 23-3. Template With Simple Formatting for a Word-Processed Paper

```
                              [right justify, 12-point Helvetica]
                                              *Type your full name here.
                                          *Type your student number here.
                                             *College de Maisonneuve
                                             *English 101 Section 1
                                                *Dr. Beller-Kenner
                                                   *Today's date
                                          [end right justify]
```

[center, bold]Your Title Here[end center, bold]

[left justify, double space]*Replace everything that has a * in front of it.

Then replace this whole paragraph with yours. Indent your first sentence. Make

sure that the other sentences follow, from margin to margin, until the end. Check

your spelling, and have a classmate read it before you give it to me. [end left

justify, double space]

---

checklists for the leader, the correct disk name, and the prepared files with the correct names. Also include more detailed directions for each exercise on the disk or network space with more detailed instructions. Students can print these directions out (about 75% of the students do) or read them from the disk.

Multimedia Software

Multimedia software introduces additional hardware, which brings the learning curve up one step. For the students to use the headphones, VCR, microphones, or audiotape recorders in my lab, they first have to learn how to deal with a very complex mixer to which all the peripheral hardware is attached. Neither the students nor I can ever remember all the steps required for each piece of equipment. Even with less complex equipment, by going through each step and writing it down you will come to realize that using almost any hardware and software is not simple for the neophyte.

For example, multimedia software usually has icons or hot buttons to make it easy for students—even students with a low level of language proficiency—to navigate the software in a nonlinear fashion. However, like many so-called international signs, some of these icons baffle me completely (see Figure 23-4 to test yourself). Sometimes a software application displays a full-screen graphic, usually a room of some type, in which each item is actually an icon. Maneuvering through such graphics is not always as intuitive as publishers intend, and students will not know that they should click the mouse on any of the items in the picture to get to another page unless they are told directly on that screen or by you. In order to see the software as the students will, I always try to preview a full working version before reading either the advertisements or the manual for the software. In many cases, the students need only a few additional pointers from me to make their experience less bewildering and more successful.

E-Mail and Other Types of Electronic Communication

The complexity of sending and retrieving e-mail varies according to how students must access the e-mail software locally and what kind of e-mail software they use. Messages can be easily lost—along with the students.

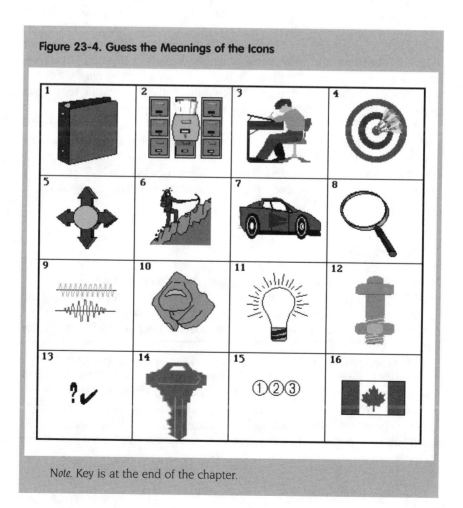

Figure 23-4. Guess the Meanings of the Icons

Note. Key is at the end of the chapter.

Make sure to go through every step in using the e-mail software. Start by having all the students send you a short message and retrieve the response from you. Then they can try sending one to another classmate and retrieving the response. You can speed up students' e-mail communication by setting up electronic bulletin boards on which all postings are public. If you have Internet access but not e-mail for your students, or of you want students to practice e-mail in a safe and manageable environment, try Web-B-Mail (free to educators; Pfaff-Harris, 1996), which allows students on the same system to send e-mail to each other using the Web. Have the students practice saving and printing e-mail files (and Web materials) with these noncrucial messages before they must complete a major project.

The World Wide Web as Research Tool

As with software, introduce Web-based tasks in stages based on their relative complexity. Using a Web browser (e.g., Microsoft Internet Explorer, 1998, or Netscape Navigator® Gold, 1997) to find information, such as an on-line article, is a fairly easy task. Initial Web sessions should include how to use the browser and how to use a simple search engine (e.g., AltaVista, http://www.altavista.com/; Lycos, http://www.lycos.com/; Yahoo!, http://www.yahoo.com/; see Appendix C). Students can report what they have found from the information on their screen.

A more complex task involves having students save a Web file, cut and paste parts of it, and print it. An even more complex task is to have students use the search function of the browser to examine a particular passage for grammatical structures, as described in Grammar Safari (Mills & Salzmann, 1998). Keep in mind how each part of the activity increases the level of computer skill required.

Conclusion

Most teachers have only a limited amount of time to spend with students in the CALL environment but have much to introduce them to. With careful planning and much consideration of abilities and motivations, you can avoid misunderstandings that might cause you to waste your students' time in the lab.

Don't lose sight of the language learning goal or the makeup of your ESL class. Have your students use the computer when it will strengthen their learning experience. Keep the focus on the language rather than on the computer. The amount of time you invest in ensuring a positive experience with the computers, right from the introductory lesson, will be repaid tenfold when you see happy students eager to use the technology in their language learning.

Key to Figure 23-4, Guess the Meaning of the Icons

1. Student work and scores
2. Student work and scores
3. Take a test
4. Take a test
5. Choose another activity
6. Choose a higher level activity
7. Go to the next exercise
8. Read
9. Pronunciation exercise
10. Your turn to speak
11. Brainstorming/prewriting activity
12. Grammar explanation
13. Check your answers
14. Answer key
15. Check your scores
16. Canadian adventure game (earned after a certain number of points)

Explorations

Projects

1. Do your students have computer anxiety? How would you find out? Develop a way to measure this variable for your students.

2. Visit a multiuser object-oriented domain (MOO). Describe how specific features of the MOO might affect the atmosphere in a language learning classroom.

3. Describe a task you might have students do in the CALL classroom. Suggest ways in which you can tell when your students are experiencing the appropriate amount of stress. What can you do to help them experience the optimal amount of stress?

Guided Research

1. How can teachers help students get into the flow of learning in the classroom? Develop a proposal for an action research study in which you will describe when and how students are optimally stressed.

2. To what extent does MOO use contribute to oral proficiency? Observe, take notes, and audio- or videotape a group of students using a MOO over a period of time. Examine the audio- or videotaped record of students' use of oral language when engaged in MOOing in groups. Examine the written language students generate: Which elements relate most closely to oral language? Which written elements are reflected in their oral language? You will need to research specific linguistic elements to complete this assignment successfully.

3. Collect data to determine how MOO use affects learners' attitudes toward speakers of the target language and toward their culture. What specific cultural considerations play a role in MOO use?

Questions for Further Investigation

1. What area(s) of current language learning curricula could be diminished or eliminated in order to free up time for MOO use? Does language learning similar to that provided in the eliminated areas take place via MOO use?

2. How many hours of MOO use contribute, to any significant degree, to the acquisition of a second language?

3. What aspects of MOO use are most motivating to learners? Do these aspects contribute to second language acquisition? What aspects dampen learners' motivation?

PART VIII

Control

Chapter 24 ▦

Theory and Research:
Autonomy in Language Learning

Deborah Healey

The term *autonomy* can evoke a number of images: fierce independence, like the frontier spirit of the U.S. West; an isolation that can border on loneliness; an adult maturity that is different from childlike dependence. *Learner autonomy* in language learning is often set in contrast to dependence on the teacher and is also discussed as *learner control*. This chapter follows Dickinson (1987) in using the term *self-direction* to refer to learners' attitudes and *autonomy* to refer to the instructional framework: the degree of independence the learner is given in setting language learning goals, the path to the goal, the pace of learning, and the measurement of success. Educators can only hope to encourage learners to take on the attitude of greater self-reliance and independence that will let them actively seek out ways to enhance their own learning. However, teachers can control the environments they establish and can choose to design classrooms and labs so that the equipment, software, and staff move in concert to enable learners to be self-directed.

Much work has been done on finding ways to encourage self-directed learning. The Centre de Recherches et d'Applications Pédagogiques en Langues (CRAPEL) began conducting research on self-directed learning in 1974 at the Université de Nancy II in France. A major focus of its work has been on teaching learners how to work in autonomous settings, often with explicit instruction about learning strategies. The Open University in the United Kingdom, a center for correspondence courses and distance education, has also long been involved in seeking ways to encourage learners to be comfortable with learning independently. Candy's *Self-Direction for Lifelong Learning* (1991) is a very helpful and comprehensive look at self-direction and autonomy in adult learners. A number of other writers have explored the role of learning strategies, including autonomy, in language teaching, among them Dickinson (1987), O'Malley and Chamot (1990), Oxford (1990, 1996), and Wenden and Rubin (1987).

Candy (1991) points out some factors in the recent surge in the popularity of self-directed learning, including "the democratic ideal, the ideology of individualism, the concept of egalitarianism, subjective or relativistic epistemology, the emphasis on humanistic education, and the construct of adulthood and adult education's search for an identity" (p. 32). Although Candy's focus is adult learners, children also benefit from being encouraged to become independent learners. They need to be prepared for the lifelong learning that awaits them, which is propelled in many ways by changes in the workplace (Guglielmino & Guglielmino, 1994; Naisbitt, 1984; Rosow & Zager, 1988). As teachers of individuals from a variety of cultures, however, it behooves ESL/EFL professionals to keep in mind that learner self-direction and autonomous learning are Western concepts that fit smoothly into U.S. culture in particular. These concepts may not be as logical to others, particularly when children are concerned. Parents in many immigrant communities in the United States, for example, already feel that their children are far too independent and too likely to break from parental guidance and control. Teachers need to tread carefully in how they encourage learners, especially children, to seek their own paths. The benefits are clear for language learners who actively seek out opportunities to practice and who formulate and test theories about how the language works; such learners achieve more (Rubin, 1979). The task for teachers is to establish frameworks for autonomous learning that can work in conjunction with the cultural values learners (and their parents) bring rather than in opposition to their basic beliefs.

Settings for Autonomous Learning

In a classroom situation, teachers, especially those preparing students for a U.S. academic setting, often encourage students to take control of their learning in a variety of ways. Certainly, few if any teachers expect to be the sole source of language learning for their students—for one thing, it would be nearly impossible for one person alone to provide the extensive access to language data that is essential to learning, much less to make the interconnections among the data that allow creative language use. Teachers can guide students to seek out language data for themselves and try to fit those data into their own knowledge frameworks. Students can generally be expected to participate actively in their own learning in this way. In settings offering large quantities of language data that are presented in a variety of forms to appeal to different learning styles, students should be able to work on their own as well as in class.

Depending on the age, maturity, and language proficiency of the students, teachers can allow varying degrees of choice to their learners. Adults generally prefer to have some choice in their activities. With teenagers and adults at intermediate and higher proficiency levels, teachers can leave the topics for some papers and projects to the student. Beginners may not be able to find the information they need in the target language on their own, so they may work better using teacher-provided material and preset topics.

The different autonomous learning settings that have been described generally vary according to whether the content is fixed or variable and according to whether the teacher or instructional designer or the learner has the larger role in structuring the learning. These settings can be seen as a table with four cells, A–D (see Table 24-1), although the structure source and content variables should be thought of as continua rather than as discrete units, and students may not fit perfectly into any of these settings.

In a learning situation with no autonomy, the teacher sets requirements for every aspect of learning, including the time and pace. However, the representation in Table 24-1 assumes that there are some opportunities for autonomous learning in the classroom. In settings where the teacher structures the learning by fixing the content (Cell A in the table), the learner usually controls the pace through the material and the time of study. The content and sequence, as well as the form of evaluation, usually come from the teacher or instructional designer. Cell A represents the *programmed learning* model of instruction that was quite popular in computer-assisted instruction circles in a range of fields and has been used for language learning in PLATO, a mainframe computer–based courseware system designed in the early 1980s (now redesigned as NovaNet; see http://

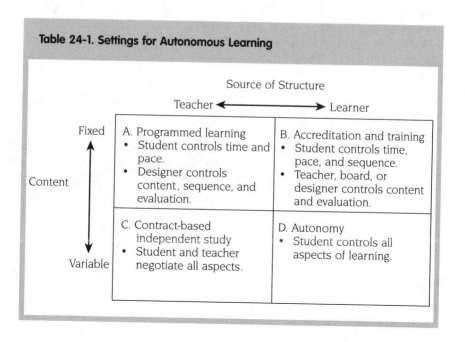

Table 24-1. Settings for Autonomous Learning

| | | Source of Structure | |
		Teacher ⟵⟶ Learner	
Content	Fixed	A. Programmed learning • Student controls time and pace. • Designer controls content, sequence, and evaluation.	B. Accreditation and training • Student controls time, pace, and sequence. • Teacher, board, or designer controls content and evaluation.
	Variable	C. Contract-based independent study • Student and teacher negotiate all aspects.	D. Autonomy • Student controls all aspects of learning.

www.nn.com/). A good designer will build in ways to account for learners' preferences, at least to some extent. Correspondence and many distance education courses follow this model.

Learning that is structured by the learner with fixed content (Cell B in the table) is characterized by a fixed body of content, usually set by an external authority such as a teacher or accreditation board. Learners can choose the time, the pace, and the order of progression through the material. This type of setting works best when the body of material to be learned is well defined and learners are able to organize their own learning effectively. The teacher or group that sets the content also typically decides how evaluation will take place.

The third type of autonomous learning setting is structured by the teacher with variable content (Cell C in the table). The learner generally decides the content in this setting, with the teacher serving as a facilitator or guide. The teacher may suggest the route and rate through the material, but the final decision is made jointly or by the learner. Here teachers should work with learners to design a course of study that fits their individual preferences. Contract-based independent study courses often follow this model. Evaluation is more difficult with this setup and should be agreed on ahead of time.

The final type, a setting structured by the learner with variable content (Cell D in the table), is the most flexible. A teacher is involved only as an optional source of information and guidance, if at all. A research project of the learner's choice would fall into this category, as would certain Open University courses (Nobel, 1980). Dickinson (1987) describes this type of learning as autonomy, in which a fully autonomous learner would not even necessarily need a teacher or an institution for learning to occur. The learner is responsible for all elements in this setup, including deciding how evaluation will take place.

Conditions That Enhance Autonomy and Learning

Learning can take place in all four of the autonomy quadrants described above or in none of them, depending on the learner and the resources available. Both issues centering on the learner and issues involving learning come into play in the search for the appropriate degree of autonomy for an individual learner or a group of learners.

Learner Issues

Learner issues include

1. degree of self-motivation
2. preference for an independent style

3. knowledge of how one learns best

4. knowledge of what one needs to learn

Self-Motivation

As regards self-motivation, many language learners and teachers come from educational backgrounds in which teachers are expected to control all knowledge in their realm. The pedagogical image is often that of the learner as empty vessel, waiting to be filled with the teacher's flowing knowledge. Such a background is not autonomous, and it actively discourages learners for being independent. It is often difficult to convince learners who have always been taught this way, and teachers who have learned this way, that giving some control to learners carries certain advantages. As Oxford (1990) remarks, "Just teaching new strategies to students will accomplish very little unless students begin to *want* greater responsibility for their own learning" (p. 10). The issue of self-direction sometimes seems like a chicken-and-egg problem: Unless learners have strategies, they can't be self-directed, but learners may have no interest in the strategies until they start to take some control into their own hands.

Independent Style

Ideal self-directed learners are always motivated to learn by some internal fire that never needs stoking from a teacher-facilitator. Such people are able to organize their learning independently, knowing when to ask for assistance but not seeking it otherwise. A former student who had learned an appreciable amount of English just from Beatles recordings and a dictionary is an example of such a person. He was, needless to say, quite unusual in both his motivation for learning and his method. Learners who are not very self-motivated and independent in their learning—that is, most people—need more assistance in an autonomous setting to define and then focus on specific language learning goals. Impossible goals can cause learners to lose heart, but a series of smaller, achievable goals can encourage learners to continue. Keep in mind that simply telling someone to be motivated and independent will not cause a personality change; incentives for new attitudes need to be built into the learning setting (Hiemstra & Brockett, 1994). Teachers can begin this process by accounting for student preferences in content, pace, media, and other areas as much as possible (Areglado, 1996; Dudley-Marling & Searle, 1995).

Knowledge of How One Learns

As discussed in chapter 18, most language teachers have noted a clear difference between students who are learning a second language and those who are learning their third or fourth language. The latter generally have a clearer idea than the former of both the possible ways to organize human language and the way they themselves operate as language learners.

People exhibit certain tendencies in how they learn. Individuals who are more visually oriented learn best from information presented as text or graphics; other people are auditorily oriented and learn best from listening; some are tactile, and touching an object or a physical representation of a concept helps them remember it best; others are kinesthetic and learn best when they can move to act out ideas or manipulate objects. People are quite capable of learning information presented in a format that is not in their strongest area. However, those who know how they learn can structure their learning in a way that will help them the most. They also know how to compensate for information presented in a format from which they do not learn well, often by translating it for themselves into their preferred mode. (See chapters 18–20 for a full discussion of learning preferences and styles.)

Knowledge About the Target Area

The learner's knowledge of the target content area is another very important factor in self-direction. As Brookfield (1985) puts it,

> An adult can embark on independent exploration of a field of knowledge with no real idea of how to design learning activities that will result in the development of a certain level of proficiency. It is only as the adult becomes aware of the standards, operations, procedures, and criteria deemed intrinsic to that skill or knowledge area that he or she can begin to set short- and long-term learning goals. (p. 10)

Research by Chapelle and Mizuno (1989) shows that learners are not necessarily good judges of their own skill level, at least in certain areas of language, and may assume they know more than they actually do as a result. Furthermore, work by Johanesen and Tennyson (1983) indicates that learners given advice about their level of knowledge practice for a more appropriate time—usually longer—than if they do not have that information. Goforth's (1994) meta-analysis of learner control studies confirms the importance of information given to learners when they are empowered to make decisions. Again, the framework needs to be in place to help independent learners know what they are trying to learn.

Content Issues

The content to be learned also affects the degree of autonomy. Content issues include the following three conditions:

1. The path to the goal is relatively unambiguous.
2. What is to be learned can be explained clearly.
3. Appropriate resources exist for self-directed language learning.

Clear Path to the Goal

The first issue, that the path to the goal be clearly defined, is not particularly easy in language learning. To begin with, the target of learning varies with the individual needs of the learner (Widdowson, 1983). Someone who wants to be an airline pilot needs a different subset of English from a person whose main goal is to negotiate with a car dealership in California.

In addition, many aspects of grammar, such as negation, word order, and question formation, seem to be acquired in a specific sequence. Work by Ellis (1984) and Long (1987) indicates that the formal study of grammatical forms at the appropriate stage in the acquisition sequence can be helpful; possibly, learners become aware of the forms they are using and should use through formal study. A focus on form, though, may also slow learners' speech, making it appear more grammatical but less fluent. Beyond these general guidelines in grammar, the path to linguistic proficiency is quite murky.

Clear Explanations of the Target Area

To approach the second content-related issue, clear explanations of what is to be learned, learners must be as specific as possible about their language learning goals—the more well defined the subset of language to be learned, the more readily the teacher-facilitator can suggest materials and approaches to study. Learners who are uncertain about why they are studying the target language are the hardest to help. The issue moves back to the learners again: Those who are better able to set their own goals are easier to serve in an autonomous setting.

Resources Available

The best intentioned of learners will not get far without resources, that is, language data to work with. Learners also need an organizational system that will help them find what they need, either by themselves or with assistance from a facilitator. Such a system needs to take into account the factors mentioned earlier—the subset of language the learner wishes to work on, the learner's stage of acquisition, the learner's degree of motivation and independence, the learning style the material fits best, and the background knowledge the learner brings to the learning task. A wide variety of well-organized material and an easy way to find it are thus essential to learners' success in an autonomous setting.

Technology and Learning

Good and Brophy (1987) suggest five preconditions for motivation that must be set by the teacher-facilitator in classroom learning:

1. an appropriate level of challenge or difficulty
2. learning objectives that are meaningful to the learner

3. variation in the teaching methods used

4. intrinsic and extrinsic feedback about success

5. no barriers to learning

These considerations are important for managers of autonomous learning settings and for software developers as well.

Appropriate Level of Challenge or Difficulty

Although technology is often touted as the great salvation of education—an easy way to customize learning to individual needs—it rarely lives up to this broad expectation. Even if technology is not all things to all learners, it can help most learners in some ways. For example, developers can create language teaching software that assesses learners in the areas of instruction the software will offer, then presents the information customized to the learner's needs. This individualized approach means that, at least within the subset of language the software deals with, learners can work on an area that fits their skill level. An alternative and less expensive approach—and the most common one—is for the software developer to create an index and let learners choose for themselves the level they feel is appropriate. Software that allows students these kinds of choices, thus giving them control, often enhances learning (Goforth, 1994). The developer still needs to make sure that the software includes enough information to meet the range of levels the application is intended for.

Meaningful Learning Objectives

Given the wide variation in personal goals that students bring to learning language, setting learning objectives that are meaningful to the learner may be more the task of the teacher-facilitator and lab manager than of the software developer. With enough different software available, learners in an autonomous setting should be able to find something that will meet their needs, at least in part. Software that can be customized (authored) to fit specific learners generally requires time and effort on the part of the teacher but may be the best approach to take, especially if learners have specific needs that are not met by currently available software.

The material itself is not the only factor in setting learning objectives; defining paths to reach these objectives is also part of the task. At present, second language acquisition research has not come up with any universal, easy, step-by-step methods for language acquisition. Developers and facilitators therefore need to build in guidelines that help learners decide why they want to learn the target language and how they plan to learn it.

A Variety of Teaching Methods

Multimedia software, which presents data in different ways, certainly offers the possibility of varying the teaching methods used. Also, it is a rare multimedia program that does not have at least two instructional modes, such as less structured and more structured, practice-and-test or game, and individual and group. Most multimedia programs also provide information simultaneously in some combination of textual, graphical, and auditory form. The tactile and kinesthetic possibilities when a learner is sitting at a computer or in front of a videocassette recorder are not as extensive as what is available in a classroom, generally being limited to moving the mouse or using the keyboard. The virtual reality technology now under development may help, because in virtual reality software learners at least have the impression that they are manipulating objects and moving in space even though they may be moving only their head and hands.

The facilitator in an autonomous setting has a substantial role to play in encouraging learners to use a variety of materials and methods and in explaining how to go about it. Although most software developers create material for learners to use individually, learners working in pairs often achieve better results. For example, in doing a cloze exercise, learners spend more time guessing words before giving up and checking the answer when they work in pairs than when they work alone (Healey, 1993). Students who are social rather than individual learners may need help with the logistics of finding others with the same learning objectives to work with. The physical layout of the CALL environment also needs to be conducive to pair work; there should be enough space and enough chairs at individual machines for learners to work together.

Feedback

A commonly noted problem with autonomous learning is that students sometimes have trouble seeing the progress they have made and become discouraged when they think about how much farther they need to go. Explicit assessment from time to time helps provide mileposts for learners. Most software activities offer learners feedback in one way or another. At the simplest level, using a word processor to produce a good-looking printout gives learners an intrinsic sense of satisfaction. At the other end of the intrinsic-extrinsic continuum, grammar software may keep student records over time and generate a score for the immediate exercise as well as for the learner's overall work with the software.

Unfortunately, current software rarely gives more than a limited snap-shot of learners' performance on a given task. Unless the software has been customized to meet the specific language learning goals of individual learners, it won't give learners a sense of where they stand in meeting those goals. Facilitators can ask learners to keep records of what they worked on and how they did as a way to assess themselves on a more global level. In the Individualized Directed Learning class at Oregon State University's English Language Institute, for example, learners' midterm and final grades depend in large part on the self-assessment they conduct based on the records they have kept (Healey, 1992).

No Barriers to Learning

As mentioned in chapter 23, for software the issue of barriers to learning generally centers on user-friendliness. Software that regularly crashes falls into the worst-case category, causing a total loss of the learner's control over the activity. Software that requires reference to a manual in the target language generally doesn't work well for language learners, either. Software can set up barriers to learning when it is cumbersome to use, requiring unnecessary keystrokes or memorization of obscure commands to accomplish basic tasks. Learners who have to struggle just to operate a program are engaged in inauthentic labor—the only struggle necessary should be to meet the reasonable cognitive demands involved in actual language learning.

Another type of barrier set up by technology can be psychological. Many learners are excited by what computers can offer, but others feel anxious and uncertain. They may be threatened by the unfamiliar technology and completely lost when software does not work the way they imagined it would. The self-esteem of older learners in particular may be damaged if they feel that younger learners are more skilled with the technology than they are (especially if the younger learners are also more skilled with the language); such older learners may hesitate to ask for help for fear of exposing their weakness and losing face. As suggested in chapter 23, facilitators may need to make an extra effort to avoid such problems and create a climate conducive to learning by, for example, pairing learners thoughtfully for group work and holding individual help sessions to bring learners up to speed with the technology.

Conclusion: Autonomy and Technology

For full autonomy, a learner must be able to control the content and the structure of the learning, including the time, the pace, the path to the goal, and the measurement of success.

Control Over Time

Extensive reliance on technology requires access to the technology at a time convenient to the learner; however, staffing and maintaining a lab on a

24-hour basis can be quite expensive, putting it out of the reach of smaller institutions. Learners who do not live near the lab will have more difficulty making use of it. However, the increase in on-line resources accessible from home has made autonomous learning more feasible in many cases by removing time- and location-related constraints on access to technology. As more resources become available on-line, particularly through the multimedia World Wide Web, autonomous learning may become more widespread.

Control Over Pace

Most current computer software gives users full control over the pace of learning. Learners can choose how often and how long to work on a particular program. Context-sensitive help is increasingly offered on demand, giving learners the option to proceed through material at a faster or slower pace depending on how often help is requested and how extensively it is read. A language learning course with the usual term deadlines may remove some of the learner's control over the pace, but those constraints will be imposed by human demands, not by language learning technology.

Control Over the Path to the Goal

The path to the goal is a complicated area in autonomous learning. As mentioned, there is no consensus among linguists and language teachers on the optimum way to take a learner from zero proficiency in the target language to a near-native level. Learners must be able to define their learning objectives as the first step, deciding which subset of language is most important to them. Technology could come into play in the form of automated questionnaires that help learners figure out their learning styles and then match their needs to specific items in a database of available resources. Another advantage of multimedia technology is that current multimedia software for language learning can provide for several learning styles, being especially useful for visual (textual and graphical) and auditory learners (see chapters 9, 10, and 13).

As mentioned, current software does not meet the needs of tactile and kinesthetic learners well; a flat screen is just not three-dimensional. Social learners also need to make more effort when working in a technology-intensive setting to find people to work with, although Internet connections can help in that regard. With fast, reliable connections, learners can take advantage of real-time interaction in multiuser object-oriented domains (MOOs) and chat areas. Learners can also use the delayed interaction mode of e-mail for peer review of writing and other project work, an option that is especially useful for those without full Internet access or with slow connections.

Access to the Measurement of Success

A necessary part of learning is assessment, an arena in which technology can be quite helpful. Individual applications can track not only how learners did on tests but also how they worked through material, including the time they spent on individual items, the words they looked up, the help they requested, and the guesses they made in doing an exercise. When learners look back on what they've done, they can see what they worked on and check to see if they now know the words they looked up and the grammar and other rules they asked for help with. As another example, software that tracks reading speed can help learners see their progress over time. By logging users' actions automatically, the computer can take some of the record-keeping burden off the learners. However, a truly autonomous setting clearly would have the learners, not the technology, evaluate the learning.

In general, technology can be a valuable tool for autonomous learning, providing help in setting goals, making progress toward achieving them, and gathering information for self-assessment. As in other areas of education, technology is not an end in itself; it is only as useful as learners and teachers make it in working toward the goal of language acquisition.

Chapter 25 ⊡

Classroom Practice: Autonomy Through Authoring Software

Robert Wachman

Autonomous CALL environments benefit learners in a number of ways (see chapter 24). In this chapter, I discuss software that can, at least in part, assist teachers and learners in constructing autonomous modes of language learning: software that can be customized or authored to fit teachers' or learners' needs (*authorable* software) and software expressly designed for the development of one's own educational materials (*authoring* software). Because software is developing and changing rapidly, this discussion is not intended to be exhaustive but rather to provide examples of these two kinds of software and ways they can benefit both teachers and learners in their quest for an optimal language teaching and learning environment.

Authorable Software

Authorable software consists of programs that can be customized by adding data, usually in the form of text, to fit specific learners' needs in terms of degree of difficulty, interest, culture, and so on. Two authorable programs used in the ESL Lab at Yuba College in Marysville, California, are Eclipse (Higgins, 1989) and MacReader (McVicker, 1992).

Eclipse is a story reconstruction program for computers running the MS-DOS® operating system. In it, learners read a story on the screen, the letters of each word then automatically become blank squares, and the learners are prompted to type any word they recall. The software then puts the correctly typed words into the proper spots in the story. Students may peek at the complete story for a few seconds any time they wish. This full-cloze activity gives students practice with typical structures and vocabulary in a text, and the reconstruction of the original is a gamelike activity with intrinsic motivation: The student wants to see the text made whole.

As pointed out in chapter 24, most contemporary language learning software gives users control over various aspects of their learning experience. In Eclipse (Higgins, 1989), learners start and stop the software, select stories, control the time they spend on a particular story, create their own input, and decide when to peek at the full text. What makes Eclipse authorable is that you can scan any story or type it using any word-processing software and then import and use the story with Eclipse. In my lab, teachers have imported a series of stories that are easier than those provided with the software and that focus on the cultures of the students who use them (see Figure 25-1 for one story in the process of reconstruction). This addition has greatly increased low-intermediate students' interest in and ability to use this software.

MacReader (McVicker, 1992), a reading program developed for Macintosh® computers, is designed to increase reading speed and improve comprehension. Activities include untimed and timed reading, paced reading, cloze, and jumbled-sentence and -paragraph exercises. A built-in notebook automatically keeps a record of the current work session. Users may view or print this information, as well as any personal notes they want to type, and choose any activity, via clickable buttons, at any time. (A newer version, NewReader, McVicker, 1995a, with even more activities, is also available.) In the untimed reading mode, users may click the mouse on a word and see a definition from the software's built-in glossary (see Figure 25-2). Definitions

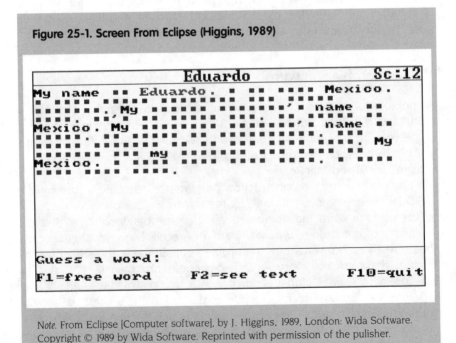

Figure 25-1. Screen From Eclipse (Higgins, 1989)

Note. From Eclipse [Computer software], by J. Higgins, 1989, London: Wida Software. Copyright © 1989 by Wida Software. Reprinted with permission of the pulisher.

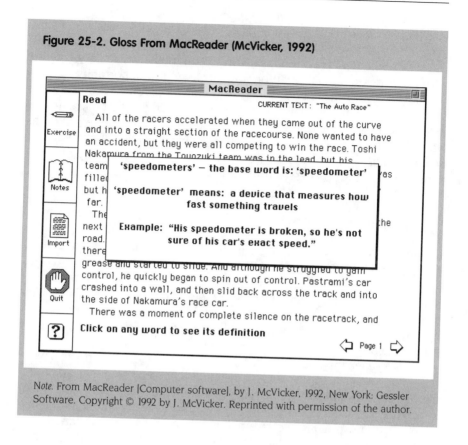

Figure 25-2. Gloss From MacReader (McVicker, 1992)

Note. From MacReader [Computer software], by J. McVicker, 1992, New York: Gessler Software. Copyright © 1992 by J. McVicker. Reprinted with permission of the author.

are followed by a dialogue box in which the user is asked to type one of three things to aid retention: (a) the learner's own definition, (b) an original sample sentence, or (c) a translation of the word in the learner's own language.

Like Eclipse (Higgins, 1989), MacReader (McVicker, 1992) allows any text to be imported and used with the various activities. The glossary of definitions and follow-up dialogues can also be modified and expanded. When I have typed and imported short stories read in class and added simple definitions to the glossary, students having difficulty understanding a story have been able to use MacReader for assistance.

More advanced students can load their own word-processed or scanned essays into MacReader (McVicker, 1992) for other students to use. Often it is helpful for students to see the level of reading difficulty of their writing, which the software can assess using several different readability scales, or to create glossary definitions for their readers, particularly in relation to a content area or adjunct class.

Many game programs, such as MacTrivia (Killion, 1985), Phraze Craze

Plus (Pettit, 1986), and any of a number of hangman and crossword puzzle generators available as shareware or freeware, allow the user to add words, clues, or whole data files. You may wish to control the vocabulary entered, which provides one level of autonomy. However, the opportunity to write the files for each other forces students to engage with the vocabulary in a very direct way. When students write files in groups, the authorable software makes the task collaborative. Many computerized word games, such as HangMan Plus (Winograd, 1991), have this editing capability. A student may add a word from the vocabulary lesson and then turn the computer over to another student, who guesses the word.

Authoring Software

Chapter 13 describes the primitive authoring tools available in multimedia software, such as Storybook Maker (1994) and Storybook Weaver (1992), which allow students to cut and paste settings and characters, write text, make audio recordings, and even have their text read back to them. With higher level authoring software, educators without technical expertise can not only modify software developed by others but also create their own from scratch.

Authoring means using tools within the software to make it do what you, the author, want it to. Far less demanding than programming, authoring allows flexibility and a degree of creativity within predefined (programmed) structures. The extent of creativity allowed varies greatly among programs. In this section I discuss two levels of authoring software: (a) that created especially for language teaching and learning and (b) the more flexible and powerful general multimedia authoring software.

Authoring Software for Language Teaching and Learning

Examples of authoring software created expressly for language educators include Dasher (Otto & Pusack, 1994) and MacLang (1987). Both are billed as foreign language authoring systems, but they may also be used to teach ESL/EFL. Though not as flexible as high-end authoring packages, these programs allow you not only to supply the content but also to choose the mode of presentation and testing from the templates offered.

In Dasher (Otto & Pusack, 1994), for either Macintosh computers or those running the Microsoft® Windows® operating system, you can create activities of the following types with your own content: story-writing exercises, substitution drills, sentence-combining exercises, multiple-choice questions, scrambled sentences, vocabulary-building exercises, dialogue presentations and reviews, sentence transformation tasks, true-false questions, fill-in-the-blank sentences, dictations, translation exercises, and "synthetics," a combination of several of these types. Samples provided with the demo version for Macintosh computers each begin with a text-based introduction. The material may be presented in the form of text, graphics, audio, or video. Follow-up questions are text based. Users type in their answers, which are then evaluated, and appropriate responses are given. Dasher gets its name from its manner of response: It marks incorrect portions of learners' responses with dashes and arrows (see Figure 25-3). Responses may also have an audio component. Audio-based and image-based exercises (see Figure 25-4) have similar formats. In audio-based exercises, learners play an attached audio file by clicking the mouse.

Like Dasher, MacLang (1987), for Macintosh computers, provides a variety of exercise types: vocabulary, fill-in-the-blank, cloze paragraph (see Figure 25-5), multiple choice, jumble (scrambled words), and multiformat. Exercises may be linked to audio or interactive video. Positive or negative feedback follows each of the learner's responses, and scores are reported at the conclusion of an exercise.

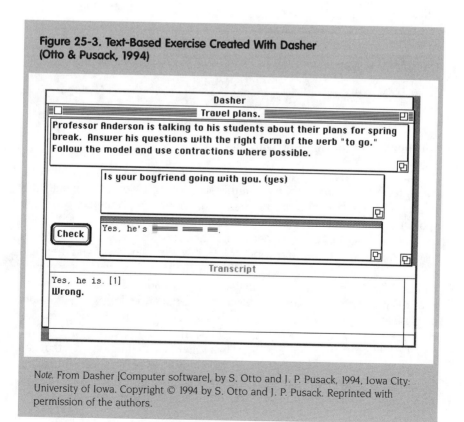

Figure 25-3. Text-Based Exercise Created With Dasher (Otto & Pusack, 1994)

> **Dasher**
> **Travel plans.**
> Professor Anderson is talking to his students about their plans for spring break. Answer his questions with the right form of the verb "to go." Follow the model and use contractions where possible.
>
> Is your boyfriend going with you. (yes)
>
> [Check] Yes, he's ▬▬ ▬ ▬ ▬.
>
> **Transcript**
> Yes, he is. [1]
> **Wrong.**

Note. From Dasher [Computer software], by S. Otto and J. P. Pusack, 1994, Iowa City: University of Iowa. Copyright © 1994 by S. Otto and J. P. Pusack. Reprinted with permission of the authors.

Figure 25-4. Image-Based Exercise Created With Dasher (Otto & Pusack, 1994)

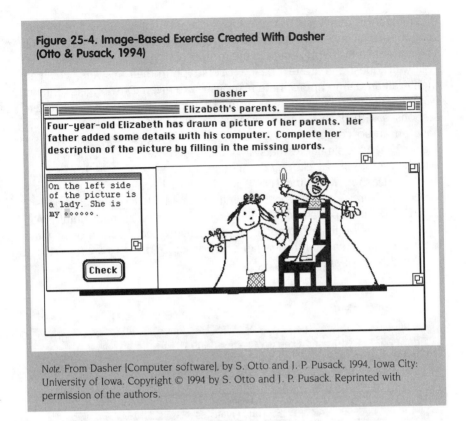

Note. From Dasher [Computer software], by S. Otto and J. P. Pusack, 1994, Iowa City: University of Iowa. Copyright © 1994 by S. Otto and J. P. Pusack. Reprinted with permission of the authors.

Multimedia Authoring Software

Although authoring software for language teaching and learning allows a higher level of autonomy than the authorable software described earlier, it is still far less powerful and flexible than multimedia authoring software, the subject of the balance of this chapter. Examples are HyperCard® (1995, 1997; for Macintosh computers), HyperStudio (1997; for Macintosh computers or those running Windows), and ToolBook II (1996; for Windows), and there are many more such tool applications, some written specifically for young authors. With these software applications, you and your learners can use your own content to create a wide variety of educational programs that are highly interactive, fully media capable, easy to use, and enjoyable. You can create, import, and display text, graphics, animations, video, and sound, and the resultant programs are saved in a *player*, or run-time version, that can be operated without a copy of the full authoring application. End-users (students) merely point and click the computer mouse to change screens, view graphics and animations, play sounds, read text, see video clips,

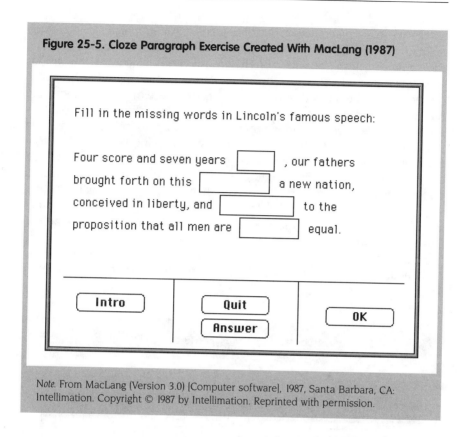

Figure 25-5. Cloze Paragraph Exercise Created With MacLang (1987)

> Fill in the missing words in Lincoln's famous speech:
>
> Four score and seven years [____], our fathers
> brought forth on this [____] a new nation,
> conceived in liberty, and [____] to the
> proposition that all men are [____] equal.
>
> [Intro]   [Quit]   [OK]
>   [Answer]

Note. From MacLang (Version 3.0) [Computer software], 1987, Santa Barbara, CA: Intellimation. Copyright © 1987 by Intellimation. Reprinted with permission.

activate other software on the computer or on a CD-ROM or videodisc player, or even link to the Internet.

These features, plus the ability to create buttons, fields, and animations easily, give educators without true programming skills the ability to modify programs developed by others and to create their own software virtually from scratch. Most of the examples given here are based on HyperCard (1995), the software with which I, as principally a Macintosh computer user, am most familiar. Authoring programs such as Director (1998) and AuthorWare Star (1994) are more powerful and sophisticated, but they are much more complex and difficult to learn as well as considerably more expensive. My comments apply generally to these more sophisticated programs as well as to less scriptable applications, such as Microsoft PowerPoint® 97 (1996) and Digital Chisel (1996).

HyperCard (1997) and HyperStudio (1997) screens are called *cards*, and files made up of collections of cards are called *stacks*, analogous to stacks of index cards. In ToolBook II (1996), screens are called *pages*, and documents, *books*. These programs, like electronic construction sets, allow you to build stacks piece by piece, using buttons, fields, text, graphics, sound, color, animation, and video in almost any form and combination you wish. Figure 25-6, a screen from Your Tour of HyperCard (1995), illustrates the various elements of a card.

With multimedia authoring tools, you can develop presentation and practice software for virtually all language skills. The feature that most fully sets these full-blown authoring applications apart from those described in the previous section is that each employs a scripting language in which authors can write simple programs, or *scripts*, to make the software do almost anything they want. Scripting languages, which have syntax similar to that of English, are much simpler to learn than true programming languages, such as Microsoft C++ or Pascal. In Figure 25-7, the script tells the computer to highlight a button when the mouse clicks on it, wait 1 second, and then go to another card.

One of the most powerful characteristics of software created with these multimedia tools is its nonlinearity, or branching ability. The screens or

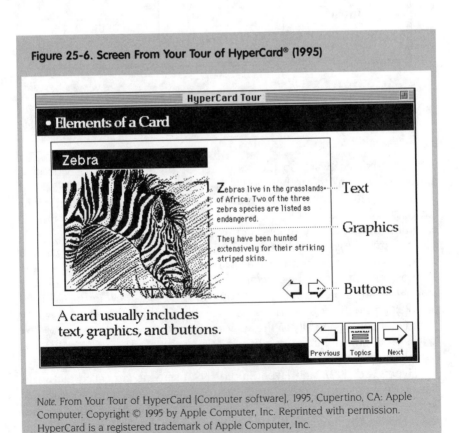

Figure 25-6. Screen From Your Tour of HyperCard® (1995)

Note. From Your Tour of HyperCard [Computer software], 1995, Cupertino, CA: Apple Computer. Copyright © 1995 by Apple Computer, Inc. Reprinted with permission. HyperCard is a registered trademark of Apple Computer, Inc.

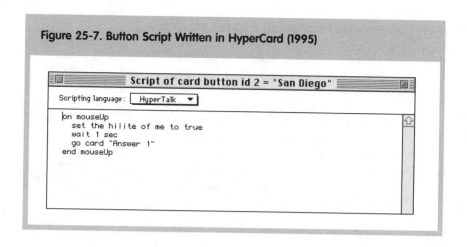

Figure 25-7. Button Script Written in HyperCard (1995)

```
Script of card button id 2 = "San Diego"
Scripting language:  HyperTalk  ▼

on mouseUp
    set the hilite of me to true
    wait 1 sec
    go card "Answer 1"
end mouseUp
```

cards in a stack (or pages in ToolBook II, 1996) need not be viewed in order. The click of a button can lead not only to the next card in the stack but to any card in the current stack or in any other stack; a button can even lead to and open another program or application. And buttons are used for myriad functions besides navigation, for example, to view a hidden text field or graphic, access questions, indicate or check an answer to a question, play a sound, or even record one.

Perhaps the best feature of most multimedia authoring software is its user-friendliness. You can learn the rudiments of authoring in the software in a matter of hours or days—on your own—with tutorials that come with the software or from introductory books. HyperStudio (1997) is renowned for its ease of authoring. A free demo version on CD-ROM from the publisher includes a basic tutorial, sample stacks, and the capability to create a working four-card stack for practice. The catalogue of the International Society for Technology in Education (see Appendix A) lists numerous books, including *HyperStudio in One Hour!* (Sharp, 1994), explaining how to use these authoring applications; often the books are accompanied by software. For a more extensive but still quick, user-friendly start with HyperCard (1997), I recommend *HyperCard 2.3 in a Hurry* (Beekman, 1996). Hands-on introductory workshops offered at professional conferences and institutes, such as the TESOL Academies, can be a good way to get started. In a very short time, you can learn enough to modify existing stacks or begin to create your own.

Stack development is enjoyable for learners as well as for teachers. You can let students field-test your efforts and make modifications as needed. With a little instruction, learners, too, can create stacks. HyperStudio (1997) makes authoring especially easy: Even elementary school children have produced interesting and colorful projects with it, as described below.

A Teacher's Progression into Authoring

Before getting involved with CALL, I specialized in second language teaching methodologies and gave conference workshops and in-service training on the Silent Way, the natural approach, and total physical response (TPR). To this day I stress active listening comprehension activities in classes for low-level listening and speaking; by *active* I mean the learner must do something to show understanding of the material. The software that hooked me on the use of computers for language learning was HyperCard (1997). Not only was it easy to learn, but I immediately realized its potential to engage students actively. After attending a 1-hour conference presentation demonstrating the ease of recording and incorporating sound files in stacks, I created a simple vocabulary stack (see Figure 25-8 for a sample). It was easy and enjoyable to copy and paste clip-art graphics onto electronic cards; add text, sound, and buttons for navigation; and play the sounds.

Another early endeavor was to modify a text-and-picture-matching vocabulary stack called HyperFlash (Seyler, 1987). In this stack, users click the mouse on the picture that they think depicts the word shown on the left side of the screen. If they choose the correct picture, a short musical jingle is played, and the next word appears (on a new card). A wrong selection results in a "boing" sound only. In the original stack, clicking a "Hint" button

Figure 25-8. Simple Vocabulary Stack Created With HyperCard (1995)

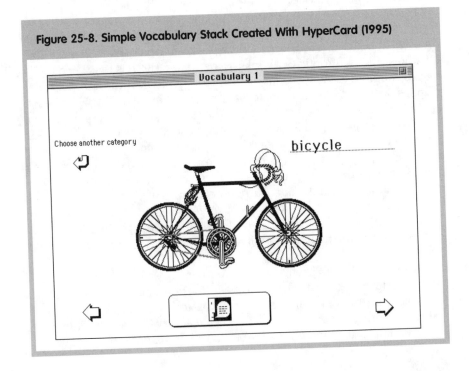

displayed a syllabicated version of the word. I replaced this option with a button that, when clicked, plays a spoken version of the word (Figure 25-9). I found this much more useful to my students for pronunciation and reading development.

These two projects were just warm-ups for my most ambitious stack modification, the conversion of a lesson for learning and practicing preposi-tions of location in Spanish, called "Preposiciones" (1990), a card in a stack called Classroom Ideas. To my excitement, I realized that this lesson was TPR on a computer! Learners click the picture of "la Señorita" to hear and see a command involving putting the hat, the ball, or the cup in a specific location in the bedroom; with the mouse, they then click and drag the object (actually, a movable button) to accomplish the task. If they are correct, la Señorita praises them and tells them to try another command. If they are wrong, she says the equivalent of, "No, not there," and repeats the original command. When I saw this lesson, I said to myself, "If I can get into the script, I can convert this wonderful exercise to English." After about 3 months of working with scripting way beyond my understanding, I managed

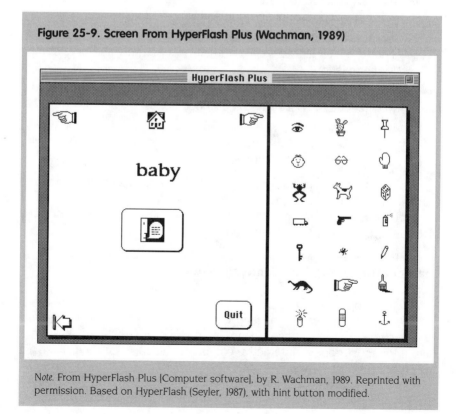

Figure 25-9. Screen From HyperFlash Plus (Wachman, 1989)

Note. From HyperFlash Plus [Computer software], by R. Wachman, 1989. Reprinted with permission. Based on HyperFlash (Seyler, 1987), with hint button modified.

to make the software work in English to my own satisfaction. Wrestling with any of the freeware and shareware scripts found in such collections as TESOL/CELIA '96 (1996) is a good way to learn how to author at more advanced levels.

Admittedly, my first several stacks do not meet all the software design criteria set out in chapters 11 and 27. However, these stacks actively engage learners and give them control over the pace of their learning, so they are useful in the CALL classroom.

Authoring for Autonomy and User Control

Using multimedia authoring software such as that just described, you can develop programs with any degree of user control, ranging from virtually none to full. HyperCard (1995) is by far the most common authoring program used by educators to develop their own software, and it allows the creation of language learning applications that fall into the autonomy types described in chapter 24:

1. teacher structured/fixed content (e.g., most of the early computerized tutorial and drill software)

2. learner structured/fixed content (e.g., software such as MacESL, 1992, in which learners choose their own pathway and time frame for completion)

3. teacher structured/variable content (e.g., authorable software like MacReader, McVicker, 1992, described above)

4. learner structured/variable content, achieved by allowing learners to become authors themselves using one of the authoring applications described above

Type 1 software is represented by programmed-learning software, exemplified by the stacks described previously, and are not considered further here. Type 3 applications are covered in the section on authorable software. Types 2 and 4 are described in more detail below.

Learner-Structured/Fixed-Content Software

Commercial Software

Numerous commercial language learning products based on HyperCard (1995) provide for a wide range of learner- and teacher-structured autonomy. One of the most popular interactive computer games, Myst (1995) is also a HyperCard product.

One of my favorite HyperCard-based programs, MacESL (1992; developed by the Hacienda–La Puente Unified School District and reviewed by

Wachman, 1995), gives learners fixed content and activities, but learners may choose their preferred methods of presentation and practice by navigating the list of lessons that serves as the main menu. Lessons include nine typical adult education situations, for example, talking to the landlord, making a doctor's appointment, and looking for a job. Clicking on the name of a lesson takes the user to the activities menu (Figure 25-10). Activities consist of a story presented in two formats—first animated with sound and then with text and sound—followed by six vocabulary and comprehension exercises. In all but the first activity, learners can take as much time as they want; they may repeat any activity as many times as they want and perform the activities in any order. Within some activities, they can look back at the story for help. Immediate visual feedback is given within exercises, and scores are shown on completion.

In pronunciation activities, learners see and hear words from the lesson. They can record their own pronunciation, listen to the software's model or their own production as many times as desired, and re-record in an attempt to improve their pronunciation. The learner decides when to go on to the

Figure 25-10. Activities Menu From "Looking for a Job" (MacESL, 1992)

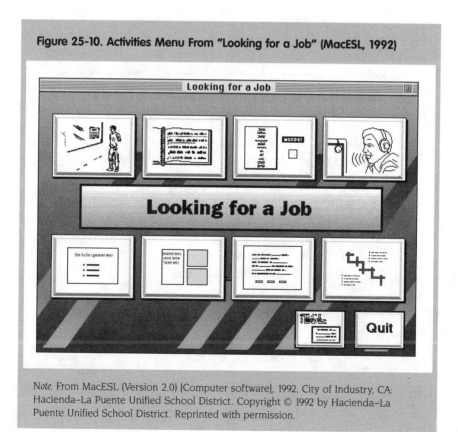

Note. From MacESL (Version 2.0) [Computer software], 1992, City of Industry, CA: Hacienda-La Puente Unified School District. Copyright © 1992 by Hacienda-La Puente Unified School District. Reprinted with permission.

next word in the lesson. Within a lesson, therefore, the content is fixed, but the learner has total control over the pace and the selection of activities.

Teacher-Made Applications

Classroom teachers have used HyperCard (1997) and other authoring software packages to create language learning applications that provide learner control. For example, Reading the Classifieds (Egbert, 1992; see Figure 25-11) uses sound, text, graphics, and an external newspaper to help beginning students read and understand the classified ads. Users look for love, a job, and a place to live, making their own life choices as they go. Using the same newspaper and advertisements as in Reading the Classifieds, learners can plan a spring trip in Travelling in the USA (Egbert & Stepanova, 1992; see Figure 25-12) or add the use of a special map and ride a bus around "The City" discovering information needed to create a guide for newcomers in CityGuide (Egbert & Jessup, 1991).

In Karaoke Conversation (Bradin, 1994; see Figure 25-13), students listen and then take one of the parts in a role play, recording their own voice and

Figure 25-11. Instruction Page From Reading the Classifieds (Egbert, 1992)

Reading the Classifieds

Introduction

The classified ads are an important part of the newspaper. They can help you find many things. For example, you can find a new car or a place to live.

This computer program will help you to understand and use the classified ads. To use this computer program, please read your ads carefully and choose the answers that you think are the best. There are no right or wrong answers! You can get vocabulary help by clicking on the words in boxes, like the word "ads" in the first sentence.

As you complete each part of the program, please answer the questions on the worksheet. When you are finished with the program, answer the questions on the "Personal Information" sheet. Give the sheet to your teacher, or share it with a friend.

I'm ready.

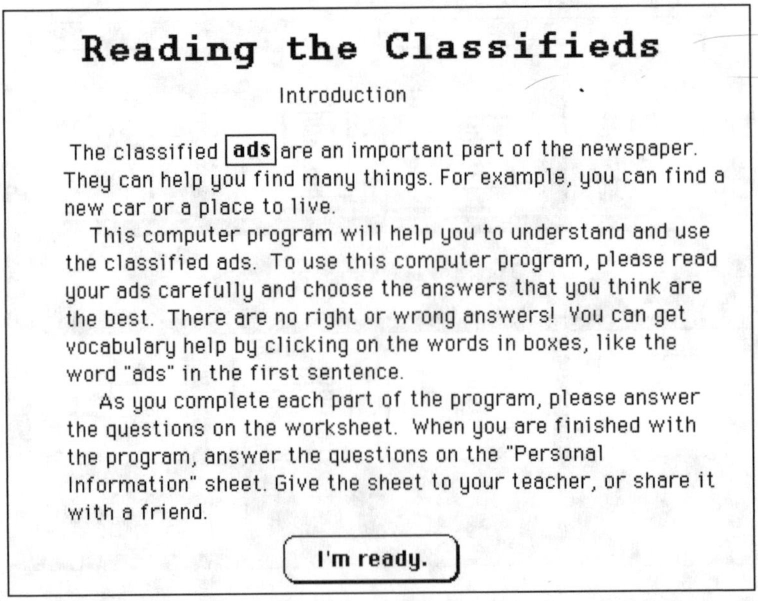

Note. From Reading the Classifieds [Computer software], by J. Egbert, 1992. Copyright © 1992 by J. Egbert. Reprinted with permission.

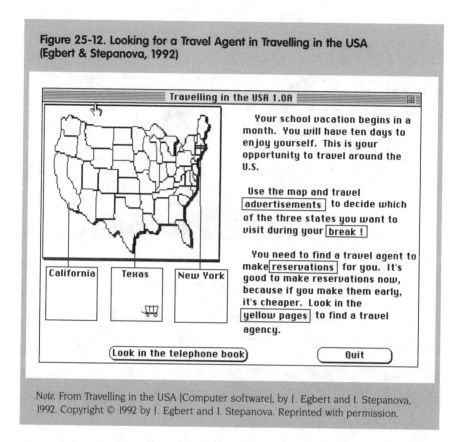

Figure 25-12. Looking for a Travel Agent in Travelling in the USA (Egbert & Stepanova, 1992)

Note. From Travelling in the USA [Computer software], by J. Egbert and I. Stepanova, 1992. Copyright © 1992 by J. Egbert and I. Stepanova. Reprinted with permission.

then playing back the whole conversation with their part included. In What Do You Say? (Egbert, 1995b; see Figure 25-14), learners hear a dialogue and read about a potential problem in six different social contexts. They then must choose an appropriate response or solution. When a less-than-correct answer is chosen, learners receive clear feedback about the possible consequences of their choice and can either stick with their solution or choose another.

Many other teacher-developed applications are found in freeware, shareware, and demo collections such as TESOL/CELIA '96 (1996) or the CD-ROMs produced by Computer-Using Educators (see Appendix A); others are available from the developer or from freeware and shareware archives (see chapter 14 and Appendix D).

Software Allowing Variable Autonomy: Learners as Authors

Engaging learners themselves in authoring can give them maximum autonomy, but if you desire more structure, you can author software in any of

Figure 25-13. Screen From Karaoke Conversation (Bradin, 1994)

Note. From Karaoke Conversation [Computer software], by C. Bradin, 1994. Copyright © 1994 by C. Bradin. Reprinted with permission.

the autonomous styles listed above. For example, you can supply the content and dictate exactly how the students will construct the software product (Type 1); provide the content but let the learners develop their own structure for presentation (Type 2); give learners free choice of content but prescribe the steps and structures to build (Type 3); or, after giving basic instruction on authoring operations, set learners free to decide on their own content as well as its form (Type 4).

Egbert (1995a) and Hanson-Smith (1997b) describe activities that promote self-direction by learners. Egbert describes the technologizing of a formerly nontechnological language learning strategy: the construction and solution of *action mazes*, a Type 3 activity (teacher structured/variable content). Action mazes are communication problems that are usually written out on paper cards. Learners proceed from card to card in search of a solution. An example cited by Egbert deals with choosing between "doing what's right and doing what your friends want" (p. 11). As the author says, "Action mazes seem to lend themselves particularly well to electronic forums" (p. 9). She goes on to suggest that this activity can be changed from a Type 3 to a Type 4, noting that "asking learners to find information and

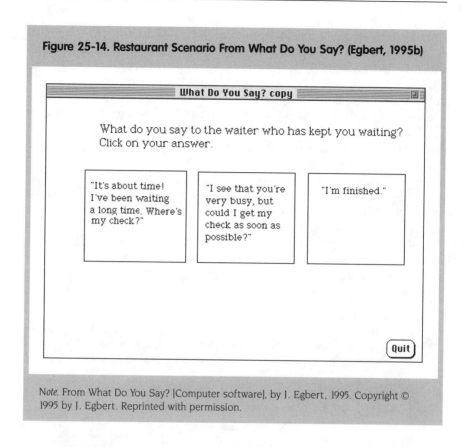

Figure 25-14. Restaurant Scenario From What Do You Say? (Egbert, 1995b)

> **What Do You Say? copy**
>
> What do you say to the waiter who has kept you waiting? Click on your answer.
>
> | "It's about time! I've been waiting a long time. Where's my check?" | "I see that you're very busy, but could I get my check as soon as possible?" | "I'm finished." |
>
> **Quit**

Note. From What Do You Say? [Computer software], by J. Egbert, 1995. Copyright © 1995 by J. Egbert. Reprinted with permission.

assisting them in putting it together themselves may be more productive than providing learners with information and asking them to discuss and choose answers" (p. 9).

"Multimedia Projects for EFL/ESL Students" (Hanson-Smith, 1997b) is a valuable guide for developing authored projects with students. It describes in detail a 2-week summer institute in which teachers and middle and high school students authored their own multimedia projects in a Type 4 activity (variable content structured by the learners). Hanson-Smith describes the formation of collaborative teams and the planning that she believes is crucial to success. In addition to writing text, students created graphics, used a scanner to digitize some photos, obtained maps and photos from the Internet, and recorded and incorporated sounds and video into their stacks (see Figure 25-15). Projects described and illustrated include "Hometown Magazine," in which "students research their home/school locale and create a presentation that will be of interest to their peers or to other students who might want to come to their school" (p. 8) and "Making Cross-Cultural Friends," in which "students research gestures, common greetings, and some of the background of their countries in order to make other students aware of possible cross-cultural conflicts" (p. 9). Hanson-Smith chose HyperStudio (1997) as the authoring medium because of its extreme ease of operation and fully integrated color. As she explains, multimedia projects can "give students control of the creative process, enhance cognitive and language learning skills, and result in finished products that they can take home or send out to the world electronically." Further, this project demonstrates that "students of almost any age or level of language proficiency can create exciting presentations" (p. 3).

Adult ESL students can create a variety of applications, from electronic portfolios to vocabulary quizzes. Figure 25-16 shows a screen from Jeopardize, created by international students to test their classmates' knowledge of U.S. culture. Figure 25-17 shows a problem-setting screen from the HyperCard (1995) application Friends, created by adult students to help elementary school students think about the topic of child abuse. In this software, decisions made by the user lead to a variety of outcomes.

Figure 25-15. Card from a Student-Created HyperStudio (1997) Stack

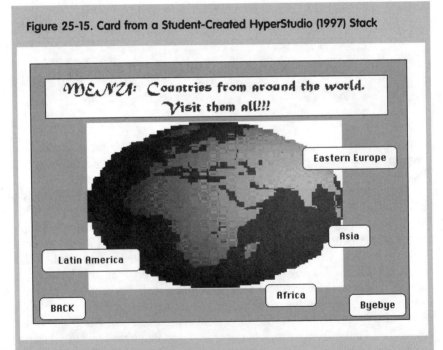

Note. Produced by the Internationally Cool Team (L. Anguiano, L. Ayrapetyan, Y. Berhane, E. Contreras, A. Divakov, T. Fayyer, G. Guevara, M. Luc, W. Najera, H.-T. Nguyen, E. Vlayov), 1996, Title VII Summer Institute, Jonas Salk Middle School/ Encina High School Academies, Sacramento, CA.

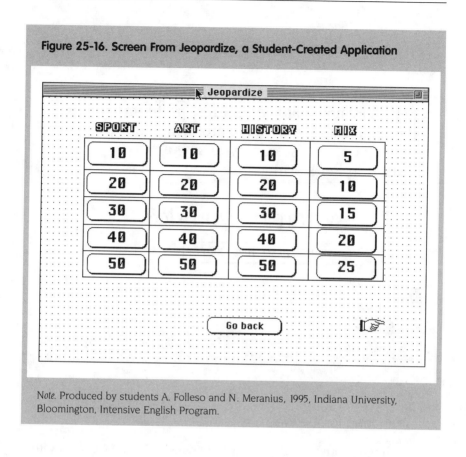

Figure 25-16. Screen From Jeopardize, a Student-Created Application

Note. Produced by students A. Folleso and N. Meranius, 1995, Indiana University, Bloomington, Intensive English Program.

Students as young as elementary-school age can readily master such software as HyperStudio (1997), which has a mini–drawing program, colors, ready-made templates, a built-in tutorial, numerous sample programs for inspiration, an electronic bulletin board on which teachers share ideas, and a World Wide Web site for instant upgrades and the exchange of information. Students can paste in their own photos and drawings from a scanner, add a video, play a laser disc or audio file, record their own voices and sound effects, or use the hundreds of clip-art and audio files that come with the software. For older students, Microsoft PowerPoint 97 (1996), a presentation graphics program that is often loaded on new computers as part of software bundles, is a good choice, and although its templates are more adult in appearance, it too is very flexible as a tool for presenting students' original work. Either program can be learned in just a few hours, and because most such programs use a fairly standard interface for their tools, the students are also learning highly transferable computer skills as they create their own presentations.

Figure 25-17. Problem Setting in Friends, a Student-Created Application

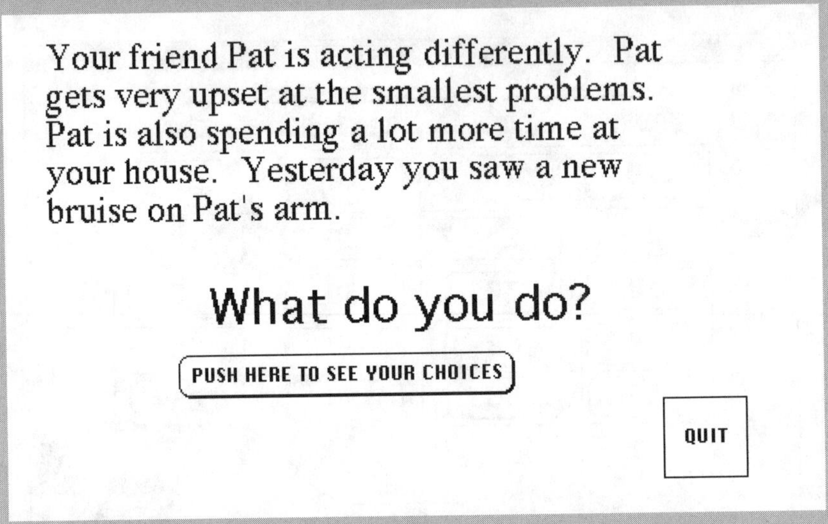

Your friend Pat is acting differently. Pat gets very upset at the smallest problems. Pat is also spending a lot more time at your house. Yesterday you saw a new bruise on Pat's arm.

What do you do?

(PUSH HERE TO SEE YOUR CHOICES)

QUIT

Note. Produced by members of the Technology and Language Learning class, 1995, Washington State University, Pullman, Department of Teaching and Learning.

Authoring for the Web

Most authoring software, such as HyperStudio (1997), now comes with a Web interface that allows the stacks to be converted to Hypertext Markup Language (HTML) and played on the Internet, giving students the opportunity to show their work to a wide authentic audience. (For more information on Web projects, see chapter 7.) However, students can learn fairly easily how to write Web pages in HTML or use a simple HTML editor, such as Microsoft FrontPage® 98 (1998). The resulting activities are either Type 3, in which the teacher specifies the structure, or Type 4, in which the students are turned loose in the medium as they master the code.

Beginning HTML is fairly simple with a Web browser, such as Netscape Navigator® Gold (1997). Students can download and study the document source code of a favorite page by selecting that item in the "View" menu. (Note that commands written in Common Gateway Interface [CGI], which allows input into forms, searchable databases, and other types of file manipulation on-line, are not available through this method.) They can copy the source code, paste it into the HTML editor, and then paste their own text, photo file references, audio file references, and navigation links (universal resource locators [URLs]) over the appropriate places in the document source page. A built-in editor, such as the one in Netscape Navigator Gold (1997; Figure 25-18) allows students to make changes and add pictures, buttons, and links with the same intuitive graphics tools used in multimedia presentation software. Figures 25-19 and 25-20 illustrate a simple Web page created by ESL students and its document source code in HTML.

Students quickly learn some of the HTML code from this copying and pasting process. For more advanced students, or for those who wish to gain more mastery of the Web medium, learning HTML from scratch is not difficult. Free on-line lessons and directions for using HTML can be downloaded at many Web sites, and many publishers, such as Claris and Macromedia, sell HTML authoring software for less than $100. Most Web

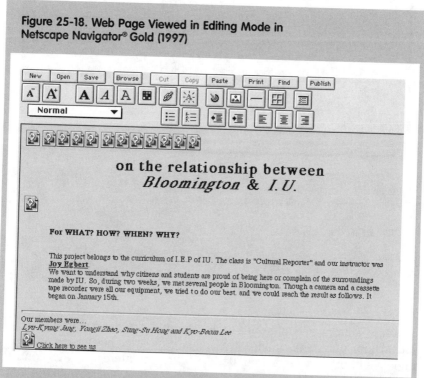

Figure 25-18. Web Page Viewed in Editing Mode in Netscape Navigator® Gold (1997)

Note. Squares designate graphics and buttons corresponding to other files not located on the same hard drive. Produced by students L.-K. Jang, Y. Zhao, S.-S. Hong, and K.-B. Lee, 1996, Indiana University, Bloomington, Intensive English Program. From Netscape Navigator Gold (Version 3.02) [Computer software], 1997, Mountain View, CA: Netscape Communications. Portions copyright © 1998 by Netscape Communications Corporation. All rights reserved. Netscape and Netscape Navigator are registered trademarks of Netscape Communications Corporation in the United States and other countries.

Figure 25-19. Web Page in Figure 25-18 Viewed in a Browser Window

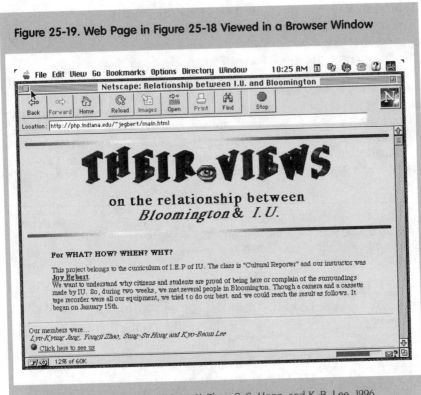

Note. Produced by students L.-K. Jang, Y. Zhao, S.-S. Hong, and K.-B. Lee, 1996, Indiana University, Bloomington, Intensive English Program. From Netscape Navigator Gold (Version 3.02) [Computer software], 1997, Mountain View, CA: Netscape Communications. Portions copyright © 1998 by Netscape Communications Corporation. All rights reserved. Netscape, Netscape Navigator, and the Netscape N logo are registered trademarks of Netscape Communications Corporation in the United States and other countries.

browsers, editors, and authoring tools offer templates as a starting point. If your school, university, or intensive language program has its own Web site, student-authored projects are a perfect source of interesting Web content. In an on-line school literary journal, poets can read their own work in an audio file; a sculpture can be displayed in a video taken in the round and manipulated by dragging with the mouse; and photos and drawings can be viewed as in a paper journal, but the electronic version can incorporate animated cartoons and student-produced videos. In addition to contributing significantly to autonomy in learning, a student-produced Web page is also an excellent way to advertise a school globally.

Figure 25-20. HTML Document Source Code for Web Page in Figures 25-18 and 25-19

```
<HTML><HEAD>
<TITLE>Relationship between I.U. and Bloomington
</TITLE>
</HEAD>

<body bgcolor="#ebc79e">  [This makes the background light orange.]

<img src="rainban.gif">  [This is a horizontal line graphic.]

<center><img src="T.GIF"><img src="H.GIF"><img
src="E.GIF"><img
src="I.GIF">
<img src="R.GIF"><img src="eye.gif"><img
src="V.GIF"><img src="I.GIF"><img
src="E.GIF"><img src="W.GIF"><img src="S.GIF">  ["gifs" are
graphics.]

<h1>on the relationship between<br><EM>Bloomington</EM>
&amp;<EM>
I.U.</EM></h1></center></h2>  ["H1" signifies "header" plus size]

<img src="rainban.gif"><p>

<blockquote>
<B>For WHAT? HOW? WHEN? WHY?</B><br><p>  ["B" means "bold," and
"br" and "p" are line break and paragraph break]
  This project belongs to the curriculum of I.E.P of IU.
The class is
"Cultural Reporter" and our instructor was <a
href="http://ezinfo.ucs.indiana.edu/~jegbert/">
<b>Joy Egbert</a></b>.
<br>  [This link takes you to Egbert's home page]
We want to understand why citizens and students are
proud of being here or complain of the surroundings
made by IU. So, during two weeks, we met several people
in Bloomington. Though a camera and a cassette tape
recorder were all our equipment, we tried to do our
best. and we could reach the result as follows. It
began on January 15th.<p>
</blockquote>
<hr size=3>
Our members were...<br>
<I>Lyu-Kyung Jang, Yongji Zhao, Sung-Su Hong and Kyo-
Beom Lee</I><br>
<img src="pupleball.gif"><a href="every.html"> Click
here to see us</a>
<hr size=3><br><p>
</body>  [This signifies the end of the body and then the end of the document]
</HTML>
```

Summary

This chapter has looked at authorable software—applications that you can adapt to your students' needs by adding your own material—and a range of authoring software—which you and your students can use to modify or create applications. Each type of software can help you and your students enhance language learning in one or more of the autonomous styles described in chapter 24.

Chapter 26

CALL Issues: Language Learning Over Distance

Ruth Vilmi

In this chapter, I describe some of the many activities that come under the umbrella of language through distance for the independent learner. The Internet has provided a whole new world: first, the world of electronic mail and multiuser domains (MUDs) and object-oriented MUDs (MOOs) for virtual conferencing, and since 1995, the World Wide Web, which brings with it the ability to send pictures, sounds, and video all over the world within seconds and to create interactive documents that respond directly and immediately to students' input. This rapidly developing technology is bound to change teaching methods and enhance distance education for the independent learner. This chapter examines how the Internet is being used for language learning at present, explores the new learning opportunities that the Internet has enabled, and touches on how it may affect language learning in the future.

Distance learning is not a new concept. For years, people have been taking correspondence courses, in which the learners receive written materials and tasks by surface mail and return the completed tasks to a tutor to be marked and graded. At the end of the course the learner might take a final test or a public examination arranged locally, such as the University of Cambridge Local Examinations Syndicate's tests or the Test of English as a Foreign Language. After World War II, the British Broadcasting Company (BBC) was a pioneer of language courses on the radio, which have been enjoyed by enormous audiences since the 1920s. Then came the era of television. In 1963, Harold Wilson launched the *University of the Air* and in 1964, after he became the British prime minister, asked his minister for the arts, Jennie Lee, to develop the Open University. The first 24,000 students were admitted in 1971. Students met for the occasional seminar and followed courses on television. Since then, Open Universities have sprung up all over the world.

Radio and television still are very popular and effective media for language learning. Audio- and videotapes are also quite popular for learning foreign languages. Nowadays, some distance-learning courses are sold on video, and some courses consist of a combination of video and conferencing. For example, at the University of Massachusetts, the course *Oral Skills Improvement for Foreign-Born Professionals* (Dauer, 1998) consists of 10 hours of videotapes for lease; learners can call in with questions. Teleconferencing, a useful tool for distance learning in which subscribers are linked to the televised instructor through an open telephone line, is becoming increasingly popular, too.

As a medium of instruction, the Internet (and its multimedia component, the World Wide Web) is truly global, and it is interactive in a way that none of the aforementioned media were; it is also time and place independent. Language teachers saw the potential of the Internet as a tool for learning before teachers in other fields did, even though mathematics had always been the main subject associated with computers. Already by 1990, pioneering language teachers had formed discussion groups. The discussion list TESL-L (see chapter 6 and Appendix B) was started in 1991 for teachers of ESL. I created a local newsgroup for my students at Helsinki University of Technology (HUT) in 1992 and, in 1994, created an international newsgroup for teachers who were interested in starting e-mail projects (see Vilmi, 1994). In 1995, at the 29th Annual TESOL Convention, a core group of computer-using language teachers gave presentations about the Internet and what it could mean for language teaching and learning. After that convention, the discussion list NETEACH-L (see Moody, n.d., http://www .ilc.cuhk.edu.hk/english/neteach/main.htm; and Appendix B) emerged for teachers interested in using the Internet in language education. Teachers worldwide continued to exchange ideas, and mailboxes overflowed. Soon afterward, Kristina Pfaff-Harris had the brilliant idea of creating ESLoop (see ESLoop Index, n.d., http://www.webring.org/cgi-bin/webring?index&ring =esloop) to link ESOL teachers who were active on the Internet, thus providing easy access to many language learning sites for English learners. ESLoop may be accessed at any member site, but you might begin at Pfaff-Harris's site, *Linguistic Funland* (http://www.linguistic-funland.com/), which contains an index to the 90 or so member sites. ESLoop is well worth a visit for language learners or people interested in finding out about ESL/EFL learning on the Internet.

Although very few distance courses, and perhaps none in the traditional sense, exist specifically for language learning according to the information I have found on-line so far, language learners will find more and more ways to use the Internet. In the following sections I list ways in which autonomous language learners have used the Internet along with some sites to browse for an idea of the rich opportunities the Web offers.

The Internet has been used in language learning for

- finding references and doing research (e.g., discovering vocabulary and collocations typically used in content areas)
- locating listening resources
- finding grammar rules (e.g., using on-line writing labs [OWLs])
- finding interactive exercises, activities, or drills for vocabulary, grammar, listening, and reading
- analyzing texts, concordancing, and searching for structures, thus deducing rules
- publishing writing with the opportunity to receive feedback from readers
- communicating internationally with e-mail keypals or newsgroups
- communicating in real time (e.g., synchronous conferencing, Internet Relay Chat [IRC], MOOs, videoconferencing, text-based chat rooms)
- on-line courses with tutors or teachers

Reference and Research

The World Wide Web as a reference tool is a global library on the desktop. When learning to use the Web for research purposes, independent learners need to learn two very important skills: (a) how to use a search engine (e.g., AltaVista, http://www.altavista.com/; Excite, http://www.excite.com/; Yahoo!, http://www.yahoo.com/; see also Appendix C) and (b) how to discriminate.

The ability to distinguish high-quality from low-quality material has always been important, even in examining textbooks, but not as critical as it is when doing research on the Web. Books are edited and deemed to be worthy of selling before being published and, furthermore, have usually been selected by the teacher or the education authority for a particular level, class, and culture. However, on the Internet, anybody with space on a Web server can publish whatever he or she chooses. Thus the Internet contains both the best and the worst kinds of literature—dictionaries and encyclopedias as well as pornography. Some universities publish their research papers, providing the public with a mine of specialized information. The Web abounds with possibilities for broadening independent learners' vocabulary in English while they search and read for content. However, time is always limited, and students have to learn how to select suitable material for the task at hand and disregard the rest. A highly recommended on-line resource for this purpose is *Evaluating Web Resources* (Alexander & Tate, 1997, http://www.science.widener.edu/~withers/webeval.htm).

In addition to all the wonderful content sources on the World Wide Web, many *push* services, particularly for news and stock quotes, transmit content to users according to their specifications. Push services can be extremely useful for language learners, who can specify content that they are particularly interested in. Two examples are CNN *Custom News* (http://customnews.cnn.com/), for news, and *My Yahoo!* (http://my.yahoo.com/), for a wide variety of areas, such as stock quotes, health tips, sports scores, and technology news. Collins Cobuild offers *Wordwatch* (n.d., http://titania.cobuild.collins.co.uk/wordwatch.html), an unusual service for individuals wishing to develop their vocabulary. Responses to questions about vocabulary and other English matters are sent directly to the user by e-mail. (To subscribe, see Collins Cobuild's Web site, http://titania.cobuild.collins.co.uk/.)

Listening Resources

Among other useful resources for the independent learner on the Internet, many Web pages offer audio files and corresponding transcripts, which are useful for listening practice. Users need only download RealPlayer™ (1998; for audio and video) and QuickTime® (1998) software, both free at the developers' respective Web sites. Audio files may then be played through a Web site or downloaded and saved to the hard drive for repeated practice off-line. I mention here only three important resources. (See chapter 9 for a complete discussion of listening skills activities; also see Appendix F.) Voice of America's Web site (http://www.voa.gov/) and BBC *World Service: Listen Live 24 Hours a Day* (1998, http://www.bbc.co.uk/worldservice/) contain audio archives of radio programs around the world in many different languages. *The World Wide Web Virtual Library: Audio* (Bowen, 1998, http://www.comlab.ox.ac.uk/archive/audio.html) contains a list of Web sites with audio files, including a sound library of spoken excerpts from famous novels, topics related to computing and broadcasting, and music channels, both classical and pop.

Grammar Rules

Many Web sites offer grammar rules and exercises, but probably the most comprehensive is *Online Writing Lab* (OWL; http://owl.english.purdue.edu/), created by Muriel Harris at Purdue University (see Figure 14-5). The *Resources for Writers* page contains links to hundreds of useful handouts on grammar rules and writing as well as exercises (see Figure 9-2). Since OWL's inception, many other labs offering pages that resemble mini–traditional grammar books in digital form have sprung up. These labs are places for the independent learner to get expert advice from native speakers (see Appendix G).

Interactive Drills and Practice Activities

The Internet is also a resource for interactive exercises: multiple-choice drills, reading comprehension practice, and listening exercises that are scored and corrected as the learner watches. Grammar drills written by myself and my students can be found at *Grammar Help* (Vilmi, 1998a, http://www.hut.fi/~rvilmi/LangHelp/Grammar/).

Drills do not suit everyone, but certainly many students like them, and because the computer never tires, it is an excellent tool for doing drills. *Dave's ESL Café* (http://www.eslcafe.com/; created by Dave Sperling), which has interactive quizzes and all kinds of bulletin boards, is a big hit with autonomous learners and teachers alike. It offers a wide variety of pages for the autonomous learner, including *One-Stop Search, Quiz Center, Help Center, Idea Page, Graffiti Wall, Question Page, Links for Students, Links for Teachers, Message Exchange, E-Mail Connection,* and *Student Connection.* On many of these pages, the independent learner can find other learners to practice with. Sperling's site is a good example of how independent learners can work collaboratively on the Web. The quizzes are limited neither to grammar exercises nor to Sperling's work alone. Dennis Oliver, for example, has contributed a large collection of phrasal verbs and idiom exercises. Sperling and Oliver (1997, http://www.eslcafe.com/animals.cgi) have also created Hangman, an on-line word game (see Figure 26-1).

Figure 26-1. Hangman Game From *Dave's ESL Café* (Sperling & Oliver, 1997)

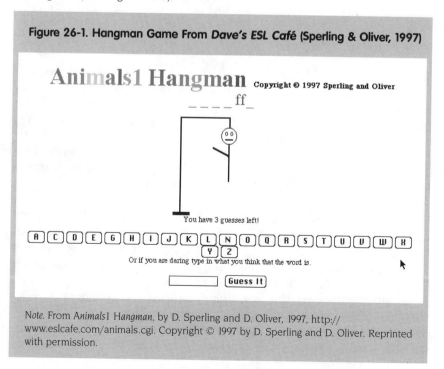

Note. From *Animals1 Hangman,* by D. Sperling and D. Oliver, 1997, http://www.eslcafe.com/animals.cgi. Copyright © 1997 by D. Sperling and D. Oliver. Reprinted with permission.

The *English Grammar Pages* (Revusky, 1997, http://web.jet.es/jrevusky /esl.html) offer both rules and examples. Other pages have foreign language (bilingual) exercises, such as *Schumann's Foreign Language Tests/Exercises* (Schumann, 1998, http://ourworld.compuserve.com/homepages/joschu/).

For listening exercises, *Learning Oral English Online* (Li, 1998, http:// www.lang.uiuc.edu/r-li5/book/) gives several examples of the use of sound files played on RealPlayer (1998) software, with such dialogues as "Making Friends" and "Asking for the Way," written by ESL/EFL teachers from around the world. Students listen on-line and may replay the file as often as they wish.

Reading comprehension for the beginning learner can be found at CNN *San Francisco: Interactive Learning Resources* (1998, http://www.cnnsf.com/education/education.html), cosponsored by the Outreach and Technical Assistance Network. News stories are rewritten in special English for learners and are followed by a series of reading comprehension questions of various types, such as multiple choice and sequencing. Students also have the opportunity to write about the news and read and comment on what other learners have written.

Among many other sites, *The Internet TESL Journal* (1998, http://www .aitech.ac.jp/~iteslj/) brings together many teachers' work, such as on-line crossword puzzles (see Figure 26-2) and grammar and vocabulary exercises based on such topics as the U.S. holidays.

Deduction of Rules

Several Internet sites offer the opportunity to analyze language with concordancers, search engines that arrange all found items in a list, usually in the center of the page, with their surrounding context (see Appendix G). Thus users can examine grammar structures, vocabulary, tense sequences, and so on in focused, highly contextualized groups in authentic texts. Outstanding work in this area is found in *Tim Johns' Data-Driven Learning Page* (Johns, 1998, http://web.bham.ac.uk/johnstf/timconc.htm), which is certainly of interest to language learners and teachers. The site contains bibliographic references, links to interesting software, and samples of lessons using data-driven learning. Collins Cobuild's Web site (http://titania .cobuild .collins.co.uk/) also offers all kinds of ways to use concordancers in analyzing and learning about the English language. Fill-in-the blank exercises using authentic reading matter are found at the site of a competition to win a dictionary; past contests are used for practice.

Another interesting site is *Grammar Safari* (Mills & Salzmann, 1998, http://deil.lang.uiuc.edu/web.pages/grammarsafari.html; see Figure 26-3). *Grammar Safari* is somewhat more difficult to use than a concordancer; students use the Web's search engines to look for particular words or

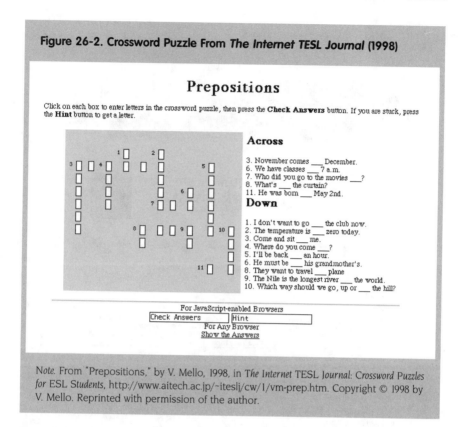

Figure 26-2. Crossword Puzzle From *The Internet TESL Journal* (1998)

Prepositions

Click on each box to enter letters in the crossword puzzle, then press the **Check Answers** button. If you are stuck, press the **Hint** button to get a letter.

Across

3. November comes ___ December.
6. We have classes ___ 7 a.m.
7. Who did you go to the movies ___?
8. What's ___ the curtain?
11. He was born ___ May 2nd.

Down

1. I don't want to go ___ the club now.
2. The temperature is ___ zero today.
3. Come and sit ___ me.
4. Where do you come ___?
5. I'll be back ___ an hour.
6. He must be ___ his grandmother's.
8. They want to travel ___ plane
9. The Nile is the longest river ___ the world.
10. Which way should we go, up or ___ the hill?

For JavaScript-enabled Browsers

Check Answers   Hint

For Any Browser
Show the Answers

Note. From "Prepositions," by V. Mello, 1998, in *The Internet TESL Journal: Crossword Puzzles for ESL Students,* http://www.aitech.ac.jp/~iteslj/cw/1/vm-prep.htm. Copyright © 1998 by V. Mello. Reprinted with permission of the author.

collocations, thus providing a wealth of vocabulary as it is used in authentic communication. This site makes the most of the Web's potential. On a related page, *World Wide Web Activities That Work (and Why),* Salzmann (1998, http://deil.lang.uiuc.edu/resources/TESOL/Ann/grammarcorpus_index.html) has posted handouts to teach others how to take advantage of the Internet's search potential.

Electronic Publication

Many sites offer learners the opportunity to publish on the Web and receive responses to their writing as content (see Appendixes F and G). CNN *San Francisco: Interactive Learning Resources* (1998, http://www.cnnsf.com/education /education.html), mentioned above, offers this feature, as does *Graffiti Wall* in *Dave's ESL Café* (http://www.eslcafe.com/). More extended work can be found at *Fluency Through Fables* (1997, http://www.comenius.com/fable/), where readers of fables are encouraged to write about them and post their

Figure 26-3. Welcome Page in *Grammar Safari* (Mills & Salzman, 1998)

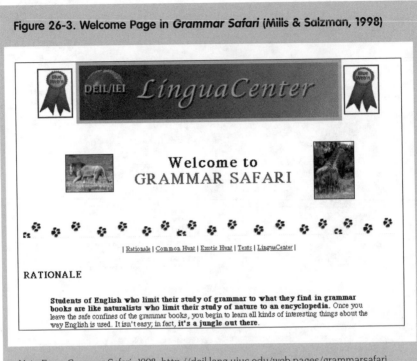

comments for others to read. *Heinle & Heinle Museum of Cultural Imagery* (1996, http://www.thomson.com/heinle/museum/welcome.html) includes a "school," which has photos and short essays to inspire composition as well as a place for independent learners to post their writing and read and write about others' work. A particularly attractive magazine is TOPICS, *An Online Magazine by and for Learners of English* (Peters & Peters, 1997, http://www .rice.edu/projects/topics/Electronic/main.html; see Figure 26-4).

International Keypals

As discussed in chapters 2 and 12, learners writing to others in the fairly rapid exchanges of e-mail gradually adjust their expressions to the forms and collocations of their correspondents. There is also evidence that keypalling is inspiring a new interest in the structures and expressions of informal oral language.

Figure 26-4. Home Page of *TOPICS* (1997)

TOPICS

An Online Magazine by and for Learners of English

TOPICS is an electronic magazine where learners of English as a second language consider topics of interest to them, express their ideas and opinions, and illustrate their writings with drawings and photographs.

Note. From TOPICS: *An Online Magazine by and for Learners of English*, by S. Peters and T. Peters, 1997, http://www.rice.edu/projects/topics/Electronic/main.html. Copyright © 1997 by S. Peters and T. Peters. Reprinted with permission.

The Internet is readily used for communicating internationally by e-mail (see Appendix B). Never before has the autonomous learner been so easily able to communicate globally with both native and nonnative speakers of English and other languages. Independent learners may participate in discussion groups and mailing lists on areas of professional concern or just discuss hobbies and general interests.

Many thousands of newsgroups operate on the Web; luckily, there is also a Web page on which to search for these newsgroups: *Deja News* (http://www.dejanews.com/), a free service that allows the independent learner to seek others with similar interests.

Synchronous Communication

As described in chapter 22, MOOs and MUDs are popular places in which learners communicate in real time (see Appendix B for a list of MOOs and MUDs). MUDs are very popular with HUT students, and sometimes hundreds of players are connected to the same game at the same time. MOOing is a hands-on approach to learning over distance while communicating with other people, often strangers, and interest in MOOs seems to be growing. Students can also use the MOO environment completely independently once they understand the software commands. A number of sites provide information about how to use a MOO and access MOO lessons independently (see Falsetti, n.d., http://schmooze.hunter.cuny.edu:8888/).

When I wanted to establish a MUD for my students to use for their collaborative work, a capable team and I built HUT *Virtual Language Centre* (VLC; Vilmi, 1997a, http://www.hut.fi/~rvilmi/Project/VLC/). The MUD experienced technical difficulties with international communications systems and problems caused by time differences of up to 14 hours among users. However, all agreed that VLC was an essential part of HUT *Internet Writing Project* (Vilmi, 1998b, http://www.hut.fi/~rvilmi/Project/; a class-to-class exchange is described at the site), as it allows students access to each other in real time across distance.

Educational MOOs and MOOs for learners of many different foreign languages also exist. Lists of MOOs can be found at HUT *Virtual Language Centre*; among them is *schMOOze University* (Falsetti, n.d., http://schmooze .hunter.cuny.edu:8888/; see chapter 22).

On-Line Feedback

An astonishing feature of the Internet in its present chaotic state is the number of sites that offer free assistance to language learners. Also becoming popular are sites that use Internet features to edit students' written work. *Using* HTML *for Online Editing* (Bowers, 1997, http://www.tnis.net /rbowers/demo.html) shows how frames in a Web browser can be used to link student errors to a prepared set of grammar queries and instructor comments (see Figure 26-5).

Another example of on-line editing is found in *Business English and Academic Writing* (1997, http://www.comenius.com/writing/). The pages include an explanation of how the instructors of a course on business writing used e-mail and the special editing features of a word processor to correct students' writing.

On-Line Course Work

On the Internet, students may enroll in an increasing number of courses in a variety of subjects at all levels—including degree and advanced degree programs—anywhere in the world (see Appendix H). However, as of this writing very few EFL/ESL courses are found on the Web. David Winet's courses, about 14 in all at this writing, were perhaps the first on-line, and he offers them free of charge on an experimental basis in *English for Internet* (http://www.study.com/). When asked about on-line ESL/EFL courses, Winet wrote,

Figure 26-5. Model of the Use of Hyperlinking and Frames to Comment on Written Work (After Bowers, 1997)

• _Class home page_ • _E-mail Instructor_ • _grammarON LINE_ • _Grammar Safari_ • _OWL_	STUDENT ESSAY The student's essay appears in this window. Various passages in the essay are hyperlinked (the underlined portions), so that they will jump to instructor's notes (in the lower right-hand box) or to grammar points (in the lower left-hand window), which may in turn be linked to some of the grammar help pages on the Web. The instructor could set up the templates and teach students how to insert their text in the HTML page, and then send it to him or her electronically. Or the instructor could simply copy in the students' essays, which would be delivered electronically, either by e-mail or on a diskette. Students might also post their essays in draft to each other for comments, and pursue the search for grammar assistance on the Web, using for example, the Grammar Safari page at the DEIL LinguaCenter.

	GRAMMAR ASSISTANCE be linked to - see Passive Voice at this Web page grammar points - check out Mark Wade Lieu's grammar help at grammarONLINE	INSTRUCTOR'S COMMENTS student's essay - It would be good to use a real student essay as an example. hyperlinked - a hyperlinked word is underlined. Use your BACK button to return to this page.

Note. Underlined terms are hyperlinks to comments in other frames or pages.

I'm getting more and more student applications; there's definitely interest out there. Teachers work for the experience, as we have no money as yet. Those who want the experience, teach. The others, of course, don't. The key problem, as David Paul has pointed out, is retention of students. I believe that fundamentally learning English is a chore, so in the absence of 1) constraint 2) live encouragement 3) investment of one's own cash—that is, the student's own cash—and 4) fear of looking bad in front of other students, a high dropout rate is going to be the norm, no matter how great the teaching or how cool the approach. (personal communication, April 1997)

A few EFL/ESL courses are being produced at universities, and more are being developed all the time. A list of both teacher-training and EFL courses can be seen at *On-Line Courses* (Vilmi, 1997c, http://www.hut.fi/~rvilmi /online/).

One potentially interesting site for EFL/ESL teaching is *Merlin: World Class* (1997, http://www.hull.ac.uk/merlin/; see Figure 26-6). Approximately 30 learners worldwide followed a 15-week Internet-based EFL course in fall 1997. The group was supported by a live tutor and help desk. The courses

Figure 26-6. Home Page of *Merlin: World Class* (1997)

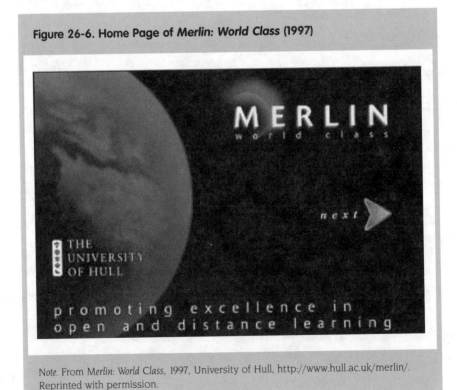

Note. From *Merlin: World Class*, 1997, University of Hull, http://www.hull.ac.uk/merlin/. Reprinted with permission.

English for Business and English for Communication were offered in spring 1998, with a week's free trial.

Most of the fully developed language learning courses on-line seem to be writing courses, for example, UVic Online English Writing Course (Holmes, 1997c, http://web.uvic.ca/hrd/OLCourse/; see chapter 14). Holmes believes that the teaching of writing is ideally suited to the Internet environment:

> This site is an on-line textbook. The objective of the project is to deliver interactive instruction in writing skills to students working on any computer platform running a current browser, anywhere on the Internet. (Holmes, 1997c, n.p.)

At the heart of the course are many practice exercises and assignments, which students submit to the instructor on Web forms. The degree of interaction between student and instructor is intended to be high, and much of the real learning is likely to take place by e-mail as the instructor responds to exercises and assignments and deals with questions. This course is not intended to be an automatic one that requires little time on the part of the teacher; teaching a class in this way, although involving little or no classroom time, would in fact take as much time as or more time than teaching any conventional course (Holmes, 1997c).

According to Holmes (personal communication, April 1997), one probable reason why very few EFL/ESL courses are found on the Internet is the enormous amount of time that it takes to create such a course. He also noted that being a teacher of a distance-learning course is very demanding. Only one chapter of Holmes's course is accessible to the public; to view the rest requires a password. This fact leads me to believe that there indeed must be many other courses on-line, but perhaps the majority of them are closed to public view—understandably so, given the time and energy involved in creating them.

An unusual on-line language learning project is International Tandem Network (http://www.slf.ruhr-uni-bochum.de/), in which students exchange e-mail in order to learn languages together. Designed as a supplement to foreign language classes, the Network states on its home page that its goal is "autonomous and intercultural language learning in tandem." The network has been funded since July 1994 by the Commission of the European Union. Twelve universities from 10 European countries have been working together to expand the network and develop didactic materials designed for tandem partners, organizers, and foreign language teachers. Their materials, including bibliographies and a guide to the Internet, are free for individual users and for institutions if they do not use the material commercially. The Tandem Server database contains tasks for remote and face-to face activities and has mirrors at universities in several countries.

Non-ESL, noncredit courses, particularly those on using the Internet and Hypertext Markup Language (HTML), abound. For example, *EnglishNet: Writing for the Web* (Hammersmith, 1997, http://www.uic.edu/depts/tie/net/) is an elective class at the Tutorium in Intensive English at the University of Illinois at Chicago. The 4-day class was designed to introduce students to the World Wide Web as a tool for practicing and improving their English through the research and development of collaborative Web sites. Students' final projects for the course each semester are posted at the site.

On-line classes such as those described above can be valuable for language learning, and they have the advantage of helping the independent learner gain further access to Internet resources.

A Look at the Future

Using the resources of the Internet, students in the future will no doubt be able to take classes anywhere, anytime, with peers and teacher-mentors from around the globe. Asao's (1997) *Evaluating Evaluation: Online Instruction of EFL/ESL* brings to light some very important matters concerning language teaching and the Internet:

> When students exchange email with their peers from different cultures and create their web pages, their interest is directed to the content of their messages. Language learning on the Internet is a different kind of educational experience from the language learning experience in the traditional classroom setting. When EFL/ESL instruction is done on a network, educational activities assume a new meaning and we need a new paradigm for evaluating the educational experience of the students. (n.p.)

I believe that the methods for teaching languages, now for English but in the near future for all languages, are about to change dramatically. The artificial teacher–student–classroom peer environment (in which the student writes or speaks for the purposes of improving accuracy and receiving a grade) will gradually be replaced by authentic, dynamic student–teacher–global peer situations.

Classroom lessons will always be useful for many students, particularly when they are learning a new language. However, once they have acquired the basics, students need to practice in real situations. They need to use their language skills to exchange ideas, learn about other cultures, get expert advice from people living in totally different environments, make personal contacts, and learn the technical and social skills necessary for surviving in today's rapidly evolving world. Autonomous learning, made possible by technology, is a significant aspect of this new approach to global education.

The technology for audio- and videoconferencing exists and is improving rapidly. In the not too distant future, I believe that Internet technology, three-dimensional multimedia, and television will be combined and readily available in many homes around the world. It is time for teachers to start developing suitable interactive, collaborative language courses for the autonomous students of tomorrow. (See chapter 28 for a discussion of other challenges that technology will bring to teachers.) The teacher's role in these courses is that of a facilitator. Accuracy alone is not enough; students need to be encouraged to search for knowledge critically, develop intercultural awareness, and use their language skills for meaningful communication with their global peers.

Chapter 27

CALL Issues:
Designing CALL Software

Elizabeth Boling and Keng-Soon Soo

In designing and developing software or World Wide Web sites, language educators and their students should follow many of the guidelines for software evaluation outlined in chapter 11 (see chapter 25 for a discussion of authoring). However, software designers and developers have greater command over specific aspects of software design than educators choosing commercial software do, and they therefore must consider more specifically how to incorporate certain important features into their products. One such feature is how much autonomy the software allows the user; this characteristic and other design features are the focus of this chapter.

Characteristics of Well-Designed Software

Some design characteristics (see the box) are considered to be essential for the effectiveness and ease of use of any software (Boling & Yi, 1996; Heinich, Molenda, Russell, & Smaldino, 1996; Leshin, Pollock, & Reigeluth, 1992; Shneiderman, 1998). You can share these characteristics, which are explained below, with learners as an important component of the task of developing software or Web sites. These features provide a friendly interface that users do not have to master before they gain access to the content and instruction in the program.

Consistency

The visual design of the software interface needs to be consistent. Consistency reduces the amount of mental energy users expend on mastering the software and allows them to concentrate on mastering the content. In software design, consistency means that the placement of elements on the screen remains stable from one display to the next; color, layout, capitaliza-

---

Essential Elements of Good Software Design

- The interface and terminology are consistent from screen to screen.
- The layout of each screen makes good use of space.
- Legibility and readability are high.
- The software makes good use of contrast, repetition, alignment, and proximity.
- Serious navigational errors are prevented.
- Undesired actions are easily reversed.
- Audio and video playback (where applicable) are of good quality.

---

tion, and fonts are consistent within each major segment of the software; and the terminology used in prompts, menus, and help screens is consistent from one part of the software to another.

The programs ELLIS Middle Mastery (1998; see Figure 27-1) and ELLIS Senior Mastery (1998) both show a very high level of consistency. The control panel appears at the bottom of the screen. Speakers in the dialogue are clearly identified in a separate color panel (here appearing as a darker gray). Because ELLIS Senior Mastery uses the same interface, a user moving to the higher level program in the series would have no difficulty finding the appropriate controls.

Good Use of Space

People perceive divisions of space more readily than they perceive typographical cues (Millet & Sano, 1995). In software design, therefore, each section of content should fit onto one screen, and different parts of the information should be distinguished from one another spatially rather than through variations in color, style, or other treatments. Too many other treatments (e.g., lines, bullet points, bold or underlined text) can clutter the screen with visual noise, which distracts from the content being presented. In the screen in Figure 27-1, space distinguishes the content from the navigational features.

Legibility

At all times, the text on the screen must be legible (i.e., the letter forms must be easy to see) and readable (i.e., lines of text must be easy to scan in

Figure 27-1. Design Elements in ELLIS Middle Mastery (1998)

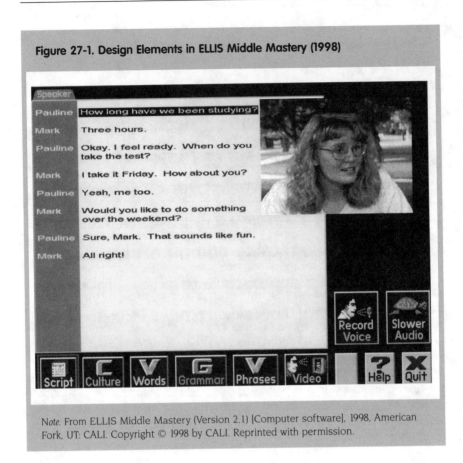

Note. From ELLIS Middle Mastery (Version 2.1) [Computer software], 1998, American Fork, UT: CALI. Copyright © 1998 by CALI. Reprinted with permission.

normal reading patterns). For the sake of legibility, developers should avoid the use of elaborate typefaces on screen, and text in paragraphs should not be smaller than 12 points. For readability, lines of English text should be aligned on the left (left justified), not on the right, and individual lines of text in any language should be at least several pixels apart.

Contrast, Repetition, Alignment, Proximity

Effective screen design exhibits good use of contrast, repetition, alignment, and proximity, which are four basic principles of visual design (Williams, 1994). Different elements should contrast clearly with each other, whereas common elements, like logos and navigation buttons, should be repeated in order to unify the various screens in the same section. Each element on the screen should be aligned either horizontally or vertically against a few locations on an invisible, consistent grid that gives structure to the individual displays while uniting all the screens of a program in a consistent design. Related items should be placed close to each other, and unrelated items placed farther apart, because users assume that items in close proximity are related.

Ease of Navigation and Recovery

Good design prevents users as much as possible from making serious errors with the interface of the software, for example, accidentally quitting the program before finishing a quiz or throwing away long documents without saving them. The software should ignore nonsensical choices or commands and provide clear instructions for recovery if users get into trouble. In addition, even fairly trivial undesired actions, like advancing the screen display or starting to play an audio segment, should be easy to reverse.

High-Quality Playback

Audio and video playback must be of sufficiently high technical quality. The synchronization of video with audio is more important than the quality of the video display, as poor synchronization distracts learners from the content (Schwier & Misanchuk, 1997). Obviously, poor-fidelity audio poses a problem for language learners both in recognizing language and in using it as a model for their own pronunciation.

Control Profiles for Language Learning Software

The general guidelines above present design characteristics that are important for all software; software designed with a set amount of user autonomy in mind requires additional characteristics that make it effective for the target user. In the terms used to describe autonomous learning environments in chapter 24, a software package is characterized by the combination of teacher-determined and learner-determined structure it supports. This description is the *control profile* of the software, and you should make the initial decision to design (or choose) software based on whether or not its profile is well suited to the characteristics of your particular learners. Once this decision is made, you can focus on the functional, visual, and navigational aspects of the design.

General guidelines in professional software development often suggest that the user's control over all aspects of a piece of software is a critical indicator of the software's quality (Apple Computer, 1987; Preece et al., 1994), and this view sometimes translates to the general public as "more user control is always better." However, researchers and developers of instructional software recognize that giving learners a high degree of control over all aspects of their interaction with software does not always promote the greatest amount of learning (Hannafin & Sullivan, 1995; Steinberg, 1989; Weller, 1988). Chapter 24 suggests that teachers can determine what mix of control is appropriate for various language learning situations by looking at whether the teacher or the learner structures the content, pacing, and sequence in a learning environment. You can use this model to evaluate the design of language learning software by categorizing it into one of the following profiles:

- *high teacher control*: The teacher structures the content, pacing, and sequence. When the language learners are novices with little or no prior knowledge of the content and have to start with the very basics of the subject, it may be appropriate for you to control content, pacing, and sequence in order to reduce learners' anxiety and ensure that they have opportunities to learn. When learners have to internalize the basics correctly and quickly, they need to proceed through the content systematically without going wrong too often or too seriously. For these types of learners, you should design software that allows you to structure most of the learning experience.

- *high learner control*: The learner structures the content, pacing, and sequence. Advanced learners have already mastered the basics and need to experiment actively and creatively with that basic knowledge in order to solve problems. The freedom to formulate and test hypotheses against authentic data (frequently using high-fidelity audio and video) and to collaborate with peers is important. For these types of learners, you and your students should design software that allows them to structure most of the learning experience.

- *moderate teacher control*: The teacher guides the pacing and sequence, and the learner structures the content. When learners know what they want to learn but face time constraints, they may need to structure their own content while relying on you for guidance on the optimal pacing and sequence of the learning experience. Workers who study English for specific purposes, such as hotel receptionists and airplane pilots, need only to master the specific vocabulary and constructions necessary for them to do their jobs or to refresh their mastery of particular aspects of the language from time to time, especially when new technology requires them to update their working vocabulary. Such learners have a good idea of the content they need to learn and might select only a few modules from a large database of learning materials, but they may follow the specified sequence and pacing within those modules.

- *moderate learner control*: The learner structures the pacing and sequence, and the teacher structures the content. When learners have mastered the early basics, you may still need to retain control of the content because your state or another accrediting agency stipulates it. If you follow a mastery learning approach, you may also determine content but want to give learners the freedom to structure the pacing and sequence of their learning (Heinich et al., 1996).

Software exhibiting moderate or high learner control shares some advantages. Giving learners control over pacing and sequence allows them to learn at their optimal speed so that they are neither pressured to go faster than they can absorb the material nor bored by waiting for others to catch up. If the software includes audio and video, it can also cater to visual and auditory learning styles (see chapter 18 for a discussion of learning styles). Learners can also arrange the content in the sequence most comfortable or useful to them, which may enhance their satisfaction with the learning experience.

You may use software exhibiting moderate learner control in learning situations with a high level of teacher control if you provide the sequence for the learners to follow and limit the time they can spend on each unit.

Software Design Elements for High Teacher Control

The checklist in the box contains the design elements necessary for the novice learner, for whom you may need to structure content more tightly. Each item is explained below.

Chunking and Sequencing

When the learner does not control the presentation of textual content, it should be divided into digestible "chunks." As a rule of thumb, Boling and Yi (1996) suggest that most chunks should not exceed 12–15 lines of 12-point text, the amount that fits comfortably on one monitor screen. Leshin et al.

Design Elements for High Teacher Control

- The content is divided into relatively small units.
- The chunks are sequenced from simple to difficult.
- Feedback is provided constantly and instantly.
- Navigation is well controlled.
- The software guides the learners through the content.

(1992) suggest further that 8–10 words per line of text is optimum for comprehension. Text that does not fit onto one screen should be presented on another screen rather than require users to scroll down one screen. Even in World Wide Web documents, which learners may become accustomed to reading by scrolling down the screen, learners are apt to miss segments of content that lie outside the immediately visible area of the screen. Chunks of content should represent logically complete units and should be presented progressively from simple to difficult.

Feedback

Because sequencing is out of the learners' control, feedback regarding right and wrong responses should tell learners clearly why they are or are not moving ahead in the sequence. Feedback that offers remediation (an explanation of why the learner was wrong) and reinforcement (an explanation of why the learner was right) is much more effective than simplistic "Good work!" or "Wrong, try again" messages because learners receiving only short messages as feedback cannot discover such explanations on their own. In addition, the explanation offered should not be more difficult for the learner to understand than the initial test or practice item was.

Navigation

Users' ability to move from one chunk of content to another should be tightly controlled in software supporting this profile. Strict control forces learners to concentrate on one task or subtask at a time and allows them to move on to the next task only after they have performed in the desired manner. Novice computer users tend to do better with more rigid navigation control, without which they may get lost in the software.

Guidance

The software interface should indicate clearly when it is time for learners to give a response and in what way they should give it. When learners perceive that the software (i.e., the teacher) is controlling all the interaction, they will not initiate actions without specific prompting to do so. By the same token, the software should be unresponsive to learners' attempts to explore by clicking the mouse around the screen or entering random keyboard characters. Also, warning beeps and visual messages may become annoying for learners who encounter them inadvertently and may be the focus of unproductive play for younger learners who are tired of the software-controlled lesson.

Example

Software with a high degree of teacher control is good for carefully structured learning and is most useful for novice learners and remediation. An example is The Rosetta Stone (1995; see Figure 13-1). Such applications divide the content into small concepts, which are presented to learners one at a time. Learners cannot choose which topic they want to learn; the content is sequenced—usually from simple to complex. Therefore, navigation options are restricted to only what is appropriate at a certain point. In programs with very high control (so-called *programmed learning*) learners have to complete a whole exercise before going on to the next concept. They may check their answers or ask the software to show the correct answers. Essentially, learners have little choice of what to do. In some software, if they fail to answer even one item, the software will not allow them to go on until they correct that omission. In The Rosetta Stone, a graphical navigation system assists learners, who quickly come to understand the button functions. Buttons are consistently placed throughout the series.

Software Design Elements for High Learner Control

Software with a high degree of learner control demands more freedom in the user interface and in learners' experience with the content. The checklist in the box is described in more detail below.

Chunking

In software with a high degree of learner control, content is organized in large, coherent chunks rather than small, discrete chunks. Large chunks of content portray language in context and allow a degree of authenticity that supports a sufficiently complex simulation of the real-world problem being studied.

Feedback

When learners have a high level of control, feedback spells out what the results of the learners' hypotheses will be if they are played out to their logical end but does not judge whether the answer is right or wrong. The learners themselves decide if the projected results are satisfactory and if they need to learn more.

Navigation

Learners should be able to move from one part of the software to another with ease. All possible navigation options should be available to

---

Design Elements for High Learner Control

- The content is presented in sufficiently large chunks.
- The chunks are sufficiently authentic and complex.
- Feedback is accurate and nonjudgmental.
- The learner can freely navigate through the entire program.
- The learner is an initiator of actions.
- The learner can save and recover work if necessary.

learners at all times. Because many navigation options are likely to be available in this kind of software, the representations of those options (e.g., buttons, icons, menu items) must be organized into groups (e.g., navigation, program functions, content items) with the most frequently used in convenient positions and the least frequently used placed out of the way, perhaps at the edges of the visual display. Although icons or buttons may be used to conserve space, they should be labeled on screen or with pop-up text to minimize errors in determining their functions (Boling et al., 1997).

Interface Control

In software of this type, learners initiate all actions, and the software should respond to every request without mandating particular paths or sequences to be followed. Even when learners initiate an action that takes control of the interface (e.g., playing video or audio segments), they should be able to stop the action and regain control. Learners should be able to save a bookmark in a lesson or save a file containing complicated work (e.g., a personalized vocabulary list, a complex translation project, constructed audio dialogues) and return to the software at any later time.

Example

Figure 27-2 shows a screen from the American Sign Language Dictionary (Sternberg, 1998), a good example of software with high learner control. The learner sees multiple methods of accessing content. In the lower left part of the screen, the learner can choose to "Find," "Browse Category," or "Browse A–Z" (alphabetically) using the buttons provided. Learners can start with any item and continue in no particular sequence. They can also add words to a list by clicking the mouse on the "List" button and can practice them later. All information—text, graphics, full-motion video, and audio—related to a particular word appears on screen at the same time. There is high-fidelity reproduction of the language. The layout is systematic and consistent among all screens: The content to be learned is displayed on the left half of the screen, and the right half is devoted to the video representation of the content.

Learners also have full control over the video. They can increase or decrease the tempo, play the video frame by frame, or double the size of the video. Control functions pertaining to the video are grouped with the video window and clearly separated from the navigational functions through the use of a frame. This clear separation prevents confusion. It makes the software easier and quicker to use because learners soon associate particular functions with particular areas of the screen and, provided all screens have a consistent layout, move instinctively toward the part of the screen they want.

Figure 27-2. Software With High Learner Control

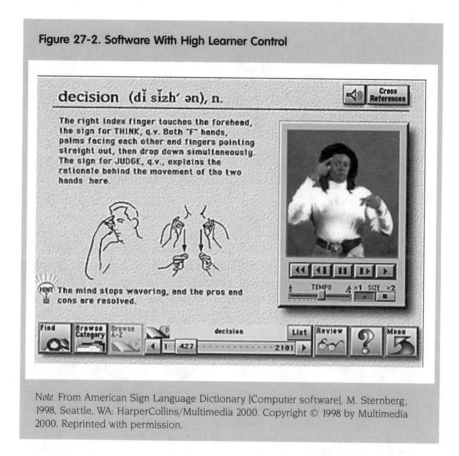

Note. From American Sign Language Dictionary [Computer software], M. Sternberg, 1998, Seattle, WA: HarperCollins/Multimedia 2000. Copyright © 1998 by Multimedia 2000. Reprinted with permission.

Software Design Elements for Moderate Teacher Control

Moderate teacher control is appropriate in software for learners who have a good idea of what they need to know but who may need help planning and organizing the pace and the sequencing of the content (see the box).

Design Elements for Moderate Teacher Control

- The content is presented in independent modules.
- The content and selection menus are clearly labeled.
- Feedback is explicit.
- Navigation is strictly controlled.
- The software guides the learners through the content.

Content Presentation

To support this profile, the content must be divided into freestanding modules that are clearly labeled so that learners can select them easily.

Navigation

Because the learner is not controlling pacing or sequencing within modules, the software should follow several of the design guidelines for high teacher control. In brief, feedback should be explicit and timely, navigation should be restricted within modules, and the software should guide the learner through each self-selected segment of content, ensuring that the learner has mastered each part before going on to the next.

Example

Figure 27-3 shows a screen from the Expert English Tutor, a conceptual mock-up of software in which the learner controls the content but the teacher controls the pacing and sequence. In this example, developed for the purposes of this chapter only, the learner has chosen to practice a single communicative function—denials (refusals). Learners exercise control over content when they select this particular module. Once the learners begin the

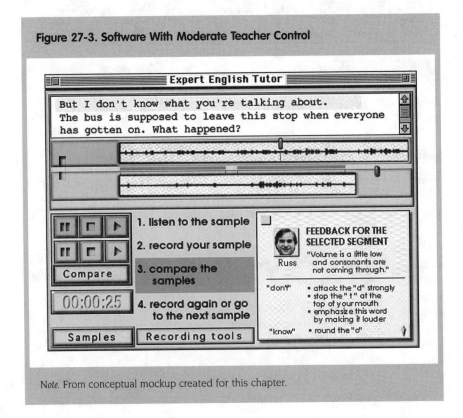

Figure 27-3. Software With Moderate Teacher Control

Note. From conceptual mockup created for this chapter.

module, they have to follow a strict sequence of actions: listen to the sample, record their own sample, compare the samples, and, finally, repeat the previous steps or go on to a new sample. Because the learners have to familiarize themselves with this content to the point of automaticity, a timer limits the amount of time in which they can reproduce the sample. At higher difficulty levels, the amount of time can be decreased. Feedback is both textual (in the box) and graphical (in the two frequency graphs).

As in Figure 27-2, the screen shows consistent and systematic clustering of functions, a feature that becomes even more important as the number of controls on-screen increases. The audio control functions and timer are located in the lower left part of the screen; the textual feedback from the computer tutor is in the lower right part of the screen. Located between them is the checklist of actions the learner has to go through. This type of software forces learners to become faster and more accurate in whatever topic they wish to improve themselves.

Software Design Elements for Moderate Learner Control

In this type of software, the learner takes charge of the pacing and the sequencing of the content presentation. The software developer controls the content and must ensure that it is clearly organized and presented (see the box). This profile may be the most flexible one because it offers the learner control over pacing and sequencing while allowing the teacher to control the language learned.

Design Elements for Moderate Learner Control

- The learning objectives are clear.
- The content is divided into relatively small units.
- The chunks are sequenced from simple to difficult.
- Feedback is provided constantly and instantly.
- Branching is available and is based on an adequate assessment tool.
- Navigation gives the learners the choice of what and how fast to learn.
- An anchor or bookmarking system brings learners back to the main pages.
- The learners are initiators of actions, including assessment.
- The software guides the learners through the content.

Objectives

The software should communicate clear objectives to the learners, as the teacher (or developer) is determining what content they must master.

Chunking

As in high-teacher-control software, the content should be chunked into relatively small units, and the chunks should progress from simple to difficult. The software should give frequent explanatory feedback.

Navigation

Slower learners should be able to branch to chunks that offer more detail on the content in the main path, and learners should receive clear recommendations on which paths to follow next based on an accurate assessment of their performance. For learners who have branched off, tools such as bookmarking or menu buttons should lead clearly back to the main path. Learners should have access to testing software at any point during their learning in case they feel they have already mastered the content in a module.

Because the learner has control over the pacing and sequence of learning, most of the guidelines applicable to the high learner control profile also apply here. In brief, the software should allow for easy navigation, quick error recovery, and simple reversal of actions. The learner should initiate all actions and should be able to insert a bookmark in a lesson and return to the same place in the software later.

Example

In Clinton Debate (Duber, 1994; see Figure 27-4), the teacher controls the content, but the learner controls the pacing and sequence. The screen contains a limited amount of content and is designed for maximum readability (black text on a white background). The content box itself is set against a dark but interesting background that attracts the learners' attention. The blanks signaling the answers required are underlined in color to highlight their positions in a crowded screen. There is only one navigation function—"Click here when done"—because the learners are not supposed to control the content. They may, however, listen to the passage or parts of the passage as often as they wish using the standard audio control bar, slider, and buttons under the picture of Bill Clinton.

As is typical in software with moderate control, students may not change the content, but they may choose a variety of activities and access them in any order. Activities include a comprehension test of main ideas (the "?s" button), a true-false quiz on details, vocabulary words and definitions, and a cloze passage (as seen in Figure 27-4, accessed by the "Text" button). The buttons are somewhat cryptic, but this is not a major drawback if the teacher can explain them to the students in class before they start the exercise. In all the activities, students must write answers to the questions

Figure 27-4. Software With Moderate Learner Control

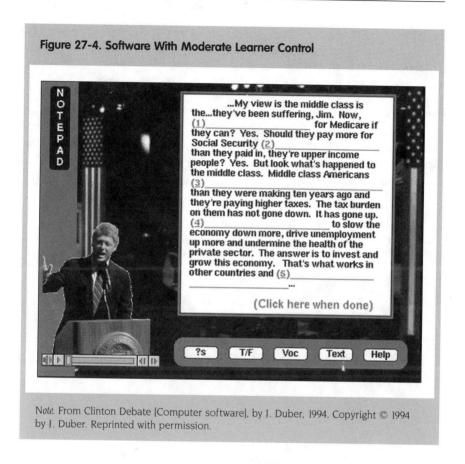

Note. From Clinton Debate [Computer software], by J. Duber, 1994. Copyright © 1994 by J. Duber. Reprinted with permission.

on paper or open the Notepad (upper left corner), where they may type and copy the contents to a word processor. The function buttons related to the content are visually clustered in the lower right part of the screen on a red bar, while the Notepad, which serves a different function from the others, is separated visually. Software with moderate student control often may be adjusted for higher teacher control. In this software, the Teaching Tips included provide worksheets and suggest an order for the activities and ways for the students to work in pairs or small groups.

Conclusion

To fit well into the intended curriculum and learning environment, language learning software must support the appropriate mix of teacher and learner control over content, pacing, and sequencing. A complex language curriculum may demand a range of control profiles and may demand software that fits more than one profile. You will most probably need to find or design software to fit into various parts of the curriculum (Kluge, 1996), and achieving the correct mix of control profiles can be more conducive to language learning than strictly adhering to a single profile (Cobb & Stevens, 1996). Even a software package that falls into the right control profile must be designed to meet the other criteria for an optimal CALL environment (see chapter 1), or it will not function adequately in the role that it is supposed to play.

Explorations

Projects

1. Design an ESL class that you might teach over the World Wide Web. Consider what degree of control you as a teacher will have. How autonomous do you expect your students to be?

2. In your local lab, find an authoring program, such as Microsoft® PowerPoint® 97 (1996) or HyperCard® (1997), or obtain a fully functioning demo of HyperStudio (1997) directly from Roger Wagner Publications (http://www.hyperstudio.com/). Complete the tutorial accompanying the software, and create a short program (of three or four screens or cards) displaying what you know, think, and believe so far about autonomy in language learning. Use sound files and photographs, drawings, or charts to illustrate your project. If possible, collect authentic samples from students for these illustrations.

3. Create a project for your learners in which they learn to use an authoring package with which you are familiar. How does your project meet the conditions for optimal language learning set forth in chapter 1?

4. Using the design criteria set forth in chapter 18, analyze at least two different software programs. Which program better meets the conditions of appropriate technology? Illustrate your report with screen shots.

Guided Research

1. How do the roles of teacher and student in the electronic or virtual classroom differ from those roles in the conventional classroom? Are teachers generally satisfied with the virtual classroom? What problems exist for teachers? For students? How may they be overcome? Contact the authors of some of the many

academic courses that exist solely or in part on-line to collect information.

2. What are the differences between discourse over distance and discourse in a classroom? Collect samples of student output in both an on-line course and a face-to-face course. Include oral and informal samples, for example, a tape recording of a group discussion in class and an on-line peer-editing session or paper comments by peers in a chat room. A survey of on-line courses (such as that suggested in Guided Research, No. 1) may also help you determine differences in discourse in distance as opposed to face-to-face instruction.

3. Investigate a variety of local classrooms, including at least one on-line course, using the paradigm set forth in chapter 24. Are students presumed to share authority, or is power centered in the teacher or the computer? How do classrooms that differ in this regard differ in other ways? Perform a search of the literature to find other studies that examine the same question.

Questions for Further Investigation

1. What kind of learner is most successful at distance learning?

2. In what circumstances are learners more successful when they have control, and in what circumstances are they less successful? Why?

3. How can classroom teachers determine which learners need how much control in which contexts?

Chapter 28 ⊞

Conclusion:
20 Minutes Into the Future

Carla Meskill

The year is 2005. It's 2:45 p.m. A high school ESL class is winding down, and students are beginning to pack up to leave their classroom. Thong, age 16, disconnects his 8-1/2-in.-by-11-in. digital notebook computer from the plug on his desk. During this month's 90-minute real-time class, Thong's desk outlet has transferred image and sound files of all class activities to his notebook computer. Thong places the computer in his ergonomic pack, says good-bye to his classmates and teachers, and leaves the classroom.

On the high-speed train that transports him from his class in Albany, New York, to his home on Lake Champlain, Thong takes advantage of the quiet, takes out his computer, opens it on his lap, and spends this time reviewing what occurred in his ESL class.

When his notebook computer pops open, his private tutor (a video image on the computer's screen) greets him and asks how he liked today's class, what he learned, what understandings he gained, and what kinds of questions remain in his mind. Thong indicates that he greatly enjoyed today's activities and that he is interested in reviewing the U.S. courtroom simulation he and his classmates undertook that day. As a previewing strategy, he tests his retention of new vocabulary, structures, and language functions in a dialogue with his on-line tutor. He then spends several minutes examining the interactional dynamics and accompanying discourse he and his classmates employed in their simulation. He uses zoom, playback, and annotation utilities in conjunction with the numerous files of videoconferences he has had over the past month with field experts and peers around the world and of courtroom scenarios and documents he has carefully included in his personal ESL work database. Using a combination of finger-controlled and voice-generation tools, he edits errors and enhances the video. He then tackles tomorrow's assignment: recast the courtroom simulation by selecting new characters and a new problem and design the outcome. Using video and audio morphing tools, Thong builds his own courtroom simulation. He employs his evolving subject-area and linguistic knowledge and his imagination in conjunction with an extensive database of images and audio options and texts. By the time he arrives at

Lake Champlain, a first draft of his version of the courtroom simulation is almost complete. At home he will eventually plug his notebook computer into the jack in the wall of his room and transmit the completed assignment to his fellow team members and to his ESL teacher's computer for feedback. He then turns to his other high school course work.

This glimpse of the not-too-distant future may inspire awe or skepticism in the late 1990s. However, such technological power is clearly just around the corner. What is less clear is how language teaching professionals can prepare to make the kind of pedagogically grounded use of technology that is depicted here. This chapter explores teachers' preparation for integrating and using instructional technologies, both now and in the future. Central to this discussion is the role of the teaching professional as a mediator of instruction, with technology called into the service of the mediation process. Professional skills—perceptual, technical, and instructional—that are essential now and for the near future are suggested.

Some History to Consider

Instructional technologies have been in existence as long as the notion of teaching and learning has. Chalkboards, manipulatives, and audiovisual aids have long been standard fare in instruction. Language instruction especially is notoriously resourceful in terms of the kinds of physical objects that are used as illustrations of and catalysts for language. Hardware and software of all kinds have been used to their maximum instructional potential—and sometimes to less than their minimum (Cuban, 1986). What is particularly interesting is the extent to which historical forces affect the adoption of technologies and influence how they come to be used in teaching and learning. The technologies that have become most common to instruction in the past three decades—video and computers—are relevant in this respect.

The "Hand-Me-Down" Syndrome

The technologies used in education very rarely originate there. Teachers borrow them from other sectors that have their own special driving forces: the government, the military, industry, and consumer markets. For example, in recent times the home entertainment industry has supplied education with the videocassette recorder, the videodisc player, the CD-ROM, and the camcorder. They all become accessible, inexpensive, and extremely easy to use, not in consideration of the needs of, goals for, and beliefs about what constitutes good instruction but because of a vast consumer market. Likewise, the speed of microcomputer processing has grown not in response to the needs, goals, and processes of schools but in response to the requirements of the military, government, business, and entertainment.

This hand-me-down syndrome can be considered both a positive and a negative force in how technologies are used in schools and how they come to influence instruction. The positive side is that teachers reap benefits from other professions' research and development dollars. The negatives are that (a) instructional beliefs, goals, and practices have to be applied to technologies that are designed for something other than teaching and learning; (b) the technology, which was designed for quite a different purpose, may shape teaching and learning; and (c) good pedagogical uses, when they do evolve, take a long time to do so.

The "Because-We-Can" Syndrome

Neither the printing press nor the photocopy machine was invented to be used in schools, yet teachers were quick to appropriate both. Their lasting impact on instructional practice cannot be disputed. One need only walk into any language classroom in the country to witness the phenomenon of the photocopied handout. Like any technology, photocopying can be overused, used poorly, or used to its maximum pedagogical benefit. What is clear is that when photocopying is misused, for example, in creating worksheets simply to keep students quiet and busy, the technology has shaped the instruction, not the other way around.

A contemporary example of this phenomenon comes from a developing country, although such a thing could happen anywhere: Told that the audiotape player was an essential tool in language teaching, a well-meaning instructor recorded and then played back for his students a story using his own voice. Another example might hit closer to home for the TESOL professional. It wasn't that long ago that teachers used video playback merely as it was designed to be used in consumer contexts, that is, for passive, entertainment-oriented viewing. Teachers had students watch videotapes because they could, not necessarily because of a solid pedagogical rationale. One need only look at the work of TESOL's Video Interest Section to see how far the field has come in providing the needed conceptual work and, in turn, in developing pedagogically grounded uses for this hand-me-down technology.

History shows that there are reasons technologies are used well or poorly. The bottom line is that good use of a new technology requires some conceptual work to retrofit that technology to teaching practice. Using a new approach "because we can" is not good enough.

The Role of Technology in Instruction

The learning and teaching in the ESL scenario at the beginning of this chapter is not that much different from scenarios in ESL classrooms today.

The emphasis is on communication, and the bulk of learning is socially mediated. The teacher, who has maintained an ongoing electronic conversation with the group during the month leading up to the real-time, face-to-face session, has employed her knowledge of the individual learners, their interpersonal dynamics, and their current language needs in designing and orchestrating tasks that make optimal use of the face-to-face learning opportunity in the classroom. Student interaction is therefore treated as central. Using her knowledge, her skills, and some very handy electronic tools, the teacher has planned, orchestrated, and facilitated the kind of communicative activities that strike the right chord in the hearts of turn-of-the-millennium TESOL professionals: Students are engaged in constructive discourse. The teacher supports and reinforces critical aspects of that discourse through the appropriate tools.

What role does technology play in this scenario? Certainly not a large, looming one. The technology is instead very quiet and very powerful, used much as technologies are used well now. The hardware is secondary and subservient to the larger goals and social processes of learning. The video storage, playback, and manipulation technologies are pulled into the service of a real-time communicative activity: the courtroom simulation. Before coming to the classroom, students have used technology in collaboratively researching, preparing for, and rehearsing the simulation through video-conferencing and on-line collaborative tasking that the teacher has designed and orchestrated. The technology provides resources for and a record of what is central to the students' language. Both the students and their teacher are thus empowered by electronic databases, e-mail, and video-conferencing—tools with which they can make greater sense of the language and nuances contained within that record. Teaching and learning continue in this vein when Thong leaves the classroom and is at a distance from the other learners on his collaborative team.

The salient aspect of this scenario is that learning processes are human, not technology, driven. Rather than being involved with technology, students are involved in their learning through negotiations of meaning with one another in electronic contexts—synchronously and asynchronously—and in face-to-face contexts. The teacher is involved in orchestrating and facilitating these processes, not in the cumbersome manipulation of buttons, wires, and peripherals, thanks to a voice-activated control panel that responds to simple commands. The technology serves her need to seamlessly document learning processes, provide individual support and feedback, and engage students in relevant learning activities when they are not in the classroom. Technology complements and enhances these pedagogical processes.

Agency: Who's in Charge?

As expressed by both the language used to talk about computers and the attempt to build software to emulate thinking behaviors, people tend to perceive that the computer can act on its own—that it has powers independent of its user. In short, people attribute agency to a box of plastic parts. Many teachers have been guilty of resorting to "The machine did it!" when something goes wrong and even have thought, "The machine doesn't like me!" when things go really wrong. Much of this tendency to anthropomorphize the computer is due to bad interfaces that cause the user to feel disoriented and not in control (Laurel, 1991; see also chapter 23). Interface design is improving, but the attribution of agency to computers continues to present singular and sometimes difficult challenges in conceptualizing their role in instruction.

Risks of the Agency Fallacy

Inadequate interfaces can be very limiting, especially for teachers who are new to computers. First, they fear that the machine will do something unpredictable and irrevocable. This can result in two additional fears for teachers: (a) that they will become forever lost and at the mercy of something they don't understand and (b) that they will look foolish in front of their peers or students.

The fact is, computers are fundamentally dumb. Relative to human intelligence, they will most likely remain that way (Dreyfus & Dreyfus, 1986). The video tutor on Thong's notebook computer screen gives cues and canned suggestions to guide Thong. The tutor's main function is to serve as a record keeper that makes suggestions to Thong from a closed list of possibilities. Selecting from this list is a matter of smoke and mirrors: The tutor cannot perform its function unless Thong and his teacher enter specific information into the tutor and direct it to respond. Likewise, as a communication tool, the computer holds no mystery: It is merely a fancy device for sending and receiving messages. The human communicator is in charge of that which is uniquely human: decision making and communication that is based in thought.

Another risk comes wrapped up in the agency fallacy. When too much power or agency is attributed to the computer, it risks being used as an *electronic baby-sitter* (Branscum, 1992). The thinking goes something like this: Computers are supposed to be able to teach, so let the computer teach Jorge. Jorge is consequently sent off to the computer so it can teach him something. In this way, both the teacher's time and the student's time are seen as more productive. The idea that computers are good because they free up the teacher is a two-edged sword: True, computers can free the teacher from center stage and allow students some control over their learning, but, particularly for language minority students in mainstream classrooms, computers can also be used as a way to absolve teachers, administrators, programs, and schools from the responsibility for the challenges some students represent.

Traditional kudos for CALL include the message that individualized instruction has merit. So it does, but only when the activity is valued by and integrated into the larger community and learning context (Meskill & Mossop, 1997; Meskill & Shea, 1994). In other words, the activity or task that an individual student does with the computer needs to fit into the big curricular and social picture. More specifically, machines need to be cast in the role of mediators, not sources, of learning. Unfortunately, software sales techniques send subtle messages portraying computers as teaching machines that offer solutions to problems. This conception of the role of computers in instruction, in combination with the notion of agency in computers themselves, raises issues that are both prevalent and problematic. These notions reinforce the idea of standardizable instruction delivery rather than the enslavement of technology for larger, human-centered pedagogical purposes.

Revising the Conceptions

The conceptual work needed on the role of computers in ESL instruction can begin with merely taming the beast. Teachers need to understand that the computer is stupid and that, without their skills, knowledge, and humanity, it is little more than a home entertainment system that rewards, punishes, or baby-sits. Teachers need not feel like unskilled, nonknowers of special formulas or tricks; rather, they should feel empowered by the fact that, given the goals and processes of language teaching and learning, without mediation by smart teachers the machine's role is very limited. Fortunately, new and better interfaces and technical support will eventually help teaching professionals see the soul in the machine as the pile of silicon it truly is. The teacher in the futuristic scenario has no wires, no code, no mystery buttons to push to make her class happen. The interface she uses on her notebook computer could be used by anyone. Happily, the goal of the better, more thoughtful software producers is to eliminate any sense of powerlessness and to promote a sense of what Winograd and Flores (1988) call *at-handedness* in user interface design, meaning that computer interfaces will eventually become so accessible that their use will be as much second nature to the learner as switching on a light or hammering in a nail is.

The second bit of conceptual work is also related to the notion of agency. Historically, instructional technologies have been designed and used based on the transmission model of learning, which sees the learner in a passive or receptive mode and, consequently, sees any learning that takes place as the direct result of teaching (see Figure 28-1). The transmission model thus sees the teacher possessing and purveying knowledge. Many of the media used in instruction—filmstrips, audiotapes, computers—have likewise been conceived as conveyances of knowledge. One need only look

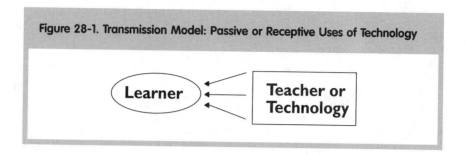

Figure 28-1. Transmission Model: Passive or Receptive Uses of Technology

at the vast number of comparison studies of the use of media—studies that use a classic research design with a control group and a treatment-medium group—to note this prevalent conceptual framework: Learning is seen as the direct result of the medium's actions. Any involvement on the part of the learner is only peripherally taken into account. This concept needs modification if instructional technology is to fit the needs, goals, and beliefs of contemporary language teaching.

The fundamental weakness of the transmission model is that it is based on older notions of teaching and learning. Constructivist, and in the realm of language teaching, communicative schools of thought have since brought a shift away from thinking of the teacher as knower toward the notion of learning as social and collaborative (see Figure 28-2; also see Laurel, 1991). The basic concept of the role of instructional technology, however, has been slower to evolve in a like direction. A sense persists that technology, especially computers, exerts some power and effects some learning independent of other processes and concerns. Probably the first credo for teachers learning about computers, then, is that *teachers teach; machines don't.* Machines are tools for, not agents of, learning. In a communicative framework, they are at their best when supporting social and collaborative

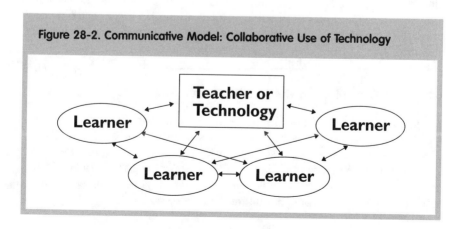

Figure 28-2. Communicative Model: Collaborative Use of Technology

processes. In other words, machines can be catalysts and tools for thinking and communicating. Their use can be integral to learning activities but cannot be their source.

Multimedia Literacy in Language Learning

How do you as a teacher go about evolving pedagogically driven uses for technology in your classroom? A useful starting point is your already extensive knowledge of multimedia.

For teachers, adapting computers to language learning can represent a cultural as well as a methodological transition (Poole, 1995). Fortunately, understanding multimedia and its potentialities for ESL represents less a cultural transition than a cultural expansion. First, like it or not, much of the world, regardless of nationality, socioeconomic status, or cognitive ability, is media literate, having lived on a rich, steady diet of popular media from birth. People know how to watch TV and films and listen to the radio. They understand well, but mostly unconsciously, the intricate conventions the media use to inform and entertain.

I define *multimedia literacy* as what teachers already know about media elements and how they can interact to affect language learning. Teachers know, for example, the power of visuals in teaching and learning. Teachers use visuals—both still and moving—frequently in language classrooms, insofar as they are available. Likewise, teachers use charts, diagrams, photographs, slides, and video as tools for many purposes, such as activating schema, providing context within which meaning can be more effectively portrayed and analyzed, stimulating associations, encouraging connections between what is known and what is new, provoking discussion, illustrating, defining, motivating, and clarifying. Teachers also understand the many roles that audio, whether audiotape or audio with video accompaniment, can play. Audio- and videotape bring the target of language study into an accessible and controllable format. It can be the direct object of practice or be used much as visuals are used, for example, to stimulate or illustrate.

What Can Control Over Multimedia Do for Educators?

You know that visual and audio media can be employed in numerous ways and in many combinations as tools for instruction. Your extant familiarity with these elements combined with how you use text in teaching and learning form the basics of multimedia literacy. You need now only add the control and manipulation of these elements, which is becoming ever more feasible with computer-based multimedia technologies.

What does this control gain you as an educator? In the 2005 scenario, the classroom is connected to and managed by a central processing system built specifically to assist in the management of instructional processes. The system facilitates the process of gathering, storing, sharing, and managing background information for the courtroom simulation as well as for the documentation of the activity itself. In preparation for the group activity, the instructor most likely taps into the system to call up visual aids—perhaps video clips of actual court cases or audiovisual samples of the kinds of language students may want to use in their simulation—and to present a searchable database of appropriate texts, possibly based on transcripts of real court cases. In turn, students can save, in a searchable format, a complete audiovisual record of the information gathered and the in-class performance. The simulation was in no way technology dependent, but the enhancement furnished by the technology is called into the service of instruction by virtue of (a) its visual, auditory, and textual elements and (b) streamlined access to and control over that information. As such, this enhancement is not that different from ESL instructors' scavenging a resource room for the tools of their trade—there are just more resources, and they are more at hand.

What about the out-of-class work Thong undertakes on his notebook computer? This work exemplifies the power of controlling and manipulating information—the true hallmark of computers. Note, however, that the material being controlled and manipulated by Thong originated in the social context of his classroom and through on-line collaboration with his teacher and peers. As such, the material is both human and properly valued and integrated into the larger instructional process.

Human values and instructional integration are critical aspects of instructional technology right now. When examining hardware and software for potential use in the classroom, you can begin by asking

- whether the media elements—aural, visual, and textual—can be used in ways that make sense
- whether the kind of manipulation and control of material is complementary to and translatable to existing classroom contexts
- what adjustments might be necessary in the existing classroom context
- whether the technology is valuable pedagogically, or an instance of the because-we-can syndrome

Where to Begin?

If you want to begin to use some of the new instructional technologies, reading the other chapters in this volume is a good start. Examining exemplary uses of computers and considering whether and how they might be adapted to your own situation serves many purposes, letting you learn from others' mistakes and successes. You can also start with what you know:

- what the needs, goals, and constraints of your teaching context are
- how to learn with and from your students and colleagues
- what the optimal roles are for visual, aural, and textual materials in the instructional process

and believe:

- Machines are servants to your needs and the needs of your students.
- Machines don't teach, teachers teach.
- Machines thoughtfully integrated into classrooms can mediate and support instructional processes.

Is the specific software used important? According to the research of recent years and the experience of long-term computer-using language professionals, the answer is a resounding no. Even the most simply constructed software can induce rich constructivist learning if it is used thoughtfully, with communicative principles firmly in mind. The process of considering the adoption of instructional technologies should be grounded in reflective teaching, not in the bells, whistles, and agenda of a given software package. The processes of adopting and integrating software should in effect mirror the kinds of thinking and discourse that teachers orchestrate for their ESL students: Teachers need to talk to one another and share their thoughts and experiences with various media. It is, after all, the negotiation of meaning that instantiates teachers' thoughts and beliefs. Teachers' talk about instruction with, through, and around computers is particular to the technology and becomes a place where meaning is made, a process through which understandings are constructed, and a dialogic space where craft is further crafted. As in other aspects of pedagogical implementation, a supportive administration can do much to assist the dialogic process (see the box).

Conclusion

Cast in a role subservient to the goals and processes of language teaching, technologies such as those in the 2005 scenario break away from the transmission model of learning and teaching. Language teachers, however,

---

A Note to Administrators on Assisting the Pedagogic Dialogue

- Remember that training and adoption require rethinking the curriculum and the act of teaching. This rethinking takes more time than learning which buttons to push.
- Help teachers stay informed. Keeping abreast of the technological tools that are available is a daunting task.
- Encourage teachers to resist the "because-we-can" and "everybody-else-is" syndromes.
- Be aware that software and hardware vendors are selling you hand-me-downs from other sectors and that you therefore will need to retrofit these products by applying good practice to them. This takes time.
- Resist the temptation to buy. Let your teachers select what they need. Support them in discovering what works best for them.
- Don't let buttons and cables get in the way of teaching and learning. A technical support staff on-site is an essential investment.
- Promote the attitude that technology represents opportunity, not imposition.

---

seem to feel a strong impetus to do something now with the technology currently available. Doing so carries a great deal of both risk and promise. In the ESL classroom in 2005, the craft of teaching and learning will be supported by technology, as long as teachers remember who they are.

References

A&E Classroom: Classroom materials pages. (1997). A&E Television Networks. Retrieved November, 7, 1997, from the World Wide Web: http://www.aetv.com/class/teach/.

Accelerated English (Demo version) [Computer software]. (1995). Cupertino, CA: Courseware Publishers International/Harcourt Brace.

Accent Lab (Version 2) [Computer software]. (1995). Los Angeles: Accent Technologies.

Africa Inspirer (Version 4.0) [Computer software]. (1997). Watertown, MA: Tom Snyder Productions.

Ahmad, K., Corbett, G., Rogers, M., & Sussex, R. (1985). *Computers, language learning, and language teaching.* Cambridge: Cambridge University Press.

Alderson, J. C., & Hamp-Lyons, L. (1996). TOEFL preparation courses: A study of washback. *Language Testing, 13,* 280–297.

Alderson, J. C., & Urquhart, A. H. (1985). The effect of students' academic discipline on their performance on ESP reading tests. *Language Testing, 2,* 192–204.

Alexander, J., & Tate, M. (1998). *Evaluating Web resources.* Widener University, Wolfgram Memorial Library. Retrieved April 15, 1998, from the World Wide Web: http://www.science.widener.edu/~withers/webeval.htm.

Allwright, D. (1988). *Observation in the language classroom.* London: Longman.

Allwright, D., & Bailey, K. M. (1991). *Focus on the language classroom: An introduction to classroom research for language teachers.* Cambridge: Cambridge University Press.

The Amazing Writing Machine [Computer software]. (1994). Novato, CA: Brøderbund Software.

The Amazon Trail (Version 1.0) [Computer software]. (1994). Minneapolis, MN: MECC.

American Council on the Teaching of Foreign Languages. (1986). ACTFL *proficiency guidelines.* Hastings-on-Hudson, NY: Author.

American University and English as a second language information service (AUESLIS). (1997). Conversa Language Center. Retrieved May 1, 1998, from the World Wide Web: http://www.iac.net/~conversa/S_homepage.html.

Anderson, R. (1994). Anonymity, presence, and the dialogic self in a technological culture. In R. Anderson, K. N. Cissna, & R. C. Arnett (Eds.), *The reach of dialogue: Confirmation, voice, and community* (pp. 91–110). Cresskill, NJ: Hampton Press.

angus1@cris.com. (1998, August 30). *Virtual reality in education: Education and Moo, Mud, Mush.* Retrieved October 13, 1998, from the World Wide Web: http://angus.interspeed.net/eduvr/.

Antommarchi, C., Ngeow, K., & Yajima, R. (1996). *Using technology for collaborative learning in the ESL classroom.* Unpublished manuscript, Indiana University, Bloomington.

Apple classrooms of tomorrow (1997). Apple Computer. Retrieved May 1, 1998, from the World Wide Web: http://www.research.apple.com/go/acot/.

Apple Computer. (1987). *Apple human interface guidelines: The Apple desktop interface.* Reading, MA: Addison-Wesley.

Areglado, R. J. (1996). *Learning for life: Creating classrooms for self-directed learning.* Thousand Oaks, CA: Corwin Press.

Asao, K. (1997, April). *Evaluating evaluation: Online instruction of EFL/ESL.* Paper presented at the Second Annual Teaching in the Community Colleges Online Conference. (Available from the author, e-mail koji@lb.u-tokai.ac.jp)

Aspects (Version 1.5) [Computer software]. (1994). Arlington, VA: Group Logic.

Association for Supervision and Curriculum Development. (1997). *The annual guide to the highest-rated educational software and multimedia.* Alexandria, VA: Author.

Authorware Star (Version 2.2.0 academic) [Computer software]. (1994). San Francisco, CA: Macromedia.

Backer, J. (1997, October 10). IRC for ESL/EFL. TESLCA-L [Discussion list]. Retrieved October 12, 1997, by e-mail: listserv@cunyvm.cuny.edu.

Bakhtin, M. M. (1986). *Speech genres and other late essays* (V. W. McGhee, Trans.). Austin: University of Texas Press.

Baltra, A. (1984). An EFL class in a mystery house. TESOL *Newsletter*, 18(6), 5–6.

Barlow, M. (1996). MonoConc for Windows [Computer software]. (1996). Houston, TX: Athelstan.

Batson, T., & Williamson, J. (1998). *The Epiphany Project: Strategies and structures for pedagogical change in the age of the electronic text.* Retrieved April 29, 1998, from the World Wide Web: http://mason.gmu.edu/~epiphany.

BBC World Service: Listen live 24 hours a day. (1998). Retrieved October 20, 1998, from the World Wide Web: http://www.bbc.co.uk/worldservice/.

Beach, R., & Liebman-Kleine, J. (1986). The writing/reading relationship: Becoming one's own best reader. In B. T. Petersen (Ed.), *Convergences: Transactions in reading and writing* (pp. 64–81). Urbana, IL: National Council of Teachers of English.

Beekman, G. (1996). *HyperCard 2.3 in a hurry.* Berkeley, CA: Peachpit Press.

Bell, A. (1984). Language style as audience design. *Language in Society*, 13, 145–204.

Bender, T. (1989). Eliza (Version 1.5) [Computer software]. San Angelo, TX: Trans-Tex Software. Retrieved November 20, 1998, via the World Wide Web and FTP: http://chiron.latrobe.edu.au/www/education/celia/celia.html, FTP Directory: english Subdirectory: mac Subdirectory: discussion File: eliza.hqx.

Bereiter, C., & Scardamalia, M. (1987). *The psychology of written composition.* Hillsdale, NJ: Erlbaum.

Berge, Z., & Collins, M. (1995). Computer-mediated communication and the on-line classroom: Overview and perspectives. *Computer-Mediated Communication Magazine*, 2(2), 6–17. Retrieved June 12, 1998, from the World Wide Web: http://www.december.com/cmc/mag/1995/feb/berge.html.

Biber, D. (1988). *Variation across speech and writing.* Cambridge: Cambridge University Press.

Bickel, B., & Truscello, D. (1996). New opportunities for learning: Styles and strategies with computers. TESOL *Journal*, 6(1), 15–19.

Biography.com: Biography magazine. (1997). A&E Television Networks. Retrieved November 7, 1997, from the World Wide Web: http://www.biography.com/read/.

Bishop, A. (1996, January). How to select bilingual software. NABE News 19(5), 1ff. (ERIC Document Reproduction Service No. ED 399 824)

Bishop, A. (1997). Checklist for ESL software. (Available from the author, e-mail: abishop@interport.net)

Black, S. D., Levin, J. A., & Mehan, H. (1983). Real and non-real time interaction: Unraveling multiple threads of discourse. Discourse Processes, 6, 59–75.

Blue Web'n: A library of blue ribbon learning sites on the Web. (1998, May 1). San Diego State University, Pacific Bell Fellows Applications Design Team, & Wired Learning. Retrieved May 8, 1998, from the World Wide Web: http://www.kn.pacbell.com /wired/bluewebn/.

Boling, E., Beriswill, J., Xaver, R., Hebb, C., Kaufman, D., & Frick, T. (1997). Text labels for hypermedia navigation buttons. International Journal of Instructional Media, 25(4), 1–15.

Boling, E., & Yi, Q. (1996). Design process and guidelines for language learning sites on the World Wide Web. The Dong-Eui International Journal, 2, 5–23.

Bonk, C. & Kim, D. (Eds.). (1998). Electronic collaborators: Learner-centered technologies for literacy, apprenticeship, and discourse. Mahwah, NJ: Erlbaum.

Boswood, T. (Ed.). (1997). New ways of using computers in language teaching. Alexandria, VA: TESOL.

Bowen, J. P. (1998, March 25). The World Wide Web virtual library: Audio. Retrieved April 15, 1998, from the World Wide Web: http://www.comlab.ox.ac.uk/archive/audio.html.

Bowers, R. (1997). Using HTML for online editing. Retrieved May 2, 1998, from the World Wide Web: http://www.tnis.net/rbowers/demo.html.

Bradin, C. (1994). Karaoke Conversation [Computer software]. Retrieved October 20, 1998, from the World Wide Web: http://edvista.com/claire/hypercard/templates .html. (Also available from the author, e-mail: bradincl@pilot.msu.edu)

Branscum, D. (1992, September). Educators need support to make computing meaningful. Macworld Special Edition, 83–88.

Breen, M. P. (1985). Authenticity in the language classroom. Applied Linguistics, 6, 60–70.

Breen, M. P. (1987). Learner contributions to task design. In C. N. Candlin & D. Murphy (Eds.), Language learning tasks (Lancaster Practical Papers in English Language Education 7, pp. 23–46). Englewood Cliffs, NJ: Prentice Hall International.

Brinton, D. M., Snow, M. A., & Wesche, M. B. (1989). Content-based second language instruction. New York: Harper & Row.

Brookfield, S. (1985). Self-directed learning: A critical review of research. In S. D. Brookfield (Ed.), Self-directed learning: From theory to practice (pp. 5–16). San Francisco: Jossey-Bass.

Brooks, S. (1988). Immigrants: The Irish Experience in Boston, 1849–1859 [Computer software]. Cambridge, MA: Educational Technology Center. Retrieved November 11, 1998, via the World Wide Web and FTP: http://chiron.latrobe.edu.au/www /education/celia/celia.html, FTP Directory: english Subdirectory: mac Subdirectory: reading File: immigrants.hqx.

Brown, H. D. (1987). Principles of language learning and teaching (2nd ed.). Englewood Cliffs, NJ: Prentice Hall Regents.

Brown, H. D. (1994). Teaching by principles: An interactive approach to language pedagogy. Englewood Cliffs, NJ: Prentice Hall Regents.

Brown, R., & Gilman, A. (1960). The pronouns of power and solidarity. In T. Sebeok (Ed.), *Style in language* (pp. 253–276). Cambridge, MA: MIT Press.

Browne, M., & Keeley, S. (1990). *Asking the right questions: A guide to critical thinking* (3rd ed.). Englewood Cliffs, NJ: Prentice Hall.

Brozo, W., & Simpson, M. (1995). *Readers, teachers, learners: Expanding literacy in secondary schools.* Englewood Cliffs, NJ: Prentice Hall.

Bruner, J. (1983). *Child's talk: Learning to use language.* New York: Norton.

Buell, J., & Rule, S. (1997, September 16). *Constructivism in ESL.* Retrieved December 12, 1997, from the World Wide Web: http://lrs.ed.uiuc.edu/students/jbuell/construct_ESL/.

Burger, K. (1985). Computer assisted instruction: Learning style and academic achievement. *Journal of Computer-Based Instruction, 12,* 21–22.

Business English and academic writing. (1997). The Comenius Group. Retrieved May 2, 1998, from the World Wide Web: http://www.comenius.com/writing/.

California Confederation of the Arts. (1994). *Cultural equity position paper.* Retrieved November 9, 1997, from the World Wide Web: http://www.tmn.com/Artswire /www/CALIFORNIA/06eq.html.

Candy, P. C. (1991). *Self-direction for lifelong learning.* San Francisco: Jossey-Bass.

Cantoni-Harvey, G. (1987). *Content-area language instruction: Approaches and strategies.* Reading, MA: Addison-Wesley.

Capitalism Plus [Computer software]. (1995). Research Triangle Park, NC: Interactive Magic.

Capitalist Pig [Computer software]. (1994). Mesa, AZ: Pluma Software.

The Cat Came Back [Computer software]. (1996). San Mateo, CA: Sanctuary Woods Multimedia/Theatrix (SWMC).

CataList, the official catalog of LISTSERV *lists.* (1998, October 11). L-Soft International. Retrieved October 31, 1998, from the World Wide Web: http://www.lsoft.com /catalist.html.

Cathcart, R., & Gumpert, G. (1994). Mediated interpersonal communication: Toward a new typology. In R. Anderson, K. N. Cissna, & R. C. Arnett (Eds.), *The reach of dialogue: Confirmation, voice, and community* (pp. 157–172). Cresskill, NJ: Hampton Press.

Cazden, C. B. (1988). *Classroom discourse: The language of teaching and learning.* Portsmouth, NH: Heinemann.

CESL at SIU-C. (1997, December 11). Southern Illinois University at Carbondale, Center for English as a Second Language. Retrieved May 1, 1998, from the World Wide Web: http://www.siu.edu/~cesl/.

Chamot, A. U., & O'Malley, J. M. (1989). *The CALLA handbook: Implementing the cognitive academic language learning approach.* Reading, MA: Addison-Wesley.

Chantrill, R. (1997). *Links to sites with public domain EFL/ESL CALL freeware and shareware.* Retrieved April 30, 1998, from the World Wide Web: http://www.cltr.uq.oz.au:8000 /~richardc/pubsoft.html.

Chapelle, C. A. (1988, February). *Contextualized grammar practice: A problem for CALL?* Paper presented at the Computer-Assisted Language Instruction Symposium, Atlanta, GA.

Chapelle, C. A. (1990). The discourse of computer-assisted language learning: Toward a context for descriptive research. *TESOL Quarterly, 24,* 199–225.

Chapelle, C. A. (1995a). Field-dependence/field-independence in the L2 classroom. In

J. M. Reid (Ed.), *Learning styles in the ESL/EFL classroom* (pp. 158–168). Boston: Heinle & Heinle.

Chapelle, C. A. (1995b). A framework for the investigation of CALL as a context for SLA. *CAELL Journal, 6*(3), 2–8.

Chapelle, C. A. (1997). CALL in the year 2000: Still in search of research paradigms? *Language Learning and Technology, 1*(1), 19–43. Retrieved June 16, 1998, from the World Wide Web: http://polyglot.cal.msu.edu/llt/.

Chapelle, C. A. (in press). *Computer applications in second language acquisition: Foundations for teaching, testing, and research.* Cambridge: Cambridge University Press.

Chapelle, C., & Mizuno, S. (1989). Students' strategies with learner-controlled CALL. *CALICO Journal, 7*(2), 25–44.

Chaudron, C. (1988). *Second language classrooms: Research on teaching and learning.* Cambridge: Cambridge University Press.

Chinatown/Manpower Project and South Manhattan Development Corporation. (1997). New York State Banking Department, Business Outreach Center. Retrieved November 9, 1997, from the World Wide Web: http://www.banking.state.ny.us/tap42.htm.

Choices, Choices (Version 5.0) [Computer software]. (1994). Watertown, MA: Tom Snyder Productions.

Choices, Choices: Kids and the Environment (Version 5.0) [Computer software]. (1994). Watertown, MA: Tom Snyder Productions.

Chun, D. (1994). Using computer networking to facilitate the acquisition of interactive competence. *System, 22,* 17–33.

Clapham, C. (1996). *The development of the IELTS: A study of the effect of background knowledge on reading comprehension.* Cambridge: University of Cambridge Local Examinations Syndicate.

ClariNews. (1997). ClariNet Communications. Retrieved November 15, 1997, from the World Wide Web: http://www.clari.net/newstree.html.

Class afloat live '98. (1998). Retrieved October 28, 1998, from the World Wide Web: http://www.oceanchallenge.com/cal/98f/ca98ffin.htm.

Classline: The daily teaching system. (1997). USA Today. Retrieved November 7, 1997, from the World Wide Web: http://www.usatoday.com/classlin/clfront.htm.

CNN interactive: Feedback. (1998). Cable News Network. Retrieved June 16, 1998, from the World Wide Web: http://www.cnn.com/feedback/.

CNN San Francisco: Interactive learning resources. (1998). Cable News Network, California Distance Learning Project, Outreach and Technical Assistance Network, California Department of Education, & Sacramento County Office of Education. Retrieved April 29, 1998, from the World Wide Web: http://www.cnnsf.com/education/education.html.

Cobb, T., & Stevens, V. (1996). A principled consideration of computers and reading in a second language. In M. C. Pennington (Ed.), *The power of CALL* (pp. 115–136). Houston, TX: Athelstan.

Coley, R. J., Cradler, J., & Engel, P. K. (1996). *Computers and classrooms: The status of technology in US schools* (Policy Information Report). Princeton, NJ: Educational Testing Service. Retrieved November 8, 1997, from the World Wide Web: http://www.ets.org/research/pic/compclass.html.

CommonSpace (Version 2.0) [Computer software]. (1997). Boston: Houghton Mifflin College Division/Sixth Floor Media.

Community Exploration [Computer software]. (1994). Lansing, MI: Hartley Courseware/ Jostens Learning.

Computer-Assisted Language Learning, a TESOL interest section. (1998). University of Oregon. Retrieved October 14, 1998, from the World Wide Web: http://darkwing .uoregon.edu/~call/.

Cooper, S. E., & Miller, J. A. (1991). MBTI learning style-teaching style discongruencies. *Educational and Psychological Measurement, 51,* 699–706.

Creative Writer (Version 2.0) [Computer software]. (1993). Redmond, WA: Microsoft.

Crookall, D., & Oxford, R. (Eds.). (1990). *Simulation, gaming, and language learning.* New York: Newbury House.

Crosscountry Canada [Computer software]. (1992). Burnaby, Canada: Ingenuity Works.

Crosscountry USA [Computer software]. (1992). Burnaby, Canada: Ingenuity Works. (Demo version available from Ingenuity Works, http://www.vrsystems.com/)

Csikszentmihalyi, M. (1991). *Flow: The psychology of optimal experience.* New York: HarperCollins.

Csikszentmihalyi, M. (1996). *Creativity: Flow and the psychology of discovery and invention.* New York: HarperCollins.

Csikszentmihalyi, M. (1997). *Finding flow: The psychology of engagement with everyday life.* New York: HarperCollins.

Cuban, L. (1986). *Teachers and machines: The classroom use of technology since 1920.* New York: Teachers College Press.

Cultural Debates [Computer software]. (1996). Watertown, MA: Tom Snyder Productions.

Cultural Reporter (Version 1) [Computer software, videotape, workbook]. (1995). Watertown, MA: Tom Snyder Productions.

Culture and Technology [Computer software]. (1996). Armonk, NY: The Learning Team.

Cummins, J., & Sayers, D. (1995). *Brave new schools: Challenging cultural illiteracy through global learning networks.* New York: St. Martin's Press.

Cunningham, P. A. (1995). Evaluating CALLware for your classroom. CAELL Journal, 6(3), 13–19.

Curran, K. (1976). *Counseling-learning in second language.* East Dubuque, IL: Counseling-Learning Publications.

CU-SeeMe (Version 3.0.0) [Computer software]. (1997). Nashua, NH: White Pine Software.

Daedalus Integrated Writing Environment [Computer software]. (1997). Austin, TX: The Daedalus Group.

Daedalus Integrated Writing Environment Guided Tour [Computer software]. (1989). Austin, TX: The Daedalus Group.

Dauer, R. M. (1998). *Oral skills improvement for foreign-born professionals* [Study guide and videotapes]. Amherst: University of Massachusetts, Video Instructional Program. Information available from *Professional development:* O3SC. (1998). Retrieved April 14, 1998, from the World Wide Web: http://www.ecs.umass.edu/vip/spring98/03sc.html.

Davidson, C., & Tomic, A. (1994). Removing computer phobia from the writing classroom. *English Language Teaching Journal, 48,* 205–213.

Day, E., & Shapson, S. M. (1991). Integrating formal and functional approaches to language teaching in French Immersion: An experimental study. *Language Learning*, 41, 25–58.

Day, R. (Ed.). (1986). *Talking to learn: Conversation in second language acquisition*. Rowley, MA: Newbury House.

Decisions, Decisions (Version 5.0) [Computer software]. (1996). Watertown, MA: Tom Snyder Productions.

Decisions, Decisions: Prejudice (Version 4.0) [Computer software]. (1994). Watertown, MA: Tom Snyder Productions.

DeMello, C. (1996). *College and university home pages—Alphabetical listing*. Massachusetts Institute of Technology. Retrieved May 1, 1998, from the World Wide Web: http://www.mit.edu:8001/people/cdemello/univ.html.

Destination: Ocean (Imagination Express) [Computer software]. (1995). Redmond, WA: Edmark.

Destination: Rain Forest (Imagination Express) [Computer software]. (1995). Redmond, WA: Edmark.

Dialectical Notebook [Computer software]. (1996.) Santa Barbara, CA: Intellimation/Academic Technologies.

Dickinson, L. (1987). *Self-instruction in language learning*. Cambridge: Cambridge University Press.

Digital Chisel (Version 2.1.6) [Computer software]. (1996). Portland, OR: Pierian Spring Software.

DiMatteo, A. (1990). Under erasure: A theory for interactive writing in real time. *Computers and Composition*, 7(Special issue), 71–84.

Director (Version 6.0.2) [Computer software]. (1998). San Francisco: Macromedia. (Available from http://www.macromedia.com /software/director/)

Discoveries: In the Desert [Computer software]. (1995). Boston: D.C. Heath/Houghton Mifflin.

Discovering America: The Adventure of Spanish Exploration [Computer software]. (1993). Galesburg, MI: Lawrence Productions.

Diversity University main campus MOO: Student union lounge. (n.d.). DU Educational Technology Services. Retrieved November 1, 1998, from the World Wide Web: http://moo.du.org:8000/99anon/anonview.

Dockterman, D. (1991). *Great teaching in the one-computer classroom*. Watertown, MA: Tom Snyder Productions.

Do Not Disturb (Version 2.0 Demo) [Computer software]. (1996). DeSoto, TX: Macmillan/McGraw-Hill.

Donath, J. (1996). *The electric postcard*. Massachusetts Institute of Technology Media Lab. Retrieved November 15, 1997, from the World Wide Web: http://persona.www.media.mit.edu/postcards/.

Doughty, C. (1991). Second language instruction does make a difference: Evidence from an empirical study of SL relativization. *Studies in Second Language Acquisition*, 13, 431–469.

Douglas, D. (in press). *Testing language for specific purposes: Theory and practice*. Cambridge: Cambridge University Press.

Dreyfus, H., & Dreyfus, S. (1986). *Mind over machine: The power of human intuition and expertise in the era of the computer*. New York: Free Press.

Duber, J. (1994). Clinton Debate. [Computer software]. Retrieved November 21, 1998, from the World Wide Web: http://www.duber.com/~dub/docs/portfolio.html.

Duber, J. (1997). *Cutting edge CALL demos*. University of California, Berkeley, College Writing Programs. Retrieved October 9, 1997, from the World Wide Web: http://www-writing.berkeley.edu/chorus/call/cuttingedge.html.

Duber, J. (Ed.). (1998). *Computer-assisted language learning@Chorus*. University of California, Berkeley, College Writing Programs. Retrieved October 14, 1998, from the World Wide Web: http://www-writing.berkeley.edu/chorus/call/.

Dudley-Marling, C., & Searle, D. (Eds.). (1995). *Who owns learning? Questions of autonomy, choice, and control*. Portsmouth, NH: Heinemann.

Duff, P. (1993). Tasks and interlanguage performance: An SLA perspective. In G. Crookes & S. M. Gass (Eds.), *Tasks and language learning: Integrating theory and practice* (pp. 57–95). Philadelphia: Multilingual Matters.

Dukes, R. L., Discenza, R., & Couger, J. D. (1989). Convergent validity of four computer anxiety scales. *Educational and Psychological Measurement, 49*, 195–203.

Dunn, R. S. (1996). *How to implement and supervise a learning style program*. Alexandria, VA: Association for Supervision and Curriculum Development.

Dunn, R., Dunn, K., & Price, G. (1989). *Learning style inventory manual*. Lawrence, KS: Price Systems.

Dunn, R., & Griggs, S. A. (1995). *Multiculturalism and learning style: Teaching and counseling adolescents*. Westport, CT: Praeger.

Dunn, R., Griggs, S. A., Olson, J., & Beasley, M. (1995). A meta-analytic validation of the Dunn and Dunn model of learning style preferences. *Journal of Educational Research, 88*, 353–362.

Dynamic English (Version 2.3) [Computer software]. (1997). Foster City, CA: DynEd International.

Ede, L., & Lunsford, A. (1984). Audience addressed/audience invoked: The role of audience in composition theory and pedagogy. *College Composition and Communication, 35*, 155–171.

Edelsky, C. (1991). *With literacy and justice for all. Rethinking the social in language and education*. London: Falmer Press.

Egbert, J. (1992). Reading the Classifieds [Computer software]. Retrieved October 9, 1997, via the World Wide Web and FTP: http://chiron.latrobe.edu.au/www/education/celia/celia.html, FTP Directory: english Subdirectory: mac Subdirectory: reading File: reading.hqx.

Egbert, J. (1993). *Learner perceptions of computer-supported language learning environments: Analytic and systemic analyses*. Unpublished doctoral dissertation, University of Arizona, Tucson.

Egbert, J. (1995a). Electronic action mazes. *CAELL Journal, 6*(3), 9–12.

Egbert, J. (1995b). What Do You Say? [Computer software]. (Available from the author, e-mail: jegbert@othello.ucs.indiana.edu)

Egbert, J. (1996a). *Computers for business and academics, Part 2*. Retrieved October 14, 1998, from the World Wide Web: http://php.indiana.edu/~jegbert/Part2.html.

Egbert, J. (1996b). *Cross-cultural field experience: Kids and computers*. Retrieved November 2, 1997, from the World Wide Web: http://php.indiana.edu/~jegbert/Kidsreport.html.

Egbert, J. (in press). Computers as content and context in a cross-cultural language field experience. In L. Kasper (Ed.), *Content-based ESL instruction*. Hillsdale, NJ: Erlbaum.

Egbert, J., & Jessup, L. (1991). CityGuide [Computer software]. (Available from the author, e-mail: ljessup@indiana.edu)

Egbert, J., & Jessup, L. (1996). Analytic and systemic analyses of computer-supported language learning environments. TESL-EJ, 2(1). Retrieved October 14, 1998, from the World Wide Web: http://violet.berkeley.edu/~cwp/TESL-EJ/ej06/a1.html.

Egbert, J., & Jessup, L. (in press). Integrating communities and skills: Systems analysis and design Web projects. In S. Gruber (Ed.), Weaving a virtual web: Practical approaches to new information technologies. Urbana, IL: National Council of Teachers of English.

Egbert, J., & Stepanova, I. (1992). Travelling in the USA [Computer software]. (Available from the author, e-mail: jegbert@othello.ucs.indiana.edu)

Ehrman, M., & Oxford, R. (1988). Effects of sex differences, career choice, and psychological type on adult language learning strategies. Modern Language Journal, 72, 253–265.

Ehrman, M., & Oxford, R. (1990). Adult language learning styles and strategies in an intensive training setting. Modern Language Journal, 74, 311–327.

Ehrmann, S. (1995). Asking the right question: What does research tell us about technology and higher learning? Retrieved October 14, 1998, from the World Wide Web: http://www.classweb.gatech.edu/fdw/assessment/askright.htm.

The Electronic Bookshelf [Computer software]. (1984). Frankfurt, IN: Electronic Bookshelf.

Eliason, P. A. (1995). Difficulties with cross-cultural learning-styles assessment. In J. M. Reid (Ed.), Learning styles in the ESL/EFL classroom (pp. 19–33). Boston: Heinle & Heinle.

Ellis, R. (1984). Classroom second language development. Oxford: Oxford University Press.

Ellis, R. (1994). The study of second language acquisition. Oxford: Oxford University Press.

ELLIS Master Pronunciation [Computer software]. (1994). American Fork, UT: CALI.

ELLIS Middle Mastery 2.1 [Computer software]. (1998). American Fork, UT: CALI.

ELLIS Senior Mastery 2.1 [Computer software]. (1998). American Fork, UT: CALI.

Emig, J. (1977). Writing as a mode of learning. College Composition and Communication, 28, 122–128.

ERIC on SilverPlatter [CD-ROM]. Norwood, MA: SilverPlatter Information.

Ernst, G. (1994). Talking circles. TESOL Quarterly, 28, 293–322.

ESLoop index. (n.d.). Retrieved April 14, 1998, from the World Wide Web: http://www.webring.org/cgi-bin/webring?index&ring=esloop.

Europe Inspirer (Version 4.0) [Computer software]. (1997). Watertown, MA: Tom Snyder Productions.

Exchange. (1997). University of Illinois at Urbana-Champaign, Division of English as an International Language/Intensive English Institute. Retrieved May 1, 1998, from the World Wide Web: http://deil.lang.uiuc.edu/exchange/.

Facklam, M. (1989). Do not disturb: The mysteries of animal hibernation and sleep. New York: McGraw-Hill.

The Factory [Computer software]. (1995). Pleasantville, NY: Sunburst Communications.

Falsetti, J. (n.d.). Welcome to schMOOze University. Retrieved April 29, 1998, from the World Wide Web: http://schmooze.hunter.cuny.edu:8888/.

Falsetti, J., & Schweitzer, E. (1995). schMOOze University: A MOO for ESL/EFL students. In M. Warschauer (Ed.), Virtual connections: On-line activities and projects for networking language learners (pp. 231–232). Honolulu: University of Hawaii, Second Language Teaching and Curriculum Center.

Fantin, J. P. (1997). Sounds like fun! In T. Boswood (Ed.), *New ways of using computers in language teaching* (pp. 300–301). Alexandria, VA: TESOL.

Farr, R. (1992). Putting it all together: Solving the reading assessment puzzle. *The Reading Teacher, 46,* 26–37.

Faulkner, G., & White, G. (1993). Who lives and works at the zoo? *CAELL Journal, 4*(3), 2–5.

Ferguson, C. A. (1971). Absence of copula and the notion of simplicity: A study of normal speech, baby talk, foreigner talk and pidgins. In D. Hymes (Ed.), *Pidginization and creolization of languages* (pp. 141–150). London: Cambridge University Press.

Fidelman, C. G. (1996). A language professional's guide to the World Wide Web. *CALICO Journal, 13*(2, 3). Retrieved May 1, 1998, from the World Wide Web: http://agoralang.com/calico/webarticle.html.

Fillmore, L. W. (1996). *The importance of background knowledge in second-language learning.* Retrieved October 14, 1998, from the World Wide Web: http://www.scottforesman.com/sfaw/teacher/educator2educator/ltintlwf.html.

Fluency through fables. (1997). The Comenius Group. Retrieved October 29, 1998, from the World Wide Web: http://www.comenius.com/fable/.

Foelsche, O. K. E. (Ed.). (1995). *IALL foreign language software database.* International Association for Learning Laboratories & Dartmouth College. Retrieved April 30, 1998, from the World Wide Web: http://fldb.dartmouth.edu/fldb/.

Fraser, B. (1986). *Classroom environment.* London: Croom Helm.

Frizler, K. (1997, October 8). *Frizzy University Network (FUN): schMOOze directions.* Retrieved November 15, 1997, from the World Wide Web: http://thecity.sfsu.edu/~funweb/schmooze.htm.

Frommer, J. G., & Foelsche, O. (1996). SuperMacLang [Computer software]. Dartmouth, NH: Dartmouth College & Harvard University. Retrieved June 30, 1997, from the World Wide Web: http://eleazar.dartmouth.edu/SML/.

Futaba, T. (1994). *Second language acquisition through negotiation: A case of non-native speakers who share the same first language.* Unpublished doctoral dissertation, University of Pennsylvania, Philadelphia.

Gaer, S. (1997). *Email projects home page.* Staff Development Institute & Outreach Technical Assistance Network. Retrieved May 8, 1998, from the World Wide Web: http://www.otan.dni.us/webfarm/emailproject/email.htm.

Gaffin, G., with Weitkötter, J. (1993). *Big dummy's guide to the Internet: Telnet (Mining the net, part 1).* Retrieved October 14, 1998, from the World Wide Web: http://www.hcc.hawaii.edu/bdgtti/bdgtti-1.0210.html.

Gardner, H. (1983). *Frames of mind: The theory of multiple intelligences.* New York: Basic Books.

Gardner, H. (1993). *Multiple intelligences: The theory in practice.* New York: Basic Books.

Garfinkle, H. (1967). *Studies in ethnomethodology.* Englewood Cliffs, NJ: Prentice Hall.

Garrison, J. W., & Rud, A. G. (1995). *The educational conversation: Closing the gap.* Albany, NY: State University of New York Press.

Gass, S. M., & Madden, C. G. (Eds.). (1985). *Input in second language acquisition.* Rowley, MA: Newbury House.

Gattegno, C. (1972). *Teaching foreign languages in schools: The silent way* (2nd ed.). New York: Educational Solutions.

Geertz, C. (1973). *The interpretation of cultures.* New York: Basic Books.

George, E. L. (1990). Taking women professors seriously: Female authority in the computerized classroom. *Computers and Composition*, 7(Special issue), 45–52.

Giles, H., & Smith, P. (1979). Accommodation theory: Optimal levels of convergence. In H. Giles & R. St. Clair (Eds.), *Language and social psychology* (pp. 45–65). Oxford: Basil Blackwell.

Go West! The Homesteader's Challenge [Computer software]. (1997). Austin, TX: Steck-Vaughn/Edunetics.

Goforth, D. (1994). Learner control = 3D decision making + information: A model and meta-analysis. *Journal of Educational Computing Research*, 11, 1–26.

Gölz, P. (1995). Virtual classrooms: University of Victoria's "VCR MUSH." In M. Warschauer (Ed.), *Virtual connections: On-line activities and projects for networking language learners* (pp. 239–242). Honolulu: University of Hawaii, Second Language Teaching and Curriculum Center.

Gomez, L., Parker, R., Lara-Alecio, R., Ochoa, S., & Gomez, R. (1996). Naturalistic language assessment of LEP students in classroom interactions. *The Bilingual Research Journal*, 20(1), 69–92.

Good, T. L., & Brophy, J. E. (1987). *Looking in classrooms*. New York: Harper & Row.

Green, J. L., & Meyer, L. A. (1991). The embeddedness of reading in classroom life: Reading as a situated process. In C. D. Baker & A. Luke (Eds.), *Towards a critical sociology of reading pedagogy* (pp. 141–160). Amsterdam: John Benjamins.

GROUPwriter [Computer software]. (1991). Pleasantville, NY: Sunburst Communications.

Guglielmino, L. M., & Guglielmino, P. J. (1994). Practical experience with self-directed learning in business and industry human resource development. In R. Hiemstra & R. G. Brockett (Eds.), *Overcoming resistance to self-direction in adult learning* (pp. 39–46). San Francisco: Jossey-Bass.

Guiora, A., Beit-Hallahmi, B., Brannon, R., Dull, C., & Scovel, T. (1972). The effects of experimentally induced changes in ego states on pronunciation ability in a second language: An exploratory study. *Comprehensive Psychiatry*, 13, 421–428.

Halliday, M. A. K. (1977). *Explorations in the functions of language*. New York: Elsevier North Holland.

Halliday, M. A. K., & Hasan, R. (1989). *Language, context, and text: Aspects of language in a social-semiotic perspective*. Oxford: Oxford University Press.

Hammersmith, L. (1997). *EnglishNet: Writing for the Web*. University of Illinois at Chicago, Tutorium in Intensive English. Retrieved May 2, 1998, from the World Wide Web: http://www.uic.edu/depts/tie/net/.

Haney, W., & Madaus, G. (1989). Searching for alternatives to standardized tests: Whys, whats, and whithers. *Phi Delta Kappan*, 70, 683–687.

Hannafin, R. D., & Sullivan, H. J. (1995). Learner control in full and lean CAI programs. *Educational Technology Research and Development*, 43(1), 14–30.

Hanson-Smith, E. (1991). *How to set up a computer lab: Advice for the beginner*. Houston, TX: Athelstan.

Hanson-Smith, E. (1997a). Constructing the Paragraph (Color version) [Computer software]. Sacramento, CA: Computers for Education. (Available from E. Hanson-Smith, Computers for Education, 91 Sandburg Dr., Sacramento, CA 95819-1849; telephone and fax: 916-739-0662; e-mail: EHansonSmi@aol.com)

Hanson-Smith, E. (1997b). Multimedia projects for EFL/ESL students. *CAELL Journal*, 7(4), 3–12.

Hanson-Smith, E. (1997c). *Technology in the classroom: Practice and promise in the 21st century.* Alexandria, VA: TESOL.

Hanson-Smith, E., & Egbert, J. (1996). *The art of technology, Part 1: New software and multimedia.* Preconference Institute presented at the 30th Annual TESOL Convention, Chicago, IL.

Hare, A. P., Blumberg, H. H., Davies, M. F., & Kent, M. V. (1994). *Small group research: A handbook.* Norwood, NJ: Ablex.

Harnessing the power of the Web: A tutorial. (1998). Global SchoolNet Foundation. Retrieved May 1, 1998, from the World Wide Web: http://www.gsn.org/web/.

Hatch, E. (1978a). Acquisition of syntax in a second language. In J. C. Richards (Ed.), *Understanding second and foreign language learning* (pp. 34–70). Rowley, MA: Newbury House.

Hatch, E. (1978b). Discourse analysis and second language acquisition. In E. Hatch (Ed.), *Second language acquisition: A book of readings* (pp. 401–435). Rowley, MA: Newbury House.

Hatch, E. (1983). Simplified input and second language acquisition. In R. W. Andersen (Ed.), *Pidginization and creolization as language acquisition* (pp. 64–86). Rowley, MA: Newbury House.

Healey, D. (1992). Theory and practice in a learning center. CAELL Journal, 3(3), 28–36.

Healey, D. (1993). *Learner choices in self-directed second language learning.* Unpublished doctoral dissertation, University of Oregon, Eugene.

Healey, D., & Johnson, N. (Eds.). (1996). 1996 CALL Interest Section Software List [Database file]. Retrieved October 9, 1997, via the World Wide Web and FTP: http://chiron.latrobe.edu.au/www/education/celia/celia.html, FTP Directory: english Subdirectory: mac Subdirectory: teacher-utils File: 96softlist.hqx; FTP Directory: english Subdirectory: win Subdirectory: teacher-utils File: 96softlist.zip.

Healey, D., & Johnson, N. (Eds.). (1997). 1997 CALL IS *software list.* Alexandria, VA: TESOL.

Heath, S. B., & Branscombe, A. (1985). "Intelligent writing" in an audience community: Teacher, students, and researcher. In S. W. Freedman (Ed.), *The acquisition of written language: Revision and response* (pp. 3–32). Norwood, NJ: Ablex.

Hegelheimer, V., Mills, D., Salzmann, A., & Shetzer, H. (1997). WWW *activities that work (and why!).* University of Illinois at Urbana-Champaign, Division of English as an International Language/Intensive English Institute. Retrieved May 1, 1998, from the World Wide Web: http://deil.lang.uiuc.edu/resources/TESOL/www_activities .html. Earlier version delivered as Hegelheimer, V., Mills, D., Salzmann, A., & Shetzer, H. (1996). *World Wide Web activities that work (and why!).* Colloquium at the 30th Annual TESOL Convention, Chicago, IL.

Heinich, R., Molenda, M., Russell, J. D., & Smaldino, S. E. (1996). *Instructional media and technologies for learning* (5th ed.). Englewood Cliffs, NJ: Prentice Hall.

Heinle & Heinle museum of cultural imagery. (1996). Retrieved May 2, 1998, from the World Wide Web: http://www.thomson.com/heinle/museum/welcome.html.

Herren, D. (1995). CDictation [Computer software]. Middlebury, VT: Green Mountain Mac Software.

Herschensohn, J. (1994). Balancing assessment procedures in evaluation of foreign language skills. *Journal of General Education, 43,* 134–146.

Hiemstra, R., & Brockett, R. G. (Eds.). (1994). *Overcoming resistance to self-direction in adult learning.* San Francisco: Jossey-Bass.

Higgins, J. (1988). *Language, learners and computers*. New York: Longman.

Higgins, J. (1989). Eclipse (Version 1.0) [Computer software]. London: Wida Software.

Higgins, J. (1994a). Double-Up [Computer software]. Retrieved April 30, 1998, from the World Wide Web: http://www.stir.ac.uk/epd/celt/staff/higdox/software.htm.

Higgins, J. (1994b). Sequitur [Computer software]. Stony Brook, NY: RDA Mind Builders. Demo version retrieved April 30, 1998, from the World Wide Web: http://www.stir.ac.uk/epd/celt/staff/higdox/software.htm.

Higgins, J. (1995). Eclipse (Version 2.2) [Computer software]. Retrieved April 30, 1998, from the World Wide Web: http://www.stir.ac.uk/epd/celt/staff/higdox/software .htm.

Higgins, J. (n.d.). Switch [Computer software]. Retrieved April 30, 1998, from the World Wide Web: http://www.stir.ac.uk/epd/celt/staff/higdox/software.htm.

Higgins, J., & Higgins, M. (1987). Rhubarb [Computer software]. Stony Brook, NY: RDA Mind Builders.

Higgins, J., & Higgins, M. (1997, June 13). *Updates for software by John and Muriel Higgins*. Retrieved April 30, 1998, from the World Wide Web: http://www.stir.ac.uk/epd/celt /staff/higdox/software.htm.

Hinkelman, D. W., & Pysock, J. M. (1992). The need for multi-media ESL teaching methods: A psychological investigation into learning styles. *Cross Currents, 19*(1), 25–35.

History Through Art [Computer software]. (1994). Dallas, TX: Zane Interactive. (Available from AmeXpo, PO Box 2094, Carlsbad, CA 92018)

Holliday, L. (1993a, October). *A comparison of cross-sentential cues to second language syntax in the negotiated interactions of NS-NNS and NNS-NNS dyads*. Paper presented at the Linguistics Symposium, University of Wisconsin at Milwaukee.

Holliday, L. (1993b, March). *Negotiations as a source of positive data for acquisition of L2 syntax*. Paper presented at the Second Language Acquisition Forum, Pittsburgh, PA.

Holliday, L. (1995a, January). *International ESL/EFL e-mail student discussion lists for language practice with a purpose and a peer audience*. Paper presented at the 15th Annual Thai TESOL Convention, Bangkok, Thailand.

Holliday, L. (1995b). Literacy and networked computers. *Singapore Book World, 25*(Special issue), 133–150. Singapore: National Book Development Council of Singapore/ Society for Reading and Literacy.

Holliday, L. (1995c). NS *modifications in negotiated interactions as a resource for second language acquisition of syntax*. Unpublished doctoral dissertation, University of Pennsylvania, Philadelphia.

Holliday, L. (1995d, January). *The SL-LISTS: E-mail EFL/ESL student discussion lists on Internet*. Paper presented at the Australian Council of TESOL Associations and Australia TESOL New South Wales National Conference, Sydney, Australia.

Holliday, L. (1996). From CALL to CMC in ESL: Approaching communicative language teaching ideals. In P. C. Clarkson & R. Toomey (Eds.), *Computing across the secondary curriculum: A review of research* (pp. 141–182). Melbourne, Australia: National Professional Development Program.

Holliday, L. (1997a). CELIA *at La Trobe University: Computer enhanced language instruction archive*. Retrieved October 9, 1997, from the World Wide Web: http://chiron.latrobe .edu.au/www/education/celia/celia.html.

Holliday, L. (1997b, January). *The grammar of second language learners of* English EMAIL *messages*. Paper presented at the 17th Annual Thai TESOL International Conference and the First Pan-Asian Conference, Bangkok, Thailand.

Holliday, L. (1998). The grammar of second language learners of English EMAIL messages. In S. Jager, J. Nerbonne, & A. Van Essen (Eds.), *Language Teaching and Language Technology* (pp. 136–145). Lisse, Netherlands: Swets & Zeitlinger.

Holliday, L., & Robb, T. (n.d.). *SL-Lists: International EFL/ESL email student discussion lists.* La Trobe University. Retrieved June 16, 1998, from the World Wide Web: http://chiron.latrobe.edu.au/www/education/sl/sl.html.

Hollywood High [Computer software]. (1996). Emeryville, CA: Theatrix Interactive.

Holmes, M. D. (1997a). Clozemaker (Version 1.1) [Computer software]. Retrieved April 30, 1998, from the World Wide Web: http://www.net-shopper.co.uk/creative/education/languages/martin/.

Holmes, M. D. (1997b). The Evil Landlady Action Maze [Computer software]. Retrieved April 30, 1998, from the World Wide Web: http://www.net-shopper.co.uk/creative/education/languages/martin/.

Holmes, M. D. (1997c). UV*ic online English writing course.* University of Victoria, English Language Centre. Retrieved May 2, 1998, from the World Wide Web: http://web.uvic.ca/hrd/OLCourse/.

Holmes, M. D. (n.d.). *Language teaching programs from Martin Holmes.* Retrieved April 30, 1998, from the World Wide Web: http://www.net-shopper.co.uk/creative/education/languages/martin/.

Honebein, P. C. (1996). Seven goals for the design of constructivist learning environments. In B. G. Wilson (Ed.), *Constructivist learning environments: Case studies in instructional design* (pp. 11–24). Englewood Cliffs, NJ: Educational Technology.

Hooper, S. (1992). Cooperative learning and computer-based instruction. *Educational Technology Research and Development, 40*(3), 21–38.

Horowitz, D. M. (1986). Process, not product: Less than meets the eye. TESOL *Quarterly, 20,* 141–144.

A House Divided: The Lincoln-Douglas Debate [Computer software]. (1994). Colorado Springs, CO: Grafica Multimedia.

Howard, G. S. (1986). *Computer anxiety and the use of microcomputers in management.* Ann Arbor, MI: UMI Research Press.

Hubbard, P. (1987). Language teaching approaches, the evaluation of CALL software, and design implications. In W. Smith (Ed.), *Modern media in foreign language education: Theory and implementation* (pp. 227–254). Lincolnwood, IL: National Textbook Co.

Hubbard, P. (1996). Elements of CALL methodology: Development, evaluation, and implementation. In M. Pennington (Ed.), *The power of CALL* (pp. 15–32). Houston, TX: Athelstan.

Hudiburg, R. A. (1989). Psychology of computer use: XVII. The computer technology hassles scale: Revision, reliability, and some correlates. *Psychological Reports, 65,* 1387–1394.

Hudiburg, R. A. (1990). Relating computer-associated stress to computerphobia. *Psychological Reports, 67,* 311–314.

HyperACE Advanced [Computer software]. (1996) Houston, TX: Athelstan. (Demo version available from Athelstan, http://www.athel.com/)

HyperACE Intermediate [Computer software]. (1995). Houston, TX: Athelstan. (Demo version available from Athelstan, http://www.athel.com/)

HyperCard (Version 2.3.1) [Computer software]. (1995). Cupertino, CA: Apple Computer.

HyperCard (Version 2.3.5) [Computer software]. (1997). Cupertino, CA: Apple Computer.

HyperStudio (Version 3.1) [Computer software]. (1997). San Diego, CA: Roger Wagner. Demo version retrieved October 18, 1998, from the World Wide Web: http://www.hyperstudio.com/download/indbod.html.

HyperStudio Web Browser Plug-In [Computer software]. (1996). El Cajon, CA: Roger Wagner. Retrieved October 18, 1998, from the World Wide Web: http://www.hyperstudio.com/lab/plugin.html.

I*EARN Global Art Project home page: A sense of family. (1996). Washington State University. Retrieved November 2, 1997, from the World Wide Web: http://www.vpds.wsu.edu/i*earn/global_art.html.

Inspiration [Computer software]. (1988). Lake Oswego, OR: Ceres Software; Marlow, NH: MacConnection.

Interactive Internet language learning. (1997). University of Oregon. Retrieved May 1, 1998, from the World Wide Web: http://babel.uoregon.edu/yamada/interact.html.

Interactive Nova: Earth [Computer software]. (1994). Jefferson City, MO: Scholastic New Media.

International Inspirer (Version 4.0) [Computer software]. (1996). Watertown, MA: Tom Snyder Productions.

The Internet TESL Journal. (1998). Retrieved May 1, 1998, from the World Wide Web: http://www.aitech.ac.jp/~iteslj/.

Iwabuchi, T. (1998). Oregon-Senshu project. Senshu University. Retrieved May 1, 1998, from the World Wide Web: http://gkk.senshu-u.ac.jp/~tiwabuchi/o-sproject/sthomepage.html.

JALT: The Japan Association for Language Teaching. (1997, November 28). Chubu University. Retrieved December 12, 1997, from the World Wide Web: http://langue.hyper.chubu.ac.jp/jalt/.

Java [Computer programming language]. (1998). Palo Alto, CA: Sun Microsystems.

James, W. B., & Gardner, D. L. (1995). Learning styles: Implications for distance learning. In M. H. Rossman & M. E. Rossman (Eds.), Facilitating distance education (pp. 19–32). San Francisco: Jossey-Bass.

Jefferson, G. (1972). Side sequences. In D. Sudnow (Ed.), Studies in social interaction (pp. 294–338). New York: Free Press.

Johanesen, K. J., & Tennyson, R. D. (1983). Effect of adaptive advisement on perception in learner-controlled, computer-based instruction using a rule-learning task. Educational Communication and Technology, 31, 226–236.

Johns, A. M. (1986). Coherence and academic writing: Some definitions and suggestions for teaching. TESOL Quarterly, 20, 247–265.

Johns, T. (1998, February 18). Tim Johns data-driven learning page. University of Birmingham. Retrieved April 29, 1998, from the World Wide Web: http://web.bham.ac.uk/johnstf/timconc.htm.

Johnson, D. (1991). Approaches to research in second language learning. New York: Longman.

Johnson, D. W., Johnson, R. T., & Smith, K. A. (1991). Active learning: Cooperation in the college classroom. Edina, MN: Interaction Books.

Jones, B. F., Valdez, G., Nowakowski, J., & Rasmussen, C. (1995). New times demand new ways of learning. North Central Regional Education Laboratory. Retrieved October 18, 1998, from the World Wide Web: http://www.ncrel.org/sdrs/edtalk/newtimes.htm.

Jones, C. (1990). Storyboard [Computer software]. London: Wida Software. (Available from Athelstan, http://www.athel.com/; demo version available from Wida Software, http://www.wida.co.uk/)

Juilliard Music Adventure [Computer software]. (1995). Emeryville, CA: Theatrix Interactive.

Kain. (1997, September 16). *Bienvenu au MOOFrancais*. Retrieved April 29, 1998, from the World Wide Web: http://moo.syr.edu/~fmoo/fmoo/.

Kaufman, D., & Brooks, G. J. (1996). Interdisciplinary collaboration in teacher education: A constructivist approach. TESOL *Quarterly, 30*, 231–251.

Keefe, J. W. (1987). *Learning style: Theory and practice*. Reston, VA: National Association of Secondary School Principals.

Keenan, C., et al. (1996). Epiphany Project. In *Epiphany field guide: MOO resources and professional MOO meetings (What can you do in the MOO? An overview and collection of MOO lesson plans)*. Retrieved April 29, 1998, from the World Wide Web: http://mason.gmu.edu/~epiphany/docs/dointhemoo.html#resources.

Keirsey, D. M. (1984). *Keirsey temperament sorter*. Retrieved April 12, 1998, from the World Wide Web: http://www.keirsey.com/cgi-bin/keirsey/newkts.cgi.

Kelm, O. (1992). The use of synchronous computer networks in second language instruction: A preliminary report. *Foreign Language Annals, 25*, 441–454.

Kelman, P. (1990). Alternatives to integrated instructional systems. CUE *Newsletter, 13*(2), 7–9.

Kemp, F. (1993). The origins of ENFI, network theory, and computer-based collaborative writing instruction at the University of Texas. In B. Bruce, J. K. Peyton, & T. Batson (Eds.), *Network-based classrooms: Promises and realities* (pp. 161–180). New York: Cambridge University Press.

Kemp, F. (1997, January). *"Hard fun": Networks and the possibility, just maybe, of non-coercive formal learning*. Keynote address presented at the conference Astride the Divide: Mapping New Rhetorical Spaces in the Teaching of Composition, Fairfax, VA.

Kernan, M. C., & Howard, G. S. (1990). Computer anxiety and computer attitudes: An investigation of construct and predictive validity issues. *Educational and Psychological Measurement, 50*, 681–690.

Keys, K. (1996). TinyFugue (Version 3.5). [Computer software]. Retrieved October 28, 1998, via the World Wide Web and FTP: http://ftp.tcp.com/ FTP Directory: mud Subdirectory: clients Subdirectory: tinyfugue.

Kid Pix [Computer software]. (1997). Novato, CA: Brøderbund Software.

Kiesler, S., Siegel, J., & McGuire, T. W. (1984). Social psychological aspects of computer-mediated communication. *American Psychologist, 39*, 1123–1134.

Killion, K. (1985). MacTrivia [Computer software]. Retrieved October 28, 1998, via the World Wide Web and FTP: http://chiron.latrobe.edu.au/www/education/celia /celia.html, FTP Directory: english Subdirectory: mac Subdirectory: reading File: mactrivia.hqx.

King cobra: The king's armory. (1997). National Geographic Society. Retrieved October 29, 1998, from the World Wide Web: http://www.nationalgeographic.com/kingcobra /index=n.html.

Kinsella, K. (1995a). Perceptual learning preferences survey. In J. M. Reid (Ed.), *Learning styles in the ESL/EFL classroom* (pp. 221–238). (1995). Boston: Heinle & Heinle.

Kinsella, K. (1995b). Understanding and empowering diverse learners. In J. M. Reid (Ed.), *Learning styles in the ESL/EFL classroom* (pp. 170–194). Boston: Heinle & Heinle.

Kirsch, G., & Roen, D. H. (1990). Introduction: Theories and research on audience in written communication. In G. Kirsch & D. H. Roen (Eds.), *A sense of audience in written communication* (pp. 13–21). Newbury Park, CA: Sage.

Kitagawa, M. (1997). *Kyoto restaurant project.* Kyoto Sangyo University. Retrieved June 18, 1998, from the World Wide Web: http://www.kyoto-su.ac.jp/information/restaurant/.

Kitao, K., & S. K. Kitao, S. K. (1997, September 1). *Online resources and journals: ELT, linguistics, and communication.* Retrieved December 12, 1997, from the World Wide Web: http://www.ling.lancs.ac.uk/staff/visitors/kenji/onlin.htm.

Kitao, S. K., & Kitao, K. (1996, September 7). Teaching about English-speaking cultures. TESL-L [Discussion list]. Retrieved December 12, 1997, by e-mail: listserv@cunyvm.cuny.edu.

Kluge, D. (1996). Asking the basic questions about computer-assisted language learning. In S. Fotos (Ed.), *Multimedia language teaching* (pp. 21–34). Tokyo: Logos International.

Kolb, D. A. (1985). *Learning style inventory.* Boston: McBer.

Kovic, R. (1976). *Born on the fourth of July.* New York: Pocket Books.

Krashen, S. (1978). The monitor model for second language acquisition. In R. Gingras (Ed.), *Second language acquisition and foreign language teaching* (pp. 1–26). Arlington, VA: Center for Applied Linguistics.

Krashen, S. (1980). The input hypothesis. In J. E. Alatis (Ed.), *Current issues in bilingual education* (pp. 168–180). Washington, DC: Georgetown University Press.

Krashen, S. (1981). *Second language acquisition and second language learning.* Oxford: Pergamon Press.

Krashen, S. (1982). *Principles and practice in second language acquisition.* Oxford: Pergamon Press.

Krashen, S. (1985). *The input hypothesis: Issues and implications.* London: Longman.

Krashen, S., & Terrell, T. (1983). *The natural approach: Language acquisition in the classroom.* Hayward, CA: Alemany Press.

Kremers, M. (1990). Sharing authority in a synchronous network: The case for riding the beast. *Computers and Composition, 7*(Special issue), 33–44.

Kremers, M. (1993). Student authority and teacher freedom: ENFI at New York Institute of Technology. In B. Bruce, J. K. Peyton, & T. Batson (Eds.), *Network-based classrooms: Promises and realities* (pp. 113–123). New York: Cambridge University Press.

Kroll, B. M. (1984). Writing for readers: Three perspectives on audience. *College Composition and Communication, 35,* 172–185.

Langer, J. A. (1986). Musings: Computers and conversation. *Research in the Teaching of English, 20,* 117–119.

Langston, M. D., & Batson, T. (1990). The social shifts invited by working collaboratively on computer networks: The ENFI Project. In C. Handa (Ed.), *Computers and community: Teaching composition in the twenty-first century* (pp. 141–159). Portsmouth, NH: Boynton/Cook.

Language Now! (Version 5.0.2) [Computer software]. (1996). Hollis, NH: Transparent Language.

Lanier, A. (1988). *Living in the USA* (4th ed.). Yarmouth, ME: Intercultural Press.

Lapp, S., & Solé, D. (1997). Hyped communication about modern art. In T. Boswood

(Ed.), *New ways of using computers in language teaching* (pp. 293–299). Alexandria, VA: TESOL.

Larsen-Freeman, D., & Long, M. (1991). *An introduction to second language acquisition research*. London: Longman.

Laurel, B. (1991). *Computers as theater*. New York: Addison-Wesley.

Lazarus, R. S., & Launier, R. (1978). Stress-related transactions between person and environment. In L. A. Pervin & M. Lewis (Eds.), *Perspectives in interactional psychology* (pp. 287–327). New York: Plenum Press.

Learning English: Home and Family [Computer software]. (1994). Lansing, MI: Hartley Courseware/Jostens Learning.

Learning English: Neighborhood Life [Computer software]. (1994). Lansing, MI: Hartley Courseware/Jostens Learning.

Lemke, J. L. (1990). *Talking science: Language, learning, and values*. Norwood, NJ: Ablex.

Leshin, C. B., Pollock, J., & Reigeluth, C. M. (1992). *Instructional design strategies and tactics*. Englewood Cliffs, NJ: Educational Technology.

Levin, J., & Boruta, M. (1983). Writing with computers in classrooms: "You get exactly the right amount of space!" *Theory into Practice, 22,* 291–295.

Levinson, S. C. (1983). *Pragmatics*. Cambridge: Cambridge University Press.

Levy, M. (1990). Towards a theory of CALL. *CAELL Journal, 1*(4), 5–7.

Li, R. (1998). *Learning oral English online*. University of Illinois at Urbana-Champaign. Retrieved April 14, 1998, from the World Wide Web: http://www.lang.uiuc.edu/r-li5/book/.

Lian, A. (1992). Intelligence in computer-aided language learning. In M. Pennington & V. Stevens (Eds.), *Computers in applied linguistics* (pp. 66–76). Clevedon, England: Multilingual Matters.

Lieu, M. W. (n.d.). *grammarONLINE*. Retrieved May 1, 1998, from the World Wide Web: http://www.crl.com/~malarak/grammar/.

Light and Sound [Computer software and activity kit]. (1996). Austin, TX: Steck-Vaughn/ Edunetics.

Lightbown, P. M., & Spada, N. (1990). Focus-on-form and corrective feedback in communicative language teaching. *Studies in Second Language Acquisition, 12,* 429–448.

Lightbown, P. M., & Spada, N. (1994). *How languages are learned*. Oxford: Oxford University Press.

Lim, T. K. (1994). Personality types among Singapore and American students. *Journal of Psychological Type, 31,* 10–15.

Lindsey, R. (n.d.). *Rachel's super MOO list: Educational MOOs*. Retrieved May 5, 1998, from the World Wide Web: http://moolist.yeehaw.com/edu.html.

Linnell, J. (1995). Can negotiation provide a context for learning syntax in a second language? *Working Papers in Educational Linguistics, 11*(2), 83–103.

LiveCard [Computer software]. (1996). Dayton, OH: Royal Software.

LiveChat (Version 1.1) [Computer software]. (1997). Aarhus, Denmark: Cabocomm.

LiveWriter [Computer software]. (1990). Commack, NY: RDA Mind Builders.

Long, M. (1980). Inside the "black box": Methodological issues in classroom research on language learning. *Language Learning, 30,* 1–42.

Long, M. (1983a). Linguistic and conversational adjustments to non-native speakers. *Studies in Second Language Acquisition, 5,* 177–194.

Long, M. (1983b). Native speaker/non-native speaker conversation and the negotiation of comprehensible input. *Applied Linguistics, 4*, 126–141.

Long, M. H. (1985). Input and second language acquisition theory. In S. M. Gass & C. G. Madden (Eds.), *Input in second language acquisition* (pp. 377–393). Rowley, MA: Newbury House.

Long, M. H. (1987). Instructed interlanguage development. In L. M. Beebe (Ed.), *Issues in second language acquisition* (pp. 113–142). New York: Newbury House.

Long, M., & Porter, P. (1985). Group work, interlanguage talk, and second language acquisition. TESOL *Quarterly, 19*, 207–228.

Longman Multimedia Dictionary [Computer software]. (1996). New York: Addison Wesley Longman.

The Lost Mind of Dr. Brain [Computer software]. (1995). Salinas, CA: Sierra On-Line.

Lozanov, G. (1978). *Suggestology and outlines of suggestopedy.* New York: Gordon & Breach.

Lunn, F. (1996, June 18). Summary of responses to request for CALL lab info. TESLCA-L [Discussion list]. Retrieved December 18, 1996, by e-mail: listserv @cunyvm.cuny.edu.

MacESL (Version 2.0) [Computer software]. (1992). City of Industry, CA: Hacienda–La Puente Unified School District. (Available from Hacienda–La Puente Unified School District, 320 N. Willow Ave., La Puente, CA 91746; telephone 818-855-7007)

MacIntyre, P. D., & Gardner, R. C. (1991). Methods and results in the study of foreign language anxiety: A review of the literature. *Language Learning, 41*, 85–117.

Mackey, A. (1995). *Stepping up the pace: Input, interaction, and interlanguage development—An empirical study of questions in ESL.* Unpublished doctoral dissertation, University of Sydney, Australia.

MacLang (Version 3.0) [Computer software]. (1987). Santa Barbara, CA: Intellimation.

Macrorie, K. (1988). *The I-search paper.* Portsmouth, NH: Heinemann Educational Books.

Malamah-Thomas, A. (1987). *Classroom interaction.* Oxford: Oxford University Press.

Map Room [Computer software and activity kit]. (1996). Austin, TX: Steck-Vaughn/ Edunetics.

Marcoulides, G. A. (1989). Measuring computer anxiety: The computer anxiety scale. *Educational and Psychological Measurement, 49*, 733–739.

Martin, J. R. (1985). Process and text: Two aspects of human semiosis. In J. D. Benson & W. S. Greaves (Eds.), *Systemic perspectives on discourse, 1: Selected theoretical papers from the Ninth International System Workshop* (pp. 248–274). Norwood, NJ: Ablex.

May, C. (Ed.). (1993). *Fiction's many worlds.* Boston: Houghton Mifflin College Division.

May, C. (1995). HyperStory: Student Software for Macintosh [Computer software]. Boston: Houghton Mifflin College Division.

McClure, C. R., & Lopata, C. L. (1996). *Assessing the academic networked environment: Strategies and options.* Washington, DC: Coalition for Networked Information. (ERIC Document Reproduction Service No. ED 393 456)

McGregor, G., & White, R. S. (Eds.). (1990). *Reception and response: Hearer creativity and the analysis of spoken and written texts.* London: Routledge.

McInnis, D. J. (1996). An interview with Johan Galtung. *The Language Teacher, 20*(11). Retrieved November 9, 1997, from the World Wide Web: http://langue.hyper .chubu.ac.jp:8417/jalt/pub/tlt/96/nov/galtung.html.

McKenzie, J. (1997). The questioning kit. *From Now On: The Educational Technology Journal,*

7(3). Retrieved October 20, 1998, from the World Wide Web: http://www.fromnowon .org/nov97/toolkit.html.

McNamee, G. P. (1979). The social origins of narrative skills. *Quarterly Newsletter of the Laboratory of Comparative Human Cognition*, 1, 63–68.

McVicker, J. (1992). MacReader [Computer software]. New York: Gessler Software.

McVicker, J. (1995a). NewReader (Version 1.00) [Computer software]. Athens, OH: Hyperbole Software.

McVicker, J. (1995b). Verb Professor (Version 1.0) [Computer software]. Athens, OH: Hyperbole Software.

McVicker, J. (1997). NewReader (Version 1.04) [Computer software]. Athens, OH: Hyperbole Software.

Me and My World [Computer software]. (1995). Lincolnwood, IL: National Textbook Co.

Meagher, M. (1995). Learning English on the Internet. *Educational Leadership*, 53(2), 88–90.

Mejia, E. (1995). Like it was: On-line with veterans via e-mail. *CALL-IS Newsletter*, 12(2), 8.

Mello, V. (1998). Prepositions. In *The Internet TESL Journal: Crossword Puzzles for ESL Students*. Retrieved October 20, 1998, from the World Wide Web: http://www .aitech.ac.jp/~iteslj/cw/1/vm-prep.htm.

Merlin: World class. (1997). University of Hull. Retrieved May 2, 1998, from the World Wide Web: http://www.hull.ac.uk/merlin.

Meskill, C. (1987). Interactivity in CALL courseware design. *CALICO Journal*, 5(1), 9–14.

Meskill, C., & Mossop, J. (1997). *Technologies use with learners of ESL in New York State: Preliminary report*. Albany, NY: National Center for English Learning and Achievement.

Meskill, C., & Shea, P. (1994). Multimedia and language learning: Integrating the technology into existing curricula. In P. Kramer (Ed.), *Proceedings of the Third Conference on Instructional Technologies* (p. 57). Albany: State University of New York, Office of Educational Technology.

Message in a Fossil [Computer software]. (1996). Austin, TX: Steck-Vaughn/Edunetics.

Mia, V., & Walter, L. (1995). Enhancing metacognition in self-directed language learning. *System*, 23, 223–234.

Microsoft Access 98 [Computer software]. (1997). Redmond, WA: Microsoft.

Microsoft Bookshelf 95 [Computer software]. (1995). Redmond, WA: Microsoft.

Microsoft Encarta World Atlas 98 [Computer software]. (1997). Redmond, WA: Microsoft.

Microsoft Encarta Encyclopedia 98 [Computer software]. (1997). Redmond, WA: Microsoft.

Microsoft Cinemania 96 [Computer software]. (1995). Redmond, WA: Microsoft.

Microsoft FrontPage 98 [Computer software]. (1998). Redmond, WA: Microsoft.

Microsoft Internet Explorer (Version 4.0) [Computer software]. (1998). Redmond, WA: Microsoft.

Microsoft NetMeeting (Version 2.1) [Computer software]. (1997). Redmond, WA: Microsoft.

Microsoft Paint 95 [Computer software]. (1995). Redmond, WA: Microsoft.

Microsoft PowerPoint 97 [Computer software]. (1996). Redmond, WA: Microsoft.

Microsoft Publisher 97 [Computer software]. (1997). Redmond, WA: Microsoft.

Microsoft Telnet (Version 1.0) [Computer software]. (1996). Redmond, WA: Microsoft.

Microsoft Word (Version 6.0.1) [Computer software] (1995). Redmond, WA: Microsoft.

Microsoft Word (Version 7.0) [Computer software]. (1997). Redmond, WA: Microsoft.

Microsoft Works (Version 4.0) [Computer software]. (1994). Redmond, WA: Microsoft.

Miller, C., Tomlinson, A., & Jones, M. (1994). *Learning styles and facilitating reflection* (Research Report Series: Researching Professional Education). London: English National Board. (ERIC Document Reproduction Service No. ED 390 991)

Miller, J. D. (1993). Script writing on a computer network: Quenching the flames or feeding the fire? In B. Bruce, J. K. Peyton, & T. Batson (Eds.), *Network-based classrooms: Promises and realities* (pp. 124–137). New York: Cambridge University Press.

Millet, K., & Sano, D. (1995). *Designing visual interfaces: Communication-oriented techniques.* Englewood Cliffs, NJ: Prentice Hall.

Mills, D., & Salzmann, A. (1998). *Grammar safari.* University of Illinois at Urbana-Champaign, Division of English as an International Language/Intensive English Institute. Retrieved May 1, 1998, from the World Wide Web: http://deil.lang.uiuc.edu /web.pages/grammarsafari.html.

Moody, S. (n.d.). *Introduction to NETEACH-L.* Retrieved October 14, 1998, from the World Wide Web: http://www.ilc.cuhk.edu.hk/english/neteach/main.htm.

Moya, S., & O'Malley, J. M. (1994). A portfolio assessment model for ESL. *Journal of Educational Issues of Language Minority Students, 13,* 13–36.

The Multimedia Workshop [Computer software]. (1994). Torrance, CA: Davidson.

Murray, D. (1982). *Learning by teaching.* Montclair, NJ: Boynton-Cook.

Myers, I. B., & McCaulley, M. H. (1985). *Manual: A guide to the development and use of the Myers-Briggs Type Indicator.* Palo Alto, CA: Consulting Psychologists Press.

Myst [Computer software]. (1995). Novato, CA: Brøderbund Software.

Naisbitt, J. (1984). *Megatrends: Ten new directions transforming our lives.* New York: Warner Books.

Najjar, L. J. (1996). Multimedia information and learning. *Journal of Educational Multimedia and Hypermedia, 5,* 129–150.

National Center for Educational Statistics. (1995). *Student use of computers* (Indicator of the Month, NCES 96792). Washington, DC: Author. (ERIC Document Reproduction Service No. ED 391 524)

National Inspirer (Version 4.0) [Computer software]. (1996). Watertown, MA: Tom Snyder Productions.

Naumann, B. (1995). Mailbox chats: Dialogues in electronic communication. In F. Hundsnurscher & E. Weigand (Eds.), *Future perspectives of dialogue analysis* (pp. 163–184). Tübingen, Germany: Max Niemeyer.

NCSA Telnet [Computer software]. (1995). Urbana: University of Illinois, National Center for Supercomputing Applications. Retrieved June 16, 1998, from the World Wide Web: http://www.ncsa.uiuc.edu/SDG/Homepage/telnet.html.

Nelson, G. L. (1995). Cultural differences in learning styles. In J. M. Reid (Ed.), *Learning styles in the ESL/EFL classroom* (pp. 3–18). Boston: Heinle & Heinle.

Netscape Navigator Gold (Version 3.02) [Computer software]. (1997). Mountain View, CA: Netscape Communications.

The New Oxford Picture Dictionary CD-ROM (Bilingual Spanish ed.) [Computer software]. (1997). Oxford: Oxford University Press.

Newell, F. M. (1996). Effects of a cross-age tutoring program on computer literacy learning of second grade students. *Journal of Research on Computing in Education, 28,* 346–358.

Newman, C., & Smolen, L. (1993). Portfolio assessment in our schools: Implementation, advantages, and concerns. *Midwestern Educational Researcher, 6*, 28–32.

Nile: Passage to Egypt [Computer software]. (1995). Bethesda, MD: Discovery Communications. (Available from The Discovery Channel, http://shopping .discovery .com/)

Nobel, P. (1980). *Resource-based learning in post compulsory education*. London: Kogan Page.

Nobuyoshi, J., & Ellis, R. (1993). Focused communication tasks. *English Language Teaching Journal, 47*, 203–210.

Noddings, N. (1984). *Caring: A feminine approach to ethics and moral education*. Berkeley: University of California Press.

Noddings, N. (1992). *The challenge to care in schools: An alternative approach to education*. New York: Teachers College Press.

NOVA Online. (1997). WGBH Educational Foundation. Retrieved November 2, 1997, from the World Wide Web: http://www.pbs.org/wgbh/nova/.

NOVA Online: Teachers Guide. (1997). WGBH Educational Foundation. Retrieved November 2, 1997, from the World Wide Web: http://www.pbs.org/wgbh/nova /teachersguide/.

Nunan, D. (1989a). *Designing tasks for the communicative classroom*. Cambridge: Cambridge University Press.

Nunan, D. (1989b). *Language teaching methodology: A textbook for teachers*. New York: Prentice Hall.

Nyikos, M. (1990). Sex-related differences in adult language learning: Socialization and memory factors. *Modern Language Journal, 74*, 273–287.

Ocean planet: A Smithsonian Institution traveling exhibit. (n.d.). Retrieved November 15, 1997, from the World Wide Web: http://seawifs.gsfc.nasa.gov/ocean_planet.html.

Ohio University CALL lab. (1998). Retrieved May 1, 1998, from the World Wide Web: http://www.tcom.ohiou.edu/OU_Language/OU_Language.html.

Oliver, R. (1995). *Negotiation and feedback in child second language acquisition*. Unpublished doctoral dissertation, University of Western Australia, Nedlands.

O'Malley, J., & Chamot, A. (1990). *Learning strategies in second language acquisition*. New York: Cambridge University Press.

Online Writing Lab: Resources for writers. (1997). Purdue University. Retrieved May 1, 1998, from the World Wide Web: http://owl.english.purdue.edu/writers/introduction.html.

Opening Night [Computer software]. (1995). Minneapolis, MN: MECC.

Opp-Beckman, L. (1997a, August 18). OP*Portunities in ESL*. University of Oregon, American English Institute. Retrieved December 12, 1997, from the World Wide Web: http://darkwing.uoregon.edu/~leslieob/.

Opp-Beckman, L. (1997b, October 27). PIZZAZ!. University of Oregon, American English Institute. Retrieved October 29, 1998, from the World Wide Web: http:// darkwing.uoregon.edu/~leslieob/pizzaz.html.

Opp-Beckman, L. (1997c). PIZZAZ! *Magazine Marvels*. University of Oregon, American English Institute. Retrieved October 29, 1998, from the World Wide Web: http:// darkwing.uoregon.edu/~leslieob/magmarvel.html.

Opp-Beckman, L. (1998a). *Sanno College summer 1998*. University of Oregon, American English Institute. Retrieved October 29, 1998, from the World Wide Web: http:// darkwing.uoregon.edu/~aei/sanno98memories.html.

Opp-Beckman, L. (1998b, April 15). *Senshu/University of Oregon, AEI: Meet your AEI tutors!*

University of Oregon, American English Institute. Retrieved May 1, 1998, from the World Wide Web: http://darkwing.uoregon.edu/~leslieob/senshututors.html.

Oregon Trail (Version 1.1) [Computer software]. (1991). Minneapolis, MN: MECC.

Oregon Trail II [Computer software]. (1997). Minneapolis, MN: The Learning Company.

Oriti, C. (1998, May 27). *Writing projects.* Retrieved May 4, 1998, from the World Wide Web: http://137.111.169.8/writeaway/projects.htm.

Otto, S., & Pusack, J. P. (1994). Dasher [Computer software]. Iowa City: University of Iowa, Project for International Communication Studies. (Demo version available from New Horizons Software, http://newhorizsoft.com/)

Our Environment [Computer software and activity kit]. (1996). Austin, TX: Steck-Vaughn/Edunetics.

Oxford picture dictionary. (1998). Oxford: Oxford University Press.

Oxford, R. L. (1990). *Language learning strategies: What every teacher should know.* Boston: Heinle & Heinle.

Oxford, R. L. (1994, October). Language learning strategies: An update. ERIC *Clearinghouse on Language and Linguistics Digest.* Retrieved April 1, 1997, from the World Wide Web: http://www.cal.org/ericcll/digest/Oxford01.htm.

Oxford, R. L. (Ed.). (1996). *Language learning strategies around the world: Cross-cultural perspectives.* Honolulu: University of Hawaii Press.

Oxford, R. L., Hollaway, M. E., & Horton-Murillo, D. (1992). Language learning styles and strategies in the multi-cultural, tertiary L2 classroom. *System, 20,* 439–456.

Oxford, R. L., Nyikos, M., & Ehrman, M. (1988). Vive la difference? Reflections on sex differences in use of language learning strategies. *Foreign Language Annals, 21,* 321–329.

Page, L., & Sugimoto, T. (1995). *Impact! Online.* Passport Educational Publishing. Retrieved May 1, 1998, from the World Wide Web: http://lrs.ed.uiuc.edu/Impact/impact_homepage.html.

Papert, S. (1993). *The children's machine: Rethinking school in the age of the computer.* New York: Basic Books.

Parkinson, B., & Howell-Richardson, C. (1990). Learner diaries. In C. Brumfit & R. Mitchell (Eds.), *Research in the language classroom* (British Council ELT Documents 133, pp. 115–128). London: Modern English Publications.

Paul, R. (1995). *Pseudo critical thinking in the educational establishment.* Sonoma State University, Center for Critical Thinking. Retrieved October 16, 1998, from the World Wide Web: http://www.sonoma.edu/cthink/University/univlibrary/nclk/Pseudo/outline.html.

PBS *TeacherSource.* (1998). Public Broadcasting System. Retrieved April 10, 1998, from the World Wide Web: http://www.pbs.org/teachersource/.

Pearson, B., & Berghoff, C. (1996). London Bridge is not falling down: It's supporting alternative assessment. *TESOL Journal, 5*(1), 28–31.

Pennington, M. C. (1996). The power of the computer in language education. In M. C. Pennington (Ed.), *The Power of CALL* (pp. 1–14). Houston, TX: Athelstan.

Perrone, C., Repenning, A., Spencer, S., & Ambach, J. (1996). Computers in the classroom: Moving from tool to medium. *Journal of Computer Mediated Communication, 2*(3). Retrieved October 16, 1998, from the World Wide Web: http://www.usc.edu/dept/annenberg/vol2/issue3; http://jcmc.huji.ac.il/vol2/issue3.

Peters, S., & Peters, T. (Eds.). (1997). TOPICS, *an online magazine by and for learners of*

English. Retrieved April 24, 1998, from the World Wide Web: http://www.rice.edu/projects/topics/Electronic/main.html.

Pettit, B. R. (1986). Phraze Craze Plus [Computer software]. Retrieved October 9, 1997, via the World Wide Web and FTP: http://chiron.latrobe.edu.au/www/education/celia/celia.html, FTP Directory: english Subdirectory: mac Subdirectory: vocabulary File: phrazecraze.hqx.

Peyton, J. K. (Ed.). (1990a). *Students and teachers writing together: Perspectives on journal writing*. Alexandria, VA: TESOL.

Peyton, J. K. (1990b). Technological innovation meets institution: Birth of creativity or murder of a great idea? *Computers and Composition, 7*(Special issue), 15–32.

Peyton, J. K. (1991). Electronic communication for developing the literacy skills of elementary school students: The case of ENFI. *Teaching English to Deaf and Second Language Students, 9*(2), 4–9. (ERIC Document Reproduction Service No. EJ 455 957)

Peyton, J. K., & French, M. (1996). *Making English accessible: Using electronic networks for interaction in the classroom*. Washington, DC: Gallaudet University, Pre-College National Mission Programs.

Peyton, J. K., & Mackinson, J. A. (1989). Writing and talking about writing: Computer networking with elementary students. In D. M. Johnson & D. H. Roen (Eds.), *Richness in writing: Empowering ESL students* (pp. 100–119). New York: Longman.

Peyton, J. K., & Staton, J. (1993). *Dialogue journals in the multilingual classroom: Building language fluency and writing skills through written interaction*. Norwood, NJ: Ablex.

Pfaff-Harris, K. (1996). Web-B-Mail [Computer software]. Retrieved November 17, 1997, from the World Wide Web: http://www.linguistic-funland.com/scripts/.

Pica, T. (1987). Second language acquisition, social interaction, and the classroom. *Applied Linguistics, 8*, 2–21.

Pica, T. (1991a, March). *Accommodating language learners' needs through negotiation*. Paper presented at the Second Language Research Forum, University of Southern California, Los Angeles.

Pica, T. (1991b). Classroom interaction, negotiation, and comprehension: Redefining relationships. *System, 19*, 437–452.

Pica, T. (1994). Questions from the language classroom: Research perspectives. *TESOL Quarterly, 28*, 49–79.

Pica, T. (1996). Second language learning through interaction: Multiple perspectives. *Working Papers in Educational Linguistics, 12*, 1–22.

Pica, T., Holliday, L., Lewis, N., Berducci, D., & Newman, J. (1991). Language learning through interaction: What role does gender play? *Studies in Second Language Acquisition, 13*, 343–376.

Pica, T., Holliday, L., Lewis, N., & Morgenthaler, L. (1989). Comprehensible output as an outcome of linguistic demands on the learner. *Studies in Second Language Acquisition, 11*, 63–90.

Pica, T., Kanagy, R., & Falodun, J. (1993). Choosing and using communication tasks for second language instruction. In G. Crookes & S. Gass (Eds.), *Tasks and language learning: Integrating theory and practice* (pp. 9–34). Clevedon, England: Multilingual Matters.

Pica, T., Lewis, N., & Holliday, L. (1990, March). *NS-NNS negotiation as a resource for second language acquisition*. Paper delivered at the 24th Annual TESOL Convention, San Francisco, CA.

Pica, T., Lincoln-Porter, F., Paninos, D., & Linnell, J. (1995). What can second language learners learn from each other? Only their researcher knows for sure. *Working Papers in Educational Linguistics, 11,* 1–36.

Pica, T., Lincoln-Porter, F., Paninos, D., & Linnell, J. (1996). Language learners' interaction: How does it address the input, output, and feedback needs of L2 learners? *TESOL Quarterly, 30,* 59–84.

Pica, T., Young, R., & Doughty, C. (1987). The impact of interaction on comprehension. *TESOL Quarterly, 21,* 737–758.

Pinker, S. (1994). *The language instinct.* New York: HarperCollins.

Pinto, D. (1995, July). *What does "schMOOze" mean? Non-native speaker interactions on the Internet.* Paper presented at the Technology and Human Factor in Foreign Language Education Symposium of the National Foreign Languages Resource Centre Summer Institute, University of Hawai'i at Manoa.

Poole, B. (1995). *Education for an information age: Teaching in the computerized classroom.* Madison, WI: Brown & Benchmark.

Porter, P. (1986). How learners talk to each other: Input and interaction in task-centered discussion. In R. R. Day (Ed.), *Talking to learn* (pp. 200–221). Rowley, MA: Newbury House.

Practice Makes Perfect French (Version 1) [Computer software]. (1994). Fremont, CA: The Learning Company.

Preece, J., Rogers, Y., Sharp, H., Benyon, D., Holland, S. & Carey, T. (1994). *Human-computer interaction.* Wokingham, England: Addison-Wesley.

Preposiciones. (1990). In *Classroom ideas* (Educator Home Card series) [Computer software]. Santa Barbara, CA: Intellimation.

Pujol, M. (1995/1996). ESL interactions around the computer. *CAELL Journal, 6(4),* 2–12.

Purcell, R. (1996, March 12). The case for research. *Bloomington Herald-Times,* p. A6.

Quick English (Demo version) [Computer software]. (1997). Orem, UT: LinguaTech International/Delta Systems.

QuickTime (Version 3.0) [Computer software]. (1998). Cupertino, CA: Apple Computer. Retrieved April 15, 1998, from the World Wide Web: http://www.apple.com/quicktime/.

Raimes, A. (1983). *Techniques in teaching writing.* Oxford: Oxford University Press.

Raimes, A. (1991). Emerging traditions in the teaching of writing. *TESOL Quarterly, 25,* 407–430.

Rain Forest Researchers [Computer software]. (1996). Watertown, MA: Tom Snyder Productions.

RealPlayer (Version 5.0) [Computer software]. (1998). Seattle, WA: RealNetworks. (Available from RealNetworks, http://www.realaudio.com/)

Reid, J. M. (1987). The learning preference of ESL students. *TESOL Quarterly, 21,* 87–111.

Reid, J. M. (Ed.). (1995a). *Learning styles in the ESL/EFL classroom.* Boston: Heinle & Heinle.

Reid, J. M. (1995b). Perceptual learning styles preference questionnaire. In J. M. Reid (Ed.), *Learning styles in the ESL/EFL classroom* (pp. 202–207). Boston: Heinle & Heinle.

Revusky, J. (1997). *English grammar pages.* Retrieved October 16, 1998, from the World Wide Web: http://web.jet.es/jrevusky/esl.html.

Rice, P. L. (1987). *Stress and health: Principles and practice for coping and wellness.* Monterey, CA: Brooks/Cole.

Richards, J. C., & Rodgers, T. S. (1986). *Approaches and methods in language teaching:* A *description and analysis.* Cambridge: Cambridge University Press.

Rigg, P. (1991). Whole language in TESOL. *TESOL Quarterly, 25,* 521–542.

Rivers, W. (1973, June). *Testing and student learning.* Paper presented at the First International Conference of the Association of Teachers of English to Speakers of Other Languages, Dublin, Ireland. (ERIC Document Reproduction Service No. ED 086 003)

Robb, T. (n.d.-a). *Famous personages in Japan.* Kyoto Sangyo University, Department of English. Retrieved June 18, 1998, from the World Wide Web: http://www.kyoto-su .ac.jp/information/famous/.

Robb, T. (n.d.-b). *Tom's page.* Kyoto Sangyo University, Department of English. Retrieved May 1, 1998, from the World Wide Web: http://www.kyoto-su.ac.jp /~trobb/.

Robinson, G. (1991). Effective feedback strategies in CALL: Learning theory and empirical research. In P. Dunkel (Ed.), *Computer-assisted language learning and testing: Research issues and practice* (pp. 155–168). New York: Newbury House.

The Rosetta Stone (Version 2.0) [Computer software]. (1995). Harrisonburg, VA: Fairfield Language Technologies. Demo version in TESOL/CELIA '96 [CD-ROM]. (1996). Alexandria, VA: TESOL.

Rosow, J. M., & Zager, R. (1988). *Training: The competitive edge.* San Francisco: Jossey-Bass.

Rotta, L. M., & Huser, C. A. (1995). *Techniques for assessing process writing.* (ERIC Document Reproduction Service No. ED 393 893)

Rubin, J. (1979). What "the good language learner" can teach us. In J. B. Pride (Ed.), *Sociolinguistic aspects of language learning and teaching* (pp. 17–26). London: Oxford University Press.

Rush, G. M., & Moore, D. M. (1991). Effects of restructuring training and cognitive style. *Educational Psychology, 11,* 309–321.

Sachs, C. (1996, June 7). Regarding CALL/micro labs. TESLCA-L [Discussion list]. Retrieved December 18, 1997, by e-mail: listserv@cunyvm.cuny.edu.

Sacks, H., & Schegloff, E. A. (1979). Two preferences in the organization of reference to persons in conversation and their interaction. In G. Psathas (Ed.), *Everyday language: Studies in ethnomethodology* (pp. 15–21). New York: Irvington.

Sacks, H., Schegloff, E., & Jefferson, G. (1974). A simplest systematics for the organization of turn-taking in conversation. *Language, 50,* 696–735.

Salomon, G. (1990). Cognitive effects with and of technology. *Communications Research, 17,* 26–44.

Salzmann, A. (1998). *World Wide Web activities that work (and why): The WWW as a corpus for grammar exploration.* Retrieved October 18, 1998, from the World Wide Web: http:// deil.lang.uiuc.edu/resources/TESOL/Ann/grammarcorpus_index.html.

Sanchez, B. (1995). MOO-la-la—Conversing in virtual Paris. In M. Warschauer (Ed.), *Virtual connections: On-line activities and projects for networking language learners* (pp. 229–230). Honolulu: University of Hawaii, Second Language Teaching and Curriculum Center.

Sanders, D., & Kenner, R. (1984). Whither CAI? The need for communicative courseware. In D. H. Wyatt (Ed.), *Computer-assisted language instruction* (pp. 33–40). Oxford: Pergamon Press.

Savery, J., & Duffy, T. (1995). Problem based learning: An instructional model and its constructivist framework. *Educational Technology, 35*(5), 31–38.

Sayers, D. (1989). Bilingual sister classes in computer writing networks. In D. Johnson & D. Roen (Eds.), *Richness in writing* (pp. 120–133). New York: Longman.

Schegloff, E. A., Jefferson, G., & Sacks, H. (1977). The preference for self-correction in the organization of repair in conversation. *Language, 53*, 361–382.

Schegloff, E. A., & Sacks, H. (1973). Opening up closings. *Semiotica, 8*, 289–327.

Schmidt, R., & Frota, S. N. (1986). Developing basic conversational ability in a second language: A case study of an adult learner of Portuguese. In R. Day (Ed.), *Talking to learn: Conversation in second language acquisition* (pp. 237–326). Rowley, MA: Newbury House.

Schneider, D. K. (1995). WWW *virtual library: Educational technology: Educational VR (MUD) sub-page.* Retrieved April 29, 1998, from the World Wide Web: http://tecfa.unige.ch/edu- comp/WWW-VL/eduVR-page.html.

Schofield, J. W. (1995). *Computers and classroom culture.* Cambridge: Cambridge University Press.

Scholl, W. (1996). Effective teamwork—A theoretical model and a test in the field. In E. Witte & J. H. Davis (Eds.), *Understanding group behavior: Vol. 2. Small group processes and interpersonal relations* (pp. 127–146). Mahwah, NJ: Erlbaum.

Schön, D. A. (1983). *The reflective practitioner: How professionals think in action.* New York: Basic Books.

Schumann, J. (1998). *Schumann's foreign language tests/exercises.* Retrieved April 29, 1998, from the World Wide Web: http://ourworld.compuserve.com/homepages/joschu/.

Schwartz, A. H. (1995). TEAM: Technology-Enhanced Accent Management Program (Version KMA.CSU) [Computer software]. Cleveland, OH: Cleveland State University.

Schwartz, B. (1993). On explicit and negative data effecting and affecting competence and linguistic behaviour. *Studies in Second Language Acquisition, 15*, 147–163.

Schwartz, J. (1980). The negotiation for meaning: Repair in conversations between second language learners of English. In D. Larsen-Freeman (Ed.), *Discourse analysis in second language research* (pp. 138–153). Rowley, MA: Newbury House.

Schwier, R. A., & Misanchuk, E. R. (1997, June). *Technical quality and perceived quality in multimedia materials—Are they the same or different things?* Paper presented to the annual conference of the Association for Media and Technology in Education in Canada, Saskatoon.

Scott, E., Gaer, S., & Hopper, J. (1998, April 14). *Folktales from around the world.* Staff Development Institute & Outreach and Technical Assistance Network. Retrieved October 29, 1998, from the World Wide Web: http://www.otan.dni.us/webfarm/emailproject/folk.htm.

Scott, M., with Johns, T. (1994). MicroConcord [Computer software]. New York: Oxford University Press.

See It! Hear It! Say It! [Computer software]. (1996). Cupertino, CA: Courseware Publishing International.

Seyler, W. E. (1987). HyperFlash [Computer software]. Unpublished.

Sharp, V. (1994). *HyperStudio in one hour!* (2nd ed.). Eugene, OR: International Society for Technology in Education.

Shih, Y., & Alessi, S. (1996). Effects of text versus voice on learning in multimedia courseware. *Journal of Educational Multimedia and Hypermedia, 5*, 203–218.

Shneiderman, B. (1998). *Designing the user interface: Strategies for effective human-computer interaction* (3rd ed.). Reading, MA: Addison Wesley Longman.

Shockwave [Computer software]. (1995). San Francisco, CA: Macromedia. (Available from Macromedia, http://www.macromedia.com/)

Short, D. (1991). *How to integrate language and content instruction: A training manual.* Washington, DC: Center for Applied Linguistics.

Short, D. (1994). Expanding middle school horizons: Integrating language, culture, and social studies. TESOL *Quarterly, 28,* 581–608.

Sid Meier's Civilization II [Computer software]. (1997). Hunt Valley, MD: MicroProse Software.

Siembieda, K. (1995). How to play a role-playing game. In C. J. Martigena-Carella (Ed.), *Nightbane: A complete role-playing game* (p. 31). Taylor, MI: Palladium Books.

SimCity [Computer software]. (1995). Walnut Creek, CA: Maxis.

Simmons, G., & Barrineau, P. (1994). Learning style and the Native American. *Journal of Psychological Type, 28,* 3–10.

SimTown [Computer software]. (1995). Walnut Creek, CA: Maxis.

Singleton, J. (1991). The spirit of gamburu. In A. E. Finkelstein, A. E. Imamura, & J. J. Tobin (Eds.), *Transcending stereotypes: Discovering Japanese culture and education* (pp. 120–125). Yarmouth, ME: Intercultural Press.

Sirc, G., & Reynolds, T. (1993). Seeing students as writers. In B. Bruce, J. K. Peyton, & T. Batson (Eds.), *Network-based classrooms: Promises and realities* (pp. 138–192). New York: Cambridge University Press.

Sitting on the Farm [Computer software]. (1996). San Mateo, CA: Sanctuary Woods Multimedia/Theatrix (SWMC).

Skehan, P. (1996). A framework for implementation of task-based instruction. *Applied Linguistics, 17,* 38–62.

Snow, C. (1972). Mothers' speech to children learning language. *Child Development, 43,* 549–565.

Snow, C., & Goldfield, B. A. (1982). Building stories: The emergence of information structures from conversation. In D. Tannen (Ed.), *Analyzing discourse: Text and talk* (pp. 127–141). Washington, DC: Georgetown University Press.

Snow, M. A., Met, M., & Genesee, F. (1989). A conceptual framework for the integration of language and content in second and foreign language instruction. TESOL *Quarterly, 23,* 201–217.

Soo, K., & Ngeow, Y. (1996, June). The effects of an interactive learning environment on learning styles. In P. Carlson & F. Makedon (Eds.), *Proceedings of* ED-MEDIA 96— *World Conference on Educational Multimedia and Hypermedia* (p. 809). Charlottesville, VA: American Association for the Advancement of Computing in Education.

Space: A Visual History [Computer software]. (1994). San Francisco: Sumeria.

SpeechViewer III [Computer software]. (1996). Atlanta, GA: IBM.

Spell-It-Plus [Computer software]. (1991). Torrance, CA: Davidson.

Sperling, D. (1997). ESL *chat room central.* Retrieved June 16, 1998, from the World Wide Web: http://www.eslcafe.com/chat/chatpro.cgi.

Sperling, D., & Oliver, D. (1997). *Animals* 1 *hangman.* Retrieved April 13, 1998, from the World Wide Web: http://www.eslcafe.com/animals.cgi.

Spolsky, B. (1989). *Conditions for second language learning: Introduction to a general theory.* Oxford: Oxford University Press.

The sprawl! (1998). SenseMedia.Net. Retrieved April 29, 1998, from the World Wide Web: http://sensemedia.net/sprawl/.

Sproull, L., & Kiesler, S. (1991). *Connections: New ways of working in the networked organization.* Cambridge, MA: MIT Press.

Staton, J. (1984). Thinking together: The role of language interaction in children's reasoning. In D. Thaiss & C. Suhor (Eds.), *Speaking and writing, K–12: Classroom strategies and the new research* (pp. 131–135). Champaign, IL: National Council of Teachers of English.

Staton, J., Shuy, R. W., Peyton, J. K., & Reed, L. (1988). *Dialogue journal communication: Classroom, linguistic, social, and cognitive views.* Norwood, NJ: Ablex.

Steinberg, E. R. (1989). Cognition and learner control: A literature review, 1977–1988. *Journal of Computer-Based Instruction, 16,* 117–121.

Sternberg, M. (1998). The American Sign Language Dictionary [Computer software]. New York: HarperCollins Interactive.

Stevick, E. (1976). *Memory, meaning and method: Some psychological perspectives on language learning.* Rowley, MA: Newbury House.

Storybook Maker [Computer software]. (1994). Lansing, MI: Hartley Courseware/ Jostens Learning.

Storybook Weaver (Version 1.1) [Computer software]. (1992). Knoxville, TN: MECC.

Stuart, A. (1997). Student-centered learning. *Learning, 26*(2), 53–55.

Swain, M. (1985). Communicative competence: Some roles of comprehensible input and comprehensible output in its development. In S. M. Gass & C. G. Madden (Eds.), *Input in second language acquisition* (pp. 235–253). Rowley, MA: Newbury House.

Swain, M., & Lapkin, S. (1995). Problems in output and the cognitive processes they generate: A step towards second language learning. *Applied Linguistics, 16,* 371–391.

Switched-on classroom. (1994). Massachusetts Software Council. Retrieved November 11, 1997, from the World Wide Web: http://www.swcouncil.org/switch2.html.

Taber, A. (1997, June). *Volterre-Fr: Software.* WebFrance International. Retrieved April 30, 1998, from the World Wide Web: http://www.wfi.fr/volterre/software.html.

Tarone, E. (1977). Conscious communication strategies in interlanguage: A progress report. In H. D. Brown, C. Yorio, & R. Crymes (Eds.), *On TESOL '77* (pp. 194–203). Washington, DC: TESOL.

TESOL/CELIA '96 [Computer software]. (1996). Alexandria, VA: TESOL.

Thakerar, J. N., Giles, H., & Cheshire, J. (1982). Psychological and linguistic parameters of speech accommodation theory. In C. Fraser & K. R. Scherer (Eds.), *Advances in the social psychology of language* (pp. 205–255). Cambridge: Cambridge University Press.

Thalman, L. (Ed.). (1997a). *Volterre-Fr: English and French language resources.* WebFrance International. Retrieved April 30, 1998, from the World Wide Web: http://www.wfi.fr /volterre/.

Thalman, L. (Ed.). (1997b). *Volterre-Fr: Internet projects for learners and teachers of English.* WebFrance International. Retrieved May 25, 1997, from the World Wide Web: http://www.wfi.fr/volterre/inetpro.html.

Thein, M. (1994). A non-native English speaking teacher's response to a learner-centered program. *System, 22,* 463–471.

Thinkin' Things: Collection 3 [Computer software]. (1995). Redmond, WA: Edmark.

ThinkQuest. (1997). Advanced Network & Services. Retrieved May 1, 1998, from the World Wide Web: http://io.advanced.org/thinkquest/.

Thompson, D. (1993). One ENFI path: From Gallaudet to distance learning. In

B. Bruce, J. K. Peyton, & T. Batson (Eds.), *Network-based classrooms: Promise and realities* (pp. 210–227). New York: Cambridge University Press.

Thomson, J. (1991). Conc: Concordance Generating Program (Version 1.70) [Computer software]. Dallas, TX: Summer Institute of Linguistics. Also in TESOL/CELIA '96 [CD-ROM]. (1996). Alexandria, VA: TESOL.

Thornton, P., & Dudley, A. (1996). The CALL environment: An alternative to the language lab. *CAELL Journal*, 7(4), 29–34.

TimeLiner (Version 4.0) [Computer software]. (1994). Watertown, MA: Tom Snyder Productions.

Tobin, J. (1995). The irony of self-expression. *American Journal of Education*, 103, 233–258.

ToolBook II [Computer software]. (1996). Bellevue, WA: Asymetrix Learning Systems.

Towell, J., & Towell, E. (1997). Presence in text-based networked virtual environments or "MUDS." *Presence*, 6, 590–595.

TRACI Talk: The Mystery [Computer software]. (1997). Cupertino, CA: Courseware Publishing International.

Trickel, K. G. (1997). *Talking about daily routines*. Retrieved October 31, 1998, from the World Wide Web: http://grove.ufl.edu/~ktrickel/teslmini/activity.html.

Triple Play Plus! English [Computer software]. (1995). Syracuse, NY: Syracuse Language Systems/Random House.

Turbee, L. (1995a). MundoHispano: A text-based virtual environment for learners and native speakers of Spanish. In M. Warschauer (Ed.), *Virtual connections: On-line activities and projects for networking language learners* (pp. 233–234). Honolulu: University of Hawaii, Second Language Teaching and Curriculum Center.

Turbee, L. (1995b). What can we do in a MOO? Suggestions for language teachers. In M. Warschauer (Ed.), *Virtual connections: On-line activities and projects for networking language learners* (pp. 235–238). Honolulu: University of Hawaii, Second Language Teaching and Curriculum Center.

Turbee, L. (1997a, March). *Educational MOO: Text-based virtual reality for learning in community* (ERIC/IT Digest EDO-IR-97-01). Syracuse, NY: ERIC Clearinghouse on Information and Technology. Retrieved October 19, 1998, from the World Wide Web: http://ericir.syr.edu/ithome/digests/turbee.html.

Turbee, L. (1997b, December 9). *MundoHispano: The Spanish language learning MOO.* Retrieved April 29, 1998, from the World Wide Web: http://web.syr.edu/~lmturbee/mundo.html.

Turner, J. (1995). A virtual treasure hunt: Exploring the three-dimensional aspect of MOOs. In M. Warschauer (Ed.), *Virtual connections: On-line activities and projects for networking language learners* (pp. 242–244). Honolulu: University of Hawaii, Second Language Teaching and Curriculum Center.

Turner, T. (1992). *Literacy and machines: An overview of the use of technology in adult literacy programs* (Technical Report TR93.3). Philadelphia: National Center on Adult Literacy.

Tuttle, H. G. (1996). Rubrics: Keys to improving multimedia presentations. *Multimedia Schools*, 3, 30–33.

Uhlirov, L. (1994). Talk at a PC. In S. Cmejrkov, F. Dane, & E. Havlov (Eds.), *Writing vs. speaking: Language, text, discourse, communication* (pp. 275–282). Tübingen, Germany: Gunter Narr.

The U-M software archives. (1995, September 26). University of Michigan. Retrieved

November 15, 1997, from the World Wide Web: http://www.umich.edu/~archive/; via Gopher: gopher.archive.umich.edu:7055/.

The University of Maine writing center online. (1998). Retrieved May 1, 1998, from the World Wide Web: http://www.ume.maine.edu/~wcenter/.

van Lier, L. (1988). *The classroom and the learner.* London: Longman.

van Lier, L. (1996). *Interaction in the language curriculum: Awareness, autonomy and authenticity.* New York: Longman.

Ventura, F., & Grover, M. (1992). *HyperCard projects for teachers.* Grover Beach, CA: Ventura Educational Systems.

VideoVoice [Computer software]. (1995). Ann Arbor, MI: MicroVideo.

Vilmi, R. M. (1994, January). *Global communication through e-mail: An ongoing experiment at Helsinki University of Technology.* Retrieved October 19, 1998, from the World Wide Web: http://www.hut.fi/~rvilmi/Publication/global.html.

Vilmi, R. M. (1997a, October 10). *HUT virtual language centre.* Retrieved May 2, 1998, from the World Wide Web: http://www.hut.fi/~rvilmi/Project/VLC/.

Vilmi, R. M. (1997b, September 21). *King's Road 2001 Project.* Retrieved October 28, 1998, from the World Wide Web: http://www.hut.fi/~rvilmi/King/.

Vilmi, R. M. (1997c, June 12). *On-line courses.* Retrieved May 2, 1998, from the World Wide Web: http://www.hut.fi/~rvilmi/online/.

Vilmi, R. M. (1998a, January 13). *Grammar help.* Retrieved May 2, 1998, from the World Wide Web: http://www.hut.fi/~rvilmi/LangHelp/Grammar/.

Vilmi, R. M. (1998b, May 21). *HUT Internet Writing Project.* Retrieved June 12, 1998, from the World Wide Web: http://www.hut.fi/~rvilmi/Project/.

Violent Earth [Computer software and activity kit]. (1996). Austin, TX: Steck-Vaughn/Edunetics.

The virtual CALL library. (1997, December 1). University of Sussex. Retrieved April 30, 1998, from the World Wide Web: http://www.sussex.ac.uk/langc/CALL.html.

Vonck, T. (1998). *Welcome to the mIRC homepage.* Retrieved October 16, 1998, from the World Wide Web: http://geocities.com/~mirc/.

Vygotsky, L. (1962). *Thought and language* (E. Hanfmann & G. Backer, Trans.). Cambridge, MA: MIT Press. (Original work published 1934)

Vygotsky, L. (1978). *Mind in society: The development of higher psychological processes* (M. Cole, V. John-Steiner, S. Scribner, & E. Louberman, Eds. & Trans.). Cambridge, MA: Harvard University Press.

Wachman, R. (1989). HyperFlash Plus [Computer software]. (Available from the author, e-mail: Rwachman@aol.com)

Wachman, R. (1995). Review of MacESL. *CAELL Journal, 6*(2): 34–38.

Wagner-Gough, J., & Hatch, E. (1975). The importance of input data in second language acquisition studies. *Language Learning 25,* 297–308.

Wagon Train 1848 [Computer software]. (1997). Minneapolis, MN: The Learning Company.

Warschauer, M. (1995a). *E-mail for English teaching: Bringing the Internet and computer learning networks into the language classroom.* Alexandria, VA: TESOL.

Warschauer, M. (Ed.). (1995b). *Virtual connections: On-line activities and projects for networking language learners.* Honolulu: University of Hawaii, Second Language Teaching and Curriculum Center.

Warschauer, M. (1996). *Computer-mediated collaborative learning: Theory and practice* (Research Note 17). Honolulu: University of Hawaii, Second Language Teaching Curriculum Center.

Weaver, C. (1990). *Understanding whole language: From principles to practice.* Portsmouth, NH: Heinemann.

Web classes. (1998, September 6). University of New Orleans. Retrieved May 1, 1998, from the World Wide Web: http://www.uno.edu/~webclass/.

Webb, N. (1982). Student interaction and learning in small groups. *Review of Educational Research, 52,* 421–445.

Webb, N. (1985). Verbal interaction and learning in peer-directed groups. *Theory Into Practice, 24,* 32–39.

Webcrawler: People and chat. (1998). Retrieved May 4, 1998, from the World Wide Web: http://Webcrawler.com/Chat/chat.worlds.html.

Weil, M. M., & Rosen, L. D. (1997). *TechnoStress: Coping with technology @work @home @play.* New York: Wiley.

Weller, H. G. (1988). Interactivity in microcomputer-based instruction: Its essential components and how it can be enhanced. *Educational Technology, 4,* 346–355.

Wells, G. (1981). *Learning through interaction: The study of language development.* Cambridge: Cambridge University Press.

Wenden, A., & Rubin, J. (Eds.). (1987). *Learner strategies in language learning.* Englewood Cliffs, NJ: Prentice Hall.

Where in the World Is Carmen Sandiego? [Computer software]. (1996). Novato, CA: Brøderbund Software.

Who Is Oscar Lake? [Computer software]. (1996). New York: Language Publications Interactive.

Widdowson, H. G. (1983). *Learning purpose and language use.* New York: Oxford University Press.

Widdowson, H. G. (1990). *Aspects of language teaching.* Oxford: Oxford University Press.

Widget Workshop [Computer software]. (1994). Walnut Creek, CA: Maxis.

Williams, R. (1994). *The non-designer's design book.* Berkeley, CA: Peachpit Press.

Winograd, K. (1985). *Hangman* [Computer software]. Merrimack, NH: Space-Time Associates.

Winograd, K. (1991). *Hangman Plus* (Version 2.0) [Computer software]. Merrimack, NH: Space- Time Associates. Also in *TESOL/CELIA '96* [CD-ROM]. (1996). Alexandria, VA: TESOL.

Winograd, T., & Flores, F. (1988). *Understanding computers and cognition: A new foundation for design.* Reading, MA: Addison-Wesley.

Witkins, H. A., Oltman, P., Raskin, R., & Karp, S. (1971). *A manual for the Embedded Figures Tests.* Palo Alto, CA: Consulting Psychologist Press.

Witte, E., & Davis, J. H. (Eds.). (1996). *Understanding group behavior: Vol. 2. Small-group processes and interpersonal relations.* Mahwah, NJ: Erlbaum.

Wolfson, N. (1989). *Perspectives: Sociolinguistics and TESOL.* Cambridge, MA: Newbury House.

Wong, J. (n.d.). *Subscription to CALL-ED.* Retrieved May 1, 1998, from the World Wide Web: http://tiger.coe.missouri.edu/~cjw/call/call-ed.htm.

Woodbury, V., & Smith, K. (1990). *VersaText: The Hypertext Learning System* (Version 2.0) [Computer software]. Burlington, MA: NovaSoft/ICD. (Available from Athelstan, http://www.athel.com/)

Woodward, H. (1994). *Negotiated evaluation: Involving children and parents in the process*. Portsmouth, NH: Heinemann.

Wordwatch. (n.d.). Collins Cobuild. Retrieved April 15, 1998, from the World Wide Web: http://titania.cobuild.collins.co.uk/wordwatch.html.

World lecture hall. (1998, April 30). University of Texas at Austin, Academic Computing and Instructional Technology Services. Retrieved May 1, 1998, from the World Wide Web: http://www.utexas.edu/world/lecture/.

Worlds chat. (1998). Retrieved April 29, 1998, from the World Wide Web: http://www.worlds.net/wc/.

Wright, S. (1998). The effect of simulations on second language development. CAELL *Journal*, 8(2), 3–10.

Writer's Assistant [Computer software]. (1996). Hong Kong: Clarity Language Consultants. (Available from Clarity Language Consultants, http://www.clarity.com.hk)

The Writing Center [Computer software]. (1991). Freemont, CA: The Learning Company.

Yeaman, A. R. J. (1993). Whose technology is it, anyway? *Education Digest*, 58(5), 19–23.

Younger, G. (n.d.). NETEACH-L: MOO *Sessions*. Retrieved May 4, 1998, from the World Wide Web: http://spot.colorado.edu/~youngerg/netmoo.html.

Your Tour of HyperCard [Computer software]. (1995). Cupertino, CA: Apple Computer.

Yuen, C., & Lee, S. (1994). Applicability of the learning style inventory in an Asian context and its predictive value. *Educational and Psychological Measurement*, 54, 541–549.

The Yukon Trail (Version 1.0) [Computer software]. (1994). Minneapolis, MN: MECC.

Zellermayer, M., Salomon, G., Globerson, T., & Givon, H. (1991). Enhancing writing-related metacognitions through a computerized writing partner. *American Educational Research Journal*, 28, 372–392.

Appendix A: Professional Organizations

Association for the Advancement of
Computing in Education
PO Box 2966
Charlottesville, VA 22902 USA
Telephone: 804-973-3987
Fax: 804-978-7449

Association for Educational
Communications and Technology
620 Union Drive, Rm. 143 North
Indiana University–Purdue University
Indianapolis, IN 46202 USA
Telephone: 317-274-2637

Computer-Assisted Language
Instruction Consortium (CALICO)
317 Liberal Arts
Southwest Texas State University
San Marcos, TX 78666 USA
Fax: 512-245-8298
E-mail: info@calico.org
http://www.calico.org/

Computer-Assisted Language Learning
Interest Section
TESOL
1600 Cameron St., Suite 300
Alexandria, VA 22314-2751 USA
Telephone: 703-836-9774
http://darkwing/uoregon.edu/~call/

Computer Learning Foundation
Box 60007
Palo Alto, CA 94306-0007 USA
Telephone: 415-327-3347
Fax: 415-327-3349

Computer-Using Educators (CUE)
1210 Marina Village Pkwy., Suite 100
Alameda, CA 94501 USA
Telephone: 510-814-6630
E-mail: cueinc@aol.com
http://www.cue.org/

EDC Center for Children and
Technology
Education Development Center
96 Morton St., 7th Floor
New York, NY 10014 USA
Telephone: 212-807-4200

Education and Technology Resource
Center
Association for Supervision and
Curriculum Development
1250 North Pitt St.
Alexandria, VA 22314 USA
Telephone: 703-549-9110, ext. 514

International Society for Technology in
Education (ISTE)
Administrative Office
1787 Agate St.
Eugene, OR 97403-1923 USA
http://www.iste.org/

Japan Association for Language
    Teaching (JALT)
JALT Central Office
Urban Edge Building, 5F
1-37-9 Taito, Taito-ku
Tokyo 110 JAPAN
Telephone: 03-3887-1630
Fax: 03-2827-1631
http://langue.hyper.chubu.ac.jp/jalt/

Teachers of English to Speakers of
    Other Languages (TESOL), Inc.
1600 Cameron St., Suite 300
Alexandria, VA 22314-2751 USA
Telephone: 703-836-0774
Fax: 703-836-7864
E-mail: tesol@tesol.edu/
http:/www.tesol.edu/

Appendix B: Electronic Forums for Teachers and Students

Electronic Discussion Lists for Teachers

TESL-L

To subscribe, send an e-mail message to

listserv@cunyvm.cuny.edu

In the body of the message, type

sub TESL-L yourfirstname yourlastname

Either leave the subject of the message blank or type the word *subscribe*.
To join any of the branches of TESL-L, listed below, you must first become a member of TESL-L.

- TESLCA-L: TESL and technology
- TESLFF-L: fluency first and whole language pedagogy
- TESLIE-L: intensive English programs, teaching, and administration
- TESLIT-L: adult education and literacy
- TESLJB-L: jobs, employment, and working conditions in the TESL/TEFL field
- TESLMW-L: material writers
- TESP-L: teachers of English for specific purposes

A sister list, TESLK-12, is for teachers of English to children.

NETEACH-L

NETEACH-L is an electronic discussion list through which EFL/ESL teachers discuss the use of technology as an educational tool (see Moody, n.d., http://www.ilc .cuhk.edu.hk/english/neteach/main.htm).
To subscribe, send an e-mail message to

listproc@ukans.edu

In the body of the message, type

sub NETEACH-L yourfirstname yourlastname

Leave the subject of the message blank.

The owner of the list is Suzan Moody, Chinese University of Hong Kong (e-mail: smoody@cuhk.edu.hk).

Other Lists for Teachers

When you send e-mail to subscribe to one of the lists in the table on p. 508, leave the subject line blank; send the subscription request in the body of the message. Be aware that the address to which you subscribe is often not the same as the address to which you will post messages to the list.

Warning: Lists are subject to change. For a complete, up-to-date listing of educational lists, see *Liszt*, the mailing list directory (http://www.liszt.com/) or *CataList* (1998, http://www.lsoft.com/catalist.html).

Electronic Discussion Lists for Students

SL-Lists

The SL-*Lists* specialize in cross-cultural discussion and writing practice for college, university, and adult students in English language programs around the world (see Holliday & Robb, n.d., http://chiron.latrobe.edu.au/www/education/sl/sl.html). There are currently 10 lists:

- INTRO-SL: new members
- CHAT-SL: general (low level)
- DISCUSS-SL: general (high level)
- BUSINESS-SL: business and economics
- ENGL-SL: learning English
- EVENT-SL: current events
- MOVIE-SL: cinema
- MUSIC-SL: music
- SCITECH-SL: science, technology and computers
- SPORT-SL: sports

To register your class, send an e-mail message to

trobb@cc.kyotosu.ac.jp

In the body of the message, give the following information:

- your name and institution
- the number of students in your class
- the duration of the class term
- the name of the node (the part of the e-mail address following the @ sign) your students will use

| | | Instructions for subscribing | |
List	Topic	Send an e-mail message to	In the body of the message, type
BILINGUAL	Bilingual education and language planning	majordomo@ied.edu.hk	subscribe bilingual
CALL-ED	Educators interested in CALL	Majordomo@coe.missouri. edu	subscribe call-ed
CTESL-L	Christians teaching ESL	majordomo@iclnet93.iclnet.org	subscribe CTESL-L *or* info CTESL-L
EFL TEACHER TRAINERS	EFL teacher education	majordomo@list.macam98.ac.il	subscribe efltrainer-l youre-mailaddress
ESLCC	ESL at the community colleges (This list is not a TESL-L branch.)	eslccrequest@hcc.hawaii.edu	subscribe eslcc
GLESOL-L	Gay, lesbian, [bisexual] educators of ESOL (and their friends)	mailserv@uni.edu	subscribe glesol-l
The LINGUIST	Issues in theoretical and applied linguistics	listserv@tamvm1.tamu.edu	subscribe LINGUIST yourfirstname yourlastname
MULT-CUL	Multicultural education	listserv@ubvm.cc.buffalo.edu	sub MULTCUL yourname
SLART-L	Second language acquisition, research, and teaching	listserv@cunyvm.cuny.edu	sub SLART-L yourfirstname yourlastname
STORIES, HUMOR, GOOD ADVICE	Humor	listserver@graffiti.net	subscribe esl@graffiti.net

You will then be placed on a special discussion list (TCHR-SL) for teachers who are involved in this project and will receive more information about the lists.

Students can then subscribe to INTRO-SL by sending an e-mail message to

listserv@latrobe.edu.au

In the body of the message, they write

sub introsl firstname familyname

MOOs, MUDS, and Chats

ESL Chat Room Central	http://www.eslcafe.com/chat/chatpro.cgi
HUT *Virtual Language Centre*	http://www.hut.fi/~rvilmi/Project/VLC/
MOO*francais*	http://moo.syr.edu/~fmoo/fmoo/
*Mundo*Hispano	http://web.syr.edu/~lmturbee/mundo.html
*Pueblo*Lindo	http://pueblolindo.heinle.com/
sch*MOOze University*	http://schmooze.hunter.cuny.edu:8888/
WebChat Broadcasting System	http://pages.wbs.net/

Guides to Finding a Forum

CataList, the Official Catalog of LISTSERV *Lists*	http://www.lsoft.com/catalist.html
The E-Mail Key Pal Connection	http://www.comenius.com/keypal/
Rachel's Super MOO *List: Educational MOOs*	http://moolist.yeehaw.com/edu.html
Webcrawler: People & Chat	http://Webcrawler.com/Chat/chat.worlds.html
Worlds Chat	http://www.worlds.net/wc/

Appendix C: Web Sites With Lists of Links to Resources

On-Line Search Engines

AltaVista	http://altavista.com/
Dogpile: A Multisearch Engine	http://www.dogpile.com/
Excite	http://www.excite.com/
HotBot	http://www.hotbot.com/
Infoseek	http://www.infoseek.com/
Lycos	http://www.lycos.com/
Yahoo!	http://www.yahoo.com/

Teacher-Built Sites

College and University Home Pages—Alphabetical Listing	http://www.mit.edu:8001/people/cdemello/univ.html
Computer-Assisted Language Learning@Chorus	http://www-writing.berkeley.edu/chorus/call/
Dave's ESL Café	http://www.eslcafe.com/
ESLoop Index	http://www.webring.org/cgi-bin/webring?index&ring=esloop
King's Road 2001 Project	http://www.hut.fi/~rvilmi/King/
LinguaCenter	http://deil.lang.uiuc.edu/
The Linguist List	http://www.linguistlist.org/
Linguistic Funland	http://www.linguistic-funland.com/
Ohio University CALL Lab	http://www.tcom.ohiou.edu/OU_Language/
Online Resources and Journals: ELT, Linguistics, and Communication	http://www.ling.lancs.ac.uk/staff/visitors/kenji/onlin.htm
OPPortunities in ESOL	http://darkwing.uoregon.edu/~leslieob/
ThinkQuest	http://io.advanced.org/thinkquest/
Tim Johns Data-Driven Learning Page	http://web.bham.ac.uk/johnstf/timconc.htm
Volterre-Fr	http://www.wfi.fr/volterre/

Appendix D: Freeware and Shareware Archives On-Line

1996 CALL Interest Section Software List	http://chiron.latrobe.edu.au/www/education/celia/celia.html
CELIA at La Trobe University	http://chiron.latrobe.edu.au/www/education/celia/celia.html
CNET: The Computer Network	http://www.cnet.com/
Computer-Assisted Language Learning, a TESOL Interest Section	http://darkwing.uoregon.edu/~call/
Download.com	http://www.download.com
IALL Foreign Language Software Database	http://fldb.dartmouth.edu/fldb/
Jumbo!	http://www.jumbo.com/
Linguistic Funland	http://www.linguistic-funland.com/
Links to Sites with Public Domain EFL/ESL CALL Freeware and Shareware	http://www.cltr.uq.oz.au:8000/~richardc/pubsoft.html
The U-M Software Archives	http://www.umich.edu/~archive/
Updates for Software	http://www.stir.ac.uk/epd/celt/staff/higdox/software.htm
The Virtual CALL Library	http://www.sussex.ac.uk/langc/CALL.html
Volterre-Fr: Software	http://www.wfi.fr/volterre/software/

Appendix E: Software Publishers and Distributors

Agora Language Marketplace
http://www.agoralang.com:2410/

Athelstan
2476 Bolsover, Suite 464
Houston, TX 77005 USA
Telephone: 800-598-3880 (U.S. only);
    713-523-2837
Fax: 713-523-6543
http://www.athel.com/
E-mail: info@athel.com

Brøderbund Software/Electronic Arts
500 Redwood Blvd.
Novato, CA 94948 USA
http://www.broderbund.com/

The Comenius English Language Center
http://www.comenius.com/

Computers for Education
91 Sandburg Dr.
Sacramento, CA 95819-1849 USA
Telephone and fax: 916-739-0662
E-mail: EHansonSmi@aol.com

Creative Wonders (The Learning
    Company)
595 Penobscot Dr.
Redwood City, CA 94063 USA
Telephone: 650-482-2300
http://www.cwonders.com/

The Daedalus Group
Suite 510 West
1106 Clayton Lane
Austin, TX 78723 USA
Telephone: 800-879-2144
E-mail: info@daedalus.com
http://www.daedalus.com/

Davidson & Associates
Telephone: (800) 545-7677
http://www.davd.com/

DynEd International
Suite 130
989 East Hillsdale Blvd.
Foster City, CA 94404 USA
Telephone: 650-578-8067
E-mail: info@dyned.com
http://www.dyned.com/

Edmark Corporation
PO Box 97021
Redmond, WA 98073-9721 USA
Telephone: 800-691-2986; 425-556-8400
E-mail: edmarkteam@edmark.com
http://www.edmark.com/

Heinle & Heinle Publishers
20 Park Plaza
Boston, MA 02116 USA
Telephone: 800-237-0053
Fax: 617-426-4379
E-mail: reply@heinle.com
http://zelda.thomson.com/heinle
    /default.html

Heinle & Heinle Publishers (secondary
   school)
5101 Madison Rd.
Cincinnati, OH 45227 USA
Fax: 800-453-7882

Heinle & Heinle Publishers (college and
   university)
ITP Academic Resource Center
7625 Empire Dr.
Florence, KY 41042 USA
Telephone: 800-423-0563
Fax: 606-647-5020

Hyperbole Software
5 Sunnyside Dr.
Athens, OH 45701-1919 USA
Telephone: 704-594-4609
E-mail:
   mcvicker@ouvaxa.cats.ohiou.edu

Ingenuity Works
1020-720 Olive Way
Seattle, WA 98101-3874 USA
Telephone: 800-665-0667
E-mail: info@ingenuityworks.com
http://www.vrsystems.com/

Intellimation
PO Box 1922
Santa Barbara, CA 93116 USA
Telephone: 800-346-8355
http://www.callamer.com/~dave
   /intellimation/index.html

The Learning Company
One Athenaeum St.
Cambridge, MA 02142 USA
Telephone: 617-494-1200
Fax: 617-494-1219
http://www.learningco.com/

Maxis/Electronic Arts
Suite 600
2121 N. California Blvd.
Walnut Creek, CA 94596-3572 USA
Telephone: 800-245-4525
Fax: 650-513-7035
http://www.maxis.com/

MVP Software
PO Box 888281
Grand Rapids, MI 49588 USA
http://www.mvpsoft.com/

Pierian Spring Software
Suite 570
5200 SW Macadam
Portland, OR 97201 USA
Telephone: 800-213-5054; (local)
   503-222-2044
Fax: 503-222-0771
http://www.pierian.com/

Roger Wagner Publishing
1050 Pioneer Way, Suite P
El Cajon, CA 92020 USA
Telephone: 800-HYPERSTUDIO or
   619-442-0522
Fax: 619-442-0525
http://www.hyperstudio.com/

Royal Software
PO Box 9367
Dayton, OH 45409-9367 USA
E-mail: sales@royalsoftware.com
http://www.royalsoftware.com/

Steck-Vaughn Publishing
PO Box 690789
Orlando, FL 32819-0789 USA
Telephone: 800-531-5015
Fax: 800-699-9459
E-mail:
   ccumming@lnaus1.steckvaughn.com
http://www.steck-vaughn.com/

Tom Snyder Productions
80 Coolidge Hill Rd.
Watertown, MA 02172 USA
Telephone: 800-342-0236
Fax: 617-926-6222
http://www.teachtsp.com/

White Pine Software
542 Amherst St.
Nashua, NH 03063 USA
Telephone: 603-886-9050
Fax: 603-886-9051
http://www.wpine.com/

Wida Software
2 Nicholas Gardens
London W5 5 HY
UNITED KINGDOM
Telephone: 44 181 567 6941
Fax: 44 181 840 6534
E-mail: info@wida.co.uk
http://www.wida.co.uk/wida/

Appendix F: Resources for Content-Based Learning on the Internet

Student Projects and Electronic Magazines

Email Projects Home Page
http://www.otan.dni.us/webfarm/emailproject/email.htm

Exchange
http://deil.lang.uiuc.edu/ExChange/

Folktales From Around the World
http://www.otan.dni.us/webfarm/emailproject/folk.htm

I*EARN Global Art Project Home Page
http://www.vpds.wsu.edu/i*earn/global_art.html

Impact! Online
http://lrs.ed.uiuc.edu/Impact/impact_homepage.html

The Internet TESL Journal
http://www.aitech.ac.jp/~iteslj/

Kyoto Restaurant Project
http://www.kyoto-su.ac.jp/information/restaurant/

Tom's Page
http://www.kyoto-su.ac.jp/~trobb/index.html

TOPICS, An Online Magazine by and for Learners of English
http://www.rice.edu/projects/topics/Electronic/main.html

WINGS Electronic Magazine for ESL Writing and Art
http://weber.u.washington.edu/~wings/index_full.html

WriteAWAY! A Showcase of Writing by Australian Adult Migrants
http://137.111.169.8/writeaway/

News Channels

BBC World Service: Listen Live 24 Hours a Day
http://www.bbc.co.uk/worldservice/

ClariNews
http://www.clari.net/newstree.html

CNN Custom News
http://customnews.cnn.com/

CNN Interactive
http://www.cnn.com/

Deja News
http://www.dejanews.com/

Mercury Center
http://www5.mercurycenter.com/

My Yahoo!
http://my.yahoo.com/

NPR Online (National Public Radio)
http://www.npr.org/

USA Today	http://www.usatoday.com/
Voice of America	http://www.voa.gov/

Academic Information

American University and English as a Second Language Information Service	http://www.iac.net/~conversa/S_homepage.html

College and University Home Pages–
    Alphabetical Listing
	http://www.mit.edu:8001/people/cdemello
	    /univ.html

ETS Net (Educational Testing Service)	http://www.ets.org/

Other Information Resources

A&E Classroom: Classroom Materials Pages	http://www.aetv.com/class/teach/
AskERIC	http://www.askeric.org/
The Discovery Channel Online	http://www.discovery.com/
The History Channel	http://www.historychannel.com/
The Internet Movie Database	http://us.imdb.com/
MTV Online	http://www.mtv.com/
NOVA Online	http://www.pbs.org/wgbh/nova/
PBS TeacherSource	http://www.pbs.org//teachersource/
Project Gutenberg	http://www.gutenberg.net/
WWW Virtual Library: Audio	http://www.comlab.ox.ac.uk/archive/audio.html

On-Line Dictionaries

Collins Cobuild	http://titania.cobuild.collins.co.uk/
The Newbury House Online Dictionary	http://nhd.heinle.com/

Appendix G: Interactive World Wide Web Pages for Students

CNN San Francisco: Interactive Learning Resources
http://www.cnnsf.com/education/education.html

The Comenius English Language Center
http://www.comenius.com/

CRAYON: Create Your Own Newspaper
http://www.crayon.net/

Dave's ESL Café
http://www.eslcafe.com/

The Discovery Channel Online
http://www.discovery.com/

Disney.com
http://disney.com/

The Electric Postcard
http://persona.www.media.mit.edu/postcards/

English Grammar Pages
http://web.jet.es/jrevusky/esl.html

Grammar Safari
http://deil.lang.uiuc.edu/web.pages/grammarsafari.html

GrammarONLINE
http://www.crl.com/~malarak/grammar/

Heinle & Heinle Museum of Cultural Imagery
http://www.thomson.com/heinle/museum/welcome.html

The History Channel
http://www.historychannel.com/

The Internet TESL Journal
http://www.aitech.ac.jp/~iteslj/

Learning Oral English Online
http://www.lang.uiuc.edu/r-li5/book/

NASA's Quest Project
http://quest.arc.nasa.gov/

National Gallery of Victoria
http://www.ngv.vic.gov.au/

Nationalgeographic.com
http://www.nationalgeographic.com/

NOVA Online
http://www.pbs.org/wgbh/nova/

Online Writing Lab (OWL)
http://owl.english.purdue.edu/

PIZZAZ!
http://darkwing.uoregon.edu/~leslieob/pizzaz.html

Schumann's Foreign Language Tests/Exercises
http://ourworld.compuserve.com/homepages/joschu/

The Smithsonian Institution
http://www.si.edu/

Talking About Daily Routines
http://grove.ufl.edu/~ktrickel/teslmini/activity.html

The University of Maine Writing Center Online
http://www.ume.maine.edu/~wcenter/

Welcome to the White House
http://www.whitehouse.gov/

517

Appendix H: Curricular Exchanges and Courses On-Line

Curricular Exchanges

Classroom Connect   http://www.classroom.com/
De Orilla a Orilla/From Shore to Shore
  (The Orillas Project)   http://orillas.upr.clu.edu/
Email Projects Home Page   http://www.otan.dni.us/webfarm/emailproject
                              /email.htm

Intercultural E-Mail Classroom
  Connections   http://www.iecc.org/
International Tandem Network   http://www.slf.ruhr-uni-bochum.de/
King's Road 2001 Project   http://www.hut.fi/~rvilmi/King/

On-Line Courses

Blue Web'n: A Library of Blue Ribbon
  Learning Sites on the Web   http://www.kn.pacbell.com/wired/bluewebn/
Business English and Academic
  Writing   http://www.comenius.com/writing/index.html
Diversity University   http://www.du.org/
English for Internet   http://www.study.com/
EnglishNet: Writing for the Web   http://www.engl.uic.edu/tie/classes/087/
The Global Schoolhouse   http://www.gsn.org/
The Homeschool Zone   http://www.homeschoolzone.com/
Interactive Internet Language
  Learning   http://babel.uoregon.edu/yamada/interact.html
Merlin: World Class   http://www.hull.ac.uk/merlin/
On-Line Courses   http://www.hut.fi/~rvilmi/online/
SitesALIVE!   http://www.oceanchallenge.com/
UVic Online English Writing Course   http://web.uvic.ca/hrd/OLCourse/
Web Classes   http://www.uno.edu/~webclass/
World Lecture Hall   http://www.utexas.edu/world/lecture/

Appendix I: On-Line Guides to the Internet and MOOing

Apple Classrooms of Tomorrow	http://www.research.apple.com/go/acot/
Evaluating Web Resources	http://www.science.widener.edu/~withers /webeval.htm
Frizzy University Network (FUN): schMOOze Directions	http://thecity.sfsu.edu/~funweb/schmooze.htm
The Global Schoolhouse	http://www.gsn.org/
Harnessing the Power of the Web: A Tutorial	http://www.gsn.org/web/index.html
A Language Professional's Guide to the WWW	http://agoralang.com/calico/webarticle.html
Tom's Page	http://www.kyoto-su.ac.jp/~trobb/index.html
What Can You Do in the MOO?	http://mason.gmu.edu/~epiphany/docs /dointhemoo.html
WWW Activities That Work (and Why!)	http://deil.lang.uiuc.edu/resources/TESOL /www_activities.html

Contributors

Sheryl Beller-Kenner began teaching ESL in 1978 at a public elementary school in New York City, in the United States. Since then she has taught at various colleges and universities. Her students have been using computers in her classes since 1981. Currently, she teaches at College de Maisonneuve in Montreal, Canada, and serves as a consultant and teacher trainer on the effective uses of technology in language learning and teaching.

Ana Bishop is a specialist in the integration of technology into the bilingual and ESL educational environment for Grades K–12. In 1998, she was the co-chair of the National Association for Bilingual Education's Technology Interest Group and served on the planning committee for the Electronic Village at the 32nd Annual TESOL Convention. She created and managed the New York State–funded Bilingual/ESL Technology Institute for New York City's public schools, and she does long-range planning and implementation of bilingual and ESL computer software and training for a number of school districts throughout the United States.

Elizabeth Boling, an assistant professor at Indiana University, Bloomington, in the United States, teaches design and production for instructional systems technology. Previously manager of electronic graphics and production for instructional products at Apple Computer, she has worked for 15 years as a screen designer, interaction designer, and World Wide Web designer for instructional software.

Claire Bradin has worked with CALL since 1983. An associate editor of CALICO Journal and past chair of TESOL's Computer-Assisted Language Learning Interest Section, she is a doctoral student at Michigan State University, East Lansing, in the United States. Her interests center on faculty development and research on second language acquisition and CALL.

Jim Buell is a doctoral student in educational psychology and instructional technology at the University of Illinois at Urbana-Champaign, in the United States. A member of the Steering Committee for TESOL's Computer-Assisted Language Learning Interest Section, he coordinated the Electronic Village at the 32nd Annual TESOL Convention (1998) and the Authors' Showcase at the 30th and 31st Annual TESOL Conventions (1996 and 1997). He holds an MA in TESL from Ohio University and taught English for 10 years in Japan, China, Hungary, and the United States.

520

Chin-chi Chao has a master of science in instructional systems technology and is a doctoral candidate in language education at Indiana University, Bloomington, in the United States. She is an instructor and a designer of EFL and teacher education courses on the World Wide Web. Her research covers various CALL issues, including portfolio assessment, Web-based course design, and visual-spatial learning strategies.

Carol Chapelle is a professor of TESL and applied linguistics in the Department of English and the Program in Linguistics at Iowa State University, Ames, in the United States, where she teaches and conducts research in second language acquisition, language testing, and CALL.

Joy Egbert is an award-winning teacher, researcher, software developer, and materials designer. An assistant professor at Indiana University, Bloomington, in the United States, her research and teaching interests include ESL-bilingual methods and CALL. She has published and presented widely on both of these topics.

Susan Gaer is an assistant professor at the Centennial Education Center in the School of Continuing Education, Rancho Santiago College, Santa Ana, California, in the United States. She has been teaching students how to use technology since 1986. She has published in New Ways of Using Computers in Language Teaching (TESOL) and Virtual Connections: On-Line Activities and Projects for Networking Language Learners (University of Hawaii, Second Language Teaching and Learning Center), and she edits the column "Online" in CATESOL News. She has presented at both TESOL and California TESOL conventions and currently serves on the board of California TESOL as computer consultant.

Elizabeth Hanson-Smith is professor emeritus at California State University, Sacramento, in the United States, where she founded the TESOL graduate program and coordinated it for the last 10 years of her tenure. She has done teacher training for extended periods in China, Russia, Sri Lanka, Belize, and Egypt and is currently a software developer and consultant in ESL/EFL technology. Her publications include TESOL Reader and Teachers Guide (ERIC), How to Set up a Computer Lab (Athelstan), Technology in the Classroom (TESOL), and Constructing the Paragraph (computer software; Computers for Education).

Deborah Healey is the technology coordinator and an instructor at the English Language Institute, Oregon State University, Corvallis, in the United States, where she has spent some 14 of her 22 years in ESL adding technology to teaching. She is the author of Something to Do on Tuesday (Athelstan), a former editor of CAELL Journal, and a traveling consultant most recently in Brazil and Austria.

Lloyd Holliday coordinates the Applied Linguistics and TESOL Program at the Graduate School of Education, La Trobe University, Bundoora, Australia. His research interests are in second language acquisition and computer-mediated communication. He is the owner of

CELIA at La Trobe University: Computerized English Language Instructional Archive *and co-owner of the SL-Lists.*

Bill Johnston is an assistant professor of ESL at the University of Minnesota, Minneapolis, in the United States. His areas of interest include language teacher education, teacher development, language teaching methods, and classroom research.

Carla Meskill is an associate professor in the Department of Educational Theory and Practice, State University of New York at Albany, in the United States. She directs the Center for Electronic Language Learning and Research, a facility dedicated to exploring new forms of technology used in language learning.

Karen Yeok-Hwa Ngeow is a member of the faculty at Universiti Malaysia Sarawak, where she teaches CALL, teacher education, TESL methodology, and sociolinguistics. Her interests in CALL and English for specific purposes have led to publications in Proceedings of the International Conference on Computers in Education 95 *and* Proceedings of ED-MEDIA 96 (Association for the Advancement of Computing in Education), *and in* World Englishes. *She is pursuing a doctoral degree in language education and instructional systems technology at Indiana University, Bloomington, in the United States.*

Leslie Opp-Beckman is the technology coordinator and an ESL instructor for the American English Institute at the University of Oregon, Eugene, in the United States. A member of TESOL's Computer-Assisted Language Learning (CALL) Interest Section Steering Committee, she coordinated the WebFaire at the 31st and 32nd Annual TESOL Conventions (1997 and 1998) and the CALL Interest Section's World Wide Web site in 1997. She served on the board of Oregon TESOL in 1996–1997.

Joy Kreeft Peyton is a vice president at the Center for Applied Linguistics, Washington, DC, in the United States. She enjoys working with teachers to develop and study ways to use interactive writing (via dialogue journals and computer) for language and literacy. Her publications on this topic include Network-Based Classrooms: Promises and Realities *(edited with Bertram Bruce and Trent Batson; Cambridge University Press).*

Shayla Sivert directs the ESL Computer Lab at Palomar College, San Marcos, California, in the United States. She has developed and teaches a course in microcomputer applications for ESL students and is currently creating vocational ESL materials for graphics communications.

Keng-Soon Soo, a faculty member at the Centre of Applied Learning and Multimedia, Universiti Malaysia Sarawak, has published a variety of articles on ESL. He has also coauthored several ESL texts for Malaysian ESL learners.

Lonnie Turbee has extensively used e-mail, electronic discussion lists, local area networks, the World Wide Web, and multiuser object-oriented domains (MOOs) to teach Spanish and ESL. She is the founder and director of the MOO MundoHispano and continues to give presentations worldwide. At Syracuse Language Systems, Syracuse, New York, in the United States, she is developing PuebloLindo, an Internet-based multimedia language learning environment, and is director of on-line content.

Ruth Vilmi, who has taught EFL in England, Malta, France, and Nigeria, graduated as a teacher from Birmingham University, England, and did a diploma in EFL at the Institute of Education, London University. She is a lecturer at Helsinki University of Technology (HUT), in Finland, and started the HUT Email Writing Project (now the HUT Internet Writing Project) in 1993. She develops software for language teaching with students at HUT.

Robert Wachman is an ESL instructor at Yuba College in Marysville, California, in the United States. He has been involved with the use of computers for TESOL since 1987 and with HyperCard® since 1989. He is now a member of the production team for the computer software Live Action English Interactive.